A BIBLIOGRAPHY OF THE WORKS OF

W. SOMERSET MAUGHAM

CONTENTS

INTRODUCTORY NOTE   11

A BOOKS AND PAMPHLETS BY W. SOMERSET MAUGHAM

Liza of Lambeth	19
The Making of a Saint	22
Orientations	25
The Hero	27
Mrs. Craddock	29
A Man of Honour	35
The Merry-Go-Round	39
The Land of the Blessed Virgin	43
The Bishop's Apron	45
The Explorer	48
The Magician	51
Lady Frederick	55
Jack Straw	56
Mrs. Dot	56
Penelope	57
The Explorer (play)	58
The Tenth Man	59
Landed Gentry	59
Smith	60
The Land of Promise	61
Of Human Bondage	63
The Moon and Sixpence	67
The Unknown	71
The Circle	72
The Trembling of a Leaf	74
Caesar's Wife	78
East of Suez	79
On a Chinese Screen	80
Our Betters	82
Home and Beauty	83
The Unattainable	84

Contents

Loaves and Fishes	84
The Painted Veil	85
The Casuarina Tree	91
The Constant Wife	93
The Letter	94
Ashenden	96
The Sacred Flame	97
The Gentleman in the Parlour	99
Cakes and Ale	100
The Bread-Winner	103
First Person Singular	105
The Book Bag	106
The Narrow Corner	108
For Services Rendered	109
Ah King	110
Sheppey	113
The Judgement Seat	114
Don Fernando	114
Cosmopolitans	117
My South Sea Island	119
Theatre	121
The Summing Up	123
Christmas Holiday	124
Princess September and the Nightingale	125
France at War	127
Books and You	128
The Mixture as Before	129
Up at the Villa	131
Strictly Personal	132
The Hour Before the Dawn	135
The Unconquered	137
The Razor's Edge	138
Then and Now	140
Of Human Bondage (address)	141
Creatures of Circumstance	143
Catalina	144
Quartet	146
Great Novelists and their Novels	147
Ten Novels and their Authors	148
A Writer's Notebook	149
Trio	153
The Writer's Point of View	154
Encore	155

The Vagrant Mood 156
The Noble Spaniard 158
The Moon and Sixpence (opera) 159
Points of View 160
Purely For My Pleasure 161

B COLLECTED EDITIONS

Dramatic Works 164
Non-Dramatic Works 165
East and West 167
Altogether 167
Tauchnitz Edition 168
The Collected Works (Pocket edition) 169
Penguin Books 169
Samuel French's Acting Edition 170
Heron Books 170
Six Comedies 172
The Favorite Short Stories 172
The Round Dozen 173
The Somerset Maugham Sampler 173
Here and There 173
East of Suez 173
The Maugham Reader 174
The Complete Short Stories (Heinemann) 174
The Collected Plays 175
The World Over 175
The Complete Short Stories (Doubleday) 175
The Selected Novels 176
The Partial View 176
Mr. Maugham Himself 176
The Art of Fiction 176
The Travel Books 177
The Best Short Stories 177
The Kite and Other Stories 177
Husbands and Wives 177
The Sinners 178
Selected Prefaces and Introductions 178
A Maugham Twelve 178
Cakes and Ale 179
Maugham Malaysian Stories 179
Seventeen Lost Stories 179
A Baker's Dozen 180
A Second Baker's Dozen 180

C BOOKS AND PAMPHLETS EDITED, OR WITH CONTRIBUTIONS BY W. SOMERSET MAUGHAM 183

D CONTRIBUTIONS BY W. SOMERSET MAUGHAM TO PERIODICALS 198

E PLAYS NOVELISED OR BOOKS DRAMATISED BY OTHERS 218

F CHECK LIST OF WORKS CONCERNING W. SOMERSET MAUGHAM 222

G CHECK LIST OF PERIODICALS CONCERNING W. SOMERSET MAUGHAM 250

H APPENDICES 265

INDEX OF TITLES 317

TO THE MEMORY
OF
FRANCES
WITH ABIDING LOVE

INTRODUCTORY NOTE

SINCE the first edition of any bibliography can only hope to break the ground, it is perhaps not surprising that a large number of unrecorded items should have turned up since the publication of my former book *The Writings of William Somerset Maugham*. I have already recorded some of these discoveries in two Supplements, but this has made reference somewhat cumbersome and difficult to follow, and I proposed therefore to issue a second edition incorporating the Supplements and correcting any erroneous conclusions in the main bibliography, and leave it at that. However, having begun on the revision it soon became apparent that this treatment would not be adequate for so much new information had been assembled willy-nilly over the years, particularly with regard to the analyses of editions and issues that I found it necessary to alter considerably the arrangement of the book.

The plan I adopted in the main bibliography was to list the first publication of each book, irrespective of the country of origin as the real first edition of that book. This had particular significance in the case of this author, since fourteen of his books were first published in America and several English editions were bound from the American sheets.

Although bibliographically correct this treatment gave rise to some criticism across the water as it was felt that since I had collated fully all the English editions, I should do the same for the American, irrespective or not whether they were first editions.

A visit to America and an examination of the Maugham rarities in the Berg Collection in the New York Public Library and in the Library of Congress has enabled me to do this, and also to include a number of hitherto unrecorded American items of outstanding interest. The wealth of Maugham manuscripts, first editions, collections of letters, corrected galleys and typescripts that have crossed the Atlantic is quite remarkable, particularly the collection of letters in such centres of learning as the Yale University Library, The Berg Collection in the New York Public Library and the University of Texas. The latter, with the acquisition of the Jerome R. Zipkin's collection, must now have assembled the greatest collection of Maughamiana ever gathered together in one place. If one regrets their loss to this country, at least one is fortified by the knowledge that they are cared for and are made available to scholars without any tiresome restrictions and given a prominence by way of periodical exhibitions, often with useful catalogues.

I have also located and described manuscripts where they survive. Since the author's death there has been numerous changes of ownership and only very few manuscripts remain now in private hands. When in Washington I had the privilege of reading in The Library of Congress

Manuscript Division the manuscript of *The Artistic Temperament of Stephen Carey* (the first draft of *Of Human Bondage*) which is never to be printed, and in view of its importance in the Maugham canon, I have given a summary of it for the benefit of those unlikely ever to have the opportunity of reading it. I have also listed a large number of books and periodicals containing important references to Maugham, but I have made no attempt to record translations which are so numerous that it would extend the work unduly. Not has any attempt been made to record dust wrappers, except in one pertinent instance. The notes, however, have been amended where necessary and very much extended.

Otherwise, the rules and precepts I observed in my former book have been followed for the most part in the present work.

In cataloguing Maugham's periodical publications every reasonable effort was made to ensue a complete record, particularly of the short stories, the significance of which, for reasons stated elsewhere in this work has never been fully realised. One or two more 'lost' short stories have been traced, one of them a story of which all record had been lost. I again acknowledge my debt to Mr. Oliver Robinson of the National Magazine Company and Miss Alice Sheridan of Hearst's for much valuable help in sorting these out, and I have to thank the late Mr. Maugham for identifying stories subsequently printed under a different title. The best part of my own, and also the British Museum's, set of Nash's Magazine was lost in the war and has still not been replaced. Gaps in the descriptions of these serial issues, therefore, have been inevitable but all the vital information necessary to determine priority has, I think, been provided.

*   *   *

It is a pleasure to record the assistance of a number of individuals who have helped in the compilation of this work. Much of the bibliographical information was supplied by the late Mr. Somerset Maugham, to whom I have already acknowledged my indebtedness, and to his friend and Secretary, Mr. Alan Searle, who as always has been kindness itself.

It would have been impossible for me to have done this work without the help and encouragement of the private collector, and I have been fortunate in the friendship of three men who have built up Maugham collections of remarkable range and quality—Mr. Leonard Meldman of Detroit, Mr. Lynwood Giacomini of Chevy Chase, Maryland, and Mr. Grenville Cook of London. All three of them spared no effort to provide me with photostats of title pages and bindings and when this was insufficient with the actual books, but I owe most perhaps to Mr. Cook. His outstanding collection and his unrivalled knowledge of Maugham has been at my disposal whenever I needed it, and he read the final draft and made valuable suggestions and corrections. I would also like again to express my thanks to Mr. Leslie Munro, late of William Heinemann Ltd., for his unwearying research in the publisher's archives when I began this work, and to Mr. Anthony Rota who, like his father, gave me much encouragement and help.

It only remains for me to thank Mr. Maugham's publishers William Heinemann for many favours, and the directors and assistants of the Libraries where I have worked, in particular the British Museum, the Houghton Library at Harvard, the Library of Congress, Washington D.C., the Berg Collection in the New York Public Library, the Pierpoint Morgan Library, and the University of Texas Library, Austin; and to record my gratitude to Dr Frederick R. Goff, late Chief of the Rare Book Division and Dr Roy P. Basler, the Director of the Manuscript Division, The Library of Congress; Dr Lola Szladits, Curator of the Berg Collection, at The New York Public Library; Mrs. J. Boone, Manager Archives and Special Collections of the Harriet Irving Library in the University of New Brunswick; Dr Julius P. Barclay, Chief, Department of Special Collections at The Stanford University Libraries; Dr Donald C. Davidson, Librarian of the University of California, Santa Barbara, Mr. David A. Randall, the Lilly Librarian of Indiana University; Mr. A. S. Frere; Mr. Kenneth Rae, Secretary of the National Theatre; Mr. George Nash of the Theatre Collection, The Victoria & Albert Museum; Lady Glendevon; Mr. Duncan Cranford of Northport, N.Y.; Mr. G. Hattee, the Hon. Librarian of King's School, Canterbury; Mr. John A. Ford of William Collins & Sons Ltd: and in special measure to Mr. John R. Payne, of the Humanities Research Center, at the University of Texas.

I have also to express my thanks for the courtesy of the Lord Chamberlain's Office in arranging for the manuscript of *Princess September* to be brought up from Windsor for me to examine.

The Pinker letters, which the late Mr. Maugham gave me permission to publish in my former book, have changed hands and are now in the possession of the University of Texas Library. I have also included one or two quotations from the A. P. Watt letters in the Berg Collection in the New York Public Library and the Towne letters in the Yale University Library. For these and other copyright material I have to thank the Executors of the W. Somerset Maugham Estate.

Any credit which this work may have belongs to all the people named above. The responsibility for its numerous shortcomings and inequalities, of which I am fully conscious, belong only to the compiler.

NOTE

General description of the binding of the plays published by Messrs. William Heinemann in England, and The Dramatic Publishing Company and Messrs. George H. Doran in America.

1. *William Heinemann.* Cherry red buckram, blocked in black on front with author's symbol and on back with publisher's windmill device and lettered in black on front and spine. All edges cut. Size generally uniform (17.3 × 11.8 cm.), exceptions noted.

2. *William Heinemann.* Champagne wrappers, printed in reddish brown or dark brown on front, spine and inner and back wrappers; all edges cut. Size varies but average usually about 17½ × 12½ cm. The shade of the champagne varies in some plays, and the surface texture of the woven paper varies from smooth to rough, usually smooth in the earlier editions. There is a marked variation in the shade of the brown of the printing in the early and later plays. The proportion of the cloth copies to wrappers was usually one in three.

3. *Sergel's Acting Drama.* Dark blue ribbed cloth, blocked and lettered in gold on front and spine: lettered on front THE PLAYS OF W. S. MAUGHAM | [*rule*] | [*title of play in caps*]; on spine: [*thick rule*] | THE | PLAYS | OF | W. S. | MAUGHAM | [*rule*] | [*title of play running up spine*] | [*rule*] | *publisher's device* | SERGEL | [*thick rule*]: back plain. All edges cut. Size generally uniform (16.9 × 11.11 cm.).

4. *Sergel's Acting Drama.* Maize pictorial wrappers, printed in reddish brown on front and spine, with imprint at foot on front: PUBLISHED BY | THE DRAMATIC PUBLISHING COMPANY | CHARLES H. SERGEL, PRESIDENT; back wrappers advertisements. Size uniform (17.3 × 13 cm.).

5. *George H. Doran.* Grey paper boards. White paper label on front and spine. Size 18.2 × 12½ cm., top and fore-edges cut, lower edges uncut. Plays published by Doran occasionally had the Heinemann title-page. The explanation of this is that when 200 or less sets of sheets were supplied by Heinemann, the Heinemann imprint was used, but for supplies of 500 or more Heinemann printed a new title-page with the American imprint. When the Heinemann title-page was used, the verso (occasionally the recto) was rubber stamped with the words 'Made in Great Britain'.

A

BOOKS AND PAMPHLETS

BY W. SOMERSET MAUGHAM

A1   LIZA OF LAMBETH   1897

a. First edition

LIZA | OF LAMBETH | BY | William Somerset Maugham | LONDON | T. FISHER UNWIN | *Paternoster Square* | 1897
Title in red and black, the whole enclosed in a single red frame.

Collation: [viii], 248 pp. [1]^4 2–16^8 17^4.
pp. [i–ii], blank; p. [iii], half-title; p. [iv], publisher's monogram; p. [v], title; p. [vi], [*All rights reserved*]; p. [vii], dedication: in gold on spine LIZA | OF | LAMBETH | [*rule*] | W. S. MAUGHAM | To | MY GOOD FRIEND | ADNEY PAYNE; p. [viii], blank; pp. 1–242, text; pp. [243–248], advts. [dated Spring and Autumn, 1897].

Binding: Smooth laurel green cloth; blocked on front in gold with design of Coster girl enclosed within a rule frame, signed H.B., and gold lettered: LIZA | OF LAMBETH | [*rule*] | W.S. | MAUGHAM; in gold on spine LIZA | OF | LAMBETH | [*rule*] | W.S. | MAUGHAM | T. FISHER UNWIN; on back in black LIZA | OF LAMBETH | [*rule*] | BY W.S. MAUGHAM; publisher's monogram lower right-hand corner. Plain end-papers; all edges cut; leaves measure 18.3 × 12 cm.

Price: 3s. 6d. 2,000 copies were published in September 1897.

Notes: There are three issues of the first edition. The first issue is as described above, the second issue is the Colonial Edition in an identical casing to the first issue but with the words COLONIAL EDITION on the recto of the title page, the third issue is the Colonial Edition reissued in the home market with the words COLONIAL EDITION overprinted (i.e. blacked-out).

As a result of the publicity it received in the press and the pulpit, the first impression of *Liza of Lambeth* sold out very quickly. To meet the demand while the second impression was printing, the publisher drew on the Colonial Edition, which comprised first edition sheets with a new half-title and title—a quarter sheet imposition. The half-title has 'Unwin's Colonial Library' printed on the verso, followed by 23 titles, and the title page is printed only in black and enclosed in a single black frame.

It has been noted that copies of the first issue and also of the Colonial Edition exist with a variant on the verso of the title page, the words 'All rights reserved' appear without brackets. At this late date one can only surmise that the sheets of the second impression (which lacked the brackets) had somehow got mixed with the first when being stacked for the binder. Evidence that the first impression sheets did have the brackets is borne out by the Statutory Library copies, all of which possess the brackets and were received within a few days of publication.

One of the six copies given to Maugham in advance of publication (now in the University of Texas Library) also has the brackets.

The second impression has 'Second Edition' superimposed on the recto of the title page and on the verso the brackets around the words 'All rights reserved' have been removed, otherwise it is identical with the first impression.

It has been stated that the first issue had the word 'belly' instead of 'stomach' in line 20 of page 124, but this was not printed in the first edition of the book—despite the claim of a correspondent to the March 1934 issue of *The Book Collector's Quarterly* that he had seen a copy of the first edition containing the word. It was in the original manuscript, but was deleted at the publisher's request in proof. Certainly, it was not present in the first edition. The original word, however, was reverted to when Heinemann took the book over and it appeared for the first time in the *Collected Edition*.

In the New York Public Library is a unique and fascinating folder containing part of the archives of T. Fisher Unwin, the first publisher of W. Somerset Maugham, and among these papers is the author's description of the novel he submitted to Fisher Unwin called *A Lambeth Idyll* and the reports of three readers upon it.

The description what the novel is all about is in the author's own hand and was attached to the manuscript: 'This is the story of a nine days wonder in a Lambeth slum (he wrote). It shows that those queer folk the poor live and love and love and die in very much the same way as their neighbours of Brixton and Belgravia, and that hatred, malice, and all uncharitableness are not the peculiar attributes of the Glorious British Middle Class, and finally it shows that in this world nothing very much matters, and that in Vere Street, Lambeth, nothing matters at all.'

The manuscript was first sent by Fisher Unwin to Vaughan Nash, who was one of his regular readers, and his report is dated 14th January 1897. He writes 'The author shows considerable acquaintance with the speech and the customs of a certain class of the London poor and if he knew how to use his materials his work might possess a certain value. But this study shows no trace of any such power. Its details, some of which are revolting and, I should suppose, unsuitable for publication, are strung together loosely and there is no touch of romance, no sense of character, and no atmosphere from first to last. The figures are introduced apparently in order to deliver themselves of the author's collection of slum Cockneyisms. . . . Altogether I feel that as an experiment in realistic writing the story will not do. . . . But in the event of publication I would suggest that it should be carefully read in view of certain passages which strike me as particularly offensive. The

B

author's capacity for vulgarity on his own account is considerable.'

Fisher Unwin, despite what Maugham used to say about him, did have a flair for spotting talent, and he must have been very dissatisfied with this report. So he sent the MS to another reader for whom he had a great regard, Edward Garnett, who was to become one of the outstanding literary figures of his day. This is what he had to say in his report, dated 25th January 1897. 'Mr. Maugham has not produced so forceful a study as *The Jago*—but when all is said and done *A Lambeth Idyll* is *a very clever realistic study of factory girls and cosher life*. The women, their roughness, intemperance, fits of violence, kind-heartedness, slang—all are done truthfully. Liza and her mother Mrs. Kemp are drawn with no little humour and insight. The study is a dismal one in its ending, but the temper and tone of the book is wholesome and by no means morbid. The work is objective, and both the atmosphere and the environment of the mean district are unexaggerated. The question for Mr. Unwin to decide is this—the Arthur Morrison public—a slowly growing one, will understand and appreciate the book—though of course it was through Mr. Henley's backing that *Mean Streets* and *The Jago* found publisher and public, and Mr. Maugham has not got Mr. Henley at his back. If Mr. Unwin does not publish *A Lambeth Idyll* somebody else certainly will. . . . We should say *Publish*. P.S. The conversation is remarkably well done.'

There could not have been a more confident report than this and Fisher Unwin must have been duly impressed. However, it would seem he was still not quite happy about certain passages in the book or its 'realism' for he decided to seek the opinion of yet another reader, a certain Mr. W. H. Chess. His report is dated 2nd February 1897. He writes 'This is interesting, impressive and truthful. It might be described as an attempt to do for the South East of London what Mr. Morrison has done for the Bethnal Green district. Both from the moral and artistic point of view we should advise the publication of this study. . . . We have said that it is also a story to "take or leave". A process of pruning down would be absurd. If people don't like to read of a love that takes the form of a "swinging blow in the belly" they won't; if they do, they will. Yet one feels that Mr. Maugham knows his people and between those and these there is not a great gulf fixed after all.'

This last report evidently enabled Fisher Unwin to make up his mind and despite the fact that the office 'was in a state of nervous apprehension on the day of publication.'[1] *Liza of Lambeth* (to give the novel its new title) duly came forth and a new young author made his debut upon the literary stage.

[1] According to Mr. A. D. Marks, then Trade Manager to Mr. T. Fisher Unwin.

Not all the reviews, it may be remarked, of Maugham's first book were favourable. The reviewer in *The Athenaeum* (11.9.97) wrote that '*Liza of Lambeth* is emphatically unpleasing as literature,' while the reviewer in the *Academy* (11.9.97) after reading the novel felt as if he had taken 'a mud bath in all the filth of a London street.'

A1   LIZA OF LAMBETH   (1921)

b. First American edition:
Liza of Lambeth | By | W. Somerset Maugham | Author of "The Trembling of a Leaf," "The Moon and Sixpence," "Of Human | Bondage," Etc. | New [*publisher's monograph device*] York | George H. Doran Company.

> *Collation:* 222 pp. [unsigned 1⁶ 2¹⁰ alternatively to 12¹⁰ 13⁶ 14⁹] p. [1], half-title; p. [2], By W. Somerset Maugham [listing 7 titles]; p. [3], title; p. [4], Printed in the United States of America; p. [5], fly-title; p. [6], blank; pp. 7–221, text; p. [222], blank.
>
> *Binding:* Hemp beige linen cloth, blocked and lettered in front in plum ornamental lettering; Liza of Lambeth | by | W. Somerset Maugham; on spine LIZA OF | LAMBETH | [*cross of Loraine*] | Maugham | DORAN.
> Plain end-papers; top and lower edges cut, fore-edges rough trimmed; leaves measure 19 × 13 cm.
>
> *Price:* $1.75. Published in September 1921.

Notes: On page 87 a line is transposed.

A1   LIZA OF LAMBETH   1904

c. Second edition:
LIZA OF LAMBETH | BY | WILLIAM SOMERSET MAUGHAM | *Author of* | "*The Hero,*" "*Mrs. Craddock,*" "*The Merry-go-Round,*" | "*The Making of a Saint*" and "*Orientation.*" POPULAR EDITION, REVISED | LONDON | T. FISHER UNWIN | PATERNOSTER SQUARE | 1904 | (*All rights reserved.*)

> *Collation:* 96 pp. [unsigned 1–3¹⁶].
> pp. [1–2], advts.; p. [3], half-title LIZA OF LAMBETH; p. [4], advts.; p. [5], title; p. [6], To | MY GOOD FRIEND, STILL | WALTER PAYNE | 1897 1904; pp. 7–95, text; p. [96], blank.
>
> *Binding:* Dark blue pictorial wrappers, stamped and lettered in black, inside front and back wrappers advts. Text in double columns.

Variant Binding: See below.
All edges cut; leaves measure 21.7×14 cm.

Price: 6d. Number of copies unknown. Published in May 1904.

Notes: There are two issues of this edition. The first is as described above, in the second the date '1904' has been removed and 'Adelphi Terrace' substituted for 'Paternoster Square'. A page of advertisements replaces the dedication to Walter Payne. There are also variations in the colour printing of the front wrapper. The background is ivory instead of blue, the border is red instead of black, as also are the top and lower panels. The jackets of the two men are in Royal blue instead of black. The advertisements are also different.

Another interesting variation is that the first edition is dedicated to Adney Payne, whereas the second edition is dedicated to Walter Payne.[1] A comparison of the text of the first and second editions reveals that the author made a large number of small revisions, particularly to the Cockney dialogue, as for example changing 'ter' to 'to'. On the title page the title of the novel 'Orientations' is wrongly spelt.

A1   LIZA OF LAMBETH   1915

d. Cheap edition:
LIZA OF | LAMBETH | BY | W. SOMERSET MAUGHAM | T. FISHER UNWIN, LTD | ADELPHI TERRACE, LONDON

Collation: [i–iv], 244 pp. [1]² 2–16⁸ 17².
p. [1], half-title; p. [ii], listing 6 titles; p. [iii], title; p. [iv], First published in 1897 (and listing later "Impressions" in 1897, 1904, 1906, 1914 and 1915) (All rights reserved); pp. 1–242, text; pp. [243–244], blank.

Binding: Reddish brown sand-grained cloth, lettered and blocked in blind on front within decorative frame: LIZA | OF | LAMBETH | [*rule*] | W. SOMERSET | MAUGHAM | T. FISHER | UNWIN; back plain. Plain end-papers; all edges rough trimmed. Leaves measure 18.5 × 12.2 cm.

Price: 2s. Number of copies unknown. Published in May 1915.

---

[1] Walter Payne was a qualified accountant and a barrister. He succeeded to his father's theatrical interests and became one of the outstanding figures in the theatre world. He died in 1949.

A1   LIZA OF LAMBETH   1930

e. Travellers' Library edition:
LIZA OF LAMBETH | by | W. S. MAUGHAM | [*publisher's device*] |
LONDON | WILLIAM HEINEMANN LTD

> *Pagination:* x, 214 pp. 14 pp. advts. (inserted). Navy blue cloth, gilt
> blocked. Travellers' Library No. 141. Price 3s. 6d.

Notes: Contains a new (6 pp.) preface in which the author refers to the
changes in the habits and speech of the Cockney since 1897. It has been
stated that this was withdrawn. This is not correct. There is a pencil
note in the publisher's manufacturing record—'Preface date and
author's name, if reprinted.' But the edition was not reprinted, nor is
there any record of it being withdrawn.

A1   LIZA OF LAMBETH   1947

f. Jubilee edition:
LIZA | OF LAMBETH | BY | W. SOMERSET MAUGHAM |
JUBILEE EDITION | [*publisher's device*] | LONDON | WILLIAM
HEINEMANN LTD | 1947
Title in red and black.

> *Collation:* [xvi], 140 pp. [A]⁸ B–I⁸ K⁶.
> p. [i], half-title; p. [ii], cert. of limitation: THIS EDITION | Num-
> bered and signed by the Author | is limited to 1,000 copies for sale
> in | Great Britain and Ireland | No. . . . ; p. [iii], title; p. [iv],
> bibliography; p. [v], contents; p. [vi], blank; pp. vii–xv, pre-
> face; p. [xvi], blank; pp. 1–136 [137], text; p. [138], colophon; THIS
> EDITION | Designed by Stanley Morrison | was printed and made
> at | The Windmill Press, Kingswood | Surrey; pp. [139–140],
> blank.

> *Binding:* Quarter vellum, chinese rose paper patterned boards;
> black leather label on spine blocked in gold with wavy rules and
> lettered: W.S. | Maugham | LIZA | of | Lambeth | [*author's
> symbol*]; vellum border front and back edged with gold.

> *Price:* £2 2s. od. Jubilee Edition, limited to 1,000 signed and
> numbered copies. Published 8 December 1947.

Notes: The preface to this edition consists of the Travellers' Library
edition preface, with a 4 pp. Special Supplement to the Jubilee edition.
The preface to the *Collected Edition* contains another 14 pp., in which the
author explains how he came to write not only *Liza of Lambeth* but

also all the other novels of his youth, and why he is not including them in the *Collected Edition*. It is a very important, as well as revealing, disclosure of his attitude towards his own writing, and perhaps it would not be out of place to reproduce here a very beautiful letter he wrote to a stranger who out of the blue asked his advice on how to become an author. 'What I have to say,' he writes, 'is the result of my own experience and that is this. The chances of one writing anything of permanent value before one is thirty are small. And if one is a literary man who has to earn his living the probabilities are that one will waste very good themes which one realises afterwards one could have made much more of with greater knowledge and experience. My advice to you therefore is to adopt any occupation which will give you a living and keep writing for your spare time. In that spare time you will be able to write a novel in a year or two and from its result you can judge whether it is worth your while to go on. The life of the writer is extremely specialised and by following some other avocation it is likely that he will gain experience which will be of great value to him afterwards. So far as I personally am concerned I can only wish that I had remained a doctor for three or four years instead of writing books which have long been as dead as mutton.'[1]

To those fortunate few who have read the first draft of *Of Human Bondage* which Maugham wrote in Seville in 1898, soon after *Liza of Lambeth* under the title *The Artistic Temperament of Stephen Carey*, the manuscript of which is now in The Library of Congress, the force of this argument is vividly brought home, for its rejection by Fisher Unwin (because Maugham was asking £100 for it) was one of the luckiest breaks that could ever have fallen on a young author.

A2   THE MAKING OF A SAINT   1898

a. First edition:
THE | MAKING OF A SAINT | BY | WILLIAM SOMERSET MAUGHAM | *Illustrated* | BY GILBERT JAMES | [*publisher's device*] | BOSTON | L. C. PAGE AND COMPANY | (INCORPORATED) | 1898
Title in red and black. Title page, an inset.

Collation: 352 pp. [unsigned 1–22⁸].
pp. [1–4], blank; p. [5], half-title; p. [6], blank; title page, an inset; *verso*, Copyright 1898 | By L. C. PAGE AND COMPANY | (INCORPORATED) | Colonial Press: | Electrotyped and Printed by C. H. Simonds & Co. | Boston, U.S.A.; p. [7], quotation, one verse in

---

[1] From a collection of letters in Yale University.

Italian with English translation; p. [8], blank; p. [9], Illustrations; p. [10], blank; pp. 11–15, Introduction; p. [16], blank; pp. 17–351, text; p. [352], blank.
Publisher's cat. 8 pp. undated at end, inserted.

Binding: [i] Grey linen-grain cloth, pictorially blocked on front in gold, green and black with elaborate design incorporating a rider in grey on a white horse against a background of gold sky and in the distance (top left-hand corner) a Palazzo on a hill with the wording in black: THE [*dot*] MAKING [*dot*] OF [*dot*] A [*dot*] SAINT [*in a panel at head*] and: W [*dot*] SOMERSET [*dot*] MAUGHAM [*in a panel at foot*] the whole enclosed in a double-rule border; on spine in gold: THE | MAKING | OF A | SAINT | W. SOMERSET | MAUGHAM | L [*dot*] C [*dot*] PAGE | AND | COMPANY
(ii) The lettering on the spine is in black, except for the title which is in gold.
(iii) The whole of the lettering on the spine is in black.

Illustrations: 4 illustrations in black and white by Gilbert James. (1) "As I rode along, I meditated.", front., tissue guard. (2) " 'You need have no fear about your character' I answered bitterly.", facing p. 112. (3) "It was empty but for a few rapacious men, who were wandering about, like scavengers.", facing p. 222. (4) "In a bound I had reached him.", facing p. 328.
Plain end-papers; all edges cut; leaves measure 19 × 12½ cm.

Price: $1.50. 2,000 copies were published 31 May 1898.

Notes: I do not know which is the earliest of these three states of the binding, but would incline to favour that with the additional gold blocking, particularly as the publisher states that '26 copies of the first edition were bound in some sort of special binding, possibly for presentation.' Not only is it much less frequently found than (ii) and (iii) but publishers tend to simplify rather than elaborate a binding design, for economy's sake if for no other reason.

It should be noted, however, that (ii) and (iii) contain what would appear to be earlier advertisements—in the announcement of this work on page 5 of the advertisements there is the addition '(In press)'. In the absence of any corroborative evidence, it is not possible to give priority to any of the three states.

The book was reprinted in 1900 with paper wrappers (1,500 copies) and again in 1902. In 1922 the copyright was renewed and the book reprinted under the title *The Making of a Saint. A Romance of Mediaeval Italy* by The St Botolph Society (Boston). It was again reprinted from this edition in 1966 by Farrar, Strauss & Giroux, who had absorbed the firm of L. C. Page. John Farrar writes a most interesting 20 pp. foreword to this edition giving the history of the book, and quotes a pencilled memo by L. C. Page to a member of his office staff which is of such interest that it is reproduced here: 'I purchased the American rights on my first or second visit to London, back in the 90's—probably '96 or '97. I did not make the deal with Mr. T. Fisher Unwin, an elderly man who was little at his office (although I dined with him at his London Club). The deal was made with his manager, a fair practical man who was dissatisfied with Unwin, and was even then considering going into business for himself which he later did, and like Unwin has gone out of business. He, the manager, Benn, informed me that the Saint was a first novel and was purchased outright by Unwin who yearly ran a First Novel competition, purchasing these novels outright.' Mr. Page went on to say that he purchased the American rights outright for £40.

He was not right of course in stating it was a first novel—it was in fact Maugham's second novel.

A2   THE MAKING OF A SAINT   1898

b. First English edition:
THE MAKING OF A | SAINT | BY | WILLIAM SOMERSET MAUGHAM | [*ornament*] | LONDON | T. FISHER UNWIN | PATERNOSTER SQUARE | 1898
Title in red and black.

Collation: [viii], 304 pp. a⁴ A–T⁸.
p. [i], blank; p. [ii], NOVELS AT SIX SHILLINGS EACH [listing 25 works]; p. [iii], half-title; p. [iv], announcement of 2nd edition of LIZA OF LAMBETH with extracts from reviews; p. [v], title; p. [vi], [*All Rights reserved*]; p. [vii], 4 lines of Italian verse with translation; p. [viii], blank; pp. [1] 2–5, introduction; pp. 6–303, text; p. [304], blank. 4 leaves advts. signed a–c, e–l, m–n, s–t inserted. Printer's imprint foot of p. 303: [*rule*] | *Colston & Coy., Limited, Printers, Edinburgh.*

Binding: Kendal green vertical fine ribbed cloth, gold blocked on spine only and lettered: THE | MAKING OF | A SAINT | WILLIAM SOMERSET | MAUGHAM [*these words in a single rectangular frame*] | T. FISHER UNWIN [*in a lozenge-shaped frame at tail*]
Plain end-papers; top edges cut and gilt, fore and lower edges rough trimmed; leaves measure 20 × 12½ cm.

Price: 6s. 2,000 copies were published on 25 June 1898.

Notes: There are two issues of *The Making of a Saint*, the first issue is as described above, the second issue is the Colonial edition, described below. I have come across an interesting variation identical in every respect to the first edition except that the verso of the half-title reads LIZA OF LAMBETH Second Edition. Cloth *and Paper* (my italics) instead of Cloth 3s. 6d. as in the first edition. The paper edition of *Liza* did not come out until 1904, so this would bring the volume within the orbit of the Times Book Club edition and these undoubtedly are first edition sheets remaindered to the Club several years after first publication. The sheets are considerably cut down measuring 19 × 12 cm. The binding is a dark navy blue, lettered in black on front and spine, but with no publisher's imprint.

The author has described this novel as the worst book he ever wrote.

A2 THE MAKING OF A SAINT 1897

c. Colonial edition:

THE MAKING OF A | SAINT | BY | WILLIAM SOMERSET MAUGHAM | [*ornament*] | COLONIAL EDITION | LONDON | T. FISHER UNWIN | PATERNOSTER SQUARE | 1898

Collation: [viii], 304 pp. [ ]⁴ A – T⁸.
p. [i], blank; p. [ii], UNWIN'S COLONIAL LIBRARY; p. [iii], half title; p. [iv], By the same Author (announcing the Second Edition of *Liza of Lambeth*); p. [v], title; p. [vi], [All Rights reserved]; p. [vii], 4 lines of Italian verse with translation; p. [viii], blank; pp. [1] 2–303 text; p. [304], blank, 4 leaves advts. inserted

Binding: Kendal green vertical fine ribbed cloth, lettered in gold on spine only: THE | MAKING | OF A | SAINT | WILLIAM SOMERSET | MAUGHAM | UNWIN'S COLONIAL | LIBRARY
Plain end-papers; leaves measure 19 × 12 cm. all edges cut.

A3 ORIENTATIONS 1899

a. First edition:

ORIENTATIONS | By | William Somerset Maugham | *Author of* 'Liza of Lambeth,' 'The Making of a Saint' | [*ornament*] | London | T. Fisher Unwin | Paternoster Square | 1899
Title in red and black.

Collation: [viii], 280 pp. a⁴ A–R⁸ S⁴.

p. [i], half-title; p. [ii], NOVELS AT SIX SHILLINGS EACH [listing 38 works]; p. [iii], title; p. [iv], [*All Rights reserved*]; p. [v], dedication To | MRS. EDWARD JOHNSTON; p. [vi], blank; p. [vii], contents; p. [viii], quotation in French, 4 lines; p. [1], section title; p. [2], blank; pp. 3–278, text; pp. [279–280], blank.

Binding: (i) Kendal green vertical fine ribbed cloth. Gold blocked on spine only and lettered: ORIENTATIONS | BY | W. SOMERSET | MAUGHAM [*these words in a single rectangular frame*] | T. FISHER UNWIN [*in a lozenge-shaped frame at tail*]
(ii) Lincoln green vertical fine ribbed cloth, lettered as above. These two shades of green cloth may well have been used simultaneously. I can find no evidence that one preceded the other.
(iii) Smooth olive green cloth, blocked in black but lacking the publisher's imprint at the foot of the spine. This is a remainder binding, used on some first edition sheets which were bound in a cheaper form for a wholesaler.
Plain end-papers; leaves measure 20 × 12½ cm.

Price: 6s. 2,000 copies were published in June 1899.

Notes: The first issue has the top edges cut and gilt and the other edges rough trimmed, making the pages at least 20 cm. tall. The second issue has all the edges cut, making the pages 19 cm. tall. Mr. Muir (*Points: Second Series* p. 125) describes a *third* issue as consisting of cut-down sheets, like the second issue, but with an undated cancel title-page printed in black. A number of copies in the cheap cloth casing referred to above have passed through my hands, and all of them had the title page printed in red and black, but I have never traced a copy of the issue described by Mr. Muir. I suspect, therefore, that the book Mr. Muir was handling was bound from the sheets of Unwin's Colonial Library. This edition consisted of first edition sheets with a new half-title and title-page (comprising a quarter sheet), the latter being printed only in black and undated and the former having on the verso the legend UNWIN'S COLONIAL LIBRARY, followed by a list of titles in the series. I think there is little doubt that a number of these Colonial sheets were included in the sheets the publisher sold off to the wholesaler, who then removed the half-title to disguise the book's origin, thus making the title to appear a cancel.

There is a misprint on page 66, line 27 'elasped' for 'elapsed', common to the whole printing.

In the preface to the *Collected Edition* of *Liza of Lambeth* Somerset

Maugham says that following the success of his first novel he spent 8 months in Spain writing (among other activities) some short stories and to these he added two he had previously sent to T. Fisher Unwin and so made up the volume which he called *Orientations*. These two short stories were *A Bad Example* and *Daisy* and in Eddie Ayerbach's copy of *Orientations* (now in the possession of Leonard Meldman) Maugham has written 'A Bad Example and Daisy are the first stories I ever wrote, I was then 18.'

In the folder in the Berg Collection at The New York Public Library, referred to earlier, is the reader's reports on these two stories. As they were written by 'E.G.' (Edward Garnett) they will not be without interest. Of *A Bad Example* on the 20th July 1896, he wrote: 'There is some ability in this, but not very much. Mr. Maugham has imagination and he can write prettily, but his satire against Society is not deep enough or humourous enough to command attention. He should be advised to try the humbler magazines for a time, and if he tries anything more important to send it to us.'

Of *Daisy* on the 30th December 1898, he wrote: 'In some respects this story is not very artistic. Nevertheless [it] is very effective. It is strong and able, and the end undoubtedly has emotional force. In fact, the story hits one—there is no denying that: we believe the story will hit every reader.... We believe the story will meet with a good reception, and will increase Mr. Maugham's reputation. And we should call it a publisher's mistake for Fisher Unwin to lose an opportunity of issuing a volume of such stories.'

Contents: The Punctiliousness of Don Sebastian—A Bad Example—De Amicitia—Faith—The Choice of Amyntas—Daisy.

A4   THE HERO   1901

a. First edition:
THE HERO | BY | WILLIAM SOMERSET MAUGHAM | AUTHOR OF | "LIZA OF LAMBETH," "THE MAKING OF A SAINT," "ORIENTATIONS" | [*ornament*] | London [*followed by five dots*] | HUTCHINSON & CO. | Paternoster Row [dot] 1901

> *Collation:* 352 pp. [A]⁸ B–Y⁸.
> p. [1], half-title; p. [2], two quotations from James Thomson; p. [3], title; p. [4], dedication: To | MISS JULIA MAUGHAM; pp. 5–352, text.
>
> *Binding:* Dahlia red silk-grained cloth, blocked in gold on front with author's symbol and lettered: THE HERO; spine lettered in

gold: THE | HERO | WILLIAM | SOMERSET | MAUGHAM | HUTCHINSON & CO.

Plain end-papers; all edges cut; leaves measure 18.6 × 12 cm.

Price: 6s. 1,500 copies were published on 3 July 1901.

Notes: Some first edition sheets were used for Hutchinson's Colonial Library in a similar binding, but with 'Hutchinson's Colonial Library' added on the front cover and spine.

The Hero is the author's first book to have his well known Eastern symbol on the cover, and it is the only book in which it appears in this position—upside down! There is also a dropped 'g' in 'game' on page 129 in most copies, but not in all. When I put the point to Mr. Maugham he recalled drawing the publisher's attention to the inversion of the symbol and it was corrected on a number of copies that were specially bound. Since the publication of my bibliography two copies of the book have turned up—one in England and one in America —in the second state of the binding, and one has the dropped 'g' and in the other it is present. After the lapse of time it is not possible to deduce what transpired during the printing. It is feasible that the 'g' was present when the printing commenced, and then it was pulled out by the ink roller early in the run, which would account for most of the copies lacking the 'g'. On the other hand, the compositor could accidentally have omitted the 'g' in the frame, but inserted the letter late in the run when he noticed it was missing. In the latter event, the first sheets to be printed would be the last to be folded, but again a lot would depend upon the way the sheets were fed into the machine. In those days printing machines were fed by hand and the operator would probably cut the paper in reams, two out of a sheet, and feed it in piles of 500 in order not to have the encumbrance of too big a pile on the feed board, and too big a one to move after printing. Thus feeding them in this way it could be a matter of chance as to whether the last to be printed was the first pile to be picked for folding. Obviously in the case of *The Hero* the sheets had somehow got mixed and when the binder came to bind up the special copies with the symbol the right way up, he used sheets at the bottom of the pile which contained both states of the printing. It follows, therefore, that it is not possible to give priority to either of these two states.

In a letter in 1951 to his agent A. P. Watt, Maugham comments on *The Hero:* 'It was one of my earliest novels, it was not a success when it came out, and I don't believe it has any merit at all.'

The first edition has been indifferently reproduced in facsimile, I think in America.

The Maugham symbol is an Eastern sign against the Evil Eye found in Morocco. The author's father had the sign engraved on some glass bought for a house built and newly furnished just before he died, and his son adopted and used it on the covers of all his books from *The Hero* (where it appears upside down) onwards.

A5   MRS. CRADDOCK   1902

a. First edition:
Mrs. Craddock | By | William Somerset Maugham | Author of | "Liza of Lambeth," "Making of a Saint," | "The Hero" | London | William Heinemann | 1902

> *Collation:* [viii], 376 pp. [ ]⁴ A–Z⁸ 2A⁴.
>
> A blank leaf, not included in pagination: p. [i], half-title; p. [ii], [15] *New 6s. Novels*; p. [iii], title; p. [iv], blank; p. v–vi, Epistle Dedicatory signed W.M.; pp. [1] 2–373, text; pp. [374–376], blank. 32 pp. advts., unnumbered, undated, inserted.
>
> *Binding:* Petrol blue cloth, blocked in black on front with author's symbol and on back in blind with publisher's windmill device; gold-lettered on front: Mrs. Craddock; and on spine: Mrs. | Craddock | W. S. | Maugham | Heinemann
>
> Plain end-papers; all edges cut; leaves measure 18.3 × 12 cm.
>
> *Price:* 6s. 2,000 copies were published in November 1902.

Notes: 618 sets of first edition sheets printed for Heinemann's Colonial Edition were sold to the Times Book Club and bound for the Club in putty coloured cloth, lettered in black on the spine only, with the Club's device and imprint at the foot. These copies have a cancel title page, dated 1903. Most copies contain 32 pp. publisher's advertisements, but I have no evidence whether these have any significance for issue. The author's copy and all the Statutory Libraries' copies have the advertisements.

The notable fact about *Mrs. Craddock* is that it is the only one of this author's early novels (with the possible exception of *Liza*) that is today at all readable. Here for the first time one catches unexpected flashes of the later Maugham, with his worldly wisdom and uncanny, intuitive understanding of human nature, breaking through the somewhat hackneyed prose.

After the publication (for those days) of the somewhat 'daring' *Mrs. Craddock*, Mr. Maugham evidently suffered some rebuffs from

publishers and editors, for he is constantly stressing in his letters to
Pinker, that 'I can be trusted to be suitably moral . . .' and again 'My
new work (The Bishops Apron) is different from anything I have
hitherto done in that it is exceedingly decent and is presumed to be
humourous.' In a letter to his agent written from Capri about 1905,
asking him to protect the American rights of *Loaves and Fishes*, later
published under the title *The Bishop's Apron*, he declared, 'My novels
have apparently been too shocking for the American public. Only one
was published there and that was six years ago by Page of Boston, I
think . . . I don't know if it had any success. I should think not. I don't
think there is in *Loaves and Fishes* anything that would bring a blush to
the cheek of an American matron.'

A5   MRS. CRADDOCK   1903

*b. First edition sheets remaindered to the Times Book Club, with new title
page.*
MRS. CRADDOCK | BY | WILLIAM SOMERSET MAUGHAM |
AUTHOR OF | "LIZA OF LAMBETH," "MAKING OF A
SAINT," | "THE HERO" | LONDON | WILLIAM HEINEMANN
| 1903

> *Binding:* Violet cloth, lettered in black on front: Mrs. Craddock;
> and on spine: Mrs. | Craddock | W.S. | Maugham | [*device*] |
> The Times.
> On verso of title page 'All rights reserved'. No prelims, apart
> from title page (a cancellans), blank leaf at end of volume. Sheets
> cut down to 18.1 by 12 cm.

Notes: Collectors who have the Times Book Club issues of *Mrs.
Craddock* and *The Merry-go-Round* are often puzzled to account for
the dates on the title pages, i.e. 1903 and 1905 (see P. H. Muir's *Points:
Second Series*, pages 126–7) when, according to the publisher's records,
the sheets were not remaindered to the Club until April 1906 and at
that time the Club, formed 11th September, 1905, had been in existence only a few months. The explanation is that the sheets remaindered
to the Club were the balance of the Colonial editions, new titles for
which had been printed with the dates 1903 and 1905—the year
following English publication in each case. It was common practice at
this time for Heinemann to date their Colonial editions a year later,
partly because the new titles were not printed until the English impression had been run off but mainly so that the edition should not
appear an old one when it arrived in the Colonies.
The stock remaindered to *The Times Book Club* was made up partly

of sheets and partly of bound copies. The bound copies were invariably cased in the familiar blue cloth, though variations are to be met with in the type of brasses used for the blocking, and the blocking of the windmill and symbol is usually in blind instead of gold. Copies cased in other coloured cloths (i.e. lilac, smooth navy blue, putty, chestnut etc.) with the Club device or imprint at the foot of the spine, were bound by the Club. It was the practice for the Club to rebind copies of books discarded by their lending library for sale to the public, and the *Times* imprint on these copies is usually lacking. In the case of *The Merry-go-Round* Heinemann loaned the dies to the Club to save the expense of making new brasses. This accounts for the identical blocking on the covers of both issues.

All the copies I have examined of this remainder issue bound in the Heinemann blue cloth lack the half-title page, and the title page and verso have a variant text. The title page is always set in caps. This is explained by the fact that most of the sets of sheets remaindered to *The Times Book Club* originally formed part of the Colonial edition for which a new half-title and title page had been printed. The half-title page was removed before binding because the text disclosed it was the Colonial edition. This half-title page reads as follows: Heinemann's Colonial Library of Popular Fiction | [*rule*] | Issued for Sale in the British | Colonies and India, and not | to be imported into Europe or | the United States of America. Verso blank. The Colonial edition also usually had inserted at the end of the volume four to eight additional leaves of advertisements captioned 'Heinemann's Colonial Library', and was bound in straw coloured wrappers. I have to thank Mr. Leslie Munro and Mr. S. H. Herbert of Messrs. Heinemann for help in elucidating this problem.

It may interest collectors to know something of the origin of *The Times Book Club*. It aroused one of the most bitter and drawn-out controversies of the 1900's and became known as the 'War of the Books'. It was formed and financed by *The Times* newspaper ostensibly to break the 'net-book' system—'a monopoly trust' as *The Times* described it—but was really a newspaper stunt to increase the *Thunderer's* circulation and finances, which were then at a very low ebb. The 'net-book' system, which has been operating successfully for over 70 years (it was inaugurated at the turn of the century) and received the blessing of the Monopolies and Restrictive Practices Commission in 1962, was formed by the Publisher's Association to stop the price-cutting that had almost brought ruin to certain sections of the book trade.

In exchange for an order for *The Times* newspaper for a year, subscribers 'would be able to read the newest books without buying them, or paying a circulation library for the use of them' and also to buy on special terms any book that seemed worth buying after reading it 'at a discount of 35% off the published price of ordinary books and 20% off net books'. One of the first publications *The Times Book Club* handled was a Supplement edition of the *Encyclopaedia Britannica* and it sold—according to an advertisement in *The Times*—'like hot cakes on a cold morning'. The Club followed up this success by opening up a bookshop in the West End and starting a circulating library and book club.

To make a success of the venture, however, the Club had to obtain books and it was soon brought home to its organisers that this was going to prove a difficult and costly business, for no sooner had the publishers got wind of what was happening than they acted quickly. They combined with the booksellers' association to boycott the Club and prevent books reaching it through ordinary trade channels, except at net-book prices. The Club did its utmost to circumvent the boycott by coming to an arrangement with certain publishers outside the scheme, but it still had to secure for subscribers books which could only be purchased under the 'net-book' agreement, and these it sold at a loss. Only a year after its establishment—as the purchase of the Maugham sheets indicates—the Club had, for all intents and purposes, given up the idea of selling new books at a reduced rate inside the 'net-book' close period—i.e. at least six months from the date of publication—and had to a large extent fallen back on 'remainders'.

Despite repeated appeals to the public for support, it was palpably clear to everyone that *The Times* was fighting a losing battle and that there was nothing for it but to take the advice of *The Spectator* 'to stick to its last and be the best newspaper in the world, rather than turn itself into a cheap lending library and a bookseller at cut-throat prices'. Ultimately, of course, the Club had to change its tactics, with the result that until its absorption a few years ago *The Times Bookshop* was one of the largest and most esteemed booksellers in the trade.

A5   MRS. CRADDOCK   (1920)

c. First American edition:
[*within a double-rule border*] MRS. CRADDOCK | BY | W. SOMER-SET MAUGHAM | AUTHOR OF "THE MOON AND SIX-PENCE," | "OF HUMAN BONDAGE," ETC. | NEW [*publisher's monogram device*] YORK | GEORGE H. DORAN COMPANY

Collation: [viii] 9–318 pp. [unsigned 1–20⁸]
pp. [—], blank leaf; p. [i], half-title; p. [ii], BY W. SOMERSET

MAUGHAM [listing 4 titles]; p. [iii], title page; p. [iv], Printed in the United States of America; p. v–vi, Epistle Dedicatory; p. [vii], fly-title; p. [viii], blank; pp. 9–313, text; pp. [314–318], blank.

Binding: Mortlake brown open thread cloth, blocked in peat brown on front with two ornamental brackets resting on a third and lettered Mrs. Craddock | by | W. Somerset Maugham; and on spine: MRS. | CRADDOCK | [*ornament*] | Maugham | DORAN Fancy or ornamental lettering has been ignored.
Plain end-papers; all edges cut; leaves measure 19 × 13 cm.

Price: $1.90. Number of copies unknown. Published March 1920.

Notes: This copy is inscribed 'For my dear Barbara this novel of my early youth published in 1900. Willy.' and came from the author's library. It is now in the University of Texas Library.

A5 MRS. CRADDOCK (1937)

d. The Collected Edition:
W. SOMERSET MAUGHAM | [*rule*] | MRS. CRADDOCK | [*star*] | [*publisher's windmill device*] | LONDON | WILLIAM HEINE-MANN LTD

Collation: x, 302 pp. [A]⁸ B–T⁸ U⁴.
p. [i], half-title; p. [ii], The Collected Edition of the Works of W. Somerset Maugham [listing 14 non-dramatic works and 6 vols. plays]; p. [iii], title; p. [iv], FIRST PUBLISHED 1902 ... | COLLECTED EDITION 1937 | Printed in Great Britain | at The Windmill Press, Kingswood, Surrey; p. v–vii, Preface; p. [viii], blank; pp. ix–x, Epistle Dedicatory; pp. [1] 2–302, text.

Binding: Smooth red cloth, blocked on front in blind with author's symbol and on back with publisher's windmill device; gold-lettered on spine between double-rules THE WORKS | of | W. SOMERSET | MAUGHAM | [*dot*] | MRS. | CRADDOCK | HEINEMANN Plain end-papers; all edges cut; leaves measure 18.2 × 12 cm.

Price: 3s.6d. Number of copies unknown. Published February 1937.

Notes: The author made considerable textual revisions to this edition, tidying up the grammar and the punctuation, as will be seen from the illustration of one of the pages which Mr. Grenville Cook has annotated, showing the revisions (see illus.).

A5   MRS. CRADDOCK   1955

e. New and Revised edition:
W. SOMERSET MAUGHAM | [*rule*] | MRS. CRADDOCK |
[*star*] | [*publisher's windmill device resting on base*] | WILLIAM HEINE-
MANN LTD | MELBOURNE [*square of 4 dots*] LONDON [*square of
4 dots*] TORONTO

> *Pagination:* [xii], 339 [340] pp. Scarlet cloth, gilt.
> 18.5 × 12.1 cm. 18s.

Notes: The first reprint of this novel appeared in the *Collected Edition*
in 1937 and was reprinted from the original manuscript with the
passages that William Heinemann found shocking left in. Mr. Maugham
had forgotten what they were and, on the contrary, says the propriety
of the book seemed to him almost painful. However, for the reader
interested in bibliographical niceties, the texts of two of the passages
are extracted and compared below. They appear towards the end of the
book when Mrs. Craddock is contemplating eloping with her young
lover.

First edition	Collected edition
p. 316 . . . person	p. 291 . . . body
. . . they might be separated by ten thousand miles, but they would always be joined together. How else could she prove to him her wonderful love, how else could she show her immeasurable gratitude?	. . . they might be separated by ten thousand miles, but there would always be the bond between them. Her flesh cried out to his flesh, and the desire was irresistable. How else could she prove to him her wonderful love? How else could she show her immeasurable gratitude?
p. 321. . . . She gave way; she no longer wished to resist. She turned her face to Gerald.	p. 296. . . . She gave way, she no longer wished to resist, flesh called to flesh, and there was no force on earth more powerful. Her whole frame was quivering with passion. She turned her face to Gerald. . . .

The author states in the preface to the new edition that he has made
minor amendments in the text and corrected the 'haphazard punctuation', but otherwise left it as it was with 'all its faults'. The Epistle

Dedicatory (2 pages) was dropped with this edition, and the preface expanded.

A6   A MAN OF HONOUR   1903

a. Separate issue:
A MAN OF | HONOUR | A PLAY IN FOUR ACTS | BY | W. SOMERSET MAUGHAM | As performed by the Stage Society at the Imperial | Theatre, Westminster, on | MONDAY, FEBRUARY 23rd, 1903 | LONDON: | CHAPMAN AND HALL, LIMITED | 11 HENRIETTA STREET, COVENT GARDEN | 1903 [*the foregoing is enclosed in a double frame, outside border being thicker than inside*] **Price Two Shillings net**
Cover title.

> *Collation:* 50 pp. a¹⁶ b⁸ c¹.
> p. [1], A MAN OF HONOUR. | A PLAY IN FOUR ACTS. | BY WILLIAM SOMERSET MAUGHAM. | [*rule*] | CHARACTERS [*followed by list of 10 characters with John Halliwell's role left blank*] | TIME: The Present Day: pp. 2–50, text.

> *Binding:* Stiff light cream wrappers, printed in black (as above); inner and back wrappers blank. Sewed.
> All edges cut. 24.4 × 16 cm. Published 22 February 1903.

> *Binding Variant:* A few copies were bound in thick pink paper for the use of the actors during the rehearsals. These precede those in light cream wrappers sold in the theatre. This information was given me by the author. I have never met with a copy, but Sir Gerald Kelly once owned one, presented to him by the author. Mr. Grenville Cook tells me, however, that he once handled one after the last war and the colour was a "rich buff".

Supplement issue:

[*top left-hand corner*] Literary Supplement | A MAN OF HONOUR. | A PLAY IN FOUR ACTS. | BY WILLIAM SOMERSET MAUGHAM | [*rule*] | CHARACTERS. [*followed by list of 10 characters with John Halliwell's role left blank*] | TIME: The Present Day.

> *Collation:* Collation same as in the copy described above.
> 23.9 × 15.3 cm.
> Issued as a Supplement to the March issue of *The Fortnightly Review.*

A Man of Honour was published in two states—as a single play in wrappers and in the unusual form as a supplement to *The Fortnightly Review*. Indeed, had it not appeared in this latter form, it is unlikely that it would ever have been printed. It may be of interest to recount how this came about. When the play was accepted for production by The Stage Society, one of the members on the committee was W. L. Courtney, who was also editor of *The Fortnightly Review*. He liked the play and offered to publish it as a Supplement to that magazine. Mr. Maugham was, of course, delighted. Apart from the satisfaction it would give him to see his first play in print, it was a signal honour for a comparatively unknown author to have his work accepted for an important and influential magazine as *The Fortnightly Review* then was.

Just before the play was due to go into rehearsal Mr. Maugham approached the editor and asked him if he would run off a few copies for use at rehearsal and also for sale as a souvenir on the opening night. Mr. Courtney obliged, and 150 copies were put at the author's disposal and published under the imprint of the magazine's publishers, Messrs. Chapman and Hall. The only variation in the two issues was the addition of the two words 'Literary Supplement' in the top left-hand corner of the Supplement's title page.

The circulation of *The Fortnightly Review* at that time was about 5,000 or 6,000 copies, and there is little question that the procedure followed by the printer was to print the several thousand copies of the Supplement, then remove from the type the words 'Literary Supplement' and run off Mr. Maugham's copies. A reverse of this procedure was most unlikely. The 'Supplement issue', therefore, preceded in actual printing the separate Maugham issue. It is important to note, however, that the Supplement was printed separately and not as part of the sheets of the magazine, as an examination of the signatures reveals, and it was bound in at the end of the magazine. This the author confirms.

Unfortunately, it has not been possible to ascertain the exact date of publication of the two issues. Mr. Maugham states that the 'separate issue' was on sale in the theatre on February 22nd (which the publisher confirms) despite the fact that in *The English Catalogue* the month of publication is given as March. The fact, however, that the 'separate issue' was on sale at the theatre on the opening night definitely establishes that it was published on or before February 22nd.

The date of publication of *The Fortnightly Review* (March issue) is uncertain. The British Museum copy is stamped April 3rd, but this signifies very little as periodicals normally take about three weeks to a month after delivery to be stamped. The scanty evidence available, however, would seem to point to the magazine having been received some time in March.

In all the circumstances, I regard the *Supplement issue* in the original magazine wrappers as the true first edition, but collectors of the *Separate issue* may be encouraged to know that the late Mr. Michael Sadleir, who was faced with a parallel problem in his Trollope bibliography (see *Ralph the Heir*, pages 124–127 and pages 298–299) sides with them. This is what he has to say on the point: 'I belong to the somewhat pedantic school who give to any item wrappered separately and with no magazine material within its covers priority over a serial issue in periodical magazine form. So I should regard the Maugham *A Man of Honour* as the true first. But I should "collect" the Supplement series all the same. One cannot ignore a second issue of such intimate interest and one as vital to the complete *A Man of Honour* as are the back legs of a pantomime horse.' The 'supplement issue' must be as common or as rare as are copies of *The Fortnightly Review* for March 1903 *which survive in their original wrappers*—for, of course, it is only in that form that it is of real importance to collectors.

A Man of Honour was the author's first acted full-length play. The separate issue consisted of only 150 copies. Very few were sold and the remainder were sent to the author at his flat in Portland Place shortly before the war and, according to the author, disappeared when the house was bombed. This, however, is not in accord with the facts. The true story of the whereabouts of these remainder copies is revealed in the correspondence between the author and Fred Bason, the Cockney bookseller, author and broadcaster, from which it would appear that Fred Bason sold six of them for him on a commission basis and the remainder were divided, some going to friends as gifts and some being retained by the author.

The play is a dramatisation of one thread of *The Merry-go-Round*, which provided the author with several plots for later books. It was written in Rome in 1898. A year after its production by the Stage Society (the first night of which, incidentally, was a Sunday, the 22nd February), the play was put on at the Avenue Theatre for a short run with a revised ending, but was not a financial success.

A6 A MAN OF HONOUR (1911) 1912

b. First Heinemann edition:
A MAN OF HONOUR | A TRAGEDY | *In Four Acts* | BY W. S. MAUGHAM | LONDON: WILLIAM HEINEMANN | MCMXII

Collation: xvi, 160 pp. [   ]⁸ A–K⁸.
p. [i–ii], blank; p. [iii], half-title; p. [iv], HEINEMANN'S MODERN
PLAYS; p. [v], title; p. [vi], *Copyright: London William Heinemann*
1912; p. [vii], dedication: TO | GERALD KELLY; p. [viii], quotation
from Eckermann; pp. ix–xii, General Preface; p. xiii, list of cast;
p. [xiv], blank; p. xv, Characters; p. xvi, note on performing
rights; pp. 1–158, text; p. [159], printer's imprint; p. [160],
blank.

Binding: Cherry red buckram (2s.6d.) and champagne wrappers
(1s. 6s.). *See prelim Note.*
Plain end-papers; all edges cut; leaves measure 17.3 cm. (wraps.
17.6 cm.).

1,500 copies of the second (first Heinemann) edition were published on 11th December, 1911.

First American edition: (1912) Chicago (The Dramatic Publishing
Co.).
    Reissue of the first Heinemann edition with new American title
leaf. Heinemann sheets, comprising 500 copies, were despatched to
Chicago in 1912.
    Two typescript copies of *A Man of Honour* were deposited in Mr.
Maugham's name with the Library of Congress in 1903. These
copies were transferred from the copyright office, apparently non-
registerable. Under the terms of copyright that prevailed at that time,
dramatic composition in unpublished form could be deposited for
purposes of copyright on the understanding that, if the particular
work was printed, two additional copies of the printed text would
also be deposited. After 1909, unpublished works by both American
and foreign authors could still be accepted for copyright; if these
unpublished works, however, were published, copyright in America
was effective only if the work itself was published in that country.
This provision of course in no way affected material already deposited
prior to 1909 in unpublished form.
    This copyright question has given rise to much confusion, par-
ticularly in regard to the Maugham plays published in Chicago by
The Dramatic Publishing Company under the series *Sergel's Acting
Drama*—a similar organisation to the present day Samuel French. It
has been stated in print (as recently as 1950) that there are earlier
American editions than Heinemann's of *Smith*, *The Explorer* and
Penelope, and also a Chicago 1903 edition of *A Man of Honour*. This is
not correct, despite the fact that the date of this latter publication is
given in The Library of Congress Catalogue as 1903, an error that

will be adjusted in the next edition. All the *Sergel* editions of the plays are made up of Heinemann sheets, including in some cases the new American title page, and these dates—which are usually indicated only by a rubber stamp on the verso of the American title page— are the dates of the original copyright. The so-called 1903 edition of *A Man of Honour* is made up of sheets of the 1912 Heinemann edition and contains the new preface and the announcement 'Heinemann's Modern Plays' (facing title page), a study of which alone reveals a much later printing than 1903. Most of the plays have the printer's imprint at the end of the volume or state 'Printed in England' on the verso of the title page.

A letter received by The Library of Congress from Messrs. Doubleday, Doran in 1937, relating to *Smith*, touches on this point: 'Copyright in England, which in those early times initiated with production rather than publication, began in the fall of 1909. That accounts for the 1909 copyright, and is supported by a U.S.A. copyright registration for the unpublished manuscript. In 1913, when Heinemann brought out their first publication of *Smith*, sheets were sent to Chicago, to The Dramatic Publishing Company, with the legend 'Copyright 1909'. Those sheets were for the purposes of distribution disposed of among play producers. One of that small edition bound up by The Dramatic Publishing Company, it now seems, was actually deposited in the U.S.A. Copyright Office. That fortunately completes the American copyright through meeting the requirements of Section 11 Copyright Act. . . .'

Notes: Contains a new 3½ pp. preface by the author. It is one of the more scarce of the Heinemann series, especially in buckram. *See* Appendix 1.

A7   THE MERRY-GO-ROUND   1904

a. First edition
The Merry-go-round | By | William Somerset Maugham | Author of | 'Liza of Lambeth', 'The Hero,' 'Mrs. Craddock' | [*publisher's windmill device in box*] | London | William Heinemann | 1904

> *Collation:* [viii], 400 pp. [ ]⁴ 1–25⁸.
> p. [i–ii], blank; p. [iii], half-title; p. [iv], [9] press opinions of *Mrs. Craddock*; p. [v], title; p. [vi], *This Edition enjoys Copyright in all | countries signatory to the Berne | Treaty, and is not to be imported | into the United States of America*; p. [vii], dedication: To HERBERT AND MARGUERITE BUNNING | [4 lines of verse foot of page]; p. [viii], blank; pp. [1] 2–398, text; pp. [399–400], blank.

Binding: Petrol blue cloth, blocked in gold on front with author's symbol and on back in blind with publisher's windmill device in box; gold-lettered on front: The Merry-Go-Round; and on spine: The | Merry- | Go-Round | W. S. | Maugham | Heinemann.
Plain end-papers; top edges cut, fore and lower edges rough trimmed; leaves measure 19 × 12.8 cm.

Binding Variant: Smooth chestnut cloth, identically blocked, except that the blocking is in black instead of gold, and the publisher's imprint is lacking at the foot of the spine. The blocking was done with the original dies. This is a remainder binding used on some first edition sheets which were bound in a cheaper form for a wholesaler.
Plain end-papers; all edges cut; leaves measure 18.2 × 12 cm.

Price: 6s. 3,000 copies were published on 19 September, 1904.

Notes: There are two issues of the first edition. The first issue is as described above, the second is the Times Book Club issue described below **A7b**.

A7   THE MERRY-GO-ROUND   1905

b. First edition sheets remainder to the Times Book Club, with new title-page.
THE | MERRY-GO-ROUND | BY | WILLIAM SOMERSET MAUGHAM | AUTHOR OF | "LIZA OF LAMBETH," | "THE HERO," "MRS. CRADDOCK" | LONDON | WILLIAM HEINEMANN | 1905

Binding: Petrol blue cloth, blocked in blind on front with author's symbol; gold-lettered on front The Merry-Go-Round | W. S. | Maugham | HEINEMANN.

Notes: Apart from the copies sold to the Times Book Club in the Heinemann binding as described above, the Club also received 290 sets of first edition sheets printed for Heinemann's Colonial edition which were bound for the Club in smooth navy blue cloth, lettered in gold on spine only, with the Club's device and imprint at the foot. These copies have a cancel title page, dated 1905, and the blank leaf at the end of the volume has been removed, leaving a stub. On verso of title-page 'All rights reserved'. The leaves measure 18.2 × 12 cm. *See Note to* **A5b**.

A7   THE MERRY-GO-ROUND   1904

c. American Copyright issue, lodged with the Library of Congress (not for sale):
[*within a double-rule border, divided into 3 compartments and lettered: at top*] The Merry-go-round | [*centre*] By W. Somerset Maugham | [*publisher's device—book lying on stand*] | [*at base*] NEW YORK | DOUBLE, PAGE & COMPANY | 1904

> *Collation:* pp. [i–ii], blank; p. [iii], half-title; p. [iv], blank; p. [v], title; p. [vi], COPYRIGHT, SEPT., 1904, BY | W. SOMERSET MAUGHAM; p. [1], PART ONE; p. [2], blank; pp. 3–42, text.

> *Binding:* Greenish (now much faded) wrappers, printed on front within double-rule border: The | Merry-go-round | By W. Somerset Maugham.
> All edges cut; leaves measure 24 × 15 cm.

Notes: Contains Chapter 1 of Part One, pp. 3–11; and Chapter 1 of Part 11, pp. 15–28 and Chapter XV, pp. 29–42. Only parts of the chapters are printed, but sufficient to comply with the requirements of American copyright.

A7   THE MERRY-GO-ROUND   (1916)

d. First cheap edition:
THE | MERRY-GO-ROUND | BY | WILLIAM SOMERSET MAUGHAM | AUTHOR OF | "OF HUMAN BONDAGE," "THE EXPLORER," ETC. | [*publisher's windmill device in box*] | LONDON | WILLIAM HEINEMANN

> *Collation:* [iv], 252 pp. [ ]² A–G¹⁶ H⁸ [I]⁴ [K]².
> The first two leaves are an insert.
> p. [i], half-title; p. [ii], Heinemann's 1s. net Novels, listing 34 titles; p. [iii], title; p. [iv], *First published 6s., September*, 1904 | CHEAP 1s. CLOTH EDITION, *July* 1916; pp. [1] 2–241, text; pp. [242–248], advts.; pp. [249–250], free end-paper (advts.) conjugate with pp. [251–252] lining paper pasted down K².

> *Binding:* Red ribbed cloth, blind blocked on front with elaborate design of leaves and flowers within a two-rule border and lettered in blind THE MERRY- | GO-ROUND | WILLIAM SOMERSET MAUGHAM; gold-lettered on spine in panels THE | MERRY- | GO- | ROUND | [*ornament*] | WILLIAM | SOMERSET | MAUGHAM; and at base HEINE-MANN; on back publisher's windmill device in blind.

Binding Variant: I have met with a variant binding—the binding blocked and lettered in black instead of in blind.
Yellow front end-papers with double border in yellow and publisher's windmill device in box; back plain.

Price: 1s. Number of copies unknown. Published in September 1916.

Notes: The break between Maugham and his first literary agent William Maurice Colles, who was a barrister by profession but carried on a literary agency, came about as a result of the failure of *The Merry-go-Round*. Colles had persuaded Heinemann to accept the book but he evidently did so reluctantly, and only after the author had made considerable cuts. He did very little to promote the novel and when sales continued to drag Maugham put the blame not on the book's shortcomings but on his agent's lack of initiative in not pressing the publisher to do more advertising. He then began looking around for a new literary agent and on Arnold Bennett's recommendation contacted J. B. Pinker who agreed to handle his new novel (The Bishop's Apron). Thereupon he wrote to Colles from Capri, where he was staying, informing him that owing to the lamentable failure of *The Merry-go-Round* he proposed to make his own arrangements with regard to his next novel.[1] Evidently Colles protested, for then Maugham revealed how deeply he felt about the whole business. 'With regard to *The Merry-go-Round* I think we must agree to differ; I do not wish to break into recriminations; but I cannot help thinking that what is obvious to me now, your experience might have suggested to you then, namely, that when a publisher does not like a book and has made up his mind that it will not sell, one might just as well throw it in the Thames as let him publish it.'[2]

In his next letter to Pinker, Maugham declared that he did not want his new novel (The Bishop's Apron) offered to Heinemann. '. . . he has grown slack of late and he does not seem to me to advertise well. My last novel (The Merry-go-Round) he only sold two thousand copies of.'[3]

---

[1] Grenville Cook Collection.
[2] Yale University Library.
[3] The University of Texas Library.

A8   THE LAND OF THE BLESSED VIRGIN: 1905
Sketches and Impressions in Andalusia

First edition:
THE LAND OF | THE BLESSED VIRGIN | SKETCHES AND
IMPRESSIONS IN | ANDALUSIA | BY | WILLIAM SOMERSET
MAUGHAM | (WITH FRONTISPIECE) | [*publisher's windmill
device in box* | LONDON | WILLIAM HEINEMANN | MCMV

Collation: viii, 228 pp. [ ]⁴ A–O⁸ P². Front, tissue guard, a
single inset.
p. [i], half-title; p. [ii], announcement of four books within rule
border; p. [iii], title; p. [iv], *All rights reserved*; p. [v], dedication;
TO | VIOLET HUNT; p. [vi], blank; pp. vii–viii, contents; pp. 1–
227 [228], text.

Binding: Madonna blue boards, parchment spine, blocked in
gold on front with author's symbol; gold-lettered on front;

THE LAND OF THE | BLESSED VIRGIN; and on spine: THE LAND |
OF THE | BLESSED | VIRGIN | W. SOMERSET | MAUGHAM | HEINEMANN
Plain end-papers; top edges uncut, fore and lower edges rough
trimmed; leaves measure 20.4 × 14.6 cm.

Price: 6s. 1,250 copies were published in January 1905. About
half the edition was remaindered.

Binding Variants: There are 3 variants of the casing of the first
edition, their chronological order being as follows:
(i) the width of the lettering on the spine measures THE LAND
3.3 cm. (or 1 9/32 in.), OF THE 1.8 cm. (or 22/32 in.), BLESSED 2.9 cm.
(or 1.4/32 in.), VIRGIN 2.4 cm. (or 30/32 in.).
(ii) the lettering is appreciably smaller. THE LAND measures 2.6 cm.
(or 1 1/32 in.). OF THE 1.4 cm. (or 18/32 in.), BLESSED 2.4 cm.
(or 30/32 in.), VIRGIN 1.9 cm. (¾ in.).
(iii) this variant has a white *flat* cloth back with identical lettering
to (ii) and with all edges uncut.
The measurements I have taken differ slightly from Mr. Muir's
(*see Points: Second Series*, page 126). I have measured the lettering
by taking a rubbing and then measuring the width of the rubbing,
in this way making allowance for the rounded spine.

First American edition: July 1920. New York (A. A. Knopf). $3.
The title of the first American edition reads: *The Land of the Blessed
Virgin: Sketches and Impressions in Andalusia.* There are two 1920 Knopf
editions of this travel book. The first is made up from sheets of the

1905 English printing with a new title page which is on a stub. This follows the text of the English title page except for the imprint, which reads: [*publisher's device*] | NEW YORK | ALFRED A. KNOPF | MCMXX. Bound in light blue-green paper boards with white cloth spine and with a paper label. The second Knopf edition, published later the same year, reads: ANDALUSIA | SKETCHES AND IMPRESSIONS | BY W. SOMERSET MAUGHAM | AUTHOR OF "THE MOON AND SIXPENCE," ETC. | NEW YORK [*publisher's device*] MCMXX | ALFRED A. KNOPF. Bound in red paper boards with black cloth spine with yellow label on front cover printed in red. This edition has the note 'A small edition of this book (printed in England and bound in the United States) was published in the Spring of 1920 by Mr. Knopf under the title THE LAND OF THE BLESSED VIRGIN.'

Notes: This book was written from notes made by Maugham while living in Seville for eight months in 1898. A draft of the book was ready the following June and Maugham suggested to his agent that he should try and get the book serialised in a magazine and perhaps get a Spanish artist to do some sketches, as to illustrate it with photos 'would be absurd.'[1] But these ideas came to nothing for no publisher would have the book at any price. It was entirely rewritten in 1902 and by the beginning of 1903 it was in Heinemann's hands, though he did not want to publish it '. . . this year because he has in hand another book of the same class.'[2]

Ultimately, Heinemann signed an agreement with Maugham in June 1904 though this of course was before it had become evident through the failure of *The Merry-go-Round* that he was not the go-ahead publisher that Maugham had been led to believe. In any event it was too late to do anything about *The Land of the Blessed Virgin* even if he had wanted to, but having got it off his hands after seven years, this seems most unlikely.

However, Heinemann remained under a cloud and in 1905 Maugham was writing from Paris to Pinker '. . . Heinemann has published my last three books, but I am tired of him.' Again, the same year, he was writing '. . . There is no reason to leave Heinemann to fare worse, and he will give me a substantial advance. But if I can help it I do not want to go to him as I think his day is over.' The fact of the matter was that the young novelist was beginning to fall on his feet and his experience with his first publisher, Fisher Unwin who, he declared

[1] Grenville Cook Collection.
[2] Yale University Library.

in a letter to Pinker, did him 'thoroughly in the eye' over *Liza of Lambeth* had probably done more than anything else to strengthen the shrewd business acumen which, as the Pinker correspondence discloses, stood him in good stead in his future relations with publishers. He was not destined, however, to continue with the struggle to make a living out of novel writing. Success was just around the corner and within eighteen months *Lady Frederick* had relieved him of the necessity of ever again having to write 'for money'. He was not to write another novel for nearly eight years, by which time he was a famous playwright, and then followed *Of Human Bondage* and a relationship with William Heinemann that was to endure for over half a century. *See* Appendix V, Note 1.

A9   THE BISHOP'S APRON   1906

a. First edition:
THE BISHOP'S APRON | A STUDY IN THE ORIGINS | OF A GREAT FAMILY | BY | W. S. MAUGHAM | AUTHOR OF "LIZA OF LAMBETH", "MRS. CRADDOCK," | "THE MERRY-GO-ROUND" | LONDON | CHAPMAN AND HALL, LTD. | 1906

> *Collation:* [viii], 312 pp. [A]⁴ B–U⁸ X⁴.
> p. [i–ii], blank; p. [iii], half-title; p. [iv], blank; p. [v], title; p. [vi], printer's imprint: RICHARD CLAY & SONS, LIMITED, | BREAD STREET HILL, E.C., AND | BUNGAY, SUFFOLK; p. [vii], dedication: TO | HARRY PHILIPS; p. [viii], blank; pp. [1] 2–311 [312], text. At foot of p. [312], printer's imprint: [*rule*] | *Richard Clay & Sons, Limited, London and Bungay*.

> *Binding:* Cardinal linen grain cloth, blocked in gold on front with author's symbol and gold-lettered: THE BISHOP'S APRON; and on spine: THE | BISHOP'S | APRON | W. Somerset | Maugham | CHAPMAN AND HALL
> Plain end-papers; all edges cut; leaves measure 18.4 × 12.4 cm.

> *Price:* 6s. No record is now available of the number of the first edition. The author believed it was 1,500 but the book's scarcity suggests it was small. It was published in February 1906. There is no American edition of the novel.

Notes: There are two issues of *The Bishop's Apron*, the first issue is as described above, the second issue is Bell's Indian & Colonial Library edition comprising cut down sheets of the first edition with a new half-title page, and which is described below.

Copies of the novel, in all respects identical to the first edition
except for the addition 'Second Edition' 'Third Edition' or 'Fourth
Edition' on the title page, have been traced. In the absence of any
explanation from the publishers, who state that their records are no
longer available. I had to rely on the author's memory and he affirmed
that the book did not sell particularly well and he believes that the
whole edition did not exceed 1,500 copies. A comparison of the sheets
of the first edition and the so-called 'Second' 'Third' and 'Fourth'
editions shows that all these 'editions' were run off the same casting of
type. I am confident that the novel was never reprinted by the original
publishers, and conclude that these additions to the title-page were
made to give a spurt to sales that were lagging—a not uncommon
contrivance in those days, even among established publishers. It is
probable that the reprint of the novel by Newnes in 1908 was inspired
by the publicity Maugham had gained through having four plays
running in the West End at the same time.

Arthur Waugh, head of Chapman and Hall, the publishers, writing
to Pinker to inform him that he would be glad to read the MS. of
The Bishop's Apron, said 'As a rule I have not cared for his stories as I
think they are too gloomy and pessimistic for the general public to
take to them.'

A9   THE BISHOP'S APRON   1906

b. Bell's Indian & Colonial Library edition:
THE BISHOP'S APRON | A STUDY IN THE ORIGINS | OF A
GREAT FAMILY | BY | W. S. MAUGHAM | AUTHOR OF
"LIZA OF LAMBETH," "MRS. CRADDOCK," | "THE MERRY-
GO-ROUND" | [*publisher's bell device*] | LONDON | GEORGE
BELL & SONS | AND BOMBAY | 1906

Collation: [viii], 312 pp. [A]⁴ B–U⁸ X⁴.
pp. [i–ii], blank; p. [iii], half-title: ***Bell's Indian and Colonial
Library*** | [*rule*] | THE BISHOP'S APRON; p. [iv], *This Edition is issued
for Circulation in* | *India and the Colonies only*; p. [v], title; p. [vi],
printer's imprint: RICHARD CLAY & SONS, LIMITED, BREAD STREET
HILL, E.C., AND | BUNGAY, SUFFOLK; p. [vii], TO HARRY PHILIPS;
p. [viii], blank; pp. [1] 2–311 [312]; 4 leaves of advts. on India
paper printed in reddish brown + 9 leaves of advts. of Bell's
Indian & Colonial Library and Bohn's Library on India paper
dated September, 1905, the list running on to the inside of the
back wrapper, inserted.
At foot of p. [312], printer's imprint: [*rule*] | *Richard Clay &
Sons, Limited, London and Bungay.*

Binding: Red stiff wrappers, printed in black on front within a black rule border: BELL'S INDIAN & COLONIAL LIBRARY | [*within an ornamental frame of leaves and flowers*] The Bishop's | Apron | BY | W. S. MAUGHAM; [*at base*] LONDON: GEORGE BELL & SONS; on spine: THE BISHOP'S | APRON | W.S. | MAUGHAM | No. 652 | [*publisher's bell device*] | LONDON | BELL & SONS; on back advts. of BELL'S COLONIAL EDITIONS OF STANDARD BOOKS.
All edges cut; leaves measure 18.3 × 12.2 cm.

Notes: The number of sets of sheets sold by Chapman and Hall to Bell is not known, but it is not likely to have been more than a few hundred.

A9   THE BISHOP'S APRON   1908

c. Second and First Illustrated edition:
THE BISHOP'S | APRON | BY W. SOMERSET MAUGHAM | [*publisher's device*] | ILLUSTRATED BY | JOSEPH SIMPSON | [*ornament*] | [*on a plaque at foot*] GEORGE NEWNES LIMITED | SOUTHAMPTON STREET | STRAND LONDON W.C.
Title within an ornamental frame, the whole within a rule border.

Collation: 126 pp. [A]¹⁶ B–D¹⁶.
pp. [i–ii], advts. *Bryant & May Swan Vestas* and *Epps Cocoa* not incl. in pag.; p. [1], title; p. [2], advts. *Grand Cut*; p. [3], TO | HARRY PHILIPS; p. [4], advts. *Wood-Milne*; p. [5], Contents; p. [6], advts. *Hartmann's Towels*; p. [7], Illustrations; p. [8], advts. *Fry's Cocoa*; pp. [8] 10–120, text; pp. [121–126], advts.

Binding: Art paper wrappers printed in brown, red and white and lettered in white: NEWNES SIXPENNY NOVELS ILLUSTRATED. | The BISHOP'S | APRON | [*in red*] W. S. MAUGHAM; inside and back wrappers advts.

Illustrations: 2 illus. in black and white by Joseph Simpson.
(1) "Ponsonby, have you any—white satin in the house?" front.
(2) He stood up, and without another word left her, facing p. 28.
The illustrations are on art paper, and comprise a quarter octavo sheet wrapped round sig. [A].
All edges cut. Leaves measure 21.3 × 14.7 cm. Test in double columns. Newnes' Sixpenny Novels, 160.

Price: 6d. Number of copies unknown. Published 22 December 1908.

A10   THE EXPLORER   (1907) 1908

a. First edition:

The Explorer | By | William Somerset Maugham | Author of | "The Merry-go-round," "Mrs. Craddock," "'Liza of Lambeth," | etc. | [*publisher's windmill device in box*] | London | William Heine-mann | 1908

> *Collation:* 304 pp. [1]⁸ 2–19⁸.
> p. [1], half-title; p. [2], New 6s. Novels [*listing 11 titles*]; p. [3], title; p. [4], *Copyright 1907, by William Heinemann*; p. [5], dedication: To | My Dear Mrs. G. W. Steevens; p. [6], blank; p. [7] 8–297, text; p. [298], blank; pp. [299–302], advts.; pp. [303–304], blank.

> *Binding:* Petrol blue cloth, blocked in gold on front with author's symbol and on back in blind with publisher's windmill device in box; gold-lettered on front: The Explorer; and on spine: The | Explorer | W.S. | Maugham | Heinemann.

> Plain end-papers; top edges cut, fore and lower edges rough trimmed; leaves measure 19 × 12.4 cm.

> *Price:* 6s. 2,500 copies (less 600 to Colonial edition) were pub-lished in December 1907. New impressions January, November 1908.

Notes: There are three issues and a second state of the second issue of the first edition. The first issue is as described above, the second issue is the Colonial edition in an identical casing to the first issue but with a new half-title and title—a quarter sheet imposition—and with the title page all in caps instead of in upper and lower case as with the first issue, and with the words COLONIAL EDITION on the verso of the half-title, followed by a short list of the author's earlier works. The second state of the second issue is identical with the second issue except that the half-title leaf has been removed. This was because the publishers wished to disguise the fact that the Colonial issue had been drawn upon to supply more copies for the home market while the new impression was being printed. The third issue is the Times Book Club issue described below A10b.

Sir Gerald Kelly's copy bore this inscription from the author 'Gerald Kelly from W. S. Maugham, his worst book.' Maugham also con-sidered *The Making of a Saint* as his 'worst book' and the truth of the matter is that he would have liked, as he said in *The Summing Up*, to have supressed much of his early literary work because of its im-maturity.

A10   THE EXPLORER   1908

b. First edition sheets remaindered to The Times Book Club, with new title page
THE EXPLORER | BY | WILLIAM SOMERSET MAUGHAM |
AUTHOR OF | "THE MERRY-GO-ROUND," "MRS. CRAD-
DOCK," "LIZA OF LAMBETH," ETC. | LONDON | WILLIAM
HEINEMANN | 1908

Notes: Identical with the first edition, except that there are no prelims,
apart from the title-page which has on the verso 'All rights reserved'.
4 pp. advertisements end of volume listing Heinemann's Six Shilling
Novels. Sheets cut down to 18.2 × 12.2 cm.

Cut down copies exist in a triton green cloth of similar quality, but
these are copies bound by The Times Book Club or remainder copies.
See Note to A5b.

A10   THE EXPLORER   1909

c. First American and First Illustrated edition:
The Explorer | By | William Somerset Maugham | New York |
THE BAKER & TAYLOR CO. | 1909

> *Collation:* 300 pp. [1]⁸ 2–18⁸ 19⁶.
> p. [1], half-title; p. [2], blank; p. [3], title; p. [4], COPYRIGHT 1907,
> BY | WILLIAM HEINEMANN | [*rule*] | COPYRIGHT, 1909, BY | THE
> BAKER & TAYLOR COMPANY | [*rule*] | *Published, January, 1909* |
> THE PREMIER PRESS, NEW YORK, U.S.A.; p. [5], To | My Dear Mrs.
> G. W. Steevens; p. [6], blank; pp. [7] 8–297, text; pp. [298–300],
> blank.

> *Binding:* Sage green ribbed cloth, lettered in gold on front within
> a cream panel with gold border THE | EXPLORER; [*outside panel in
> gold*] WILLIAM SOMERSET MAUGHAM; gold-lettered on spine:
> THE | EXPLORER | [*ornament*] | WILLIAM | SOMERSET | MAUGHAM | THE
> BAKER & | TAYLOR CO.
> Plain end-papers; all edges trimmed; leaves measure 18.7 × 12.5 cm.
> *Price:* $1.50. Number of copies unknown. Published January 1909.

> *Illustrations:* Col. front, with tissue guard, and 3 illus. in black and
> white by J. Graham Coates. (1) Col. front. (2) "She gave a gasp as
> she saw Alec's face," facing p. 198. (3) "Alec," facing p. 170.
> (4) "Lucy," facing p. 252.

Notes: A comparison of the English 1907 and the American 1909
editions would suggest that the latter was bound from the English

D

sheets, with new preliminary matter. This was not the case, however, the sheets of the American edition having been printed in America. The illustrations appeared only in the American edition. The English publisher reprinted the book in his *Sevenpenny Novel Series* (*see below*). *The Explorer* is a novelisation of a play written in 1899 (which had been rejected) and took a month to write. The play was not published in book form until 1912.

A10   THE EXPLORER   1915

d. Second and First Illustrated English edition:
The Explorer | By | W. S. Maugham | [*publisher's windmill device in box*] | London | William Heinemann | 1915
Title within ornamental border.

> *Collation:* 256 pp. [A]¹⁶ B–H¹⁶.
> A 2-leaf insert on art paper, not included in pagination, containing p. [i], FIRST PUBLISHED, 6s., *December* 17, | 1907; NEW IMPRESSIONS, *January,* | *November,* 1908 | HEINEMANN'S SEVENPENNY | NOVELS, *April,* 1915; p. [ii], illustration front; p. [iii], title-page; p. [iv], HEINEMANN'S Sevenpenny Net Novels [listing 24 authors]; p. [1] 2–256, text.
>
> *Binding:* Red sand-grained cloth, blocked on front and back with decorative frame in blind and on back with publisher's windmill device in blind; lettered in gold on front THE | EXPLORER | W. S. MAUGHAM; spine blocked in gold with conventionised flowers and leaves and gold-lettered in panels: W. S. | MAUGHAM [at top] | THE | EXPLORER [centre] | HEINEMANN [at base]. With age the cheap gilt has become tarnished and appears to be black.
> White end-papers with yellow broken-rule border and publisher's monogram device centre in yellow; all edges cut; leaves measure 17×10.7 cm.
>
> *Price:* 7d. Number of copies unknown. Published in April 1915
> *Illustrations:* The front. illus. ("Alec led the way") and the engraved title-page, printed on art paper and forming a quarter octavo sheet, is inserted before the title-page and not included in the pagination.

Notes: Mrs. G. W. Steevens, whose name figures on the title page of *The Explorer* got 'the grandest whitewashing that ever came the way of erring mortal,' according to Sir John Pollock in the October 1966 issue of *The Quarterly Review*. She was the prototype of Lady Frederick Berolles in *Lady Frederick*. When Maugham met her she was well on the way to old age, the widow of the brilliant reporter and special correspondent of the then young *Daily Mail*. Of her Henry James said 'If she had been beautiful and sane, she would have been one of the world's great wicked women.'

When she was approaching seventy years, she became manageress of an hotel in Holborn. At earlier dates she had run a large soup kitchen in Marylebone with immense success, a day nursery for the poor, probably the first of its kind to exist, suggests Sir John, 'and an orphanage for 30 children in the country, only to drop them like hot potatoes when she became bored with them.'

Happily for Mrs. Steevens she did not live long enough for Somerset Maugham in turn to see through her. 'He gave her an apotheosis; but she gave him Lady Frederick, fame and fortune.'

A11   THE MAGICIAN   1908

a. First edition:
The Magician | By | William Somerset Maugham | Author of | "The Explorer," "The Merry-go-round," etc. | [*publisher's windmill device in box*] | London | William Heinemann | 1908

> *Collation:* [iv], 316 pp. [1]⁸ 2–20⁸.
> p. [i], half-title; p. [ii], New 6s. Novels [listing 14 titles]; p. [iii], title; p. [iv], *Copyright, London, 1908, by William Heinemann | and Washington, U.S.A., by Duffield & Company*; p. [1], fly-title; p. [2], blank; pp. [3] 4–310, text; pp. [311–313], advts.; pp. [314–316], blank.

> *Binding:* River blue cloth, blocked in gold on front with author's symbol and on back in blind with publisher's windmill device in box; gold-lettered on front: The Magician; and on spine: The | Magician | W. S. | Maugham | Heinemann.
> Plain end-papers; top and fore-edges cut, lower edges rough trimmed; leaves measure 19 × 12½ cm.

> *Price:* 6s. 3,000 copies (less 900 to Colonial edition) were published in November 1908.

Notes: There are two issues of the first edition of *The Magician*. The first issue is as described above, the second issue is the Colonial edition, as described below.

Forwarding the MS. of *The Magician* to his agent, Maugham wrote: 'Here is the book. I have come to the conclusion it is very dull and stupid: and I wish I were an outside Broker, or——— (naming a best-seller novelist), or something equally despicable!'

AII   THE MAGICIAN   1908

b. First Colonial edition:
THE MAGICIAN | BY | WILLIAM SOMERSET MAUGHAM |
LONDON | WILLIAM HEINEMANN | 1908

> *Collation:* [iv], 316 pp. [1]⁸ 2–20⁸.
> p. [i], half-title; Heinemann's Colonial Library of Popular
> Fiction | [*rule*] | *Issued for Sale in the British* | *Colonies and India, and*
> *not* | *to be imported into Europe or* | *the United States of America*;
> p. [ii], BY THE SAME AUTHOR [listing 3 works]; p. [iii], title; p. [iv],
> *First printed, November, 1908* | *All rights reserved*; p. [1], fly-title;
> p. [2], blank; p. [3] 4–310, text; pp. [311–313], advts.; pp. [314–
> 316], blank.

> *Binding:* Yellow ripple grain cloth, lettered in gold on front and
> enclosed by an elaborate border of panels incorporating a galleon
> or windmill on a plum-red background: THE | MAGICIAN |
> W. S. MAUGHAM; blocked on spine with 2 panels one of a galleon
> and the other a windmill both on a plum-red background and
> lettered in gold: THE | MAGICIAN | [2 dots] W. S. [2 dots] | MAUGHAM
> | HEINEMANN'S | COLONIAL | LIBRARY
> Plain end-papers; all edges cut; leaves measure 18.3 × 11.4 cm.

> *Price:* 6s. 900 copies were published in November 1908.

AII   THE MAGICIAN   1909

c. First American edition:
THE MAGICIAN | By | W. SOMERSET MAUGHAM | *Author of*
"Jack Straw," "Lady Frederick," "The | *Explorer," etc., etc.* | [*publisher's*
device] | NEW YORK | DUFFIELD & COMPANY | 1909

> *Collation:* [vi], 314 pp. [unsigned 1–20⁸].
> pp. [i–ii], blank; p. [iii], half-title; p. [iv], blank; p. [v], title;
> p. [vi], COPYRIGHT 1908 BY | DUFFIELD & COMPANY | THE PREMIER
> PRESS | NEW YORK; p. [1], fly-title; p. [2], blank; p. [3] 4–310,
> text; pp. [311–314], blank.

> *Binding:* Blue ribbed cloth, blocked in blind, orange and green
> on front with title within an elaborate frame, composed of cobras
> and lettered in orange: THE MAGICIAN | [below] W. Somerset
> Maugham; on spine blocked with smaller but identical cobra
> ornament in green and lettered in orange: THE | MAGICIAN |
> W. | Somerset | Maugham | DUFFIELD.
> Plain end-papers; all edges cut; leaves measure 18.6 × 12.4 cm.

> *Price:* $1.50. The first edition was published in February 1909.

Two copies of an advance proof state were deposited for copyright with the Library of Congress November 5 1908, collating the same as above, but bound in sage green wrappers, printed on front in black: THE MAGICIAN | By | W. SOMERSET MAUGHAM | Author of "Jack Straw," "Lady Frederick," "The Explorer," etc., etc. | [*ornament*] | NEW YORK | DUFFIELD & COMPANY | 1909. All edges cut; leaves measure 19 × 12.7 cm.

Notes: A collation of the text with the English version reveals that Maugham made several revisions in the text of the American edition, in some instances considerably expanding it, i.e. *see* p. 236.

The book was acquired by George H. Doran in 1921 and it was reprinted in that year.

A11   THE MAGICIAN   1914

d. Second and First Illustrated edition:
The Magician | By | W. S. Maugham | Author of "Explorer," etc. | [*publisher's windmill device in box*] | London | William Heinemann | 1914 Within an ornamental border.

Collation: 312 pp. [1]^{16} 2–9^{16} 10^{12}.
p. [1], half-title; p. [2], blank; pp. [3] 4–310, text; pp. [311–312], advts.

Binding: Red sand-grained cloth, blocked on front and back with decorative frame in blind and on back with publisher's windmill device in blind; lettered in blind on front: THE MAGICIAN | [dot] | W. S. MAUGHAM; spine blocked in gold with conventionised flowers and leaves and gold-lettered in panels: W. S. | MAUGHAM [at top] | THE | MAGI- | CIAN [centre] | HEINEMANN [at base].

Illustrations: The front. illus. ("I won't help you. I'm afraid.") and the engraved title-page, printed on art paper and forming a quarter octavo sheet, are inserted between the half-title and p. [3].

Plain end-papers with yellow broken-rule border and publisher's monogram device centre in yellow; all edges cut; leaves measure 17 × 10.6 cm.

Price: 7d. Number of copies unknown. Published April 1914.

Notes: The Magician had a somewhat chequered career. It was accepted by Methuen and Maugham signed an agreement with them for three novels under which he obtained an advance of £75. Then it was returned to him by the publishers when already set up 'owing' as

Maugham says in his preface to *Liza of Lambeth* 'to one of the partners reading it in proof and being shocked by it.' Nothing more was heard of the arrangement until Heinemann published *The Magician*, by which time the erstwhile young novelist had become a successful and popular playwright, having created a theatrical record by having four original plays performing in London concurrently. Then came a reminder from Methuen that they had an agreement with him for three books. No doubt suspecting that Methuen was not unaware of his new standing in the literary world the young dramatist wrote indignantly to his agent Pinker and a long correspondence ensued, culminating in a letter in which he set out very clearly the full facts of the matter. 'Upon Methuen's refusal to publish the first novel' he wrote, 'I gathered the agreement was cancelled by mutual consent, and I returned the amount I had received upon signing it. Referring to your letter . . . I certainly have never understood that the agreement was to remain in existence, to come into operation whenever I might like to write a novel. For in that case it might have remained dormant for twenty years. This is a position I should certainly not have agreed to; nor do I think you would have advised me to. If you have not already done so you might remind Methuen that since the cancellation I have published a novel *The Explorer*; and their silence at that time makes their present contention the more incomprehensible. I should like to hear definitely from Methuen that they have abandoned their contention, for if they have not I propose to take steps to have the Agreement declared at an end by the Courts.' In the end the affair fizzled out. But it is interesting to speculate what might have been the outcome if, by fulfilling their contract with the young novelist, Methuen had been given the opportunity to become his publisher instead of Heinemann.

AII   THE MAGICIAN   (1956)

e. New edition, with 'Fragment of Autobiography'.
W. SOMERSET MAUGHAM | [*rule*] | THE MAGICIAN | A NOVEL | together with | A FRAGMENT OF AUTOBIOGRAPHY | [*ornament*] | [*publisher's windmill device*] | WILLIAM HEINEMANN, LTD. | MELBOURNE: LONDON: TORONTO

> *Pagination:* [xx], 233 [234] pp. Scarlet cloth, gilt. 18.5 × 12.1 cm 15s.

Notes: Mr. Maugham wrote a considerable 'Fragment of Autobiography' as preface to this new edition of his novel *The Magician* first published in 1908. The fragment begins in 1897 when he had left

St Thomas's Hospital and had published *Liza of Lambeth*. Among the many interesting anecdotes of his early struggles is one which tells of his meeting in Paris with Aleister Crowley, who was 'dabbling in Satanism, magic and the occult'. Crowley became the model of his character Oliver Haddo in *The Magician*.

A12   LADY FREDERICK   (1911) 1912

First edition:
LADY FREDERICK | A COMEDY | *In Three Acts* | BY W. S. MAUGHAM | LONDON: WILLIAM HEINEMANN | MCMXII

> *Collation:* vii, 164 pp. [ ]⁴ A–K⁸ L².
> p. [i], half-title; p. [ii], HEINEMANN'S MODERN PLAYS; p. [iii], title; p. [iv], *Copyright: London William Heinemann* 1912; p. v, list of cast; p. [vi], blank; p. vii, characters; p. viii, note on performing rights; p. 1–163, text; p. [164], blank.

> *Binding:* Cherry red buckram (2s. 6d.) and champagne wrappers (1s. 6d.). *See prelim. Note.*
> 17.3 cm. (wraps. 17.6 cm.). All edges cut. 1,500 copies were published in December 1911.

> *First American edition:* 1912. Chicago (The Dramatic Publishing Co.) Reissue of the first English impression with new American title leaf, printed in England. Heinemann sheets, consisting of 500 copies, were despatched to Chicago in July 1912.
> George H. Doran received 100 copies of the 1927 reprint.

Notes: Lady Frederick was written in 1903. It was produced at the Court Theatre on October 26 1907, with Ethel Irving and W. Graham Browne in the cast.

This was the author's first commercial play and it brought him fame overnight at the age of 33. He was soon to have the distinction of having four plays running in London at the same time, and the event was recorded by a cartoon drawn by Bernard Partridge in an issue of *Punch* (June 24, 1908) in which Shakespeare was shown biting his fingers in front of the boards advertising Maugham's plays. 'I did not make a lot of money,' Mr. Maugham wrote in *The Summing Up*, 'for in those days the takings of a popular play were much less than they are now, and my royalties were small, but I was at all events relieved from financial anxiety and my future seemed sure . . . I was much photographed and much interviewed. Distinguished people sought my acquaintance. My success was spectacular and unexpected.'

A13   JACK STRAW   (1911) 1912

First edition:
JACK STRAW | A FARCE | *In Three Acts* | BY W. S. MAUGHAM |
LONDON: WILLIAM HEINEMANN | MCMXII

> *Collation:* viii, 156 pp. [   ]⁴ A–I⁸ K⁴ L².
> p. [i], half-title; p. [ii], HEINEMANN'S MODERN PLAYS; p. [iii] title;
> p. [iv], *Copyright: London William Heinemann* 1912: p. v, list of
> cast; p. [vi], blank; p. vii, characters; p. viii, note on performing
> rights; pp. 1–156, text.

> *Binding:* Cherry red buckram (2s. 6d.) and champagne wrappers
> (1s. 6d.). *See prelim. Note.*
> 17.3 cm. (wraps. 17½ cm.). All edges cut. 1,500 copies were
> published in December 1911.

> *First American edition:* 1912. Chicago (The Dramatic Publishing
> Co.) Reissue of the first English impression with new American
> title leaf, printed in England. Heinemann sheets, consisting
> of 1,000 copies, were despatched to Chicago in July 1912. George
> H. Doran received 100 copies of the 1913 reprint in 1923.

Notes: Jack Straw was produced at the Vaudeville Theatre on March
26, 1908, with Charles Hawtrey and Lottie Venne in the cast. The
play was written in 1907.

A14   MRS. DOT   1912

First edition:
MRS. DOT | A FARCE | *In Three Acts* | BY W. S. MAUGHAM |
LONDON: WILLIAM HEINEMANN | MCMXII

> *Collation:* viii, 176 pp. [   ]⁴ A–L⁸.
> p. [i], half-title; p. [ii], BY THE SAME AUTHOR [listing 9 dramatic
> works]; p. [iii], title; p. [iv], *All rights reserved*; p. v, list of cast;
> p. [vi], blank; p. vii, characters; p. viii, note on performing rights;
> pp. 1–172 [173], text; p. [174], printer's imprint: PRINTED BY |
> BALLANTYNE & COMPANY LTD. | AT THE BALLANTYNE PRESS |
> TAVISTOCK STREET COVENT GARDEN | LONDON; pp. [175–176],
> blank.

> *Binding:* Cherry red buckram (2s. 6d.) and champagne wrappers
> (1s. 6d.). *See prelim Note.*
> 17.3 cm. (wraps. 17.6 cm.). All edges cut. 2,000 copies were
> published in November 1912.

First American edition: (December 1912). Chicago (The Dramatic Publishing Co.) Reissue of the first English impression with new American title leaf, printed in England. Heinemann sheets, consisting of 1,000 copies, were despatched to Chicago in 1912.

Notes: This play was originally called *Worthley's Entire.* In a bibliography of the author issued by Heinemann in 1934, containing Desmond MacCarthy's *Appreciation,* it was stated that the first edition was published in 1904 and a new edition in 1912. This is incorrect. The play was written in 1904.

Mrs. Dot was produced at the Comedy Theatre on April 26th, 1908, with Marie Tempest, W. Graham Browne and Fred Kerr in the cast. Mr. Maugham said it was the most successful of the three—the other two being *Lady Frederick* and *Jack Straw.*

A15   PENELOPE   1912

First edition:
PENELOPE | A COMEDY | *In Three Acts* | BY W. S. MAUGHAM | LONDON: WILLIAM HEINEMANN | MCMXII

> *Collation:* [viii], 216 pp. [   ]⁴ A–N⁸ O⁴.
> p. [i], half-title; p. [ii], THE PLAYS OF | WILLIAM SOMERSET MAUGHAM [listing 5 dramatic and 4 non-dramatic works]; p. [iii], title; p. [iv], *Copyright* 1912; p. v, list of cast; p. [vi], blank; p. vii, characters; p. [viii], note on performing rights; pp. [1] 2–213, text; p. [214], printer's imprint; pp. [215–216], blank.

> *Binding:* Cherry red buckram (2s. 6d.) and champagne wrappers (1s. 6d.). *See prelim. Note.*
> 17.3 cm. (wraps. 17.6 cm.). All edges cut. 2,000 copies were published in November 1912.

> *First American edition:* (December 1912). Chicago (The Dramatic Publishing Co.). Reissue of the first English impression with new American title leaf, printed in England. Heinemann sheets, consisting of 1,000 copies, were despatched to Chicago in November 1912.
> George H. Doran received 100 copies of the 1913 reprint.

Notes: This play was originally called *Man and Wife.* It was written in 1908, and produced at the Comedy Theatre on January 9th, 1909, with Marie Tempest (for whom it was written), Grahame Browne and Kate Bishop in the cast.

A16   THE EXPLORER   1912

First edition:
THE EXPLORER | A MELODRAMA | *In Four Acts* | BY W. S.
MAUGHAM | LONDON: WILLIAM HEINEMANN | MCMXII

Collation: viii, 152 pp. [   ]⁴ A–I⁸ K⁴.

p. [i], half-title; p. [ii], BY THE SAME AUTHOR [listing 9 works];
p. [iii], title; p. [iv], *All rights reserved*; p. v, list of cast; p. [vi],
blank; p. vii, characters; p. viii, note on performing rights;
pp. 1–152, text.

Binding: Cherry red buckram (2s. 6d.) and champagne wrappers
(1s. 6d.). *See prelim. Note.*
17.3 cm. (wraps. 17½ cm.). All edges cut. 2,000 copies were
published in November 1912.

First American edition: (December 1912). Chicago (The Dramatic
Publishing Company). Reissue of the first English impression
with new American title leaf, printed in England. Heinemann
sheets, consisting of 1,000 copies, were despatched to Chicago
in 1912. *See Note to A6b.*

Advance Proof state: pp. viii + 152. Plum green wrappers, all
edges untrimmed. 19 cm.

Notes: The Explorer was produced at the Lyric Theatre on June 13th,
1908, with Lewis Waller, Eva Moore and Evelyn Millard in the cast.
It was omitted from the *Collected Plays.*

This was the play Maugham wrote in 1899 after writing *A Man
of Honour* and Maurice Colles, his agent, after submitting it unsuccess-
fully to several managements, sent it to Lewis Waller, the actor
manager. He was interested but said he could not entertain it in its
present form and advised him to try elsewhere, but if he met with no
success, to come back to him. Maugham then withdrew the play
from Maurice Colles and sent it to two other agents. In 1905 he
altered the play and added the first act, turning it into a four act play.
He then re-submitted it himself to Lewis Waller and it was accepted.
It was produced in 1908 and folded after only 48 performances, but
Maugham still had faith in it and was prepared to re-write the last act
for a production in 1909 that was even more of a flop.

It was also in 1909 that Maurice Colles brought an action against
Maugham in the High Court for his commission on *The Explorer* on
the grounds that it was his introduction to Lewis Waller that led
eventually to the play being accepted, and he won his case.

A17   THE TENTH MAN   1913

First edition:
THE TENTH MAN | A TRAGIC COMEDY | *In Three Acts* | BY
W. S. MAUGHAM | LONDON: WILLIAM HEINEMANN |
MCMXIII

> *Collation:* [viii], 216 pp. [   ]⁴ A–N⁸ O⁴.
> p. [i], half-title; p. [ii], BY THE SAME AUTHOR [listing 13 works];
> p. [iii], title; p. [iv], *All Rights Reserved*; p. [v], list of cast; p. [vi],
> blank; p. [vii], characters; p. [viii], notes on performing rights;
> pp. 1–214, text; p. [215], printer's imprint; PRINTED AT | THE
> BALLANTYNE PRESS | LONDON; p. [216], blank.

> *Binding:* Cherry red buckram (2s. 6d.) and champagne wrappers
> (1s. 6d.). *See prelim. Note.*
> 17.2 cm. (wraps. 17.4 cm.). All edges cut. 2,000 copies were
> published in December 1913.

> *First American edition:* (1913) Chicago (The Dramatic Publishing
> Company). Reissue of the first English impression with new
> American title leaf, printed in England. Heinemann sheets,
> consisting of 1,000 copies, were despatched to Chicago in Nov-
> ember 1913. George H. Doran received 100 copies of the 1913
> imprint in 1923.

Notes: The Tenth Man, written in 1909, was produced at the Globe
Theatre on the 24th February, 1910, with Arthur Bouchier, Godfrey
Tearle and Frances Dillon in the cast. It was omitted from the *Collected
Plays*.
    The whole of the issue of *The Playgoer and Society Illustrated* No. 6
(1910) was devoted to a summary of *The Tenth Man* with excerpts
from the dialogue as captions to the photographs illustrating scenes
from the play.

A18   LANDED GENTRY   1913

First edition:
LANDED GENTRY | A COMEDY | *In Four Acts* | BY W. S.
MAUGHAM | LONDON: WILLIAM HEINEMANN | MCMXIII

> *Collation:* [viii], 169 pp. [   ]⁴ A–K⁸ L⁴.
> p. [i], half-title; p. [ii], BY THE SAME AUTHOR [listing 13 works];
> p. [iii], title; p. [iv], *All Rights Reserved*; p. v, list of cast; p. [vi],
> blank; p. vii, characters; p. [viii], note on performing rights;
> pp. 1–168, text.

Binding: Cherry red buckram (2s. 6d.) and champagne wrappers (1s. 6d.). *See prelim. Note.*
17.3 cm. (wraps. 17½ cm.). All edges cut. 2,000 copies were published in November 1913.

First American edition: (1913) Chicago (The Dramatic Publishing Company). Reissue of the first English impression with new American title leaf, printed in England. Heinemann sheets, consisting of 1,000 copies, were despatched to Chicago in November 1913.

Notes: The play was originally produced under the title *Grace*. at the Duke of York's Theatre, October 15th, 1910, with Dennis Eadie, Leslie Faber, Arthur Wontner, Edmund Gwenn, Irene Vanburgh, Lady Tree and Lillah McCarthy in the cast. It was written in 1910, and is omitted from the *Collected Plays*. The whole of the issue of *The Play Pictorial* No. 100 (1910) was devoted to a summary of *Landed Gentry* with excerpts from the dialogue as captions to the photographs illustrating scenes from the play.

A19 .   SMITH   1913

First edition:
SMITH | A COMEDY | *In Four Acts* | BY W. S. MAUGHAM | LONDON: WILLIAM HEINEMANN | MCMXIII

Collation: [viii], 200 pp. [ ]⁴ A–M⁸ N⁴.
p. [i], half-title; p. [ii], BY THE SAME AUTHOR [listing 13 works]; p. [iii], title; p. [iv], *All rights reserved*; p. v, list of cast; p. [vi], blank; p. vii, characters; p. [viii], note on performing rights; pp. 1–200, text; Printer's imprint foot of p. 200; PRINTED AT | THE BALLANTYNE PRESS | LONDON.

Binding: Cherry red buckram (2s. 6d.) and champagne wrappers (2s.). *See prelim. Note.*
17.4 cm. (wraps. 17½ cm.). All edges cut. 2,000 copies were published in December 1913.

First American edition: (1913). Chicago (The Dramatic Publishing Company). Reissue of the first English impression with new American title leaf, printed in England. Heinemann sheets, consisting of 1,000 copies were despatched to Chicago in November 1913. See Note to A6b.

Notes: In some copies the words 'All rights reserved' on verso of title page are only partly impressed.
The wrappers state has a printed label pasted on to the front cover

stating that the price of the paper covered plays is 'temporarily raised from 1s. 6d. to 2s.'

Smith was written in 1909, and was produced at the Comedy Theatre on September 30th, 1909, with Robert Loraine, A. E. Matthews, Kate Cutler and Marie Lohr in the cast.

A20   THE LAND OF PROMISE   1913

a. First Copyright edition:
THE LAND OF | PROMISE | A COMEDY IN FOUR ACTS | BY | W. S. Maugham | ALL RIGHTS RESERVED | Copyright in the United States of America | LONDON: | BICKERS & SON, LTD. | LEICESTER SQUARE, W.C. | 1913

> *Collation:* 80 pp. [1]⁸ 2–5⁸.
> p. [1], title; p. [2], blank; p. [3], characters; p. [4], scenes; pp. 5–78, text; p. [79], blank; p. [80], printer's imprint: The Westminster Press (Gerrards Ltd.) | 411a Harrow Road London, W.

> *Binding:* Stiff silver grey wrappers flecked with white, lettered in black on front: THE LAND OF | PROMISE | A COMEDY IN FOUR ACTS | By | W. S. Maugham | LONDON: | BICKERS & SON, LTD. | LEICESTER SQUARE, W.C. | 1913.
> All edges cut. 18½ × 12.3 cm.

Notes: This play was printed by Messrs. Bickers & Son for purposes of copyright only. It does not appear in *The English Catalogue*. Not more (probably less) than 25 copies were printed. It is the scarcest of all Mr. Maugham's works.

I am indebted to Mr. M. B. Piper (a member of Messrs. Bickers staff in 1913) whom I was able to contact through the kind offices of the Liquidator of the Company, for this information. The Company went into voluntary liquidation some years ago.

A20   THE LAND OF PROMISE   (1914)

b. Second Copyright (Canadian) edition:
[*within a broken lozenge frame, divided into two compartments by a broken lozenge rule: upper compartment*] The | Land of Promise | [*lower compartment*] A COMEDY IN FOUR ACTS | By | W. S. Maugham | GEO A. POPHAM, OTTAWA, CAN.
Cover title.

> *Collation:* 80 pp. 40 leaves in 1 gathering, unsigned.
> p. [1], characters; p. [2], acts; pp. 3–77, text; pp. [78–80], blank.

Binding: Stiff biscuit wrappers, lettered in front in black, as above; on back: PRINTED BY | GEO H. POPHAM | OTTAWA, CANADA; inside front wrapper: Copyright—Canada, 1914, by W. S. Maugham | Copyright—United States of America, 1914 | by W. S. Maugham.
All edges cut. 20 × 12.3 cm.

Notes: This edition is similarly scarce, as it was printed for purposes of copyright only.

A20   THE LAND OF PROMISE   1922

c. First Published edition:
THE LAND OF | PROMISE | A COMEDY IN FOUR ACTS | BY | W. S. MAUGHAM | [*windmill device resting on base with date* 1922] | LONDON: WILLIAM HEINEMANN

Collation: [viii], 160 pp. [ ]⁴ 1–10⁸.
p. [i], half-title; p. [ii], *By the same Author* [listing 12 works]; p. [iii], title; p. [iv], LONDON: WILLIAM HEINEMANN, 1922; p. [v], dedication: TO | IRENE VANBRUGH; p. [vi], note on performing rights; p. [vii], list of cast; p. [viii], characters; pp. [1] 2–159, text; p. [160], blank. Printer's imprint at foot of p. 159: PRINTED IN GREAT BRITAIN BY | BILLING AND SONS, LTD., GUILDFORD AND ESHER.

Binding: Cherry red buckram (3s.) and champagne wrappers (2s. 6d.).
17.3 cm. (wraps. 17½ cm.). All edges cut. 2,000 copies were published in June 1922.

First American edition: 1923. New York (George H. Doran) Reissue of the Heinemann edition with new American title leaf, printed in America. Heinemann sheets, consisting of 100 copies, were despatched to New York in February 1923.

Notes: The Land of Promise was suggested to Mr. Maugham by Charles Frohman, who told him that he would like him to write a modern play on the theme of *The Taming of the Shrew*.
It was written in 1913 and first produced in New Haven, Conn, at the Hyperion Theatre with Billie Burke and Lumsden Hare in the cast. In London, it was produced at the Duke of York's Theatre on February 26th, 1914, with Godfrey Tearle and Irene Vanburgh in the cast.
The whole of the issue of *The Play Pictorial* No. 144 (1914) was devoted to a summary of *The Land of Promise* with excerpts from the

dialogue as captions to the photographs illustrating scenes from the play.

A21 OF HUMAN BONDAGE (1915)

a. First edition:
OF | HUMAN | BONDAGE | By | W. Somerset Maugham | New York | George H. Doran Company [*the foregoing within a double-rule border outside line slightly thicker than the inside*]

> *Collation:* [vi], 650 pp. [unsigned [ ]⁴ 1–40⁸ 41⁴].
> p. [i], half-title; p. [ii], blank; p. [iii], title; p. [iv], Copyright, 1915, by | GEORGE H. DORAN COMPANY; p. [v], fly-title; p. [vi], blank; pp. [1] 2–648, text; pp. [649–650], blank.

> *Binding:* Empire green linen cloth, blocked in gold on front with the wording: OF HUMAN | [*between triangular ornaments*] BONDAGE | W. Somerset Maugham [and the single frame enclosing them standing up in relief from a crushed gold panel, the letters, frame and ornaments being actually of the texture of the cloth itself]; on spine gold-lettered: OF | HUMAN | BONDAGE | W. Somerset | Maugham | GEORGE H. | DORAN | COMPANY.

> *Presentation Binding:* A few copies of the first edition were bound in limp leather for presentation.
> Plain end-papers; all edges cut; leaves measure 19.6 × 13.3 cm. The size of the sheets appear to vary, although the style of the casing remains constant. In some copies the margins, upper and lower, are wider. The measurements vary between 19.6 and 19.8 cm.

> *Price:* $1.50. 4,336 copies (part of an impression of 5,000) were published on 12 August 1915.

Notes: The first issue of the first edition contains a misprint on p. 257, line 4, and is printed on much heavier and better quality paper than those with the misprint corrected. The comparative weights are 2 lbs. 1½ ozs. for the former, and 1 lb. 14 ozs. for the latter.

In the second issue of the first edition, which is printed on thinner paper, the misprint on p. 257, line 4, has been corrected. Both issues are identically cased.

The first edition of *Of Human Bondage* does not carry the small round monogram on the verso of the title-page, which was George H. Doran's method of identifying a first edition from about September 1921. The first Maugham book to have the monogram was *The Trembling of a Leaf. See Note to A26a and Appendix 11, Note 3.*

A copy of the first issue of the first edition with the title page on a stub has been noted, but feelers thrown out in many directions by Mr. Anthony Rota, who gave me the copy to examine, have not brought to light other copies or anyone who has previously noted the anomaly. Even if it is not possible to establish without further corroboration its precise status, it would be perhaps prudent to record its existence in view of the hair-raising bibliographical complications its proven genuineness would create. I think it unlikely, however, such a situation will arise.

A21   OF HUMAN BONDAGE   (1915)

b. First English edition. Separate issue printed in England from stereotype plates made from the American type:
OF HUMAN BONDAGE | A Novel | BY | W. SOMERSET MAUGHAM | [*publisher's windmill device in box*] | LONDON | WILLIAM HEINEMANN

> *Collation:* [viii], 648 pp. [unsigned [ ]⁴ 1–40⁸ 41⁴].
>
> p. [i], blank; p. [ii], WORKS BY | *William Somerset Maugham* [listing 5 non-dramatic and 9 dramatic works]; p. [iii], half-title; p. [iv], *New Six Shilling Novels* [listing 8 works]; p. [v], title; p. [vi], *London William Heinemann* 1915; p. [vii], fly-title; p. [viii], blank; pp. [1] 2–648, text.
>
> Printer's imprint at foot of p. 648; *Printed by* BALLANTYNE HANSON & CO. LTD | *At the Ballantyne Press* | LONDON AND EDINBURGH.
>
> *Binding:* Petrol blue linen grain cloth, blocked in gold on front with author's symbol and on back in blind with publisher's windmill device in box; gold-lettered on front: Of Human Bondage; and on spine: Of | Human | Bondage | W. S. | Maugham | Heinemann.
>
> Plain end-papers; top and fore-edges cut, lower edges trimmed; leaves measure 18.9 × 12.3 cm.

Price: 6s. 5,000 copies were published on 13 August, 1915.
Notes: The English edition of this novel was printed from stereotype plates made from the American type, with a re-set title page also set in America. There is a misprint, corrected in later editions, on p. 257, line 4, which appears to be common to the whole of the English edition. Some copies contain 16 pp. inserted advertisements, with no significance for issue. The authority's copy does not contain advertisements nor do any of the copies in the Statutory Libraries.
The first dust jacket was rejected and a further issue (5,000) printed

and delivered to the binder a day before publication. The publisher states, however, that 440 copies of the book had been received prior to this date, and it is possible that these copies had the original jacket on them. Miss Callender, a late Director of Heinemann, says that she believes the first jacket was cancelled because the 'club-foot was on the wrong foot' which corroborates the text. It shows Philip Carey wearing a black cape with a red cravat, and green trousers and on his head is a black artist's homburg with a wide brim. The jacket is lettered OF HUMAN | BONDAGE | BY | W. S. | MAUGHAM, and the front flap lists 17 1s. Novel titles. The drawing is signed 'M.B.'. *See illus.*

A21   OF HUMAN BONDAGE   (1934)

c. Presentation edition:
W. S. MAUGHAM | OF | HUMAN BONDAGE | A NOVEL | [*ornament*] | [*publisher's windmill device*] | LONDON | WILLIAM HEINEMANN LTD

> *Pagination:* [xii], 944 pp. Cigar brown cloth, gold blocked. 19.6 × 13 cm. 7s. 6d.
> Mr. Leonard Meldman has shown me a copy of this edition specially bound in red cardinal buckram, gold-lettered on spine OF HUMAN | BONDAGE | W. S. MAUGHAM | HEINEMANN which he acquired from Fred Bason. This is most probably a presentation binding, done to the publisher's special order. It may even have been Mr. Maugham's own copy.

Notes: Presentation Edition, reset, with a new preface (6½ pp.) of biographical and bibliographical interest, which has not been published in America.

A21   OF HUMAN BONDAGE   1936

d. First Illustrated edition:
W. SOMERSET MAUGHAM | OF HUMAN BONDAGE | ILLUSTRATED BY RANDOLPH SCHWABE | [*author's symbol in red*] | DOUBLEDAY, DORAN & COMPANY, INC. | Garden City MCMXXXVI New York
Title in red and black.

> *Pagination:* [xiv], 684 pp. Maize buckram, blocked on front with author's symbol in gold. 24 × 15.3 cm. In slip case with front. illus. on one side of box. $20.
> 'Of this limited printing of the first illustrated edition . . . there have been printed 751 copies signed by the author and illustrator of which this is number. . . .'

E

Notes: An edition-de-luxe on rag paper, limited to 751 copies with, 24 illustrations in colortype by Randolph Schwabe, with a new preface by the author. Later produced in a cheaper edition, using the same electros of the type but with smaller margins. The work was not published in England.

A21   OF HUMAN BONDAGE   1938

e. Limited Editions Club edition:
Of | Human Bondage | [*ornament*] | By W. Somerset Maugham. With an Intro- | duction by Theodore Dreiser & Sixteen | Etchings by John Sloan. In two volumes | Volume One [Two] | Printed for the Members of the Limited | Editions Club at the Printing-Office of | the Yale University Press New Haven | 1938
Title in black and brown.

> *Pagination:* Vol. i. xiv, 406 pp. Vol. ii. 407–805 [806] pp. paged continuously. Boards covered with coarse tan linen, flecked with green and brown spots. 24 × 15.6 cm. $10.
> 'Fifteen hundred copies of this edition have been printed . . . under the supervision of Carl Purington Rollins, the illustrations being etchings by John Sloan, who signs this copy.'

Notes: With an introduction by Theodore Dreiser and 16 etchings by John Sloan, signed by the illustrator. Theodore Dreiser's long review of this novel in *The New Republic* did a great deal to focus attention on Somerset Maugham in the United States, particularly among the more serious critics.

A21   OF HUMAN BONDAGE   1952

f. Cardinal Pocket Book edition:
Of | Human Bondage | [*rule*] | WITH A NEW INTRODUCTION BY THE AUTHOR | ESPECIALLY WRITTEN | FOR THIS ABRIDGED EDITION | [*rule*] | W. SOMERSET MAUGHAM | A CARDINAL EDITION | [*publisher's bird device*] | POCKET BOOKS, INC. | NEW YORK

> *Pagination:* vi, 373 [374] pp. Stiff printed wrappers. 35c.

Notes: The interest of this new edition lies in the two-page introduction in which Mr. Maugham characteristically points out that an author is obliged to conform to the methods of publication common to the time at which he writes, and if it is necessary to prune and cut in order to achieve a worthy object, in this case to put the novel within the reach of every pocket, then he has no legitimate right to refuse.

A22   THE MOON AND SIXPENCE   1919

a. First edition:
The Moon and | Sixpence | A Novel | By | W. S. Maugham | [*publisher's windmill device resting on rule base with date* 1919] | London: William Heinemann

> *Collation:* [iv], 268 pp. [   ]² 1–16⁸ 17⁶.
> p. [i], half-title; p. [ii], THE NOVELS OF | W. S. MAUGHAM [the foregoing within a rule border with review of 5 novels]; p. [iii], title; p. [iv], LONDON: WILLIAM HEINEMANN. 1919; pp. [1] 2–263, text; p. [264], blank; pp. [265–268], advts.
> Printer's imprint at foot of p. 263 [*rule*] | Billing and Sons, Ltd., Printers, Guildford, England
>
> *Binding:* Sage green cloth, blocked on back with publisher's windmill device boxed in black; on front in black with a panel divided into three compartments, side compartments containing a floral design and the centre compartment lettered: THE MOON AND | SIXPENCE | [*3 dots*] | W. S. Maugham; with author's symbol at foot; on spine, with four bands in black and lettered: THE MOON | AND | SIXPENCE | [*3 dots*] W. S. | MAUGHAM | HEINEMANN
> *Binding Variant:* Preserved in The Library of Congress Rare Book Department is a copy of the first edition of *The Moon and Sixpence* bound in a salmon linen cloth, lettered in gold on spine: The Moon | And | Sixpence | Maugham. There are no adverts and because the book is bound it is not possible to verify whether there are any stubs. Inserted in the book is a letter from a bookseller in England who was of the opinion that it was an advance copy issued to the publisher's traveller and that it was issued in its present state and was never in wrappers. I do not agree with this view and having examined the book, I am of the opinion that it is a rebound copy and that Heinemann would never have produced a proof copy in this format. The book is inscribed by the author.
>
> Plain end-papers; all edges cut; leaves measure 18.6 × 12.3 cm.
>
> *Price:* 7s. 6,000 copies (less 1,200 to Colonial Edition) were published in April 1919.

Notes: There are three issues of the first edition of *The Moon and Sixpence*. In the first issue the last signature consists of six leaves, the last two of which are publishers' advertisements. (The quarter sheet over from the last signature was evidently used for the preliminary two leaves.) On p. 2 of the advertisements there are listed six novels by

Eden Phillpotts, seventeen by Flora Annie Steel and three by Israel Zangwill, the last of the three being 'Jinny the Carrier. (Ready shortly).' P. 4 includes an announcement of 'The Mad House' by William de Morgan. Percy H. Muir in *Points: Second Series* (p. 129) describes incorrectly the last signature of the first issue as consisting of four leaves.

In the second issue the two leaves of advertisements have been cut out leaving the stubs. As P. H. Muir points out some copies are shorter than the first issue (which also varies in size). I think most copies of the second issue are shorter by at least 3 mm., the lower margins having been substantially trimmed.

In the third issue two new advertisement leaves have been inserted, the state of the two cancelled leaves are still showing between the text and the new advertisement leaves. The book announcements have been reprinted and there are seven works by Eden Phillpotts, seventeen by Flora Annie Steel and twelve by Zangwill, the last of which is 'Jinny the Carrier' without the '(Ready shortly)'. P. 4 includes an announcement 'The Old Madhouse (A posthumous novel)' by William de Morgan, instead of 'The Mad House'.

A22   THE MOON AND SIXPENCE   (1919

b. Colonial edition:
The Moon and | Sixpence | A Novel | By | W. S. Maugham | [*publisher's windmill device resting on rule base with date* 1919] | Lon: William Heinemann

> *Collation:* [iv], 264 pp. [ ]² 1–16⁸ 17⁶.
> p. [i], half-title; p. [ii], THE NOVELS OF | W. S. MAUGHAM [listing 5 titles]; p. [iii], title; p. [iv], LONDON: WILLIAM HEINEMANN, 1919; pp. [1] 2–263, text; p. [264], blank.
> The two leaves of advertisements have been cut out, leaving the stubs.

> *Binding:* Red ribbed cloth, blocked on back with publisher's windmill device boxed in blind; on front in blind with a panel divided into three compartments, side compartments containing a floral design and the centre compartment lettered: THE MOON AND | SIXPENCE | [3 *dots*] | W. S. MAUGHAM: on spine lettered in gold: THE MOON | AND | SIXPENCE | [3 *dots*] | W. S. | MAUGHAM | HEINE-MANN'S | COLONIAL | LIBRARY
> Plain end-papers; all edges cut; leaves measure 17.9 × 11.8 cm.

> *Price:* 7s. 1,200 copies were published in April 1919.

Notes: The Colonial edition is identical in all respects with the second issue of the first edition, except for the variant state of the binding as described above, the only indication that this impression was intended for sale in the Colonies.

A22 THE MOON AND SIXPENCE (1919)

c. First American edition:
[*within a double-rule border*] THE MOON AND | SIXPENCE | BY | W. SOMERSET MAUGHAM | AUTHOR OF "OF HUMAN BONDAGE," ETC. | NEW [*publisher's monogram*] YORK | GEORGE H. DORAN COMPANY

Collation: 320 pp. [unsigned 1–20⁸].
Blank leaf, not included in pagination; p. [1], half-title; p. [2], blank; p. [3], title; p. [4], Copyright, 1918 | By George H. Doran Company | Printed in the United States of America; p. [5], fly-title; p. [6], blank; pp. 7–314, text; pp. [315–318], blank.
Binding: Green open thread cloth, blocked in dark green on front with two ornamental brackets resting on a third and lettered: The Moon | and Sixpence | by | W. Somerset Maugham; and on spine: THE MOON | and | SIXPENCE | [*ornament*] | Maugham | DORAN
Plain end-papers; all edges cut; leaves measure 19 × 13 cm.

Binding Variant: Mortlake brown open thread cloth, blocked and lettered in peat brown as in first impression. There is a secondary state of both the green and brown cloth bindings with a misprint in the spelling of the author's name in the lettering on the front and spine – an 'n' instead of an 'm'.

Price: $1.50. 5,000 copies were published on 13 July 1919.

A22 THE MOON AND SIXPENCE (1933)

d. Collins Cheap edition:
[*within a two-rule border divided into three compartments: upper compartment*]: THE NOVEL LIBRARY: *centre:* THE MOON | AND SIXPENCE | BY | W. SOMERSET MAUGHAM | [*publisher's ship device*] | *lower compartment: Published for* | WM. COLLINS SONS & CO., LTD | *by* | THE LONDON BOOK CO., LTD.

Collation: 256 pp. [A]¹⁶ B–H¹⁶.
pp. [1–2], lining paper pasted down conjugate with [A]₁₅₋₁₆; p. [3], half-title; p. [4], This is the Story . . . ; p. [5], title page; p. [6], THE NOVEL LIBRARY [listing 39 titles]; pp. 7–250, text; pp. [251–252], advts.; pp. [253–254], blank; pp. [255–256], lining paper pasted down conjugate with H₁₋₂.

Binding: Crimson ribbed cloth, blocked in gold on front within
ornamental frame: THE MOON | AND SIXPENCE | W. SOMERSET |
MAUGHAM; spine blocked in gold with decorative bands head and
tail and gold-lettered: THE | MOON | AND | SIXPENCE | [*ornament*] |
W. SOMERSET | MAUGHAM | THE | NOVEL | LIBRARY
All edges cut; leaves measure 15.3 × 10 cm.

Price: 6d. Number of copies unknown. Published in May 1933.

Notes: In 1930 Messrs. William Collins Sons & Co was granted a
licence to publish five Maugham titles: *The Moon and Sixpence*;
The Trembling of a Leaf; *The Casuarina Tree*; *The Painted Veil* and
Ashenden at a published price not exceeding one shilling throughout
the world with the exception of the United States of America. The
licence was to last for a period of seven years from the date of publication of each book. This was not an unusual arrangement for one
publisher to make with another, particularly those with special cheap
editions as these reached an additional market and did not normally
compete with the original, more expensive edition.

The cheap editions published by William Collins were the 1s.
Fiction Library (the 'BOB' Novels), The Novel Library published
for Collins by The London Book Company and, a 7d. Novel Library.

The interesting feature of these different 'editions' is that they were
all printed from the same setting of type and so far as the 1s. and 6d.
'editions' were concerned, they collate the same, even to the first and
last leaf of the signature forming the lining paper pasted down on to
the inside of the hardback casing. The only variation were the adverts.,
announcing different publications, at the end of the book. The 7d.
edition, according to Collins, was most likely a paperback edition.
In 1932, Collins were told by Heinemann that they could not publish a
6d. edition of *The Trembling of a Leaf* because the rights at this price had
already been leased, but in 1935 they did publish a 7d. edition which
must have been legalised as they would have been rendering Royalty
Statements showing copies sold. The last title to be published under the
licence was *Ashenden* in 1937.

The 'Bob' Novels as they were familiarly known, first issued in
1928, proved a great attraction and their sale was reckoned in millions.
In 1932, when competition was very fierce, Collins improved the
format of the 'World's Best Shilling Novel' with a better grade of
paper, art cloth binding with gilt lettering, and pictorial jackets with a
standard 'green' background.[1]

---

[1] From a short history of the House of Collins by David Keir recently produced
in condensed form by John A. Ford.

To enable collectors to identify these cheap Collins' 'editions', a full collation of the 6d. edition is given above, and for the other editions the reader is referred to *The Painted Veil* (A33d), *The Trembling of a Leaf* (A25d) and *The Casuarina Tree* (i.e. *The Letter*) (A33c).

In Appendix II will be found a full list of the Maugham titles published by William Collins over the period of their licence.

A22 THE MOON AND SIXPENCE (1941)

e. First Illustrated edition:
ILLUSTRATED BY FREDERICK DORR STEELE | AND PAUL GAUGUIN | BY W. SOMERSET MAUGHAM | The Moon | AND Sixpence | The Heritage Press, New York: Publisher.

Pagination: 284 pp. Tan buckram, brown blocked. All edges cut, top edges stained brown. 23.8 × 15.9 cm. $4.25.
Illustrations: Part One contains 14 pen-and-ink illus. by Frederick Dorr Steele. Part Two contains 11 illus. in colour by Paul Gauguin (incl. front.). The end-papers, identical front and back, are from a Gauguin painting of Tahiti.

Notes: pp. 5–6 contain "EXCERPTS FROM A BRIEF CORRESPONDENCE BETWEEN THE PUBLISHER OF THIS EDITION AND THE AUTHOR OF THE NOVEL."

A23 THE UNKNOWN 1920

First edition:
THE UNKNOWN | A PLAY | *In Three Acts* | BY W. S. MAUGHAM | LONDON: WILLIAM HEINEMANN | MCMXX

Collation: [xii], 168 pp. [A]⁶ B–L⁸ M⁴.
p. [i], half-title; p. [ii], BY THE SAME AUTHOR [listing 15 works]; p. [iii], title; p. [iv], *Copyright: London William Heinemann* 1920; p. [v], dedication: To | VIOLA TREE; p. [vi], blank; p. vii, list of cast; p. [viii], blank; p. [ix], characters; p. x, author's note; p. [xi], fly-title; p. [xii], blank; pp. [1] 2–168, text.
Printer's imprint foot of p. 168: [*rule*] | PRINTED IN GREAT BRITAIN BY R. CLAY AND SONS, LIMITED, | BRUNSWICK STREET, STAMFORD STREET, S.E.I, AND BUNGAY, SUFFOLK.

Binding: Drab buff wrappers (2s.). No hardback issue. Not all the sheets were bound at the same time. On the wrappers of those bound later the price was increased to 2s. 6d.

17×12.4 cm. All edges cut. 2,000 copies were published in October 1920.
First American edition: 1920. New York (George H. Doran). Reissue of the Heinemann edition with new American title leaf, printed in America. Heinemann sheets, consisting of 100 copies, were despatched to New York in 1920.

Notes: The play was published in England in wrappers only, although it was advertised to appear in both wrappers and cloth.

In this play Maugham took up again an idea he had used many years before in his novel *The Hero.*

The Unknown was written in 1920 and was produced at the Aldwych Theatre on August 9th, 1920, with C. V. France, Basil Rathbone, Lady Tree and Haidee Wright in the cast. In the preface to the *Collected Plays* Maugham confesses that he had never seen such a moving performance as that of Miss Haidee Wright in this play.

A24   THE CIRCLE   1921

a. First edition:
THE CIRCLE | A COMEDY IN THREE ACTS | BY | W. S. MAUGHAM | [*publisher's windmill device resting on base with date* 1921] LONDON: WILLIAM HEINEMANN

Collation: [viii], 104 pp. [A]⁴ B–G⁸ H⁴.
p. [i–ii], blank; p. [iii], half-title; p. [iv], BY THE SAME AUTHOR [listing 16 works]; p. [v], title; p. [vi], note on performing rights; p. [vii], list of cast; p. [viii], blank; pp. [1] 2–103, text; p. [104], printer's imprint THE WHITEFRIARS PRESS, LTD., | LONDON AND TONBRIDGE.

Binding: (i) Champagne wrappers (2s. 6d.). (ii) Hemp beige paper boards, printed in black—lettered on front within a rule border: THE CIRCLE | [*3 dots*] | A COMEDY BY | W. S. MAUGHAM; lettered on spine between double-rules: THE | CIRCLE | [*3 dots*] | A | COMEDY | BY | W. S. | MAUGHAM | [*at foot*] HEINEMANN; on back publisher's windmill device. (3s. 6d.).
19×12½ cm. (wraps. 17.3 cm.). All edges cut. 2,000 copies were published in March 1921.

Advance Proof state: Only 13 copies of the advance proof state were assembled.

Notes: The publishers state that of 2,000 copies published 1,500 were bound in wrappers and 500 in boards. The extreme scarcity of the latter would suggest, however, that a much smaller number was involved. The publishers were experimenting with this type of casing for a series of plays (a play of Masefield's was the first to appear in the format), but it was obviously proving unsatisfactory and was soon abandoned. Possibly when this happened only a small number of copies had been bound, which would account for the play's scarcity in boards.

Copies of the issue in wrappers sometimes have a binder's leaf before the blank leaf.

The Circle was written in 1919 and produced at the Haymarket Theatre on March 3rd, 1921, with Fay Compton, Leon Quartermaine and Ernest Thesiger in the cast.

The whole of the issue of *The Play Pictorial* No. 349 (1931) was devoted to a summary of *The Circle* with excerpts from the dialogue as captions to the photographs illustrating scenes from the play. This, of course, was a revival.

A24   THE CIRCLE   (1921)

b. First American edition:
THE CIRCLE | A COMEDY IN THREE ACTS | BY | W. SOMER-
SET MAUGHAM | NEW [*publisher's monogram*] YORK | GEORGE
H. DORAN COMPANY

> *Collation:* 96 pp. [unsigned 1–6⁸].
> pp. [i–ii], blank, not incl. in pagination; p. [1], half-title; p. [2],
> BY W. SOMERSET MAUGHAM | [*rule*] | [listing 10 dramatic and 9
> non-dramatic works]; p. [3], title; p. [4], COPYRIGHT, 1921, |
> BY GEORGE H. DORAN COMPANY | All applications regarding
> [*etc.*] ... | PRINTED IN THE UNITED STATES OF AMERICA; p. [5],
> Persons of the Play; p. [6], blank; p. [7], THE FIRST ACT; p. [8],
> blank; pp. 9–92, text; pp. [93–94], blank.

> *Binding:* Grey paper boards, with paper label on spine printed
> in bluish green [*rule*] | THE | CIRCLE | [*rule*] | A | PLAY | [*rule*] |
> W. | SOMERSET | MAUGHAM | [*rule*].

> *Binding Variant:* Smooth parchment boards, with paper label
> on spine as above, but with an additional label on front lettered
> in bluish green THE CIRCLE | A COMEDY IN THREE ACTS | [*rule*] |
> W. SOMERSET MAUGHAM [*all within a rule border*].
> The significance of this variant is uncertain, but as the sheets are
> considerably cut down (18.8 × 12.4 cm.). It would seem that it is
> probably either a trial or a remainder binding.

A25 THE TREMBLING OF A LEAF (1921)

a. First edition:
THE TREMBLING | OF A LEAF | *Little Stories of the South Sea Islands* | BY | W. SOMERSET MAUGHAM | AUTHOR OF "THE MOON AND SIXPENCE," | "OF HUMAN BONDAGE," ETC. | NEW [*publisher's monogram device*] YORK | GEORGE H. DORAN COMPANY [*the foregoing within a double-rule frame, outside rule slightly thicker than the inside*]

> *Collation:* 312 [paged 304] pp. [unsigned 1–19^8 20^4].
> Lining paper and free end-paper, blank, not included in pagination (although part of first signature); p. [i], half-title; p. [ii], By w. somerset maugham [listing 6 novels]; p. [iii], title; p. [iv], copyright, 1921, | by george h. doran company [*publisher's monogram device*] | printed in the united states of america; p. [v], dedication to | bertram alanson; p. [vi], blank; p. [vii], 3-line quotation from Sainte-Beuve; p. [viii], blank; p. ix, contents; p. [x], blank; p. [xi], fly-title; p. [xii], blank; pp. 13–302, text; pp. [303–304], blank; lining paper and free end-paper, blank, part of last signature.
> The front lining paper 1$_1$ is conjugate with the fly-title 1$_8$ the free end-paper 1$_2$ with the Contents leaf 1$_5$ (p. ix); the back lining paper 20$_4$ is conjugate with 20$_1$ (pp. 301–302), the free end-paper 20$_3$ with the blank leaf 20$_2$.

> *Binding:* Mortlake brown open thread cloth, blocked in peat brown on front with two ornamental brackets resting on a third and lettered: The Trembling | of a Leaf | by | W. Somerset Maugham; and on spine: the | trembling | of a leaf | [*ornament*] | Maugham | doran.
> Fancy or ornamental lettering has been ignored.
> Plain end-papers; all edges cut; leaves measure 19 × 13 cm.
> *Price:* $1.90. 3,000 copies were published on 17 September 1921.

Notes: An examination of at least 50 Doran first editions published between 1915 and 1920, none of which carried the monogram on the verso of the title-page, has led me to deduce that Doran did not make regular use of it until late 1921, and then not only on first but also on *first* reprint library editions. The first impression of the Murray Hill Library edition of *On a Chinese Screen*, for example, carries the monogram beneath the copyright notice on the verso of the title-page, and the only evidence that this is not the first edition is the verso of the half-title, which lists works published later than the first edition. That the monogram was employed regularly after 1921 is, however, borne out by an examination of the Maugham first editions deposited for copyright in The Library of Congress, Washington. *The Moon and Sixpence* (1919) and *The Explorer* (1920), for example, lack the device, but it does appear in *The Trembling of a Leaf*, which was deposited for copyright on 29 September, 1921, the date incidentally on which the copyright copies of Dos Passos's *Three Soldiers*—lacking the monogram—were also deposited. As it would appear from a study of the announcements in *The Publisher's Weekly*, that the latter book was printed first, it is possible that the regular use of the monogram began with Maugham's *The Trembling of a Leaf*. Whether or not this assumption is correct is not important to the point under discussion, but it does determine that the monogram was first used on a Maugham book with *The Trembling of a Leaf*. Since copies of the later impression do not bear the monogram, it is the only means of identifying the first edition. The monogram appears on all subsequent first editions published by this firm until the merger with Doubleday, when it was replaced by the words 'First Edition'.

A25   THE TREMBLING OF A LEAF   1921

b. First English edition. Separate issue bound from the American sheets, with an English title page also printed in America:
THE TREMBLING | OF A LEAF | *Little Stories of the South Sea Islands* | BY | W. SOMERSET MAUGHAM | AUTHOR OF "THE MOON AND SIXPENCE," | "OF HUMAN BONDAGE," ETC. | [*publisher's windmill device resting on base with date* 1921] | LONDON: WILLIAM HEINEMANN

> *Collation:* 320 [paged 302] pp. [unsigned 1–20⁸].
> Lining paper and free end-paper, blank, not included in pagination (although part of first sig.); p. [i], half-title; p. [ii], THE NOVELS OF | W. S. MAUGHAM [listing 6 items]; p. [iii], title; p. [iv], LONDON: WILLIAM HEINEMANN, 1921; p. [v], dedication TO | BERTRAM ALANSON; p. [vi], blank; p. [vii], 3-line quotation from Sainte-Beuve; p. [viii], blank; p. [ix], contents; p. [x], blank; p. [xi], fly-title; p. [xii], blank; pp. 13–302, text; pp. [303–312], HEINEMANN'S CURRENT FICTION; lining paper and free end-paper, blank, part of last sig.

> *Binding:* Dark petrol blue cloth, blocked in black on front with author's symbol and on back with publisher's windmill device; gold-lettered on front: The Trembling of a Leaf; and on spine: The | Trembling | of a | Leaf | W. S. | Maugham; in black at foot: Heinemann.

Plain end-papers; all edges cut; leaves measure 18.8 × 12.2 cm.

Price: 7s. 6d. 3,000 copies were published on 6 October, 1921.

Notes: There are two issues of the first English edition. The first issue was printed from stereotype plates made from the American type, with a re-set title page also set in America. The second issue was printed in England and the sheets were signed.

Owing to the large demand for the book, it was quickly sold out and the English publishers reprinted the book and the sheets were signed as is the English practice. The advt. leaves were also re-set and contain books published later than in the earlier issue. *Hell's Hatches* replaces *Eli of the Downs* at the bottom of p. 2; *The Gift of Paul Clermont* replaces *Haggar's Hoard* at top of p. 4; *The Haunting* replaces *Orphan Dinah* at top of p. 5; and *To Let* replaces *In Chancery* at bottom of p. 6. The signature number '20' appears on p. 301; the advts. end on 20, followed by 2 blank leaves, but the last blank is a stub, to which the free end-paper is attached. Apart from these differences the collation agrees with the first issue. The second issue is scarce.

It should perhaps be mentioned that there are other slight variations in the first issue of the English edition, and this confusion probably arose through the scarcity of paper and the necessity for the publishers to economise and adopt the unorthodox use of end-papers as part of the sheets forming the text. This gave rise to a variation in the gathering of the first signature. In one copy I have noticed the signatures run as follows: [ ]² [ ]⁴⁺² [1]—[19]⁸, in another [1]—[20]⁸. In two such copies in the Berg Collection, the cataloguer has hazarded a query whether these form an issue, though he may have been influenced by the fact that the pages after p. 284 in the first copy have been incorrectly bound. If a bibliographical problem is involved here, it would be a 'state' and not an 'issue', but I do not consider that collectors need involve themselves with what may have been merely an accident in the folding which certainly did not occur in the American sheets.

Contents: The Pacific—Mackintosh—The Fall of Edward Barnard—Red—The Pool—Honolulu—Rain.

A25   SADIE THOMPSON: and Other Stories   (1928)
                  of the South Sea Islands

c. Readers Library edition:
[*within a double-rule border*] SADIE THOMPSON | AND OTHER STORIES OF | THE SOUTH SEA ISLANDS | BY | W. SOMERSET MAUGHAM | [*ornament*] | THE READERS LIBRARY |

PUBLISHING COMPANY LTD. | 66–66A GREAT QUEEN STREET | KINGSWAY, LONDON, W.C.2

Collation: 256 pp. [A]¹⁶ B–H¹⁶.

pp. [1–2], lining paper pasted down conjugate with [A]₁₅₋₁₆; p. [3], blank; p. [4], Foreword; p. [5], title; p. [6], Copyright Edition (*All Rights Reserved*) | Made and Printed in Great Britain | By the Greycaine Book Manufacturing Company, Limited | Watford.; p. [7], READERS LIBRARY [listing 64 authors]; p. [8] 9–10, Editor's Note: p. [11], Contents; p. [12], blank; pp. [13] 14–251 [252], text; pp. [253–254], free-end paper conjugate with pp. [255–256] lining paper pasted down.

Binding: Crimson sand-grain cloth, blocked in gold on front and spine with elaborate panel border of Eastern mosaic motifs; gold-lettered on front SADIE THOMPSON | AND OTHER STORIES OF | THE SOUTH SEA ISLANDS | [*ornament*] | W. SOMERSET | MAUGHAM; and on spine: SADIE | THOMPSON | AND OTHER | STORIES | [*ornament*] W. SOMERSET | MAUGHAM | READERS | LIBRARY.
All edges cut; leaves measure 16.3 × 10.1 cm.

Price: 6d. Number of copies unknown, but ran into many thousands. Published March 1928.

Notes: This little book has a printing and publishing background that gives it an added interest. It was the first book to be handled by Woolworth's, and was printed and bound on a new machine by the Greycaine Book Manufacturing Company which, I seem to recall, was owned by a son of Hall Caine, the famous best-seller novelist of the turn of the century. The sheets were bound on the same machine by a gutta percha process and were unsigned, but it is possible to see how the sheets were folded by removing the casing. I have an idea that the experiment was not altogether a success.

The book was reissued under the title *Rain* in Readers Library (1933); as *Sadie Thompson* etc. in The Daily Express Fiction Library (1938); as *Sadie Thompson* in the New Chevron Series, No. 98 (1940).

A25   THE TREMBLING OF A LEAF   (1932)

d. Collins cheap edition:
THE TREMBLING | OF A LEAF | *Little Stories of the South Sea Islands* | by | W. SOMERSET MAUGHAM | AUTHOR OF "THE PAINTED VEIL," "ASHENDEN," ETC. | [*publisher's monogram device*] | LONDON 48 PALL MALL | W. COLLINS SONS & CO LTD | GLASGOW SYDNEY AUCKLAND

Collation: 253 [254] + 2 pp. [A]¹⁶ B–H¹⁶.
pp. [1–2], lining paper pasted down conjugate with [A]₁₅₋₁₆;
p. [3], half-title; p. [4], This is the Story . . . ; p. [5], title; p. [6],
Copyright | PRINTED IN GREAT BRITAIN; p. [7], dedication TO |
BERTRAM ALANSON | and a 3-line quotation from Sainte-Beuve;
p. [8], Contents; pp. 9–253 (254], text; pp. [255–256], lining
paper pasted down conjugate with H₁₋₂.

Binding: Blue ribbed cloth, blocked on front with dark blue
single border; on spine blocked and lettered in dark blue between
conventional printer's ornaments; THE | TREMBLING | OF A |
LEAF | by | W. SOMERSET | MAUGHAM; on back within a lozenge
frame advert. Kolynos Dental Cream.
All edges cut; leaves measure 15.3 × 10.1 cm.

Price: 1s. Number of copies unknown. Published in March 1932.
See A22d.

A26   CAESAR'S WIFE   1922
First edition:

CAESAR'S WIFE | A COMEDY IN THREE ACTS | BY | W. S.
MAUGHAM | [*publisher's windmill device resting on base with date*
1922] | LONDON: WILLIAM HEINEMANN

Collation: [viii], 156 pp. [ ]⁴ 1–9⁸ 10⁶.
pp. [i–ii], blank; p. [iii], half-title; p. [iv], *By the same Author*
[listing 12 works]; p. [v], title; p. [vi], note on performing rights
with LONDON: WILLIAM HEINEMANN. 1922; p. [vii], list of cast;
p. [viii], characters; pp. [1] 2–156, text.

Binding: Cherry red buckram (3s. 6d.) and champagne wrappers
(2s. 6d.). *See prelim. Note.*
17.3 cm. (wraps. 17½ cm.). All edges cut. 2,000 copies were
published in June 1922.

First American edition: 1923. New York (George H. Doran).
Reissue of the English impression with new American title
lead, printed in America. Heinemann sheets, consisting of 100
copies, were despatched to New York in 1922.

Notes: In the *Collected Plays*, Somerset Maugham has this to say of
Caesar's Wife. 'It was suggested by Madame de Lafayette's *La Princesse
de Cleves* . . . one of the most exquisite novels that has ever been
written . . . [It will] to me remain a pleasing memory for the beautiful
performance that Miss Fay Compton gave in the part of Violet. The
gesture with which she held out her arms to her lover after she had

sent him away for good and all and he had miserably gone, had a grace, tenderness and beauty the like of which I have never before or since seen on the stage.'

Caesar's Wife was written in 1918 and was produced at the Royalty Theatre on March 27, 1919, with Helen Haye, C. Aubrey Smith and Fay Compton in the cast.

The whole of the issue of The Play Pictorial No. 206 (1919) was devoted to a summary of *Caesar's Wife* with excerpts from the dialogue as captions to the photographs illustrating scenes from the play.

A27 EAST OF SUEZ 1922

a. First edition:

EAST OF SUEZ | A PLAY IN SEVEN SCENES | BY | W. S. MAUGHAM | [*publisher's windmill device resting on base with date* 1922] | LONDON: WILLIAM HEINEMANN

Collation: [viii], 132 pp. [ ]^4 A–H^8 I^2.
p. [i], half-title; p. [ii], *By the same Author* [listing 13 works]; p. [iii], title; p. [iv], *Printed in Great Britain by* T. and A. CONSTABLE LTD. | *at the Edinburgh University Press:* p. [v], dramatis personae; p. [vi], list of cast; p. [vii], scenes; p. [viii], blank; pp. [1] 2–130, text; pp. [131–132], blank.

Binding: Cherry red buckram (3s. 6d.) and champagne wrappers (2s. 6d.). *See prelim. Note.*
18.4 cm. (wraps. 18.6 cm.). All edges cut. 2,000 copies were published in September 1922.

Notes: East of Suez, written in 1922, was produced at His Majesty's Theatre on September 2, 1922, with Meggie Albanesi, Basil Rathbone and Malcolm Keen in the cast.

The whole of the issue of The Play Pictorial No. 248 (1922) was devoted to a summary of the play with excerpts from the dialogue as captions to the photographs illustrating scenes from the play.

In this play Somerset Maugham attempted what was for him something quite novel—a play of spectacle. 'I had long wanted to try my hand at something of the sort,' he wrote in the preface to the *Collected Plays*, 'and a visit to China presented me with an appropriate setting . . . I cannot think that anyone who saw the play will have forgotten the thrilling and strangeness of the mob of Chinese, monks and neighbours, who crowded in when the wounded man was brought in after the attempted assassination in the fourth scene. With their frightened gestures and their low, excited chatter they produced an effect of great dramatic tension.'

Eugene Goossens wrote the incidental music to the East of Suez. The score was published in 1922:

Eugene Goossens (Op. 33) Suite from the Incidental Music to *East of Suez* (A play in seven scenes by W. Somerset Maugham). Cover design by George Harris. [London] B. Feldman & Co.: J. & W. Chester Ltd. MCMXXII.

[iv], 35 pp. Coloured Cover.

In his autobiography *Overture and Beginners* (1951) Eugene Goossens gives an amusing account of his search for Chinese musicians in order to get some idea what they sounded like, and tells how he tracked down an amateur Chinese orchestra composed of working men in a back room in one of the streets leading off Soho.

A27   EAST OF SUEZ   (1922)

b. First American edition:

EAST OF SUEZ | A PLAY IN SEVEN SCENES | BY | W. SOMER-SET MAUGHAM | NEW [*publisher's monogram device*] YORK | GEORGE H. DORAN COMPANY

Collation: [ii], 142 pp. [unsigned 1–9⁸].

pp. [i–ii], blank, not included in pagination; p. [1], half-title; p. [2], BY W. SOMERSET MAUGHAM | [*rule*] | [listing 12 dramatic and 10 non-dramatic works]; p. [3], title; p. [4], COPYRIGHT 1922, | BY GEORGE H. DORAN COMPANY | [*publisher's monogram*] | EAST OF SUEZ | [*rule*] | PRINTED IN THE UNITED STATES OF AMERICA; p. [5], Dramatis Personae; p. [6], blank; p. [7], Scenes; p. [8], blank; p. [9], Scene 1; p. [10], blank; pp. 11–138, text; pp. [139–140], blank; pp. [141–142], lining paper pasted down.

Binding: Hemp beige paper boards, label on front printed in black; [*rule*] | EAST | OF | SUEZ | [*rule*] | W. | SOMERSET MAUGHAM | [*rule*].

Plain end-papers; all edges rough trimmed; leaves measure 19 × 13 cm.

Price: $1.25. The first edition was published in November 1922. Copyright copy deposited Library of Congress 25 November 1922.

A28   ON A CHINESE SCREEN   (1922)

a. First edition:

ON A CHINESE SCREEN | BY | W. SOMERSET MAUGHAM |

NEW [*publisher's monogram device*] YORK | GEORGE H. DORAN COMPANY

Collation: 240 pp. [unsigned 1–15⁸].

p. [i], half-title; p. [ii], By w. somerset maugham [listing 8 titles]; p. [iii], title; p. [iv], copyright, 1922, | by george h. doran company | [*publisher's monogram device*] | on a chinese screen. i | [*rule*] | printed in the united states of america; p. [v], dedication for | syrie; p. [vi], blank; p. vii–viii, contents; p. [ix], fly-title; p. [x], blank; pp. 11–237, text; p. [238–240], blank.

Binding: Quarter lemon yellow cloth, Spanish orange paper backed boards, gold blocked and lettered on front within a rectangular shaped frame: on a | chinese | screen | w. [*between short rules*] | somerset | maugham; on spine in black: on a | chinese | screen | [*broken rule*] | maugham | doran. Plain end-papers; top edges cut, fore and lower edges rough trimmed. Leaves measure 19 × 13.1 cm.

Price: $2. 2,000 copies were published on 5 October 1922.

A28   ON A CHINESE SCREEN   (1922)

b. First English edition. Separate issue printed in England from stereotype plates made from the American type.
ON A CHINESE SCREEN | BY | W. SOMERSET MAUGHAM | [*publisher's windmill device resting on base with date 1922*] | LONDON: WILLIAM HEINEMANN

Collation: 240 pp. [A]⁸ B–P⁸.

p. [i], half-title; p. [ii], By w. somerset maugham | [*rule*] | [*listing 8 works*]; p. [iii], title; p. [iv], *Printed in Great Britain* | *Copyright: London, William Heinemann,* 1922; p. [v], dedication for | syrie; p. [vi], blank; p. vii–viii, contents; p. [ix], fly-title; p. [x], blank; pp. 11–237, text; p. [238], printer's imprint printed in great britain by | richard clay & sons, limited, | bungay, suffolk; pp. [239–240], blank.

Binding: Smooth black cloth, blocked on front in gold with author's symbol and a design of flying foxes and gold-lettered: on a chinese screen | w. somerset maugham; on spine with 6 gold bands and a design of a flowering tree with 8 birds and gold-lettered: on a | chinese | screen | w. somerset | maugham | heinemann; on back publisher's windmill device in blind.

F

Plain end-papers; top edges cut, fore and lower edges uncut; leaves measure 20.3 × 15.2 cm.

Price: 10s. 6d. 2,000 copies were published on 9 November 1922.

Notes: The English edition of this work was printed from stereotype plates made from the American type, with a re-set title-page also set in America. Excerpts from *On a Chinese Screen* were published in the form of sketches in *The American Bookman* (September 1922), and other periodicals prior to book publication.

A29   OUR BETTERS   1923

First edition:
OUR BETTERS | A COMEDY IN THREE ACTS | BY | W. S. MAUGHAM | [*publisher's windmill device resting on base with date 1923*] | LONDON: WILLIAM HEINEMANN LTD

Collation: [vi], 210 pp. [1]⁸ 2–13⁸ 14⁴.
p. [i], half-title; p. [ii], BY THE SAME AUTHOR [listing 14 works]; p. [iii], title; p. [iv], note on performing rights with printer's imprint PRINTED IN GREAT BRITAIN BY | BILLING AND SONS LTD., GUILDFORD AND ESHER; p. [v], list of cast; p. [vi], characters; pp. [1] 2–210, text.

Binding: Cherry red buckram (3s. 6d.) and champagne wrappers (2s. 6d.). *See prelim. Note.*
17.2 cm. (wraps. 17.4 cm.). All edges cut. 1,500 copies were published in September 1923.

First American edition: 1924. New York (George H. Doran). Reissue of the English impression with new American title-leaf, printed in America. Heinemann sheets, consisting of 200 copies, were despatched to New York in January 1924.

Notes: Our Betters was first produced at the Hudson Theatre in New York in 1917, where it created a minor sensation. In London, it was produced at the Globe Theatre on the 12th September, 1923, with Margaret Bannerman and Constance Collier in the cast. The play was written in 1915.

There was a six year gap between the New York presentation of *Our Betters* and the London presentation. When eventually it was put on at the Globe Theatre, the programme carried a printed note: 'Owing to various rumours which were circulated when the play was produced in America, the Author wishes to state that the characters in it are entirely imaginary.' That was in 1923. Almost forty years afterwards, in *Looking Back*, the author wrote: 'Gordon Selfridge had fallen madly in love with her' ('her' being Syrie Wellcome, later to become Maugham's wife) 'and had offered to settle £5,000 a year on her. She refused. She was very amusing about him and on what she told me I created a character in a play called *Our Betters.*' He called him Arthur Fenwick and the *New York Times* dramatic critic, writing in 1917, quoted the 'lobby gossips' as saying that Fenwick was a 'quite recognisable character, drawn from life.'

A30   HOME AND BEAUTY   1923

First edition:
HOME AND BEAUTY | A FARCE IN THREE ACTS | BY | W. S. MAUGHAM | [*publisher's windmill device resting on base with date* 1923] LONDON: WILLIAM HEINEMANN LTD.

> *Collation:* [viii], 184 pp. [ ]⁴ 1–11⁸ 12⁴.
> p. [i], half-title; p. [ii], *By the same Author* [listing 15 works]; p. [iii], title; p. [iv], note on performing rights, with printer's imprint PRINTED IN GREAT BRITAIN BY | BILLING AND SONS LTD., GUILDFORD AND ESHER; p. [v], list of cast; p. [vi], blank; p. [vii], characters; p. [viii], blank; pp. [1] 2–182, text; pp. [183–184], blank.

> *Binding:* Cherry red buckram (3s. 6d.) and champagne wrappers (2s. 6d.). *See prelim. Note.*
> 17.3 cm. (wraps. 17.5 cm.). All edges cut. 1,500 copies were published in December 1923.

Notes: Produced in America under the title *Too Many Husbands* See B10.

Home and Beauty was written in a sanatorium during the last winter of the first world war. 'It was an admirable opportunity to write a farce,' wrote Somerset Maugham in the preface to the *Collected Plays.* 'I never had an opportunity of seeing it, but I believe it made people laugh very much. Some of the critics called it cruel and heartless. I should not have thought it was. It was written in the highest possible spirits. It was intended to amuse.'

Home and Beauty was first produced at the *Globe Theatre*, Atlantic City on August 4th 1919 with Estelle Winwood and Kenneth Douglas, and in London at The Playhouse on August 30th 1919 with Gladys Cooper and Charles Hawtrey in the cast.

The whole of the issue of *The Play Pictorial* No. 213 (1919) was devoted to a summary of *Home and Beauty* with excerpts from the dialogue as captions to the photographs illustrating scenes from the play.

A31   THE UNATTAINABLE   1923

First edition:
THE | UNATTAINABLE | A FARCE IN THREE ACTS | BY |
W. S. MAUGHAM | [*publisher's windmill device resting on base with
date* 1923] | LONDON: WILLIAM HEINEMANN LTD.

> *Collation:* [viii], 200 pp. [ ]⁴ 1–12⁸ 13⁴.
> p. [i], half-title; p. [ii], BY THE SAME AUTHOR [listing 14 works];
> p. [iii], title; p. [iv], note on performing rights with printer's
> imprint PRINTED IN GREAT BRITAIN BY | BILLING AND SONS LTD.,
> GUILDFORD AND ESHER; p. [v], list of cast; p. [vi], blank; p. [vii],
> characters; p. [viii], blank; pp. [1] 2–197, text; pp. [198–200],
> blank.
>
> *Binding:* Cherry red buckram (3s. 6d.) and champagne wrappers
> (2s. 6d.). *See prelim. Note.*
> 17.4 cm. (wraps. 17½ cm.). All edges cut. 1,500 copies were
> published in December 1923.

Notes: Produced under the title *Caroline* at the New Theatre on
February 8th, 1916, with Irene Vanburgh, Lillah McCarthy and
Dion Boucicault in the cast.
   The author had a somewhat unusual experience with this play,
which is dealt with in the manuscript section in Appendix 1.

A32   LOAVES AND FISHES   1924

First edition:
LOAVES AND FISHES | A COMEDY IN FOUR ACTS | BY |
W. S. MAUGHAM | [*publisher's windmill device resting on base with
date* 1924] | LONDON: WILLIAM HEINEMANN LTD.

> *Collation:* [viii], 192 pp. [ ]⁴ A–M⁸.
> p. [i] half-title; p. [ii] *By the same Author* [listing 16 works];
> p. [iii], title; p. [iv], note on performing rights with printer's
> imprint *Printed in Great Britain by Woods & Sons, Ltd., London,
> N.1.*; p. [v] list of cast; p. [vi], blank; p. [vii], persons of the play;
> p. [viii], blank; pp. 1–191, text; p. [192], blank.
>
> *Binding:* Cherry red buckram (3s. 6d.) and champagne wrappers
> (2s. 6d.). *See prelim. Note.*
> 17.4 cm. (wraps. 17½ cm.). All edges cut. 2 000 copies were
> published in November 1924.

Notes: Loaves and Fishes was the author's third full length play and was
written in 1902. It was many times rejected by managers and the

novelisation of it under the title *The Bishop's Apron* was the first to appear in book form. It was not included in the *Selected Plays*.

Loaves and Fishes was produced at the Duke of York's Theatre on February 24th, 1911, with Robert Loraine and Athol Stewart in the cast.

A33 THE PAINTED VEIL (1925)

a. First and Limited edition:
THE | PAINTED VEIL | BY | W. Somerset Maugham | [*ornament*] | GEORGE H. DORAN COMPANY | ON MURRAY HILL [*square of 4 dots*] NEW YORK [*the foregoing in reddish brown and black, within a triple rule frame the inside rule being a reddish brown*]

> *Collation:* 290 pp. [unsigned [ ]¹ 1–18⁸]. Certificate of Limitation a single inset but included in the pagination.
> p. [1], cert. of limitation: This large paper edition of | THE PAINTED VEIL | is limited to two hundred and | fifty numbered copies signed by | the author, of which this is | Number ...; p. [2], blank; p. [3], half-title; p. [4], BY W. SOMERSET MAUGHAM [listing 9 works]; p. [5], title; p. [6], COPYRIGHT, 1924, 1925 | BY W. SOMERSET MAUGHAM | THE PAINTED VEIL | —B— | PRINTED IN THE UNITED STATES OF AMERICA; p. [7], fly-title; p. [8], one-line quotation; pp. 9–289, text; p. [290], blank.

> *Binding:* Pale blue boards, parchment spine and corners with dark blue leather label on spine, gold-blocked and lettered within a single frame: THE | PAINTED | VEIL | [*short rule*] | W. SOMERSET | MAUGHAM
> Plain end-papers; top edges cut and gilt, fore and lower edges uncut and unopened; leaves measure 21½×15 cm.
> *Price:* $15. 250 copies published on 20 March 1925.

Notes: The Certificate of Limitation is on vellum paper.

A33 THE PAINTED VEIL (1925)

b. First Trade edition (separate impression from the same formes):
THE | PAINTED VEIL | BY | W. Somerset Maugham | NEW [*publisher's monogram device*] YORK | GEORGE H. DORAN COMPANY

> *Collation:* [288] (paged [290]) pp. [unsigned 1–18⁸].
> p. [3], half-title; p. [4], BY W. SOMERSET MAUGHAM [listing 9 titles]; p. [5], title; p. [6] COPYRIGHT, 1924, 1925 | BY W. SOMERSET

MAUGHAM | [*publisher's monogram device*] | THE PAINTED VEIL |
—B— | PRINTED IN THE UNITED STATES OF AMERICA; p. [7], fly-
title; p. [8], one-line quotation; pp. 9–289, text; p. [290], blank.

Binding: Reddish brown fine ribbed cloth, blocked in blind
on front with two ornamental brackets resting on a third and
lettered in blind: The Painted | Veil | by | W. Somerset Maugham;
gold-lettered on spine: THE | PAINTED | VEIL | [*ornament*] | Maugham
| DORAN
Plain end-papers; all edges cut; leaves measure 19 × 12.8 cm.

Price: $2. 5,000 copies were published on 20 March 1925.

Notes: Mr. Maugham wrote a piece (which was published in Colliers)
for a booklet which Doran proposed to produce when *The Painted
Veil* was published but it did not appear, and Maugham was much
aggrieved. In a letter to Charles H. Towne[1], he said he was much
dissatisfied with the way Doran had handled *The Painted Veil*. 'He
promised,' he said, 'that he would issue a booklet about my work before
it came out and I expected him to give it individual attention. As a
matter of fact he just sent it out like a parcel of tea, and let it sell on its
own merits, without anything more than a mechanical and useless
advertising.'

An outcome of this dissatisfaction with Doran was that for a while
he played with the idea of changing his publishers, but his natural
disinclination for change eventually prevailed. 'As you know' he
wrote to Towne, 'my inclinations are very much to stick to whatever
publishers I have. I have been with Heinemanns in London for twenty
years and have resisted very substantial offers to leave them. So long
as Doran will do his best for me I am very willing to do my best by
him. I have received his letter and am about to reply to it. I do not
honestly think very much of his offer to give me a larger advance
since I cannot but feel that my books will earn that on their own
account without any pushing by a publisher and I am not so anxious
to make a large sum of money out of a book as to have it as widely
read as possible. I seek distinction rather than lucre. . . .'

A33   THE PAINTED VEIL   (1925)

*c. First English edition. Separate issue printed in England from stereotype
plates made from the American type:*
THE | PAINTED VEIL | BY | W. SOMERSET MAUGHAM |
[*publisher's windmill device in box*] | LONDON | WILLIAM HEINE-
MANN LTD.

[1] From the Charles H. Towne collection of Maugham letters in Yale University.

Binding: Canton blue linen-grain cloth, blocked on front with author's symbol in black and gold-lettered: The Painted Veil; on spine in gold: The | Painted | Veil | W.S. | Maugham | [*in black*] Heinemann.
Plain end-papers; top and fore-edges cut (or top edges cut and fore-edges rough trimmed), lower edges uncut (or rough trimmed); leaves measure 19 × 12.2 cm.
Price: 7s. 6d. The publishers state that 8,000 (in two runs of 4,000) was the original number of the first impression printing, but in view of the textual changes that were made after the sheets had been run off, and making allowance for spoilt sheets, the probability is that the final figure for the first edition was something less than 8,000. Publication date was 23 April 1925.

Advance Proof State: Buff wrappers, blank. All edges cut. Leaves measure 18.4 × 12 cm. Title page not a cancel.
292 pp. [1]^8 2–18^8 X^2.
p. [1], half-title; p. [2], BOOKS BY | W. S. MAUGHAM [listing 8 titles with extracts from reviews under each, the whole enclosed in a single rectangular frame]; p. [3], title; p. [4], *First published* 1925 | *Printed in Great Britain by* | *Woods and Sons, Ltd., London* N.1.; p. [5], one-line quotation; p. [6], blank; p. [7], fly-title; p. [8], blank; pp. 9–289, text; pp. [290–292], blank.

Collations of the Issues and States of the First English edition

First Issue, First State
Title page uncancelled. This state is known only in advance proof state. No copy known bound in cloth.
   The existence of a cancel title indicates that there was once an earlier uncancelled title. It is possible that the binders performed their task efficiently and the title-page was removed from every one of the several thousand copies bound and ready for issue. Even though no copy of the bound state is known, however, it is possible that one or more exist somewhere, bearing in mind that nearly 30 years elapsed before a copy of the advance proof state came to light. For such a contingency the bibliographer must be prepared.
   As the late Bertram Rota has pointed out, when there is evidence that a book existed in a particular form, that form should be recorded and allotted its place in a sequence of forms, whether or not copies are known to exist at this date. Or, as he once neatly put it to me 'A second son does not become a first son because his elder brother is dead, even though he may inherit the title.' This principal has been recorded recognition in such cases as those of the first states of D. H.

Lawrence's *The White Peacock* and *Sons and Lovers*, while Dodgson's *Alice in Wonderland* is an example of a first edition being relegated to a second edition status on the discovery of an earlier printing, and Dickens' *Battle of Life* provides a like example of the known issues each moving one step down the scale following Eckel's disclosure of a previously unrecorded earlier form.

First Issue, Second State
290 pp. [1]⁸ 2–18⁸ X¹.
p. [1], half-title; p. [2], BOOKS BY | W. S. MAUGHAM [listing 8 works by the same author with extracts from reviews under each, the whole enclosed in a single rectangular frame]; p. [3], title—*a cancel*; p. [4], *First published* 1925 | *Printed in Great Britain by* | *Woods and Sons, Ltd.*, *London* N.1; p. [8], blank; pp. 9–289, text; p. [290], blank.
4,000 copies printed and some distributed.

First Issue, Third State
Collates the same as in the second state, except that the verso of the half-title reads: WORKS BY | W. SOMERSET MAUGHAM | [between single rules, followed by a list of 26 titles (8 under "Novels" and 18 under "Plays")] | WM. HEINEMANN LTD [between single rules].
4,000 copies printed and some distributed.

Second Issue, First State
(292) [paged (290)] pp. [1]⁸⁺¹ [2]⁸ 3⁸ [4]⁸ 5–18⁸ X¹.
Half-title, an inset; on verso list of 26 works by W. Somerset Maugham; p. [1], title—*a cancel*—pasted on to the stub of what formerly held the half-title; p. [2], *First published* 1925 | *Printed in Great Britain by* | *Woods and Sons, Ltd.*, *London*, N.1; p. [3], Author's Note, pasted on to the stub of what formerly held the title; p. [4], blank; p. [5], one-line quotation; p. [6], blank; p. [7], fly-title; p. [8], blank; pp. 9–289, text; p. [290], blank.

Second Issue, Second State
Collation the same as in the Second Issue, First State, save that all the cancels have disappeared, and the leaves are now an integral part of the signatures. The half-title, however, is still an inset. The verso of the title-page, which is no longer a cancel, reads: First published April 1925, New Impressions April, May 1925.

Notes: The first issue of the first English edition of *The Painted Veil*, which consists at the most of 74 copies, has a cancel title and its text entirely in unaltered state with *Hong Kong, Happy Valley* and *The Peak* referred to as such instead of the later issue version of *Tching-Yen, Pleasant Valley* and *The Mount*. Kowloon is changed to *Lushan*, and all references to *Canton* because of its proximity to Hong Kong have been obliterated (or such was the intention).

There are three states of the first issue. The first state of *The Painted Veil* was never issued (so far as is known). In the second state the reverse of the half-title lists 8 titles by the same author with a review of each book, in the third state twenty-six of the author's works are mentioned.

In the second issue, first state *Hong Kong* etc, has been changed to *Tching-Yen* throughout by the insertion of cancelled leaves, and an Author's Note inserted between the title leaf and the leaf recording the single-line quotation. The half-title is now a single inset.

In the final version the whole book was reimposed, the copies of the original sheets with a full set of cancellans gatherings replacing the cancellans leaves.

Explanation: The extraordinary complexity of the various issues and states of *The Painted Veil* demand at least an attempted explanation. It arose out of two threatened libel actions which necessitated drastic alterations in the text. The first was during the serialisation of the story in *Nash's Magazine* when some people having the same names as the hero and heroine *Lane* brought an action for libel, which was settled for £250. The author says that, as a result of this action, he changed the name to *Fane*. Actually, during the run of the English serialisation, he changed it to *Forr*, and it was only in the final published form the name became *Fane*. The second alteration in the text (and a major one) occurred when the Assistant Secretary of the Hong Kong Government protested against the setting of the story and to avoid further trouble the author changed the names of the places. The second protest, however, was not made until two printings (each of 4,000) had been run off and a large number of press copies actually dispatched. These copies were recalled but not all the recipients responded and 74 copies of the two states were unaccounted for. Most of these were review copies which, on some pretext or other, were not returned. Most of the confusion associated with the first issue arose as a result of (a) being a cancel (b) some copies having eight works mentioned on the reverse of the half-title while others had twenty-six. The explanation of (a) is that the whole of the first two printings (assuming no copies were overlooked) had a cancel title (printed February 21 or March 13) including the 74 copies not returned, (b) the half-title with the eight works belonged to the first printing of 4,000, while those with the twenty-six belonged to the second printing, which was also completed before any textual changes were made. It is not possible at this late date to state definitely how copies of the two printings came to be dispatched simultaneously, but it is evident that this is what must have happened. Now we come to the second issue, first state. When the book was recalled all copies of both states, save the 74 mentioned above, were returned to the binders to have obliterated by means of cancels all reference to *Hong Kong*, *Canton*, *Happy Valley*, etc. An *Author's Note* was also printed making the usual disclaimer that the book was founded on any actual incident or persons.

The collation of the preliminary signature was now 9 leaves instead of 8 which meant, of course, that one leaf would have to be an inset. The leaves were accordingly rearranged. The half-title was removed, and the title pasted on to the stub of what was formerly the half-title's conjugate (1_8) and the *Author's Note* pasted on to the stub of what was formerly the conjugate of the title (1_7). The new half-title in the *second state* then became a single inset. This was the collation of the preliminary leaves when the book was again reissued and went forward to be newly imposed.

Ironically, despite the scrupulous care exercised by the publishers to delete all the offending passages, *Hong Kong* is still present on p. 34, 1st line and p. 56, 4th line, and the word *Canton* has been overlooked on pp. 133, 237 and 255. According to the publisher's file these errors were rectified in the 'Third Edition'.

No explanation is provided by the publisher's records for the cancellation of the title page. One can, however, offer as a possible explanation the change in the design of the windmill device revealed by a comparison of the two examples in the title-page of the advance proof state (which was uncancelled) and the cancelled title page in the second state. It will be observed that the base of the windmill is blacked out in the former, but clear in the latter and this is the form that was used in all later books and still is so today. *See illustration*.

Final Note: Book collectors do not, as a rule, trouble to collect serial publications of their favourite authors even though these almost invariably have publication priority. Nevertheless, the serialisation of *The Painted Veil* should not be overlooked, particularly in view of the important changes that occurred during its run through *Nash's Magazine* which, in the February issue, changed the names of the chief characters from *Walter* and *Kitty Lane* to *Walter* and *Molly Forr*. They were again changed in the final published form to *Walter* and *Kitty Fane*. The text of the serialisation—with the above exceptions and a few minor differences—is the same as the American text (which was never altered) and the first issue of the English book text. The *Nash's Magazine* serialisation began in the December 1924 issue and concluded in the July 1925 issue. Complete sets of all the issues are extremely scarce. The American serialisation began in the November 1924 issue of *Hearst's International Magazine* and was concluded in the March 1925 issue, but the names of the characters remained unaltered throughout (i.e. *Kitty* and *Walter* Lane). *See Appendix V, Note 4 and Illus.*

A33   THE PAINTED VEIL   (1930)

d. Collins Cheap edition:
THE | PAINTED VEIL | *by* | W. SOMERSET MAUGHAM | Author of "Ashenden," "The Moon and Sixpence," etc. | [*publisher's monogram device*] | LONDON 48 PALL MALL | W. COLLINS SONS & CO LTD | GLASGOW SYDNEY AUCKLAND

Collation: 256 pp. [A]¹⁶ B–H¹⁶.
pp. [1–2], lining paper pasted down conjugate with [A]₁₅₋₁₆; p. [3], half-title; p. [4], This is the Story . . . ; p. [5], title; p. [6], Copyright | Printed in Great Britain; p. [7], AUTHOR'S NOTE; p. [8], one-line quotation; pp. 9–248, text; pp. [249–253], advts.; p. [254], blank; pp. [255–256], lining paper pasted down conjugate with H₁₋₂.

Binding: Blue ribbed cloth, blocked on front with dark blue single border; on spine blocked and lettered in dark blue between conventional printers' ornaments: THE | PAINTED | VEIL | by | W. SOMERSET | MAUGHAM | [*between single rules*] COLLINS; back plain. All edges cut. Leaves measure 15 × 10.1 cm.

Price: 1s. Number of copies unknown. Published February 1930.

The British Museum copy was received on 10 March 1930.

A34   THE CASUARINA TREE   1926

a. First edition:
The | CASUARINA TREE | *Six Stories* | by | W. S. MAUGHAM | [*ornament*] | *London* | WILLIAM HEINEMANN LTD. | 1926

Collation: viii, 312 pp. [A]⁴ B–U⁸ X⁴.
p. [i], half-title; p. [ii], WORKS BY | W. SOMERSET MAUGHAM [listing 9 novels and 18 plays]; p. [iii], title; p. [iv], *First published 1926.* | *Printed in Great Britain by Woods & Sons, Ltd., 338–340, Upper Street, London N.1*; p. v, contents; p. [vi], blank; pp. vii–viii, author's note; pp. 1–311, text; p. [312], blank.

Binding: Dark blue linen-grain cloth, blocked on front with author's symbol in black and gold-lettered: The Casuarina

Tree; on spine in gold: The | Casuarina | Tree | W. S. | Maugham | [*in black*] Heinemann.
Plain end-papers; top and fore-edges cut, lower edges rough trimmed; leaves measure 18.8 × 12.4 cm.

Price: 7s. 6d. 5,000 copies were published on 2 September 1926.

Notes: The Outstation, a story by W. Somerset Maugham, edited by Max Moser, was published separately in Bern, Switzerland, by A. Francke AG.1942. (*Collection of English texts for use in Schools, v. 57*). Stiff orange wraps. 40p. 19½ cm. The work went into several impressions, and one or two editions. It was still being published in 1955.

A34   THE CASUARINA TREE   (1926)

b. First American edition:
The | CASUARINA TREE | *Six Stories* | By | W. SOMERSET MAUGHAM | [*publisher's tree device*] | GEORGE H. DORAN COMPANY | ON MURRAY HILL [*square of dots*] NEW YORK

Collation: 288 pp. [unsigned 1–17⁸].
p. [i], half-title; p. [ii], BY W. SOMERSET MAUGHAM | [*rule*] | [listing 10 titles]; p. [iii], title; p. [iv], COPYRIGHT, 1926 | BY W. SOMERSET MAUGHAM | [*publisher's monogram device*] | THE CASUARINA TREE | —B— | PRINTED IN THE UNITED STATES OF AMERICA; p. v–vi, THE CASUARINA TREE; p. [vii], Contents; p. [viii], blank; p. [ix], fly-title; p. [x], blank; pp. 11–288, text.

Binding: Brown smooth cloth, lettered on front and spine in dark green; on front THE CASUARINA TREE | W. Somerset Maugham; on spine The | CASUARINA | TREE | [*ornament*] | W. Somerset | Maugham | DORAN
Plain end-papers; all edges cut; leaves measure 18.8 × 12.7 cm.

Price: $2. 5,000 copies were published on 17 September 1926.

Contents: The Casuarina Tree—Before the Party—P. & O.— The Outstation—The Force of Circumstance—The Yellow Streak— The Letter—Postscript.

A34   THE LETTER   (1930)

c. Collins Detective Club edition:
[*within a black half-diamond border*] THE LETTER | STORIES OF CRIME BY | W. SOMERSET MAUGHAM | *Originally published under the title of* | *"The Casuarina Tree."* | [*vignette*] | Published by |

The DETECTIVE STORY CLUB Ltd. | for | WM. COLLINS SONS & CO. LTD.

Collation: 256 pp. [A]^{16} B–H^{16}.
pp. [1–2], lining paper pasted down conjugate with [A]$_{15-16}$; p. [iii], title; p. [4], listing titles in THE | DETECTIVE STORY | CLUB; p. [5], contents; p. [6], blank; pp. 7–254, text; pp. [255–256], lining paper pasted down conjugate with H$_{1-2}$.

Binding: Black calico cloth, blocked in gold within a design of handcuffs and chains with a vignette below of the outline of a gun pointing at the reader, and gold-lettered: THE LETTER | SOMERSET MAUGHAM | THE | DETECTIVE | CLUB; back plain; lettered in gold on spine: THE | LETTER | SOMERSET | MAUGHAM | THE | DETECTIVE | CLUB
All edges cut. Leaves measure 15 × 9.8 cm.
Price: 6d. Number of copies unknown. Published January 1930.
See A22d.

A35   THE CONSTANT WIFE   (1927)

a. First edition:
THE | CONSTANT WIFE | *A Comedy in Three Acts* | By | W. SOMERSET MAUGHAM | NEW [*publisher's monogram device*] YORK | GEORGE H. DORAN COMPANY [*the whole enclosed in a triple frame*]

Collation: 216 pp. [unsigned 1–13^8 14^4].
p. [1], half-title; p. [2], BY W. SOMERSET MAUGHAM [listing 24 works]; p. [3], title; p. [4], COPYRIGHT, 1926 | BY W. SOMERSET MAUGHAM | [*publisher's monogram*] | THE CONSTANT WIFE | —B— | PRINTED IN THE UNITED STATES OF AMERICA; p. [5], characters; p. [6], blank; p. [7], cast; p. [8], blank; p. [9], sub-title: The Constant Wife; Act One; p. [10], blank; pp. 11–216.

Binding: Black linen-grain cloth, yellow labels on front and spine, printed in black; on front, between double-rules: THE | CONSTANT WIFE | [*ornament*] | *A Comedy in Three Acts by* | W. SOMERSET MAUGHAM; on spine, between double-rules: THE | CONSTANT | WIFE | By | W. SOMERSET | MAUGHAM
Plain end-papers; top and lower edges cut, fore-edges uncut; leaves measure 19 × 13 cm.

Price: $2. 2,000 copies were published in April 1927.

Illus.: Front. port. of Ethel Barrymore, tipped in.

A35   THE CONSTANT WIFE   1927

b. First English edition:
[*within a triple-rule border*] THE | CONSTANT WIFE | *A Comedy in Three Acts* | By | W. SOMERSET MAUGHAM | [*publisher's windmill device resting on base with date* 1927] LONDON: WILLIAM HEINEMANN

> *Collation:* (220) [paged (216)] pp. [unsigned 1–13⁸ 14⁶].
> Half-title, with verso: BY W. SOMERSET MAUGHAM [listing 24 works] not included in pagination: p. [1], title; p. [2], COPYRIGHT, 1926, | BY W. SOMERSET MAUGHAM | [*publisher's monogram*] | THE CONSTANT WIFE | —B— | PRINTED IN THE UNITED STATES OF AMERICA; p. [3], dedication To | ETHEL BARRYMORE; p. [4], blank; p. [5], characters; p. [6], blank; p. [7], cast; p. [8], blank; p. [9], sub-title: The Constant Wife; Act One; p. [10], blank; pp. 11–216, text; pp. [217–218], blank.

> *Binding:* Identical with the American edition.

> *Illus.:* Front. port. of Ethel Barrymore, tipped in.

Notes: The English edition was published in September 1927. Reissue of the American impression with new English title leaf. Doran sheets, consisting of 750 copies, were despatched to London in September 1927.

   The Constant Wife was first produced in America at the Ohio Theatre on November 1 1926, with Ethel Barrymore, Mabel Terry-Lewis and C. Aubrey Smith in the cast. In London, the roles were taken by Mary Jerrold, Fay Compton and Leon Quartermaine.

A36   THE LETTER   (1927)

a. First edition:
THE LETTER | A PLAY IN THREE ACTS | BY | W. SOMERSET MAUGHAM | [*publisher's windmill device in box*] | LONDON: | WILLIAM HEINEMANN LTD.

> *Collation:* [viii], 156 pp. [A]⁴ B–K⁸ L⁶.
> p. [i], half-title; p. [ii], *By the same Author* [listing 17 works]; p. [iii], title; p. [iv], *First Published 1927* | *Printed in Great Britain*; p. [v], list of cast; p. [vi], blank; p. [vii], characters; p. [viii], blank; pp. [1] 2–156, text.

> *Binding:* Cherry red buckram (3s. 6d.) and champagne wrappers (2s. 6d.). *See prelim. Note.*

17.4 cm. (wraps. 17.6 cm.). All edges cut. 2,300 copies were published in June 1927.

Notes: This play, with its two endings, is a particularly interesting example of the author's dramatic technique.

The Letter was produced at The Playhouse on February 24th 1927 with Gladys Cooper and Leslie Faber in the cast.

The whole of the issue of *The Play Pictorial* No. 302 (1927) was devoted to a summary of *The Letter*, with excerpts from the dialogue as captions to the photographs illustrating scenes from the play.

Not included in the *Collected Plays*.

A36   THE LETTER   (1927)

b. First American edition:
[*within a double-rule border*] THE LETTER | *A Play in Three Acts* | By | W. SOMERSET MAUGHAM | NEW [*publisher's monogram device*] YORK | GEORGE H. DORAN COMPANY

Collation: 180 pp. [unsigned [1]⁴ 2–11⁸ 12⁶].
p. [1], half-title; p. [2], BY W. SOMERSET MAUGHAM [listing 13 dramatic and 12 non-dramatic works; p. [3], title; p. [4], COPYRIGHT, 1925, | By W. SOMERSET MAUGHAM | [*publisher's monogram*] | THE LETTER | —B— | PRINTED IN THE UNITED STATES OF AMERICA; p. [5], characters; p. [6], blank; p. [7], sub-title: The Letter: Act One; p. [8], blank; pp. 9–177, text; pp. [188–180], blank.

Binding: Smooth black cloth, pale yellow labels on front and spine, printed in black; on front, between double-rules: THE LETTER | [*printer's ornament*] | A Play in Three Acts by | W. SOMERSET MAUGHAM; on spine, between double-rules: THE | LETTER | By | W. SOMERSET | MAUGHAM
Plain end-papers; top and lower edges cut, fore-edges uncut; leaves measure 19.2 × 12.9 cm.

Price: $2. Number of copies unknown. Published September 1927.

Illus. Front. port. of Katharine Cornell, tipped in.

Notes: A souvenir issue of the play in orange wrappers, having the same collation as the Doran issue (save for an additional leaf listing the New York cast, tipped in) was given away with the compliments of the Producer and Publisher on the opening night.

A37					ASHENDEN: or The British Agent					1928

a. First edition:

ASHENDEN | OR | THE BRITISH AGENT | BY | W. SOMER-
SET MAUGHAM | [*publisher's windmill device in box*] | London |
William Heinemann, Ltd. | 1928

> *Collation:* [viii], 304 pp. [ ]⁴ A–T⁸.
>
> p. [i], half-title; p. [ii], BY W. SOMERSET MAUGHAM [listing 10
> non-dramatic and 18 dramatic works]; p. [iii], title; p. [iv],
> *First published* 1928 | PRINTED IN GREAT BRITAIN AT THE WINDMILL
> PRESS, | KINGSWOOD, SURREY; p. [v], dedication; p. [vi], blank;
> p. [vii], fly-title; p. [viii], blank; pp. 1–304, text.
>
> *Binding:* Dark blue linen-grain cloth, blocked in black on front
> with author's symbol and on back with publisher's windmill
> device; gold-lettered on front: Ashenden; and on spine: Ashen-
> den | W. S. | Maugham | [*in black*] Heinemann.
> Plain end-papers; all edges cut; leaves measure 18.3 × 12.4 cm.
> *Price:* 7s. 6d. 10,000 copies were published on 29 March 1928.
>
> *Contents: R—A Domiciliary Visit—Miss King—The Hairless
> Mexican—The Dark Woman—The Greek—A Trip to Paris—
> Guilia Lazzari—Gustav—The Traitor—Behind the Scenes—His
> Excellency—The Flip of a Coin—A Chance Acquaintance—Love and
> Russian Literature—Mr. Harrington's Washing.*

A37					ASHENDEN: or The British Agent					1928

b. First American edition:

ASHENDEN: *or* THE BRITISH AGENT | *by* W. SOMERSET
MAUGHAM | DOUBLEDAY, DORAN & COMPANY, INC., |
GARDEN CITY, NEW YORK [*dot*] MCMXXVIII

> *Collation:* vi, 304 [306] pp. [unsigned 1–18⁸ 19⁴ 20⁸].
> p. [i], half-title; p. [ii], Books by | W. SOMERSET MAUGHAM [listing
> 13 non-dramatic and 12 dramatic works]; p. [iii], title; p. [iv],
> COPYRIGHT 1927, 1928, BY W. SOMERSET | MAUGHAM. ALL RIGHTS
> RESERVED. PRINTED | IN THE UNITED STATES AT THE COUNTRY |
> LIFE PRESS, GARDEN CITY, N.Y. | FIRST EDITION; p. [v], dedication to
> Gerald Kelly; p. [vi], blank; pp. 1–304, text; pp. [305–306],
> blank.
>
> *Binding:* Blue linen calico cloth, blocked in reddish brown on
> front with sketch of a sea-horse and lettered in half-circle ASHEN-
> DEN; on spine blocked in reddish brown with 3 ornamental

Ley could not see a holly-tree without a little shiver of
disgust; her mind went immediately to the decorations
of middle-class houses, the mistletoe hanging from a gas-
chandelier, and the foolish old gentlemen who found
amusement in kissing stray females. She was glad that
Bertha had thought fit to refuse the display of enthusiasm
from servants and impoverished tenants, ~~which~~ *that*, on the
attainment of her majority, ~~her guardian~~ *Dr Ramsay* had wished to
arrange; Miss Ley could imagine that the festivities
possible on such an occasion, the handshaking, the making of good cheer, and the obtrusive joviality of the
country Englishman, might surpass even the tawdry
~~rejoicings~~ *celebrations* of Yule-tide. But Bertha fortunately detested
such ~~things~~ *festivities* as sincerely as did Miss Ley herself, and suggested to the persons concerned that they could not oblige
her more than by taking no notice of an event ~~which~~ *that*
really did not to her seem very significant.

But ~~Dr. Ramsay's~~ *her guardian's* heartiness could not be entirely
restrained; ~~and~~ he had ~~also~~ a fine old English sense of
the fitness of things, ~~that passion to act in a certain
manner merely because in times past people have always
so acted.~~ He insisted on solemnly meeting Bertha to
offer congratulations, a blessing, and some statement of
his stewardship.

~~Bertha~~ *un on* came downstairs when Miss Ley was already
eating breakfast, a very feminine ~~meal~~ *breakfast*, consisting of nothing more substantial than a square inch of bacon and
~~a morsel of~~ *some* dry toast. Miss Ley was really somewhat
nervous, she was bothered by the necessity of referring
to ~~Bertha's natal day~~ *her niece's birthday*.

"That is one advantage of women," she told herself,
"after twenty-five they gloss over their birthdays like

King's School Library (Somerset Maugham's). After his death a commemorative plaque was mounted under the centre windows.

WILLIAM SOMERSET MAUGHAM
K.S.C. 1885 - 1889
BORN 1874 · DIED 1965

double bands and lettered: ASHENDEN | or | THE BRITISH | AGENT | [*dot*] | W. SOMERSET | MAUGHAM | DOUBLEDAY | DORAN
Plain end-papers with sketch of sea horse centre; top edges cut and stained reddish brown, fore-edges rough trimmed, lower edges cut; leaves measure 19 × 12.9 cm.

Price: $2.50. 10,000 copies were published on 30 March 1928.

Copright copy deposited with Library of Congress May 9 1930.
Notes: In 1941 Doubleday, Doran reprinted *Ashenden* and a new 7-page preface by the author on his feelings about this book was included for the first time in this edition.

A37   ASHENDEN: or The British Agent   (1934)

c. Cheap Collins edition:
THE NOVEL LIBRARY | [*rule*] | ASHENDEN | OR | THE BRITISH AGENT | *by* | W. SOMERSET MAUGHAM | *Published for* | WM. COLLINS SONS & CO. LTD | *by* | THE LONDON BOOK CO. LTD.

Collation: 256 pp. [A]¹⁶ B–H¹⁶.
p. [1–2], lining paper pasted down conjugate with A_{15-16}; p. [3], title; p. [4], This narrative of some experiences during the Great War . . . ; pp. 5–254, text; pp. [255–256], lining paper pasted down conjugate with H_{1-2}.

Binding: Crimson ribbed cloth, blocked in gold on front within ornamental frame; ASHENDEN | SOMERSET | MAUGHAM; back plain; spine blocked in gold with decorative bands head and base and gold-lettered: ASHENDEN | [*ornament*] | SOMERSET | MAUGHAM | THE | NOVEL | LIBRARY.
All edges cut. Leaves measure 15.3 × 10 cm.

Price: 6d. Number of copies unknown. Published in January 1934.

Notes: British Museum copy received 15 January 1934. *See* A22d.

A38   THE SACRED FLAME   1928

a. First edition:
THE | SACRED FLAME | A Play in Three Acts | BY | W. SOMER-SET MAUGHAM | [*4-line quotation from Coleridge*] | GARDEN CITY, NEW YORK | DOUBLEDAY, DORAN & COMPANY, INC. | 1928

G

Collation: [x], 190 pp. [unsigned 1–10⁸ 11⁴ 12–13⁸].
p. [i–ii], blank; p. [iii], half-title; p. [iv], BY W. SOMERSET MAUGHAM [listing 13 non-dramatic and 14 dramatic works]; p. [v], title; p, [vi], [*publisher's anchor device*] | COPYRIGHT, 1928 | BY W. SOMERSET MAUGHAM | ALL RIGHTS RESERVED | PRINTED IN THE UNITED STATES AT | THE COUNTRY LIFE PRESS | GARDEN CITY, N.Y. | FIRST EDITION; p. [vii], dedication: To | HIS FRIEND | MESSMORE KENDALL | THE AUTHOR | DEDICATES THIS PLAY; p. [viii], blank; p. [ix], characters; p. [x], blank; p. [1], sub-title; The Sacred Flame: Act One; p. [2], blank; pp. 3–187, text; pp. [188–190], blank.

Binding: Black linen-grain cloth, fawn paper labels on front and spine, printed in black; on front, between double-rules: THE | SACRED FLAME | *A Play in Three Acts by* | W. SOMERSET MAUGHAM; on spine, between double-rules: THE | SACRED | FLAME | By | W. SOMERSET | MAUGHAM.
Plain end-papers; top edges cut, lower edges rough trimmed, fore-edges uncut; leaves measure 19 × 13.2 cm.

Price: $2. 2,000 copies were published in November 1928.

Notes: The Sacred Flame was produced first in New York in November 1928 where it was a 'flop', and then in London February 1929. In this play the author attempted an experiment—to introduce a literary dialogue instead of naturalistic speech. It was quite a success, but the author did not repeat the experiment.

A38   THE SACRED FLAME   1928

b. First English edition:
THE | SACRED FLAME | A Play in Three Acts | BY | W. SOMER-SET MAUGHAM | [*4 lines of verse from Coleridge*] | [*publisher's windmill device in box*] | London | William Heinemann, Ltd. | 1928

Collation: [x], 190 pp. [unsigned 1–10⁸ 11⁴ 12–13⁸].
p. [i–ii], blank: p. [iii], half-title; p. [iv], BY W. SOMERSET MAUGHAM [listing 13 non-dramatic and 14 dramatic works]; p. [v], title; p. [vi], PRINTED IN THE UNITED STATES OF AMERICA; p. [vii], dedication; p. [viii], blank; p. [ix], characters; p. [x], blank; p. [1], sub-title: The Sacred Flame: Act One; p. [2], blank; pp. 3–187, text; pp. [188–190], blank.

Binding: Identical with the American edition.

Notes: The English edition was published in February 1929. Title-page dated 1928. Reissue of the American impression with new

English title leaf. Doubleday, Doran sheets consisting of 1,000 copies were dispatched to London in 1928. Reprinted 1931 (778 copies) also with sheets from America.

A39   THE GENTLEMAN IN THE PARLOUR: (1930)
          A Record of a Journey from Rangoon to Haiphong

a. First edition:
THE GENTLEMAN | IN THE PARLOUR | A | RECORD OF |
A JOURNEY FROM | RANGOON TO HAIPHONG | By |
W. SOMERSET MAUGHAM | [*publisher's windmill device*] | [*rule*] |
LONDON | WILLIAM HEINEMANN LTD.

> *Collation:* [vi], 278 pp. [A]⁶ B–S⁸.
> p. [i–ii], blank; p. [iii], half-title; p. [iv], blank; p. [v], title; p.
> [vi], FIRST PUBLISHED 1930 | PRINTED IN GREAT BRITAIN AT | THE
> WINDMILL PRESS, KINGSWOOD | SURREY; pp. 1–276, text; pp.
> [277–278], blank.
>
> *Binding:* Smooth black cloth, blocked in gold on front with a
> design of a dragon with forked tongue and author's symbol
> and gold-lettered: THE GENTLEMAN IN THE PARLOUR | By W.
> SOMERSET MAUGHAM; on spine with 6 plain gold bands and a
> pagoda design and gold-lettered: THE | GENTLEMAN | IN THE |
> PARLOUR | [*star*] | W. SOMERSET | MAUGHAM | HEINEMANN; on
> back publisher's windmill device in blind.
> Plain end-papers; top edges cut, fore-edges uncut, lower edges
> rough trimmed; leaves measure 20.2 × 15 cm.
>
> *Price:* 8s. 6d. 5,000 copies were published in February 1930.
>
> *Advance Proof state:* pp. [vi]+276+blank leaf. Brown wrappers
> (blank). Proof has fly-title. Leaves measure 19 × 14.2 cm.

Notes: Mr. Muir states that a large number of library copies of *The
Gentleman in the Parlour* were bound by W. H. Smith & Sons in a
grey cloth, lettered in black. See B.C.Q. for January 1933, pp. 23–4.

A39   THE GENTLEMAN IN THE PARLOUR   1930
          A Record of a Journey from Rangoon to Haiphong

b. First American edition:
THE GENTLEMAN | IN THE PARLOUR | A Record of a Journey
from | Rangoon to Haiphong | BY | W. SOMERSET MAUGHAM |
[*flying bird enclosed in green frame*] | DOUBLEDAY, DORAN &
COMPANY, INC. | GARDEN CITY, NEW YORK | 1930

Collation: [iv+ii], 300 pp. [unsigned 1–19⁸]. Title page an inset.
p. [i], half-title; p. [ii], BOOKS BY | W. SOMERSET MAUGHAM [*listing 14 non-dramatic and 14 dramatic works*]; p. [iii], title; p. [iv], [*publisher's monogram*] | COPYRIGHT, 1930 | BY DOUBLEDAY, DORAN & COMPANY, INC. | COPYRIGHT, 1929 | BY INTERNATIONAL MAGAZINE COMPANY, INC. | ALL RIGHTS RESERVED | PRINTED IN THE UNITED STATES AT | THE COUNTRY LIFE PRESS | GARDEN CITY, N.Y. | FIRST EDITION; p. [v], fly-title; p. [vi], blank; pp. [1] 2–300, text.

Binding: Black linen-grain cloth, blocked on front with design of a bird flying in blue enclosed in a green frame; on spine lettered in blue between green ornamental bands THE | GENTLE- | MAN IN | THE | PARLOUR | W. | SOMERSET | MAUGHAM | [*at foot in blue*] DOUBLEDAY | DORAN.
Plain end-papers; top edges cut, fore and lower edges rough trimmed; leaves measure 21.9×14.7 cm.

Price: $3. 5,000 copies were published on 18 April 1930. Copyright copy deposited with Library of Congress May 9 1930.

A40   CAKES AND ALE: (1930)
               Or The Skeleton in the Cupboard

a. First edition:
CAKES AND ALE | OR | THE SKELETON | IN THE | CUP-BOARD | BY W. SOMERSET MAUGHAM | [*publisher's windmill device*] | LONDON | WILLIAM HEINEMANN LTD

Collation: [vi], 270 pp. B⁸+B*² C–S⁸. Quarter sheet signed B* wrapped round B₂ and B₇.
pp. [i–ii], blank; p. [iii], half-title; p. [iv], By W. SOMERSET MAUGHAM [*listing 13 non-dramatic and 20 dramatic works*]; p. [v], title; p. [vi], FIRST PUBLISHED 1930 | [*rule*] | PRINTED IN GREAT BRITAIN | AT THE WINDMILL PRESS, | KINGSWOOD, SURREY.; pp. 1–270, text.

Binding: Persian blue linen-grain cloth, blocked in black on front with author's symbol and on back with publisher's windmill device; gold-lettered on front: Cakes and Ale; and on spine; Cakes | and Ale | W. S. | Maugham | [*in black*] Heinemann.
Plain end-papers; all edges cut; leaves measure 18.5×12.2 cm.
Price: 7s. 6d. 15,000 copies were published on 29 September 1930.

Notes: It is sometimes assumed that the first issue of the first edition consists of copies with the missing 't' on p. 147, line 14. This, however, is not an issue but a state of the printing. It would appear that the error was rectified at some stage in the run. There is also a misprint on p. 181, line 4, 'in' instead of 'it' and a dropped letter 'l' on p. 63, line 22. These latter misprints appear to be common to the whole of the first printing.

Both states, however, were issued simultaneously, as is established by the copies in the Statutory Libraries, two of which have the state with the dropped 't' and three with the 't' present, and they obviously have no bibliographical significance. *Cakes and Ale* was serialised in *Harper's Bazaar*. It began in the March issue 1930 and was concluded in the following July issue.

A40   CAKES AND ALE: 1930
                     Or The Skeleton in the Cupboard

b. First American edition:
CAKES AND ALE: | OR | THE SKELETON | IN THE | CUP-BOARD | [*between single rules*] W. SOMERSET MAUGHAM | MCMXXX | DOUBLEDAY, DORAN & COMPANY, INC. | GARDEN CITY, NEW YORK

[viii], 312 pp. [unsigned 1–20⁸].
pp. [i–ii], blank; p. [iii], half-title; p. [iv], BY | W. SOMERSET MAUGHAM [listing 15 non-dramatic and 14 dramatic works]; p. [v], title; p. [vi], [*publisher's monogram device*] | COPYRIGHT, 1930 | BY DOUBLEDAY, DORAN & COMPANY, INC. | ALL RIGHTS RESERVED | PRINTED IN THE UNITED STATES AT | THE COUNTRY LIFE PRESS | GARDEN CITY, N.Y. | FIRST EDITION; p. [vii], fly-title; p. [viii], blank; pp. [1], 2–308, text; pp. [309–312], blank.

Binding: Black smooth cloth, blocked and lettered in gold on front CAKES AND ALE: | OR THE SKELETON IN THE CUPBOARD | W. Somerset Maugham | [*author's symbol*]: on spine lettered in gold CAKES | AND ALE: | OR | THE SKELETON | IN THE | CUPBOARD | W. Somerset | Maugham | DOUBLEDAY | DORAN.
Chrome end-papers, with geometrical design in white; all edges rough trimmed; leaves measure 19 × 13 cm.

Price: $2. 15,000 copies were published on 3 October 1930.

A40   CAKES AND ALE: (1950)
                     Or The Skeleton in the Cupboard

c. Another edition, with a special Introduction by the Author:
CAKES | AND | ALE | BY | SOMERSET MAUGHAM | With a special introduction | for this edition by Mr. Maugham | THE MODERN LIBRARY NEW YORK

Pagination: xii, 272 pp. Green cloth. All edges cut. Leaves measure 17.7×13 cm. $1.25.

Notes: Contains a new 8 pp. introduction by the author, in which he admits that the character of Alroy Kear in *Cakes and Ale* was based on Hugh Walpole. He confessed that Walpole had been in his mind when he described the character of Alroy Kear. He made the excuse that it was his belief that 'no author can create a character out of nothing. He must have a model to give him a starting point; but then his imagination goes to work, he builds him up, adding a trait here, a trait there, which his model did not possess. . . . It is only in this way that a novelist can give his characters the intensity, the reality which makes them not only plausible, but convincing.'

According to Alex Waugh, *Cakes and Ale* ruined the last ten years of Walpole's life. Accounts of this remarkable controversy are to be found in Hart-Davis's *Hugh Walpole. A Biography* (1952) and Myrick Land's *The Fine Art of Literary Mayhem* (1963). *See also* F.30.

A40   CAKES AND ALE: (1954)
                    or The Skeleton in the Cupboard

d. Eightieth Birthday edition:
W. Somerset Maugham | [french rule] | CAKES AND ALE | *or* | *The Skeleton* | *in the Cupboard* | WITH AN ORIGINAL LITHO-GRAPH | AND DECORATIONS BY | GRAHAM SUTHER-LAND | [*publisher's windmill device resting on base*] WILLIAM HEINE-MANN LTD | MELBOURNE [*square of 4 dots*] LONDON [*square of 4 dots*] TORONTO
Title in red and black.

Collation: xii, 256 pp. [A]⁴ B–Q⁸ R⁸⁺² Sig. R a gathering of 10 leaves. Front., a single inset; a half sheet is inserted between A₂ and A₃.
p. [i], half-title; p. [ii], cert. of limitation; front. a single inset; p. [iii], title; p. [iv], TEXT PRINTED IN GREAT BRITAIN | AT THE WINDMILL PRESS | KINGSWOOD, SURREY | LITHOGRAPH PRINTED AT | THE CURWEN PRESS, PLAISTOW, E.13; fascimile reproduction of the first and last two pages of the orig. M.S., a half sheet imposition; pp. v–xii, preface; pp. 1–255, text; p. [256], blank.
Cert. of Limitation: This Edition of *Cakes and Ale* is limited to 1,000 copies and is signed by the Author and the Artist. Number. . . .

Binding: Half mushroom calf, navy blue calf boards, divided by gold rule, front and back; on front author's symbol blocked in blind; on spine black cloth label gold-lettered CAKES | AND | ALE | W. SOMERSET | MAUGHAM [*the whole enclosed in a single frame broken top and tail*].

Binding Variant: There were a few copies specially bound for presentation in full blue and white calf. Mr. Maugham was presented with No. 1.
Plain end-papers; top edges cut and gilt, other edges uncut, unopened; leaves measure 22.7 × 15.4 cm. In slip case.

Price: £5 5s. The limited edition was published on the 25th January 1954 to celebrate the author's eightieth birthday.

A40   CAKES AND ALE: 1970
              or The Skeleton in the Cupboard

e. The Folio Society edition:
CAKES AND ALE | OR THE SKELETON IN THE CUPBOARD | W. SOMERSET MAUGHAM | MONOTYPES BY | DODIE MASTERMAN | London | The Folio Society | 1970

Collation: [ii], 190 pp. [unsigned 1–12⁸].
pp. [i–ii], blank, not included in pagination; p. [1], half-title; p. [2], frontispiece; p. [3], title; p. [4], THE FOLIO SOCIETY WISH TO THANK WILLIAM HEINEMANN LTD. | FOR PERMISSION TO USE THIS TEXT | Printed in Great Britain | *Printed by Western Printing Services Ltd, Bristol* | *Set in 11 on 12 pt Monotype* Ehrhardt | Bound by W. & J. Mackay & Co Ltd. Chatham; pp. 5–8. Author's Preface; p. 9, Illustrations; p. [10], blank; pp. 11–187, text; pp. [188–190], blank.

Binding: Lemon Dutch cloth, printed from a design by the artist in lithography, blocked in black on front with sketch of a girl in Edwardian costume riding a bicycle through some woods and on back two men riding bicycles; blocked in gold on spine with publisher's monogram device and lettered running down spine in gold: CAKES AND ALE.
Lemon end-papers; all edges cut; leaves measure 22.3 × 15.3 cm.

Price: £1.65 (for subscribers). Published in May 1970.

A41   THE BREAD-WINNER   (1930)

a. First edition:
THE | BREAD-WINNER | A COMEDY IN ONE ACT | BY | W. S. MAUGHAM | [*publisher's windmill device in box*] | LONDON: | WILLIAM HEINEMANN LTD.

Collation: [viii], 188 pp. [A]⁴ B–M⁸ N⁴ O².
p. [i], half-title; p. [ii], *By the same Author* [listing 18 works];
p. [iii], title; p. [iv], *First Published 1930* | *Printed in Great Britain*;
p. [v], list of cast; p. [vi], blank; p. [vii], characters; p. [viii],
blank; pp. [1] 2–188, text.

Binding: Cherry red buckram (3s. 6d.) and champagne wrappers
(2s. 6d.). *See prelim. Note.*
17.2 cm. (wraps. 17.4 cm.). All edges cut. 2,000 copies were
published on 29 September 1930.

Notes: There are two issues of the first edition, the second issue having
a leaf with a note on Performing Rights inserted between A¹ and B¹.
It is believed that the first issue, which lacks this leaf, consists only of a
few copies in wrappers. The leaf was pasted in, and its removal can
usually be readily discerned.

The Breadwinner was written in 1930. It was produced at the Vaudeville Theatre on September 30 1930 with Jack Hawkins, Marie Lohr
and Peggy Ashcroft in the cast.

A41   THE BREAD-WINNER   1931

b. First American edition:
THE BREADWINNER | A Comedy | BY | W. SOMERSET
MAUGHAM | [*author's symbol*] | [*thick rule, thin rule*] | DOUBLEDAY,
DORAN & COMPANY, INC. | GARDEN CITY, NEW YORK |
1931

Collation: [vi], 186 pp. [unsigned 1–12⁸].
p. [i], half-title; p. [ii], BOOKS BY | W. SOMERSET MAUGHAM [listing
16 non-dramatic and 15 dramatic works]; p. [iii], title; p. [iv],
PRINTED AT THE *Country Life Press*, GARDEN CITY, N.Y., U.S.A. |
COPYRIGHT, 1931 | BY W. SOMERSET MAUGHAM | ALL RIGHTS RE-
SERVED | FIRST EDITION; p. [v], Characters; p. [vi], blank; p. [1],
ACT ONE; p. [2], blank; pp. 3–184, text; pp. [185–186], blank.

Binding: Black matt cloth, with red label on front lettered in
black THE BREADWINNER | W. Somerset Maugham [*star*]; on spine
red label printed in black between ornamental rules: THE |
BREAD | WINNER | [*star*] | [*between double-rules*] W. Somerset |
Maugham.
Plain end-papers; top edge cut and stained red; other edges
uncut; leaves measure 19 × 13 cm.

Price: $2. Number of copies unknown. Published in October

1931. The book was copyrighted with the Library of Congress on November 7 1931.

A42 SIX STORIES WRITTEN IN THE 1931
FIRST PERSON SINGULAR

a. First edition:
SIX STORIES WRITTEN | IN THE FIRST PERSON | SIN-
GULAR | W. Somerset Maugham | [*author's symbol in red*] |
MCMXXXI | [*rule*] | DOUBLEDAY, DORAN & COMPANY,
INC. | GARDEN CITY, NEW YORK

> *Collation:* [xii] [paged x], 302 pp. [unsigned 1–18⁸ 19⁴ 20⁸].
> Title page, a single insert.
> pp. [i–ii], blank; p. [iii], half-title; p. [iv], Books by | W. SOMER-
> SET MAUGHAM [listing 16 non-dramatic and 14 dramatic
> works]; title, *with verso* PRINTED AT THE *Country Life Press*, GARDEN
> CITY, N.Y., U.S.A. | COPYRIGHT, 1923, 1924, 1930, 1931 | BY W.
> SOMERSET MAUGHAM | ALL RIGHTS RESERVED | FIRST EDITION p. [v],
> contents; p. [vi], blank; pp. vii–x, introduction; p. [1], fly-title;
> p. [2], blank; pp. 3–299, text; pp. [300–302], blank.

> *Binding:* Smooth black cloth, blocked on front in gold with
> author's symbol within an oval inlay; on spine with floral design
> above and below title and gold lettered: FIRST | PERSON | SIN-
> GULAR | W. Somerset | Maugham | DOUBLEDAY | DORAN.
> Cream end-papers; top edges cut, lower edges rough trimmed,
> fore-edges uncut; leaves measure 20×15 cm.

> *Price:* $2.50. 10,000 copies were published on the 17 September
> 1931.

A42 SIX STORIES WRITTEN IN THE (1931)
FIRST PERSON SINGULAR

b. First English edition:
W. SOMERSET MAUGHAM | [*blue rule*] | SIX STORIES |
WRITTEN IN THE | FIRST PERSON SINGULAR | [*blue rule*] |
[*publisher's windmill device in blue*] | LONDON | WILLIAM HEINE-
MANN LTD

> *Collation:* [xii], 308 pp. [A]⁸ B–U⁸.
> p. [i], half-title; p. [ii], By w. SOMERSET MAUGHAM [listing 14
> non-dramatic and 22 dramatic works]; p. [iii], title; p. [iv],
> FIRST PUBLISHED 1931 | PRINTED IN GREAT BRITAIN | AT THE WIND-
> MILL PRESS | KINGSWOOD, SURREY; p. [v], contents; p. [vi], blank;

pp. vii–xi, introduction; p. [xii], blank; pp. 1–307, text; p. [308], blank.

Binding: Blue linen-grain cloth, blocked in black on front with author's symbol and on back with publisher's windmill device; gold-lettered on front; First Person Singular; and on spine: First | Person | Singular | W. S. | Maugham | [in black] Heinemann.
Plain end-papers; top edges cut and stained blue, fore and lower edges cut; leaves measure 18.4 × 12.1 cm.

Price: 7s. 6d. 10,000 copies were published on the 28 September 1931.

Notes: In the Zipkin copy in the University of Texas, Maugham has written: '*The Alien Corn* was first published in Florence by Gino Orioli.' If the author's memory was not at fault, then this indeed is a startling revelation, as no copy to my knowledge has ever emerged from its Italian demesne.

Contents: Virtue—The Round Dozen—The Human Element—Jane—The Alien Corn—The Creative Impulse.

A43   THE BOOK BAG   1932

a. First edition:
[*within a blue double-rule frame and single-rule border*] 20 BEST | SHORT STORIES | IN | RAY LONG'S | 20 YEARS | AS AN EDITOR | [*publisher's monogram in blue*] | Ray Long & Richard R. Smith, Inc. | New York. . . . 1932

Collation: xiv [xv–xviii], 604+[2] pp. [unsigned 1–19⁸ 20⁴].
p. [i], half-title; p. [ii], blank; p. [iii], title; p. [iv], Copyright, April, 1932, by | RAY LONG & RICHARD R. SMITH, INC. | [*rule*] | All rights reserved | PRINTED IN THE UNITED STATES OF AMERICA; pp. v–xiv, Introduction; p. [xv], Contents; p. [xvi], blank; p. [xvii], fly-title; p. [xviii], blank; pp. 1–604, text; pp. [605–606], blank.

Binding: Blue calico cloth, lettered in gold within a gold panel: 20 BEST | SHORT | STORIES | IN | RAY LONG'S | 20 YEARS | AS AN | EDITOR; on spine in gold: 20 BEST | SHORT | STORIES | IN | RAY LONG'S | 20 YEARS | AS AN | EDITOR | RAY LONG & | RICHARD R. | SMITH.
Plain end-papers; all edges cut; leaves measure 21.2 × 14 cm.

Price: $3. First published in April 1932.

Notes: From Ray Long's preface it is clear that Maugham submitted *The Book Bag* to *Cosmopolitan* when most of his stories were being serialised in this magazine, but it had been rejected because Ray Long feared the subject of the story might offend many of its readers. Then, when later on he was turning over in his mind which of the stories he had published in *Cosmopolitan* were the best 20, he recalled that two of them which he ranked very high, he had rejected, and one of these was *The Book Bag*. So he wrote to Maugham and asked his permission to include it in the anthology. Presumably, because Ray Long had been very generous to him over the years, Maugham agreed, no doubt persuaded that it would hardly affect the publication of the story by Orioli in Florence in a limited edition. So the story appeared in Ray Long's anthology approximately three months before its publication in a separate edition.

Oddly enough, Ray Long lost his life because of his association with Maugham. He was sent the typescript of *The Moon and Sixpence* and after reading it decided he, too, wanted to paint. He was over 50 but he threw up his job and went to live in one of the islands in the Pacific. He painted for a number of years, then decided he had no aptitude for it, and killed himself.

A43   THE BOOK-BAG   1932

b. First Separate edition:

THE BOOK-BAG | BY | W. SOMERSET MAUGHAM | [*author's symbol*] | G. Orioli | FLORENCE | 1932

> *Collation:* 112 pp. [unsigned 1-7⁸]. Front. port. inserted.
> pp. [1–2], blank; p. [3], series title THE | LUNGARNO SERIES | No. 9 | [etching]; p. [4], PRINTED BY THE | TIPOGRAFIA GIUNTINA | FLORENCE; p. [5], half-title; p. [6], blank; p. [7], This Edition is printed on hand-made | paper, and limited to 725 copies, signed by | the Author; 700 are for sale. | This is No. . . . ; p. [8], blank; p. [9], title; p. [10], blank; pp. 11–109, text; pp. [110–112], blank.
>
> *Binding:* Half string beige canvas, mandarin blue boards, blocked in red on front with author's symbol; lettered upward in gold on spine between double-rules: W. SOMERSET MAUGHAM [*short rule*] THE BOOK-BAG.
>
> *Advance Proof State:* pp. 112. Light grey wrappers, blank, all edges uncut. Lacks portrait. This proof copy is printed on a much cheaper paper than in the published version. There is a printing error on p. 76 in the word "how" which is misspelled

"hom" and was uncorrected when the book went to press. This proof copy was purchased by an American bookseller in Rome. Plain end-papers; top edges cut, fore and lower edges uncut; leaves measure 22.3 × 16 cm.

Price: 21s. 725 copies were published in July 1932.

Notes: There are two states of this edition, identical in all respects, save for the colour of the paper, and the wording of the certificate of limitation. The first state, which is printed on blue paper, has the following wording:

"This is copy No. [1, 2] of two copies only printed on blue paper."

Some copies lack the last blank leaf, the stub of which is usually visible under the back lining paper. A photograph by Killar of the Jo Davidson bust of Mr. Maugham is tipped in as a frontispiece.

Mr. Maugham had the front. portraits forwarded to him, across which he signed his name. In a letter (in the Grenville Cook collection) written from Ormond House, St James to Orioli 11 May [1932], Mr. Maugham writes: I shall be here till May 28 and can sign the portraits if you send them.

A44   THE NARROW CORNER   (1932)

a. First edition:
W. S. MAUGHAM | [rule] | THE | NARROW CORNER | [*star*] | [*publisher's windmill device*] | LONDON | WILLIAM HEINE-MANN LTD.

> *Collation:* [viii], 296 pp. [A]⁸ B–T⁸.
> pp. [i–ii], blank; p. [iii], half-title; p. [iv], By w. SOMERSET MAUGHAM [listing 15 non-dramatic and 22 dramatic works]; p. [v], title; p. [vi], FIRST PUBLISHED 1932 | PRINTED IN GREAT BRITAIN | AT THE WINDMILL PRESS; p. [vii], 3-line quotation; p. [viii], blank; pp. 1–293, text; pp. [294–296], blank.

> *Binding:* Smooth dark blue linen-grain cloth, blocked in black on front with author's symbol and on back with publisher's windmill device; gold-lettered on front: The Narrow Corner; and on spine: The | Narrow | Corner | W. S. | Maugham | [*in black*] Heinemann.
> Plain end-papers; all edges cut; leaves measure 18.4 × 12.4 cm.

> *Price:* 7s. 6d. 10,000 copies were published on 7 November 1932.

A44 THE NARROW CORNER 1932

b. First American edition:
THE | NARROW CORNER | By | W. SOMERSET MAUGHAM
| [*author's symbol in green*] | Garden City, New York | DOUBLEDAY,
DORAN & COMPANY, INC. | 1932

> *Collation:* [vi], 314 pp. [unsigned 1–20⁸].
> p. [i], half-title; p. [ii], BOOKS BY | W. SOMERSET MAUGHAM [listing
> 17 non-dramatic and 15 dramatic works]; title-page an insert
> *verso*: PRINTED AT THE *Country Life Press*, GARDEN CITY, N.Y.,
> U.S.A. | [*publisher's monogram device*] | [rule] | COPYRIGHT, 1932 |
> BY DOUBLEDAY, DORAN & COMPANY, INC. | ALL RIGHTS RESERVED |
> FIRST EDITION; p. [iii], 3-line quotation; p. [iv], blank; p. [v],
> fly-title; p. [vi], blank; p. [1] 2–314, text.

> *Binding:* Black matt cloth, blocked in gold on front with author's
> symbol; spine divided into compartments with ornamental
> bands and two identical scenes of an island in the Indies and
> lettered in gold: THE | NARROW | CORNER | [rule] | W. SOMERSET |
> MAUGHAM | DOUBLEDAY | DORAN.
> Cream end-papers; all edges cut; leaves measure 19.7 × 13.7 cm.

> *Price:* $2.50. 10,000 copies were published on 9 November 1932.

Notes: This novel was serialised in *Hearst's International Magazine*
commencing in the October 1932 issue and it ran until the following
January. It was also serialised in *Nash's Magazine*, commencing the
following February.

A45 FOR SERVICES RENDERED 1932

a. First edition:
W. SOMERSET MAUGHAM | [*french rule*] | FOR SERVICES |
RENDERED | A PLAY IN THREE ACTS | [*star*] | [*publisher's
windmill device*] | LONDON: WILLIAM HEINEMANN LTD. | 1932

> *Collation:* [viii], 88 pp. [A]⁸ B–F⁸.
> p. [i], half-title; p. [ii], blank; p. [iii], title; p. [iv], note on perform-
> ing rights and printer's imprint PRINTED IN GREAT BRITAIN |
> AT THE WINDMILL PRESS, SURREY; p. [v], list of cast; p. [vi], blank;
> p. [vii], characters; p. [viii], blank; pp. 1–87, text; pp. [88],
> blank.

> *Binding:* Smooth chesnut cloth, blocked in gold on front with
> author's symbol and on back with publisher's windmill device
> in blind; on spine with gold bands and with the following gold

lettering: W. SOMERSET | MAUGHAM | *For* | *Services* | *Rendered* | HEINEMANN.

Advance Proof state: pp. [x]+87+[2]. Blank leaf at front and back, not repeated in published version. Royal blue wrappers, printed in black. 18.2×12.2 cm.

Plain end-papers; top edges cut and stained brown, other edges cut; leaves measure 18.4×12.4 cm.

Price: 3s. 6d. 2,000 copies were published on the 14 December 1932.

Notes: For Services Rendered was written in 1932. It was produced at the Globe Theatre on November 1 1932 with Ralph Richardson, Flora Robson and Cedric Hardwicke in the cast. *See* D97a.

A45   FOR SERVICES RENDERED   1933

b. First American edition:
W. Somerset Maugham | FOR SERVICES RENDERED | A PLAY IN THREE ACTS | [author's symbol] | DOUBLEDAY, DORAN & COMPANY, INC. | *Garden City, New York* | MCMXXXIII

Collation: [viii], 88 pp. [unsigned 1–6⁸].
p. [i], half-title; p. [ii], BOOKS BY | W. SOMERSET MAUGHAM [listing 18 non-dramatic and 16 dramatic works]; p. [iii], title; p. [iv], PRINTED AT THE *Country Life Press*, GARDEN CITY, N.Y., U.S.A. | COPYRIGHT, 1932, 1933 | BY W. SOMERSET MAUGHAM | ALL RIGHTS RESERVED | FIRST EDITION: p. [v], Characters; p. [vi], Characters (cont.); p. [vii], fly-title; p. [viii], performing rights; p. [1] 2–87, text; p. [88], blank.

Binding: Black linen cloth, blocked in blind on front with author's symbol; blocked on spine in gold with series of thick and thin rules and lettered: FOR | SERVICES | RENDERED | W. | Somerset | Maugham | DOUBLEDAY | DORAN.
Cream end-papers, top and lower edges cut, fore-edges rough trimmed; leaves measure 19×13 cm.

Price: $1.50. Number of copies unknown. Published in April 1933. Copyright copy deposited with Library of Congress May 1 1933.

A46   AH KING   (1933)

a. First and Trade edition:
W. S. MAUGHAM | [rule] | AH KING | SIX STORIES | [star] | [*publisher's windmill device*] | LONDON | WILLIAM HEINEMANN LTD

Collation: [viii], 344 pp. [A]⁸ B–U⁸ W–X⁸.
pp. [i–ii], blank; p. [iii], half-title; p. [iv], By w. SOMERSET MAUGHAM [listing 16 non-dramatic and 22 dramatic works]; p. [v], title; p. [vi], FIRST PUBLISHED 1933 | *Printed in Great Britain | at the Windmill Press, Kingswood, Surrey*; p. [vii], contents; p. [viii], blank; pp. 1–339, text; pp. [340–344], blank.

Binding: Dark blue linen-grain cloth, blocked in black on front with author's symbol and on back with publisher's windmill device: gold-lettered on front: Ah King: and on spine: Ah | King | W. S. | Maugham | [in black] Heinemann.

Advance Proof state: pp. [iv]+339+[1]+2 blank leaves. Pink wrappers, printed in black. 18.4×12.3 cm.

Cream end-papers; all edges cut; leaves measure 18.4×12.2 cm.

Price: 7s. 6d. 10,000 copies of the first trade edition were published on the 19 September 1933.

A46   AH KING   1933

b. Limited Issue, on Large Paper: (separate impression from the same formes)
AH KING | [*rule*] | W. | SOMERSET | MAUGHAM | [*publisher's windmill device resting on base*] | LONDON | WILLIAM HEINEMANN LTD. | 1933

Collation: [viii], 344 pp. [A]⁸ B–U⁸ W–X⁸.
pp. [i–ii], blank; p. [iii], half-title; p. [iv], This Edition of "Ah King" | numbered and signed by the | Author, is limited to 175 | copies, for sale in Great | Britain and Ireland. | No. . . . ; p. v, title; p. [vi], *Printed in Great Britain | at The Windmill Press, Kingswood, Surrey*; p. [vii], contents; p. [viii], blank; pp. 1–339, text; pp. [340–344], blank.

Binding: Maize buckram, blocked in gold on front with author's symbol; on spine black cloth label blocked and lettered in gold: W. S. Maugham | AH | KING | [*author's symbol*] | [*the whole enclosed in a double frame*]; [*at tail*] Heinemann.

Binding Variant: Copies exist of the limited signed edition which are unnumbered but marked "Presentation Copy". The binding is in half calf with maize buckram sides, and measures 20.5× 13½ cm., so the sheets have been markedly cut down. There are some differences in the blocking on front cover and spine. The lettering reads AH KING | [*rule*] | W. SOMERSET | MAUGHAM. The author's symbol is appreciably larger, the main stem measuring

4 cm. against 2 cm. The label on the spine is also larger and measures 4.1×3.1 cm. against 3.4×2.6 cm., although the width of the spine itself is only 3.2 cm. against 4.5 cm. in the ordinary limited edition. All edges gilt.

Presumably, there were similar presentation copies prepared of the other two limited editions *Cosmopolitans* and *Don Fernando* but I have not come across them.

Plain end-papers; top edges cut and gilt, other edges unopened; leaves measure 22×14½ cm. Cream ribbon book mark. In slip case.

Price: 42s. Date of printing: Trade edition, September 1933 limited edition, September 1933 (after the trade edition).

Notes: Contrary to usual practice, I believe, the limited editions of four of W. S. Maugham's books were printed after the ordinary trade editions, but from the same formes. The two states were issued simultaneously. I have listed the two states in order of printing as the bibliographer might be placed in an awkward dilemma if, later, it transpired that corrections had been made in the formes after the trade edition had been run off. Of course, where priority of printing is not known, then priority of publication is the only guide.

In a case of this sort, where there is no priority of publication in any absolute sense, Professor Fredson Bowers is inclined to the view that there is no priority whatsoever between trade and limited edition. He agrees, however, that in listing limited and trade edition, printed from the same formes, the governing factor must be priority of printing.

A46   AH KING   1933

c. First American edition:
AH KING | By W. Somerset Maugham | [*author's symbol in red*] | MCMXXXIII | [*rule in red*] | DOUBLEDAY, DORAN & COM-PANY, INC. | GARDEN CITY, NEW YORK

Collation: [vi], 306 pp. [unsigned 1–18⁸ 19⁴ 20⁸]. Title page an insert.
p. [i], half-title; p. [ii], BOOKS BY | W. SOMERSET MAUGHAM [listing 18 non-dramatic and 16 dramatic works]; title page an insert; *verso* PRINTED AT THE *Country Life Press*, GARDEN CITY, N.Y., U.S.A. | COPYRIGHT, 1933 | BY DOUBLEDAY, DORAN & COMPANY, INC. | COPYRIGHT, 1926, 1931, 1932 | BY W. SOMERSET MAUGHAM | ALL RIGHTS RESERVED | FIRST EDITION; p. [iii], Contents; p. [iv], blank; p. [v], fly-title; p. [vi], blank; pp. [1] 2–306, text.

Inside King's School Maugham Library.

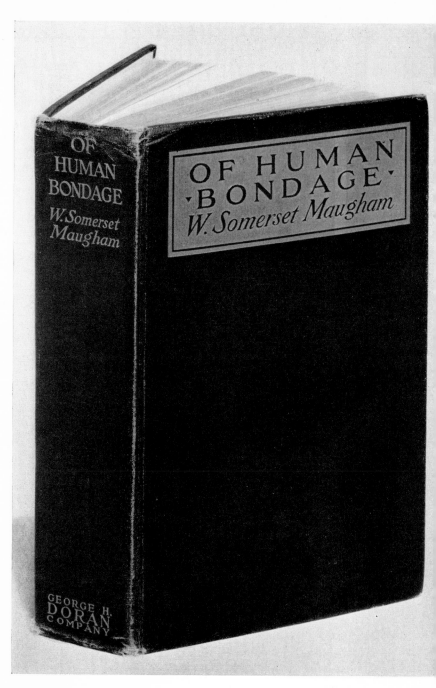

The front of the casing of the first (American) edition of *Of Human Bondage.*

Binding: Black matt cloth, blocked in blind on front with author's symbol; on spine blocked in gold with series of pagodas and flowers and leaves and single and double bands and gold-lettered: AH KING | W. SOMERSET | MAUGHAM | DOUBLEDAY DORAN. Cream end-papers; top edges cut and stained blue; fore-edges uncut, lower edges cut; leaves measure 19.9 × 15 cm.

Price: $2.50. 10,000 copies were published on November 9 1933. Copyright copy deposited with Library of Congress November 9 1933.

Contents: Footprints in the Jungle—The Door of Opportunity—The Vessel of Wrath—The Book Bag—The Back of Beyond—Neil MacAdam.

A47   SHEPPEY   1933

First edition:
W. SOMERSET MAUGHAM | [*rule*] | SHEPPEY | A PLAY IN THREE ACTS | [*star*] | [*publisher's windmill device*] | LONDON: WILLIAM HEINEMANN LTD. | 1933

Collation: [x], 118 pp. [A]⁸ B–H⁸.
p. [i], half-title; p. [ii], By w. somerset maugham [listing 17 non-dramatic and 22 dramatic works]; p. [iii], title; p. [iv], note on performing rights and printer's imprint; PRINTED IN GREAT BRITAIN | AT THE WINDMILL PRESS, KINGSWOOD, SURREY; p. [v], dedication: To | JOHN GIELGUD; p. [vi], blank; p. [vii], cast; p. [viii], blank; p. [ix], characters; p. [x], blank; pp. 1–118, text.

Binding: Smooth chestnut cloth, blocked in gold on front with author's symbol and on back with publisher's windmill device in blind; on spine with gold bands and with the following gold lettering: w. somerset | maugham | *Sheppey* | HEINEMANN.

Advance Proof state: 1 blank leaf+pp. [viii]+118. Brown wrappers, blank. Leaves measure 18.3 × 12½ cm.
In Earl Bernheimer's copy (now in the Leonard Meldman collection) Mr. Maugham has written "This is a proof copy and has several differences from the first edition."

Plain end-papers; all edges cut; leaves measure 18.2 × 12.3 cm.

Price: 3s. 6d. 2,000 copies were published on 13 November 1933.

First American edition: (1949). Boston (W. H. Baker).

Notes: Sheppey was written in 1932. It was produced at Wyndham's

H

Theatre on 14 September 1933 with Ralph Richardson and Laura Cowie in the cast.

After the production of *Sheppey*, Mr. Maugham announced that he would write no more plays.

A48   THE JUDGEMENT SEAT   1934

First edition:
[*Title-page divided into two compartments by a vertical black rule: left compartment*] THE | JUDGEMENT | SEAT | by | FRONTISPIECE | by | LONDON 1934 [*right compartment*] W. SOMERSET MAUGHAM | ULRICA HYDE | THE | CENTAUR PRESS

> *Collation:* [18] pp. [unsigned 1–2⁴]. Front., signed by the artist, tipped in.
> p. [1], half-title; p. [2], *This edition of the Judgement Seat, hand-set and | printed in 18pt. Centaur type at the Centaur Press | by Peri Cotgrave & Antony Doncaster, is limited | to one hundred and fifty copies, numbered and | signed by the Author and the Artist.* | This is Number. . . . ; p. [5], title; p. [6], blank; pp. [7] 8–17, text; p. [18], printer's imprint; *The Centaur Press, 33a, Campden Street, London W.8.*

> *Binding:* Smooth black cloth, blocked on front with gold rule dividing cover into two compartments and gold-lettered: [*left compartment*] THE | JUDGEMENT | SEAT | by | [*right compartment*] W. SOMERSET MAUGHAM.
> Plain end-papers; top edges cut and gilt, other edges uncut; leaves measure 22½ × 14¾ cm.

> *Price:* £1 1s. 150 copies were published in December 1934.

Notes: According to the certificate of limitation only 150 copies of this work were printed, but 4 of the copies I have examined (7 in number) have been out of series.

A49   DON FERNANDO   (1935)
                    or Variations on Some Spanish Themes

a. First and Trade edition:
DON FERNANDO | Or | VARIATION | ON SOME SPANISH THEMES | By | W. SOMERSET MAUGHAM | [*publisher's windmill device resting on base*] | WILLIAM HEINEMANN LTD | LONDON [*square of 4 dots*] TORONTO

> *Collation:* [iv], 272 pp. [A]⁶ B–R⁸ S⁴.
> p. [i], half title; p. [ii], By W. SOMERSET MAUGHAM [listing 16 non-

dramatic and 22 dramatic works]; p. [iii], title; p. [iv], FIRST
PUBLISHED 1935 | PRINTED IN GREAT BRITAIN | AT THE WINDMILL
PRESS, KINGSWOOD, SURREY; pp. 1–268 [269], text; pp. [270–272],
blank.

Binding: Smooth black cloth, blocked on front with author's
symbol and decorative frame in gold enclosing the lettering
DON FERNANDO | By W. SOMERSET MAUGHAM; on spine with design
incorporating a floral frame supported by two pillars resting
on standing lions with decorative bands and gold-lettered:
DON | FERNANDO | By | W. SOMERSET | MAUGHAM | HEINEMANN; on
back publisher's windmill device in blind.

Advance Proof state: pp. [iv]+269+[1]+1 blank leaf. Yellowish
brown wrappers, printed in black. 20.2×14.7 cm. Some proof
copies have an extra blank leaf and fly-title in prelims, which do
not appear in the published trade version, and the half-title is
re-set with author's name.

Plain end-papers; all edges cut; leaves measure 20.3×15 cm.

Price: 8s. 6d. 5,000 copies were published on 17 June 1935.

A49   DON FERNANDO: 1935
                or Variations on Some Spanish Themes

b. Limited Issue, on Large Paper: (separate impression from the same formes).
DON FERNANDO | [*rule*] | W. | SOMERSET | MAUGHAM |
[*publisher's windmill device resting on base*] | LONDON | WILLIAM
HEINEMANN LTD. | 1935

Collation: [viii], 272 pp. [ ]⁴ A–R⁸.
pp. [i–ii], blank; p. [iii], half-title; p. [iv], This Edition of "Don
Fernando," | numbered and signed by the Author, | is limited to
175 copies for sale in | Great Britain and Ireland. | No. ... ;
p. [v], title; p. [vi], *Printed in Great Britain* | *at The Windmill Press,
Tadworth, Surrey*; p. [vii], fly-title; p. [viii], blank; pp. 1–268
[269], text; pp. [270–272], blank.

Binding: Peridot green buckram, blocked in gold on front with
author's symbol; on spine black cloth label blocked and lettered
in gold; W. S. Maugham | DON | FERNANDO | [*author's symbol*] |
[*the whole enclosed in a double frame*]; [*at tail*] Heinemann.
Plain end-papers; top edges cut and gilt, other edges uncut and
unopened; leaves measure 22×14½ cm. Green ribbon book
mark. In slip case.

Price: 42s. Date of printing: Trade edition, May 1935, limited edition May 1935 (after the trade edition). *See* 46b.

A49　　　　　　　　　DON FERNANDO:　　　　　　　　1935
　　　　　　　　or Variation on Some Spanish Themes

c. First American edition:
W. SOMERSET MAUGHAM | [*in red*] DON FERNANDO | Or Variations on Some | Spanish Themes | [*author's symbol in red*] | *Garden City, New York* | DOUBLEDAY, DORAN & COMPANY, INC. | 1935

> *Collation:* 312 pp. [unsigned 1–17^8 18^{12} 19^8].
> p. [i], half-title; p. [ii], BOOKS BY | W. SOMERSET MAUGHAM [listing 36 titles]; title page, an insert (verso) PRINTED AT THE *Country Life Press*, GARDEN CITY, N.Y., U.S.A. | COPYRIGHT, 1935 | BY W. SOMER-SET MAUGHAM | ALL RIGHTS RESERVED | FIRST EDITION; p. [iii], fly-title; p. [iv], blank; pp. [1] 2–307, text; p. [308], blank.
> *Binding:* Black matt cloth, blocked in blind on front with author's symbol and on spine with bands and ornaments and decorative shield and gold-lettered: DON | FERNANDO | W. SOMERSET | MAUGHAM | DOUBLEDAY DORAN.
> Maize end-papers, top edges cut and stained yellow, fore-edges uncut, lower edges rough trimmed; leaves measure 19.8 × 14.1 cm.
> *Price:* $2.50. 5,000 copies were published on 19 July 1935.

A49　　　　　　　　　DON FERNANDO:　　　　　　　(1950)
　　　　　　　　or Variation on Some Spanish Themes

d. New and Revised edition:
W. SOMERSET MAUGHAM | [*rule*] | DON FERNANDO | [*star*] | [*publisher's windmill device resting on base*] | WILLIAM HEINE-MANN LTD | MELBOURNE [*square of 4 dots*] LONDON [*square of 4 dots*] TORONTO

> *Pagination:* [viii], 252 pp. Cherry red cloth, gold blocked. 18.2 × 12$\frac{1}{2}$ cm. 10s. 6d.

Notes: New and completely revised edition (in the *Collected Edition*). The Author has omitted certain details concerning ideas which he says he expressed better after further reflection, in *The Summing Up*. Chapter VII has also been omitted and Chapter IX (which becomes Chapter XIII in the revised edition) has been entirely re-written and considerably augmented. There is also an Author's note (3 pp.) on the changes.

A50   COSMOPOLITANS: 1936
                        Very Short Stories

a. First edition:
W. Somerset Maugham | COSMOPOLITANS | [*author's symbol in red*] | DOUBLEDAY, DORAN AND COMPANY, INC. | Garden City, New York | 1936

> *Collation:* [xiv], 274 pp. [unsigned 1–18⁸]. Title a single inset.
> pp. [i–ii], blank; p. [iii], half-title; p. [iv], NOVELS BY | W. SOMER-
> SET MAUGHAM [etc.] [listing 18 non-dramatic and 18 dramatic
> works]; title, an inset, with verso: PRINTED AT THE *Country Life
> Press* GARDEN CITY, N.Y., U.S.A. | COPYRIGHT 1923, 1924, 1925,
> 1926, 1927, 1928, 1929, 1936 | BY W. SOMERSET MAUGHAM | ALL
> RIGHTS RESERVED | FIRST EDITION; pp. v–x, preface; pp. xi–xii,
> contents; p. [xiii], fly-title; p. [xiv], blank; pp. [1] 2–272, text;
> pp. [273–4], blank.

> *Binding:* Black matt cloth, blocked in blind on front with author's
> symbol and on spine with willow pattern design and gold-
> lettered between ornamental bands: COSMOPOLITANS | W. SOMER-
> SET | MAUGHAM | [*at tail*] | DOUBLEDAY DORAN.
> Biscuit end-papers; top edges cut and stained yellow, fore-edges
> uncut, lower edges rough trimmed; leaves measure 20×14 cm.

> *Price:* $1. Number of copies unknown. The first edition was
> published on 21 February 1936.

A50   COSMOPOLITANS: 1936
                        Very Short Stories

b. First English and Trade edition:
COSMOPOLITANS | VERY SHORT STORIES | BY | W.
SOMERSET MAUGHAM | [*ornament*] | [*publisher's windmill device
resting on base*] | WILLIAM HEINEMANN LTD | LONDON
[square of 4 dots] TORONTO

> *Collation:* [xvi], 304 pp. [A]⁸ B–U⁸.
> p. [i], half-title; p. [ii], By W. SOMERSET MAUGHAM [listing 17
> non-dramatic and 24 dramatic works]; p. [iii], title; p. [iv],
> FIRST PUBLISHED 1936 | PRINTED IN GREAT BRITAIN | AT THE WINDMILL
> PRESS, KINGSWOOD, SURREY; pp. v–vi, contents; pp. vii–xiii,
> preface; p. [xiv], blank; p. [xv], fly-title; p. [xvi], blank; pp. 1–
> 302, text; pp. [303–304], blank.

> *Binding:* Greenish blue linen grain cloth, blocked in black on
> front with author's symbol and on back with publisher's wind-

mill device; gold-lettered on front: Cosmopolitans; and on spine: Cosmopolitans | W. S. | Maugham | [in black] Heinemann.

Advance Proof state: pp. xiii+[1]+[2]+302+blank leaf. Buff wrappers, printed in black. Leaves measure 19½ × 12½ cm.

Chalk-blue end-papers; top edges cut and stained blue, other edges cut; leaves measure 19 × 20½ cm.

Price: 7s.6d. 10,000 copies were printed on 30 March 1936.

A50   COSMOPOLITANS: 1936
                         Very Short Stories

c. Limited Issue, on Large Paper: (*separate impression from the same formes*).
COSMOPOLITANS | [*rule*] | W. | SOMERSET | MAUGHAM | [*publisher's windmill device resting on base*] | LONDON | WILLIAM HEINEMANN LTD. | 1936

Collation: [xvi], 304 pp. [A]⁸ B–U⁸.
p. [i], half-title; p. [ii], This Edition of "Cosmopolitans" | numbered and signed by the Author | is limited to 175 copies for sale in | Great Britain and Ireland | No. . . . ; p. [iii], title; p. [iv], PRINTED IN GREAT BRITAIN | AT THE WINDMILL PRESS, KINGSWOOD, SURREY; pp. v–vi, contents; pp. vii–xiii, preface; p. [xiv], blank; p. [xv], fly-title; p. [xvi], blank; pp. 1–302, text; pp. [303–304], blank.

Binding: Cardinal red buckram, blocked in gold on front with author's symbol; on spine black cloth label blocked and lettered in gold: W. S. Maugham | COSMO- | POLITANS | [*author's symbol*] | [*the whole enclosed in a double frame*]; [at tail] Heinemann.
Plain end-papers; top edges cut and gilt, other edges uncut and unopened; leaves measure 22 × 14½ cm. Red ribbon book mark. In slip case.

Price: 42s. Date of printing: Trade edition, February 1936, limited edition March 1936 (after the trade edition).

Notes: There are four issues of the first English trade edition. In the first issue pp. 5–6 are uncancelled and the half-title has 17 non-dramatic works listed on the reverse, *Ah King* being the last, followed by the Plays.

In the second issue pp. 5–6 are a cancel leaf. The pages were cancelled on account of lines 8 and 9 on p. 5 being printed in reverse order. The half-title has 17 non-dramatic works listed on the reverse, *Ah King* being the last, followed by the Plays.

In the third issue, pp. 5–6 are a cancel leaf, as is also the half-title, which has 19 non-dramatic works listed on the reverse, Don Fernando being the last, followed by the Plays.

In the fourth issue, pp. 5–6 are a cancel leaf, but the half-title in the second state is now an integral part of the first signature.

I have not seen a copy of the first issue with the second state of the half-title, but it may well exist.

The first issue is exceedingly scarce. I have only met with one copy, on the title page of which the author had written 'They tell me the second sentence of the Preface is inaccurate.' The third issue is the most common. According to Percy H. Muir, there is a small number of advance proof copies in printed wrappers in existence with pp. 5–6 uncancelled, also having 17 non-dramatic works listed on the reverse of the half-title. He also says there is another state of the proof issue with these pages uncancelled, and with a cancel half-title. It is believed there are about five copies of the first proof state and twenty of the second.

Contents: Raw Material—Mayhew—German Harry—The Happy Man— The Dream—In a Strange Land—The Luncheon—Salvatore—Home— Mr. Know-All—The Escape—A Friend in Need—The Portrait of a Gentleman—The End of the Flight—The Judgement Seat—The Ant and the Grasshopper—French Joe—The Man with a Scar—The Poet—Louise— The Closed Shop—The Promise—A String of Beads—The Bum— Straight Flush—The Verger—The Wash-Tub—The Social Sense—The Four Dutchmen.

A51   MY SOUTH SEA ISLAND   1936

a. First edition:
My South | Sea Island | By W. Somerset Maugham | Chicago, Illinois, 1936 [*sketch of a palm tree in green running up left hand of title*]. Green initial letter to opening text. Printed on one side of the leaf only.

> *Collation:* [16] ff. 16 leaves in one gathering, unsigned. Sewed. The text is foliated.
> 2 blank leaves; f. [3], title; f. [4] (verso) Copyright, 1936, by Ben Abramson; ff. 5–12, text; f. 13, blank; f. [14] (verso) BY WAY OF COLOPHON | *Printed by order of Ben Abramson without the author's* | *permission, but with a firm held hope that being done, it* | *will not be spurned nor the act censured* | [*3 dots in green*] | This brochure was designed, the type set by hand in Ludlow | Eden Light and 50 copies printed on Worthy Hand & Arrows | by Norman W.

Forgue at his Black Cat Press, Chicago, Illinois. | Cover and title-page decoration by Rex Cleveland. | Completed during the month of | August, mcmxxxvi | [green ornament] |; ff. [15–16], blank.

Binding: Stiff quartz green wrappers, printed in black on front: MY SOUTH | SEA ISLAND | BY W. SOMERSET MAUGHAM; with outsize author's symbol in limped green enclosed within a single frame. Inside and back wrappers blank.
Price $7.50. 20.6 × 13.4 cm. All edges cut.

Notes: This insignificant article about a few days spent on an island in the South Seas appeared in the *Daily Mail*, London, 31 January, 1922. According to Ben Abramson, there was a misprint in the spelling of 'Somerset' on the title page of the first printing, and all but two copies were destroyed. The pamphlet was then reprinted. *My South Sea Island* has every mark of the bibliographical fraud without finally being altogether one. If it had been an article found in manuscript among the author's papers, then there might have been some real interest in publishing it, but to pay £200 (as has been done twice recently in a London auction room) for a reprinted newspaper article seems to be bibliomania carried to extremes. For such a sum a collector could acquire a first edition of *A Man of Honour* or a first issue of *The Painted Veil*—genuine rarities which would greatly add to the value of one's collection.

As a winding up comment it might perhaps be of interest to quote from the foreword to the reprinting of this pamphlet in miniature form by the original printer, Norman W. Forgue. He writes: 'The text for this miniature, in one sense, is not original, having already been printed. However, as far as I know, this is the first printing in book form.

The original printer's dummy, badly stained with rubber cement, otherwise as it was almost thirty years ago, was found in the archives of the press—and for the record I give you a brief account of the original printing. . . . At the time I was folding and sewing the pamphlets by hand. I had the feeling something was wrong. I looked the printed sheets over several times—then I discovered a typographical error and of all places on the title page. . . . The title page was corrected and reprinted. Final count, seven copies with error on title page or first issue; forty three copies with corrected title-page or second issue of this first printing.'

The germ for *My South Sea Island* is to be found in *A Writer's Notebook* (A70) from which the author undoubtedly wrote up his article.

A51   MY SOUTH SEA ISLAND   (1965)

b. First Miniature edition:
MY SOUTH | SEA ISLAND | W. Somerset Maugham | [*ornament in brown*] | BLACK CAT PRESS | Chicago, Illinois

> *Collation:* 40 leaves. 50×39 mm. Printed on one side of the sheet only, so that when folded in 16's and uncut the inside pages are blank. The foliation ignores the blank pages.
> ff. [i–ii], blank, not included in foliation; ff. [1], half-title; ff. [2], blank; ff. [3], title; ff. [4], Copyright 1936 | by Ben Abramson; ff. 5–12, Foreword (by Norman W. Forgue); ff. 13–32, text; ff. [33–34], blank; [35–36], COLOPHON: This first printing in book form is limited to 199 copies. Printed direct from Linotype Modern on Stratmore Pastelle paper, Typography by N.W.F.; ff. [37–38], blank.

> *Binding:* Green roan with Maugham symbol on front; lettered in gold on spine MY SOUTH SEA ISLAND; back plain.
> Marbled end-papers; all edges cut; leaves measure 5.1×4 cm.

> *Price:* Unknown. 199 copies were published in February 1965. A copy at Sotheby's in December 1972 fetched £16.

A52   THEATRE. A Novel   (1937)

a. First edition:
W. SOMERSET MAUGHAM | THEATRE | A NOVEL | [author's symbol] | MCMXXXVII | [rule] | DOUBLEDAY, DORAN AND COMPANY, INC. | *Garden City New York*
Title in red and black.

> *Collation:* [viii], 296 pp. [unsigned 1–19⁸]. Title page, a single inset.
> pp. [i–ii], blank; p. [iii], half-title; p. [iv], BOOKS BY | W. SOMERSET MAUGHAM [listing 38 titles]; title, an inset, with verso: PRINTED AT THE *Country Life Press*, GARDEN CITY, N.Y., U.S.A. | COPYRIGHT, 1937 | BY W. SOMERSET MAUGHAM | ALL RIGHTS RESERVED | FIRST EDITION; p. [v], author's note; p. [vi], blank; p. [vii], fly-title; p. [viii], blank; pp. [1] 2–292, text; pp. [293–296], blank.

> *Binding:* Black matt cloth, blocked in blind on front with author's symbol and on spine in gold with an elaborate design having a foliated background, interspersed with theatrical and musical symbols, including a lyre, drums and masks, with the wording THEATRE | W. SOMERSET | MAUGHAM | DOUBLEDAY DORAN standing

up in relief from a crushed gold panel, the letters being actually of the texture of the cloth itself.

Biscuit end-papers; top edges cut and stained red, fore-edges uncut, lower edges rough trimmed; leaves measure 20 × 14 cm.

Price: $2.50. Number of copies unknown. Published 3 March 1937.

A52   THEATRE. A Novel   (1937)

b. First English edition:

THEATRE | A NOVEL | BY | W. SOMERSET MAUGHAM | [*ornament*] | [*publisher's windmill device resting on base*] | WILLIAM HEINEMANN LTD | LONDON [*square of 4 dots*] | TORONTO

Collation: [viii], 296 pp. [A]⁸ B–T⁸.

pp. [i–ii], blank; p. [iii], half-title; p. [iv], By w. SOMERSET MAUGHAM [listing 21 non-dramatic and 24 dramatic works]; p. [v], title; p. [vi], FIRST PUBLISHED 1937 | PRINTED IN GREAT BRITAIN | AT THE WINDMILL PRESS, KINGSWOOD, SURREY; p. [vii], author's note; p. [viii], blank; pp. 1–293, text; pp. [294–296], blank.

Binding: Persian blue linen-grain cloth, blocked in black on front with author's symbol and on back with publisher's windmill device; gold-lettered on front: Theatre; and on spine: Theatre | W.S. | Maugham | [*in black*] Heinemann.

Chalk blue end-papers; top edges cut and stained blue, other edges cut; leaves measure 19 × 12.8 cm.

Price: 7s. 6d. 20,000 copies were published on 22 March 1937.

Advance Proof state: pp. [viii]+293 pp.+[1]. Red wrappers, printed in black. 19 × 12.6 cm.

Notes: The first issue of the first English edition has pp. 7–8 in uncancelled state. Line 12, p. 7 reads: 'I do not eat bread. . . .' The second issue has a cancel leaf with the wording revised to 'I don't not eat bread . . .' which is the same reading as in the first (American) edition.

It is claimed that pp. 101–102 are sometimes a cancel leaf, the impression being that the last line on p. 102 which reads 'at a travel agency' read in the uncancelled state 'at Cook's', as in the American version. It is true the words 'At Cook's' are present in proof copies, but the wording was revised to 'at a travel agency' before the final run-off.

A53   THE SUMMING UP   (1938)

a. First edition:

THE SUMMING UP | BY | W. SOMERSET MAUGHAM | [*ornament*] | [*publisher's device resting on base*] | WILLIAM HEINEMANN LTD | LONDON [*square of 4 dots*] TORONTO

> *Collation:* [viii], 320 pp. [A]⁸ B–U⁸ W⁴.
> pp. [i–ii], blank; p. [iii], half-title; p. [iv], By w. somerset maugham [listing 22 non-dramatic and 24 dramatic works]; p. [v], title; p. [vi], first published 1938 | printed in great britain at the windmill press | kingswood, surrey; p. [vii], fly-title; p. [viii], blank; pp. 1–317, text; pp. [318–320], blank.

> *Binding:* Smooth black cloth, blocked in gold on front with author's symbol and on back in blind with publisher's windmill device; gold lettered on spine: The | Summing Up | W. Somerset | Maugham | [author's symbol] | Heinemann.
> Hay end-papers; all edges trimmed; leaves measure 21.6 × 14 cm.

> *Price:* 10s. 6d. 10,000 copies were published on 6 January 1938.

> *Advance Proof state:* [viii]+317+[1]+blank leaf. Pale green wrappers, printed in black. 21.5 × 14 cm.

A53   THE SUMMING UP   1938

b. First American edition:

[*in red*] The Summing Up | W. SOMERSET MAUGHAM | [*author's symbol in red*] | 1938 | Doubleday, Doran & Company, Inc. | GARDEN CITY NEW YORK

> *Collation:* [vi], 310 pp. [unsigned 1–20⁸].
> p. [i–ii], blank; p. [iii], half-title; p. [iv], books by | w. somerset maugham [listing 38 titles]; title page, an insert (verso), printed at the *Country Life Press*, garden city, n.y., u.s.a. | copyright, 1938 | by w. somerset maugham | all rights reserved | first edition; p. [v], fly-title; p. [vi], blank; pp. 1–310, text; pp. [311–314], blank.

> *Binding:* Black matt cloth, blocked in gold on front with author's symbol and on spine with rules and ornamental bands and gold-lettered: the | summing | up | w. somerset | maugham | double-day doran.
> Plain end-papers; top edges cut and stained brown; fore-edges uncut, lower edges rough trimmed; leaves measure 20 × 14 cm.

> *Price:* $2.50. 10,000 copies were published on 25 March 1938.

A53   THE SUMMING UP   1954

c. Eightieth Birthday edition:
The | Summing Up | W. SOMERSET MAUGHAM | [*author's symbol in terra cotta*] | Garden City, N.Y. | DOUBLEDAY & COMPANY, INC. | 1954

> *Collation:* [iv], 284 pp. [unsigned 1–18⁸].
> p. [iv], blank; cert. of limitation: THIS EDITION IS LIMITED TO | THREE HUNDRED AND NINETY-ONE | NUMBERED AND SIGNED COPIES PRINTED FROM TYPE WHICH HAS BEEN DESTROYED. | THREE HUNDRED AND SEVENTY-FIVE COPIES ARE FOR SALE | OF WHICH THIS IS NUMBER | . . . ; verso blank, an inset; p. [1], half-title; p. [2], blank; front. port. an inset; p. [3], title; p. [4], Library of Congress Catalog Card Number 54–5355 | COPYRIGHT, 1938, 1954, BY W. SOMERSET MAUGHAM | ALL RIGHTS RESERVED | PRINTED IN THE UNITED STATES | AT | THE COUNTRY LIFE PRESS, GARDEN CITY, N.Y. | LIMITED EDITION; p. [5], fly-title; p. [6], blank; pp. 7–279, text; p. [280], blank; p. [281], colophon; pp. [282–284], blank.

> *Binding:* Ash-grey buckram, flecked with white, bevelled edges. On front blocked in blind with author's symbol; on spine in red and gold with plain and ornamental rules and gold-lettered : The | Summing | Up | W. SOMERSET | MAUGHAM [*these words in red panel*] | DOUBLEDAY [*in a lozenge-shaped red panel at tail*] with author's symbol in gold.
> Steel blue end-papers; top edges cut and gilt, fore-edges uncut, lower edges cut; leaves measure 23.6 × 16.7 cm. In slip case.

> *Price:* $15. The limited edition was published in May 1954 to celebrate the author's 80th birthday. The partners in the firm of A. P. Watt, his literary agents, presented him with some brandy 'a little younger than yourself.'

A54   CHRISTMAS HOLIDAY   (1939)
a. First edition:

CHRISTMAS HOLIDAY | BY | W. SOMERSET MAUGHAM | [*ornament*] | [*publisher's windmill device resting on base*] | WILLIAM HEINEMANN LTD | LONDON [square of 4 dots] | TORONTO

> *Collation:* [vi], 290 pp. [A]⁸ B–S⁸ T⁴.
> pp. [i–ii], blank; p. [iii], half-title; p. [iv], By W. SOMERSET MAUGHAM [listing 23 non-dramatic and 24 dramatic works]; p. [v], title; p. [vi], PRINTED IN GREAT BRITAIN AT THE WINDMILL PRESS | KINGSWOOD, SURREY; pp. 1–289, text; p. [290], blank.

Binding: Persian blue linen-grain cloth, blocked in black on front with author's symbol and on back with publisher's windmill device; gold-lettered on front: Christmas Holidays; and on spine: Christmas | Holiday | W. S. | Maugham [*in black*] Heinemann. Chalk-blue end-papers; top edges cut and stained blue, other edges cut; leaves measure 19 × 12.4 cm.

Price: 7s. 6d. 20,000 copies were published on 6 February 1939.

Advance Proof state: pp. [vi]+289+[1]. Blue wrappers, printed in black. 19.2 × 12.6 cm.

Notes: Christmas Holiday was serialised in *Redbook Magazine* commencing August 1939, concluding in November 1939.

A54   CHRISTMAS HOLIDAY   1939

b. First American edition:
W. SOMERSET MAUGHAM | Christmas Holiday | [*author's symbol in red*] | NEW YORK | Doubleday, Doran & Company, Inc. | 1939

Collation: [iv], 316 pp. [unsigned 1–20⁸]. Title page an insert.
p. [i], half-title; p. [ii], BOOKS BY | W. SOMERSET MAUGHAM [listing 40 titles]; title page, an insert: [*verso*] PRINTED AT THE *Country Life Press*, GARDEN CITY, N.Y., U.S.A. | CL | COPYRIGHT, 1939 | BY W. SOMERSET MAUGHAM | ALL RIGHTS RESERVED | FIRST EDITION; p. [iii], fly-title; p. [iv], blank; pp. [1] 2–314, text; pp. [315–316], blank.

Binding: Black smooth cloth, blocked in blind on front with author's symbol; on spine blocked in red and gold with series of red and gold rules and gold-lettered: W. SOMERSET | MAUGHAM | Christmas | Holiday | DOUBLEDAY DORAN.
Cream end-papers; top edges cut and stained red, fore-edges rough trimmed, lower edges cut; leaves measure 20 × 14 cm.

Price: $2.75. First published 20 October 1939.

A55   PRINCESS SEPTEMBER AND THE   (1939)
                         NIGHTINGALE

a. First edition:
PRINCESS SEPTEMBER | AND THE | NIGHTINGALE | BY W. SOMERSET MAUGHAM | [*sketch in 2 colours*] | ILLUSTRATED BY RICHARD C. JONES | OXFORD UNIVERSITY PRESS | LONDON NEW YORK TORONTO

Collation: [32] pp. unpaged. [unsigned 1⁸ 2⁴ 3⁴].
p. [1], half-title; p. [2], blank; p. [3], title; p. [4], Copyright
1939 | OXFORD UNIVERSITY PRESS | New York, Inc. | *Princess
September and the Nightingale* is reprinted from *The Gentleman
in the Parlour* by W. Somerset Maugham, copyright, 1930, by
Doubleday Doran & Company, Inc., by special permission of the
author | and publisher. | PRINTED IN THE UNITED STATES OF AMERICA;
pp. [5–32], text and coloured illustrations.

Binding: Green cloth, lettered in gold running down spine:
Maugham Princess September and the Nightingale Oxford.
Decorative end-papers; all edges cut; leaves measure 24 × 18 cm.
Copyright copy deposited Library of Congress 14 October 1939.
$2.50.

Notes: A reprint in juvenile form of the fairy story which first appeared
in *Pearson's Magazine* and was later embodied in *The Gentleman in the
Parlour*. Not published in England. *See also* C6.

A55   PRINCESS SEPTEMBER   (1969)

b. First edition:
W. Somerset Maugham | Princess | September | pictures by Jac-
queline Ayer | Harcourt, Brace & World, Inc., New York

Collation: [40] pp. Unpag. Unsigned.
p. [1], half-title [with 6 black and white sketches]; pp. [2–3],
title, double-page, illustrated with coloured drawings; p. [4],
publication and copyright details; p. [5], listing other titles written
and illustrated by Jacqueline Ayer; pp. [6–38], text and illustrations; pp. [39–40], blank.

Binding: Parchment cross-grained linen cloth, blocked in black
on front with flower ornament and in right upper corner:
HB & W [*ornament*] LIBRARY EDITION; on spine lettered in black:
Maugham [dot] Ayer Princess September [publisher's monogram
device].
Decorative end-papers; all edges cut; leaves measure 21.2 ×
17.7 cm.

Price: $3.50. Number of copies unknown. Published in 1969.

Notes: Copies are known bound in red cloth, confirming in all other
respects to the binding described above, probably a secondary
binding.

A55 PRINCESS SEPTEMBER (1970)

c. First English edition:
W. Somerset Maugham | Princess | September | pictures by Jacqueline Ayer | Collins St James's Place London [*with a coloured illustration*]

Collation: [40] pp. Unpag. Unsigned.
p. [1], half-title [*with 6 black and white sketches*]; pp. [2–3], title, double-page, illus. with col. drawings; p. [4], Illustrations copyright © 1969 by Jacqueline Ayer | First published in the U.S.A. 1969 | First published in Great Britain 1970 by | William Collins, Sons & Co. Ltd. | [publication details]; p. [5], listing other titles written and illustrated by Jacqueline Ayer; pp. [6–38], text and col. illus.; pp. [39–40], blank.

Binding: Parchment cross-grained linen cloth, blocked in black on front with flower ornament; on spine lettered in black: Maugham [dot] Ayer Princess September Collins.
Decorative end-papers in green with black stalks and red and white flowers; all edges cut; leaves measure 21.2 × 16.9 cm.

Price: 80p. Number of copies unknown. Published 16 March 1970.

Notes: The English edition was bound from the American sheets.

A56 FRANCE AT WAR (1940)

a. First edition:
FRANCE AT WAR | By | W. SOMERSET MAUGHAM | [*publisher's windmill device in box*] | LONDON | WILLIAM HEINE-MANN LTD

Collation: [iv], 92 pp. [A]⁸ B–F⁸.
p. [i], half-title; p. [ii], By w. somerset maugham [listing 24 non-dramatic and 24 dramatic works]; p. [iii], title; p. [iv], first published 1940; pp. 1–89, text; p. [90], printer's imprint; pp. [91–92], blank.

Binding: Stiff pictorial wrappers, divided on front into three compartments coloured blue, white and red with royal arms of France in centre compartment; lettered [in white on blue] france | at war | [in white on red] w. somerset | maugham; lettered upward on spine [in white on red] heinemann [in blue on white] w. somerset maugham [in white on blue] france at war; on back publisher's blurb within a red, white and blue border.

All edges cut. Leaves measure 18.1 × 11 cm.

Price: 6d. 20,000 copies were published on 18 March 1940.

A56   FRANCE AT WAR   1940

b. First American edition:
W. SOMERSET MAUGHAM | FRANCE AT WAR | [*author's symbol*] | New York | DOUBLEDAY, DORAN AND CO., INC. | 1940

> *Collation:* [vi], 114 pp. [unsigned 1–5⁸ 6¹² 7⁸].
> p. [i], half-title; p. [ii], BOOKS BY | W. SOMERSET MAUGHAM [listing 43 titles]; p. [iii], title; p. [iv], PRINTED AT THE *Country Life Press,* GARDEN CITY, N.Y., U.S.A. | CL | COPYRIGHT, 1940 | BY W. SOMERSET MAUGHAM | ALL RIGHTS RESERVED | FIRST EDITION; p. [v], fly-title; p. [vi], blank; pp. 1–111, text; pp. [112–114], blank.
>
> *Binding:* Red linen cloth, blocked in black on front cover with author's symbol; on spine running down W. SOMERSET MAUGHAM FRANCE AT WAR DOUBLEDAY DORAN.
> Cream end-papers; top and lower edges cut, fore-edges uncut; leaves measure 19 × 3 cm.
>
> *Price:* $1. The first edition was published in April 1940.

Notes: This was a survey of French affairs early in the war, commissioned by what later became *The Ministry of Information.* It gave what proved to be an inaccurate picture of French morale at that time, which is surprising considering Maugham's knowledge of France and her people, but the fault was not altogether his and he sets out elsewhere the facts and obstacles he met with during its composition. Publication was discontinued on the fall of France.

A57   BOOKS AND YOU   (1940)

a. First edition:
BOOKS | AND | YOU | [*ornament*] | W. SOMERSET MAUGHAM | [*publisher's windmill device resting on base*] | WILLIAM HEINEMANN LTD | LONDON [*square of 4 dots*] TORONTO

> *Collation:* [xxii] (paged xx), 78 pp. [A]⁸ B–F⁸⁺². Sig. F a gathering of 10 leaves.
> Half-title (with verso, By W. SOMERSET MAUGHAM [listing 23 non-dramatic and 24 dramatic works]), not included in pagination; p. [i], title; p. [ii], FIRST PUBLISHED 1940 | PRINTED IN GREAT BRITAIN AT THE WINDMILL PRESS | KINGSWOOD, SURREY; p. [iii],

dedication To | BARBARA ROTHSCHILD; p. [iv], blank; pp. v–xx, preface; p. [1], fly-title; p. [2], blank; pp. 3–78, text.

Binding: Persian blue linen-grain cloth, blocked in black on front with author's symbol and on back with publisher's windmill device; gold-lettered on front: Books and You; and on spine: Books | and | You | W.S. | Maugham | [in black] Heinemann. Regency cream end-papers; all edges cut; leaves measure 19 × 12.7 cm.

Price: 3s. 6d. 3,000 copies were published on 18 March 1940.

Notes: This book was serialised in *The Saturday Evening Post*.

A57   BOOKS AND YOU   1940

b. American First edition:
W. SOMERSET MAUGHAM | Books | and | You | [*publisher's monogram device*] | DOUBLEDAY, DORAN & CO., INC., NEW YORK, 1940
Title and publisher's monogram device within a rectangular ornamental border.

Collation: 110 pp. [unsigned 1–7⁸].
Blank leaf not included in pagination; p. [1], half-title; p. [2], BOOKS BY | W. SOMERSET MAUGHAM [listing 41 titles]; p. [3], title; p. [4], PRINTED AT THE *Country Life Press*, GARDEN CITY, N.Y., U.S.A. | CL | COPYRIGHT, 1939, 1940 | BY W. SOMERSET MAUGHAM | ALL RIGHTS RESERVED | FIRST EDITION; p. 5–107, text; pp. [108–110], blank.

Binding: Light brown linen cloth, blocked in dark brown on front with author's symbol; on spine blocked and lettered in dark brown: [*rule*] | w. | SOMERSET | MAUGHAM | [*rule*] | BOOKS | AND | YOU | [*rule*] | DOUBLEDAY | DORAN | [*rule*] | [*double-rules at top and tail*].
Plain end-papers; top edges cut and stained brown, lower edges cut, fore-edges uncut; leaves measure 19 × 13 cm.

Price: $1.25. Number of copies unknown. Published on 22 March 1940.

A58   THE MIXTURE AS BEFORE   (1940)

a. First edition:
THE MIXTURE AS | BEFORE | BY | W. SOMERSET

I

MAUGHAM | [*publisher's windmill device resting on base*] | WILLIAM
HEINEMANN LTD | LONDON [*square of 4 dots*] TORONTO

Collation: [xii] (paged [x]), 292 pp. [A]⁸ B–T⁸.
Blank leaf, not included in pagination; p. [i], half-title; p. [ii],
By w. SOMERSET MAUGHAM [listing 23 non-dramatic and 24
dramatic works]; p. [iii], title; p. [iv], FIRST PUBLISHED 1940 |
PRINTED IN GREAT BRITAIN AT THE WINDMILL PRESS | KINGSWOOD,
SURREY; p. [v], contents; p. [vi], blank; pp. vii–ix, foreword;
p. [x], blank; pp. 1–288, text; pp. [289–292], blank.

Binding: Persian blue linen-grain cloth, blocked in black on
front with author's symbol and on back with publisher's windmill device; gold-lettered on front: The Mixture as Before; and
on spine: The | Mixture | as Before | W.S. | Maugham | [*in
black*] Heinemann.

Advance Proof state: pp. [i–vi] vii–ix [x]+288+2 blank leaves.
Buff wrappers, printed in black. 19.1 × 12.6 cm.

Chalk blue end-papers; top edges cut and stained blue, other
edges cut; leaves measure 19 × 12.7 cm.

Price: 8s. 15,000 copies were published on 6 June 1940.

Notes: In the foreword to *The Mixture as Before* Mr. Maugham
wrote 'I have now written between eighty and ninety stories, I shall
not write any more'. When a further volume—*Creatures of Circumstance*—appeared some seven years later he wrote another foreword in
which he explained that the typist or typesetter had left out an *m* and
that the line should have read 'I shall not write *many* more stories'. In
view of this disclaimer, it is interesting to know that it was not the
first time Mr. Maugham had threatened to retire from the short story
market. In a letter to Pinker in November 1907, he wrote—'I do not
propose to write any more short stories. I have so many commisions
for plays that I should not have time even if I had the inclination'.
Luckily for English literature he did not adhere to this resolution.

Mr. Maugham, somewhat ironically, took the title of this book
from a review in *The Times* of his last volume of short stories which
was headed *The Mixture as Before*.

*Contents: The Three Fat Women of Antibes—A Man with a Conscience—
The Treasure—The Lotus Eater—The Lion's Skin—Lord Mountdrago—
Gigolo and Gigolette—The Voice of the Turtle—An Official Position—
The Facts of Life.*

A58   THE MIXTURE AS BEFORE   1940

b. First American edition:
W. SOMERSET MAUGHAM | The Mixture | As Before | [author's
symbol] | DOUBLEDAY, DORAN & CO., INC. | NEW YORK
1940

> *Collation:* x, 310 pp. [unsigned 1–20⁸].
> p. [i], half-title; p. [ii], BOOKS BY | W. SOMERSET MAUGHAM [listing
> 43 titles]; p. [iii], title; p. [iv], PRINTED AT THE *Country Life Press*,
> GARDEN CITY, N.Y., U.S.A. | CL | COPYRIGHT, 1933, 1934, 1935, 1936,
> 1937, 1938, 1939, 1940 | BY W. SOMERSET MAUGHAM | ALL RIGHTS
> RESERVED | FIRST EDITION: p. v–vii, Foreword; p. [viii], blank;
> p. ix, Contents; p. [x], blank; pp. [1] 2–310, text.

> *Binding:* Black matt cloth, blocked on front in blind with author's
> symbol; on spine blocked with frame of rules with decorative
> corners and mid-points separated by bands and gold-lettered:
> W. SOMERSET | MAUGHAM | The Mixture | As Before | DOUBLEDAY
> DORAN.
> Cream end-papers; top edges cut and stained red, lower edges
> rough trimmed, fore-edges uncut; leaves measure 19.9 × 14 cm.

> *Price:* $2.50. 10,000 copies were published on July 12 1940.
> Copyright copy deposited Library of Congress July 18 1940.

A59   UP AT THE VILLA   1941

a. First edition:
W. SOMERSET MAUGHAM | Up At The Villa | [*author's symbol*] |
DOUBLEDAY, DORAN & COMPANY, INC., NEW YORK
1941

> *Collation:* [vi], 210 pp. [unsigned 1–10⁸ 11⁸⁺⁴ 12–13⁸]. Sig. 11 a
> gathering of 12 leaves.
> p. [i], half-title; p. [ii], BOOKS BY | W. SOMERSET MAUGHAM [listing
> 43 titles]; p. [iii], title; p. [iv], PRINTED AT THE *Country Life Press*,
> GARDEN CITY, N.Y., U.S.A. | CL | COPYRIGHT, 1940, 1941 | BY W.
> SOMERSET MAUGHAM | ALL RIGHTS RESERVED, FIRST EDITION; p. [v],
> fly-title; p. [vi], blank; pp. [1] 2–209, text; p. [210], blank.

> *Binding:* Black matt cloth, blocked in blind on front with author's
> symbol and on spine in gold with the wording: W. SOMERSET |
> MAUGHAM | UP AT | THE | VILLA enclosed in an elaborate curtain
> frame between double bands | DOUBLEDAY | DORAN.
> Biscuit end-papers; top edges cut and stained bluish green,

fore-edges uncut, lower edges rough trimmed; leaves measure
20 × 14 cm.

Price: $1.75. Number of copies unknown. The first edition was
published on April 5 1941.

Notes: Warner Bros paid Somerset Maugham $30,000 for the movie
rights of *Up at the Villa*, but although a number of experienced script
writers including Christopher Isherwood were employed on it they
were never able to produce a script that has satisfied the censor.

In the files of the American Play Company now preserved in The
New York Public Library (Berg Collection) is the typescript (carbon)
of a short story (29p.) unsigned and undated entitled *A Night in June*.
Presumably it went the round of the Editors but never found a pub-
lisher and many years later Maugham re-wrote it as a novel *Up at the
Villa* with the same characters and the names unchanged.

A59   UP AT THE VILLA   (1941)

b. First English edition:
W. SOMERSET MAUGHAM | UP AT THE VILLA | [*publisher's
windmill device resting on base*] | WILLIAM HEINEMANN LTD |
LONDON [*square of 4 dots*] TORONTO

Collation: [vi], 154 pp. [A]⁸ B–K⁸.
p. [i], half-title; p. [ii], By w. SOMERSET MAUGHAM [listing 25 non-
dramatic and 24 dramatic works]; p. [iii], title; p. [iv], FIRST
PUBLISHED 1941 | PRINTED IN GREAT BRITAIN AT THE WINDMILL
PRESS | KINGSWOOD, SURREY; p. [v], fly-title; p. [vi], blank;
pp. 1–153, text; p. [154], blank.

Binding: Persian blue linen-grained cloth, blocked in black
on front with author's symbol and on back with publisher's
windmill device; gold-lettered on front: Up At The Villa; and on
spine: Up | at the | Villa | W.S. | Maugham | [*in black*] Heinemann.
Hay end-papers; all edges cut; leaves measure 19 × 12.7 cm.

Price: 6s. 10,000 copies were published on May 12 1941.

A60   STRICTLY PERSONAL   1941

a. First and Limited edition:
Strictly Personal | BY W. SOMERSET MAUGHAM | [*author's
symbol*] | Doubleday, Doran and Company, Inc. | GARDEN CITY,
NEW YORK | 1941

Collation: [viii], 272 pp. [unsigned 1–14⁸ 15⁸⁺⁴ 16–17⁸]. Sig. 15, a gathering of 12 leaves. Photogravure front. port. and Cert. of Limitation, inserted.

pp. [i–ii], blank; cert. of limitation, inserted, with verso blank: *This edition | is limited to five hundred and fifteen copies | numbered and signed by the author | of which this is | No. . . . : p. [iii], half-title; p. [iv], BOOKS BY | W. SOMERSET MAUGHAM [listing 25 non-dramatic and 19 dramatic works]; p. [v], title; p. [vi], [*Copyright Notice, etc.*] PRINTED IN THE UNITED STATES | AT | THE COUNTRY LIFE PRESS, GARDEN CITY, N.Y. | FIRST EDITION; p. [vii], fly-title; p. [viii], blank; pp. [1] 2–272, text.

Binding: Plum buckram boards, bevelled, blocked in blind on front with author's symbol; on *flat* spine black skiver leather label gold lettered between ornamental crossbands: STRICTLY | PERSONAL | *W. Somerset | Maugham* | DOUBLEDAY DORAN. Plain end-papers; top edges cut and gilt, other edges uncut; leaves measure 21.2 × 14.4 cm. In slip case.

Price: $6. The first and limited edition was published on 3 September 1941.

A60   STRICTLY PERSONAL   1941

b. First Trade edition: (separate impression from the same formes).
Strictly Personal | BY W. SOMERSET MAUGHAM | [*author's symbol*] | Doubleday, Doran and Company, Inc. | GARDEN CITY, NEW YORK | 1941

Collation: [viii], 272 pp. [unsigned 1–14⁸ 15⁸⁺⁴ 16–17⁸]. Sig. 15, a gathering of 12 leaves. Front. port., inserted.
pp. [i–ii], blank; p. [iii], half-title; p. [iv], BOOKS BY | W. SOMERSET MAUGHAM [listing 25 non-dramatic and 19 dramatic works]; p. [v], title; p. [vi], PRINTED AT THE *Country Life Press*, GARDEN CITY, N.Y., U.S.A. | CL | COPYRIGHT, 1940, 1941 | BY W. SOMERSET MAUGHAM | ALL RIGHTS RESERVED | FIRST EDITION | AFTER THE PRINTING OF A LIMITED SIGNED EDITION | OF FIVE HUNDRED AND FIFTEEN COPIES; p. [vii], fly-title; p. [viii], blank; pp. [1], 2–272, text.

Binding: Black matt cloth, blocked in blind on front with author's symbol; spine divided into six compartments, 5 being decoratively (and identically) blocked in gold with the wording: *W. Somerset | Maugham* | STRICTLY | PERSONAL | *Doubleday Doran* in plain compartment.
Biscuit end-papers; top edges cut and stained brownish red,

fore-edges uncut, lower edges rough trimmed. Leaves measure 21.2 × 14.3 cm.

Price: $2.50. Number of copies unknown. The first trade edition was published on 5 September 1941.

A60 THE INSIDE STORY OF THE 1940
FRENCH COLLAPSE

c. First edition:
The Inside Story of the French Collapse. By W. Somerset Maugham.
Reprinted from "Redbook" October 1940 *Issue*

 Fcp. 8vo. 8 leaves unpag., printed on stiff paper, stapled and with a rice-paper cover captioned: France Fell ... on June 17, Now, just a few weeks later, w. SOMERSET MAUGHAM ... previously reported dead or captured—returns to London to give his masterful, eye-witness story of the Collapse of France—in—October REDBOOK ON SALE—SEPTEMBER 1ST. *See* D121–123.

 The greater part of this pamphlet was incorporated in *Strictly Personal*, but in the latter the author watered down his earlier impressions and was less inclined to blame himself for his lack of perspicacity in summing up the situation.

A60 STRICTLY PERSONAL (1942)

d. First English edition:
STRICTLY PERSONAL | BY | W. SOMERSET MAUGHAM | [*ornament*] | [*publisher's windmill device resting on base*] WILLIAM HEINEMANN LTD | LONDON [*square of 4 dots*] TORONTO

 Collation: vi, 198 pp. [A]⁸ B–M⁸ N⁶. Front. port., inserted.
 p. [i], half-title; p. [ii], By w. SOMERSET MAUGHAM [listing 25 non-dramatic and 24 dramatic works]; p. [iii], title; p. [iv], FIRST PUBLISHED 1942 | PRINTED IN GREAT BRITAIN AT THE WINDMILL PRESS | KINGSWOOD, SURREY; pp. v–vi, A Letter to Sir Edward Marsh; pp. 1–196, text; pp. 197–198, blank.

 Binding: Oxford blue linen-grain cloth, blocked in blind on back with publisher's windmill device; and on spine with author's symbol and gold-lettered: Strictly | Personal | W. Somerset | Maugham | Heinemann.

 Binding Variant: Bright salmon buckram, lettered on spine in black STRICTLY | PERSONAL | W. S. | MAUGHAM | HEINEMANN, conforming in all other respects with the English edition. This may be a trial binding for a limited edition that for some reason was abandoned. The reason may have been that the English publishers decided that there was not a market for two limited editions. 18 × 12 cm.

Advance Proof state: pp. vi+196+blank leaf. White wrappers, printed in black. Portrait lacking. 18.3 × 12½ cm.

Plain end-papers; all edges cut: leaves measure 18½ × 12½ cm.

Price: 8s. 6d. 10,000 copies were published on the 2nd March 1942.

Notes: The English edition contains a two-page letter addressed to Sir Edward Marsh K.C.V.O., which is not in the American edition. *Strictly Personal,* which covers the author's experiences during the first fifteen months of the war, was serialised in *The Saturday Evening Post* under dates March 22, 29, April 5, 12 1941, under the title *Novelist's Flight from France.*

A61　　　THE HOUR BEFORE THE DAWN　　　1942

a. First edition:
W. SOMERSET MAUGHAM | The Hour Before the Dawn | A NOVEL | [*author's symbol*] | Garden City, New York | DOUBLEDAY, DORAN AND COMPANY, INC. | 1942

Collation: [viii], 312 pp. [unsigned 1–20⁸].
p. [i], half-title; p. [ii], BOOKS BY | W. SOMERSET MAUGHAM [listing 26 non-dramatic and 19 dramatic works]; p. [iii], title; p. [iv], PRINTED AT THE *Country Life Press,* GARDEN CITY, N.Y., U.S.A. | CL | COPYRIGHT, 1941, 1942 | BY W. SOMERSET MAUGHAM | ALL RIGHTS RESERVED | FIRST EDITION; p. [v], 4-line quotation from Pope; p. [vi], blank; p. [vii], fly-title; p. [viii], blank; pp. [1] 2–307, text; pp. [308–312], blank.

Binding: Smooth black cloth, blocked in blind on front with author's symbol; and on spine in gold with a design incorporating the author's initials "WSM", rows of floral emblems and single and double rules, and lettered: W. SOMERSET | MAUGHAM | THE HOUR | BEFORE | THE DAWN | DOUBLEDAY | DORAN.
Plain end-papers; all edges cut; leaves measure 20 × 14 cm.

Price: $2.50. Number of copies unknown. The first edition was published on 19 June 1942.

Notes: This novel was written at the request of the Ministry of Information and was intended to show the effect of the war on a typically British family. It was written originally in the form of a documentary and serialised in *Redbook* in the January, February, March, and April 1942 issues; then expanded into a novel. It is of all Maugham's books the one he was most dissatisfied with, probably because it was written to order and was propaganda, instead of developing in his mind over a number of years as did all his other novels. In a letter to Eddie Marsh in the Berg Collection at the New York Public Library, he writes: 'No, I am not going to send you my novel to correct because I have decided not to publish it in England. It was written as propaganda, first as a picture, then as a short serial and finally as a full-length novel. How could anyone be expected to run out a decent piece of work in that way? I knew very well it was poor and I was miserable about it. I tried to console myself by looking upon it as my contribution to the war effort, but that did not help much and I prefer to think now that it will be unread in England and forgotten in America. . . .' That he had at one time, however, contemplated publishing it here is apparent from the publisher's records which show that although the type was set up and the book actually proofed at the Windmill Press, it was never produced in book form. *See* A61c.

A61   THE HOUR BEFORE THE DAWN   1945

b. First Australian edition:
W. SOMERSET MAUGHAM | The Hour Before the Dawn | A Novel | ANGUS AND ROBERTSON LTD | SYDNEY [*square of dots*] LONDON | 1945

> *Collation:* [vi], 266 pp. [A]⁸ B–R⁸.
> p. [i], half-title; p. [ii], BOOKS BY | W. SOMERSET MAUGHAM [*listing 45 titles*]; p. [iii], Set up, printed and bound | in Australia . . . 1945 . . . | COPYRIGHT, 1942 . . . ; p. [v], quotation; p. [vi], blank; pp. [1] 2–266, text.
>
> *Binding:* Brown fine cloth, lettered in blank on spine; THE | HOUR | BEFORE | THE | DAWN | [*dot*] | W. SOMERSET | MAUGHAM | ANGUS AND | ROBERTSON.
> Plain end-papers; all edges trimmed; leaves measure 18.1 × 12.4 cm.

> *Price:* 7s. 6d. 4913 copies were published on the 7th April 1945.

Notes: This copy comes from the Grenville Cook collection.

A61   THE HOUR BEFORE THE DAWN   (1942)

c. English Advance Proof state:
THE HOUR BEFORE | THE DAWN | BY | W. SOMERSET

MAUGHAM | [*publisher's windmill device resting on base*] WILLIAM HEINEMANN LTD | LONDON [*square of 4 dots*] TORONTO

> *Collation:* p. [i], half-title; p. [ii], By w. SOMERSET MAUGHAM [listing 26 non-dramatic and 24 dramatic works]; p. [iii], title; p. [iv], FIRST PUBLISHED 1942 | WAR ECONOMY ... | PRINTED IN GREAT BRITAIN AT THE WINDMILL PRESS, | KINGSWOOD, SURREY; pp. 1–216, text.

> *Binding:* White wrappers, lettered in black on front between double-rules: THE HOUR BEFORE | THE DAWN | W. SOMERSET MAUGHAM | [*at tail*] PROOF | COPY.
> All edges cut; leaves measure 18.7 × 12.7 cm.

Notes: This copy has part of pictures on the inside wrappers, suggesting that left over sheets were used for the binding, as it was not intended to complete more than a few copies for distribution. The only copy in proof form that has come to my notice is in the Leonard Meldman collection.

A62   THE UNCONQUERED   1944

First edition:
[author's symbol] | THE UNCONQUERED | W. SOMERSET MAUGHAM | HOUSE OF BOOKS, LTD. | NEW YORK [dot] 1944 | [crown]
Title page in black and dark blue.

> *Collation:* (60) [paged (58)] pp. [unsigned 1-6⁴ 7² 8⁴].
> Blank leaf, not included in pagination; p. [1], THIS FIRST EDITION IS LIMITED TO | THREE HUNDRED NUMBERED COPIES | SIGNED BY THE AUTHOR | THIS IS NO ... ; p. [2], blank; p. [3], title; p. [4], COPYRIGHT, 1944, BY | HOUSE OF BOOKS, LTD.; p. [5], half-title; p. [6], blank; pp. 7–55 [56], text; p. [57], colophon; p. [58], blank.

> *Binding:* Navy blue linen cloth, blocked on front in blind with author's symbol and gold-lettered: THE UNCONQUERED | W. SOMERSET MAUGHAM; and on spine, reading downward: THE UNCONQUERED [*dot*] W. SOMERSET MAUGHAM.
> Plain end-papers: all edges cut; leaves measure 18.8 × 12½ cm.

Price: $3.50. 300 copies were published on the 1 December 1944.

Notes: This is the original text of the short story which had appeared previously in *Collier's Magazine* in expurgated form. It was reprinted in *Creatures of Circumstance* in the original version. The certificate of limitation refers to 300 numbered copies, but there were actually

26 additional copies (lettered a–z). 12 of which were used for presentation to the author, 12 for review and presentation by the Publisher, and 2 for entry in the Library of Congress for copyright purposes.

A63   THE RAZOR'S EDGE   1944

a. First and Limited edition:
[*2-line quotation from Katha-Upanishad*] | The Razor's Edge | A NOVEL | BY W. SOMERSET MAUGHAM | Doubleday, Doran & Co., Inc., | GARDEN CITY, NEW YORK | [*author's symbol on right of imprint with date below*] 1944

> *Collation:* [vi], 346 pp. [unsigned 1–11¹⁶]. Cert. of limitation leaf, a single inset.
>
> Cert. of Limitation: *This edition* | *is limited to seven hundred and fifty copies* | *numbered and signed by the author* | *of which this is* | No. . . . ; p. [i], half-title; p. [ii], BOOKS BY | W. SOMERSET MAUGHAM [listing 28 non-dramatic and 19 dramatic works]; p. [iii], title; p. [iv], COPYRIGHT, 1943, 1944, BY THE MCCALL COMPANY | COPYRIGHT, 1944, BY W. SOMERSET MAUGHAM | ALL RIGHTS RESERVED | PRINTED IN THE UNITED STATES | AT | THE COUNTRY LIFE PRESS, GARDEN CITY, N.Y. | FIRST EDITION; p. [v], fly-title; p. [vi], blank; pp. [1] 2–343, text; pp. [344–346], blank.
>
> *Binding:* Plum buckram boards, bevelled edges, blocked in blind on front with author's symbol; on flat spine black skiver leather label gold-lettered between ornamental cross bands: THE | RAZOR'S | EDGE | *W. Somerset* | *Maugham* | DOUBLEDAY DORAN. Plain end-papers; top edges cut and gilt, other edges uncut; leaves measure 21.2 × 14.3 cm. In slip case.
>
> *Price:* $6. The first and limited edition was published on 18 April 1944.

A63   THE RAZOR'S EDGE   1944

b. First Trade edition: (separate impression from the same formes).
[*2-line quotation from Katha-Upanishad*] | The Razor's Edge | A NOVEL | BY W. SOMERSET MAUGHAM | Doubleday, Doran & Co., Inc., | GARDEN CITY, NEW YORK | [*author's symbol on right of imprint with date below*] 1944

> *Collation:* [vi], 346 pp. [unsigned 1–11¹⁶].
> p. [i], half-title; p. [ii], BOOKS BY | W. SOMERSET MAUGHAM [listing 28 non-dramatic and 19 dramatic works]; p. [iii], title; p. [iv], wartime control stamp | COPYRIGHT, 1943, 1944, BY THE MCCALL

COMPANY | COPYRIGHT, 1944, BY W. SOMERSET MAUGHAM | ALL
RIGHTS RESERVED | PRINTED IN THE UNITED STATES | AT | THE
COUNTRY LIFE PRESS, GARDEN CITY, N.Y. | FIRST EDITION AFTER THE
PRINTING OF A LIMITED EDITION OF | SEVEN HUNDRED AND FIFTY
COPIES; p. [v], fly-title; p. [vi], blank; pp. 1–343, text; pp. [344–
346], blank.

Binding: Smooth black cloth, blocked in blind on front with
author's symbol and on spine in lime yellow with head and tail
ornamental bands and lettered: W. SOMERSET | MAUGHAM | The |
Razor's | Edge | DOUBLEDAY | DORAN.
Cream end-papers; top edges cut and stained yellow, fore-edges
uncut, lower edges cut or rough trimmed. Leaves measure
19.7 × 14 cm.

Price: $2.75. The first trade edition was published on 20 April
1944.

Notes: The pagination of the limited edition runs at the head of the
page, the ordinary trade edition at the tail in brackets. *The Razor's
Edge* was serialised in *Redbook* in the December 1943, January, February, March, April and May 1944 issues.

A63   THE RAZOR'S EDGE   (1944)

c. First English edition:
THE RAZOR'S EDGE | A Novel | BY | W. SOMERSET
MAUGHAM | [*2-line quotation from Katha-Upanishad*] | [*publisher's
windmill device resting on base*] | WILLIAM HEINEMANN LTD |
LONDON [*square of 4 dots*] TORONTO

Collation: [iv], 284 pp. A–I¹⁶.
p. [i], half-title; p. [ii], By W. SOMERSET MAUGHAM [listing 25
non-dramatic and 24 dramatic works]; p. [iii], title; p. [iv],
FIRST PUBLISHED 1944 | [*wartime control stamp*] | [*short rule*] | [*printer's
imprint*]; pp. 1–284, text.

Binding: Persian blue linen-grain cloth, blocked in gold on
front with author's symbol and on back with publisher's windmill device in blind; gold-lettered on front: The Razor's Edge;
and on spine: The | Razor's | Edge | W. S. | Maugham | Heine-
mann.
Hay end-papers; all edges cut; leaves measure 18.4 × 12.3 cm.

Price: 12s. 6d. 40,000 copies were published on the 17 July 1944.

Notes: There is another edition that was issued some months later

under the Heinemann imprint with the author's signature in facsimile
on the half-title, bound from the American first edition sheets in a dull
grey cloth.

On the front of the American trade edition dust wrapper is printed
an aphorism—THE STORY OF A MAN WHO FOUND A FAITH. It does not
appear in the book nor anywhere at all in the English edition, and was
probably written by Maugham himself.

The theme of *The Razor's Edge* came from an unproduced and
unpublished play of Maugham's *The Road Uphill*.

A64   THEN AND NOW   (1946)

a. First edition:

THEN AND NOW | A Novel | BY | W. SOMERSET MAUGHAM
[*publisher's windmill device resting on base*] | WILLIAM HEINEMANN
LTD | LONDON [*square of 4 dots*] TORONTO

Collation: [vi], 230 pp. A–G¹⁶ H⁶.

p. [i], half-title; p. [ii], By W. SOMERSET MAUGHAM [listing 26 non-
dramatic and 24 dramatic works]; p. [iii], title; p. [iv], FIRST
PUBLISHED 1946 | THIS BOOK IS PRODUCED IN COMPLETE | CON-
FORMITY WITH THE AUTHORISED | ECONOMY STANDARDS | [*short
rule*] | PRINTED IN GREAT BRITAIN AT THE WINDMILL PRESS | KINGS-
WOOD, SURREY; p. [v], author's acknowledgements; p. [vi],
blank; pp. 1–229, text; p. [230], blank.

Binding: (i) Smooth Persian blue cloth, blocked in gold on front
with author's symbol and on back with publisher's windmill
device in blind; gold-lettered on front: Then and Now; and on
spine: Then | and | Now | W. S. | Maugham | Heinemann
(ii) Arabian blue matt cloth, lettered as above. (iii) Midnight
blue matt cloth, lettered as above.

(i) is the regular Heinemann Persian blue style and the B.M.
Copyright copy (received 13 May, 1946) is in this casing; (ii)
was issued simultaneously, but as it is in the same quality cloth as
(iii) which was issued several weeks later with another edition
bound by Heinemann in an identical cloth from sheets printed in
Sydney, Australia, I would incline to favour the order set out
above.

Advance Proof state: pp. [vi]+229+[1]. Buff wrappers, printed in
black. 18.3 × 12.3 cm.

Hay end-papers; all edges cut; leaves measure 18½ × 12½ cm.

Price: 10s. 6d. 50,000 copies were published on 13 May 1946.

A64 THEN AND NOW 1946

b. First American edition:
THEN AND NOW | A Novel | W. SOMERSET MAUGHAM |
[*author's symbol*] | GARDEN CITY, N.Y. | DOUBLEDAY &
COMPANY, INC. | 1946

> *Collation:* [viii], 280 pp. [unsigned 1–9¹⁶].
> p. [i], half-title; p. [ii], BOOKS BY | W. SOMERSET MAUGHAM [listing
> 48 works]; p. [iii], title; p. [iv], COPYRIGHT, 1946 | BY W. SOMERSET
> MAUGHAM | ALL RIGHTS RESERVED | PRINTED IN THE UNITED STATES |
> AT | THE COUNTRY LIFE PRESS, GARDEN CITY, N.Y. | FIRST EDITION;
> p. [v], author's note; p. [vi], blank; p. [vii], fly-title; p. [viii],
> blank; pp. [1] 2–278, text; pp. [279–280], blank.

> *Binding:* Smooth black cloth, blocked in blind on front with
> author's symbol; lettered in gold on spine between ornamental
> triple rules: THEN | and | NOW | W. SOMERSET | MAUGHAM |
> DOUBLEDAY.
> Plain end-papers; top edges cut and stained yellow, lower edges
> cut, fore-edges uncut; leaves measure 19.9 × 14 cm.

> *Price:* $2.50. 50,000 copies were published on 23 May 1946.

A65 OF HUMAN BONDAGE 1946

a. Limited edition:
Of Human | Bondage | With a Digression | on the | Art of Fiction |
An Address By | W. Somerset Maugham | [*ornament*] | MCMXLVI
[*in fancy lettering, the whole enclosed in an ornamental head-and-tail frame*]

> *Collation:* (24) [paged (16)] pp. 12 leaves in one gathering, un-
> signed, the first and last leaves used as lining papers.
> *Colophon:* [*between ornamental triple rules*] Designed and printed
> *for | The Library of Congress at | the U.S. Government Print- | ing
> Office at Washington, in | an edition of 800 copies, 500 | of which have
> been signed by | Mr. Maugham. | April 1946.*

> *Binding:* Silver grey boards, printed in black within an ornamental
> head and tail frame: Of Human | Bondage | with a Digression |
> on the | Art of Fiction | AN ADDRESS By | W. Somerset Maugham |
> [*ornament*] | MCMXLVI.
> All edges cut. Leaves measure 21.7 × 13.4 cm.

Notes: The limited edition exists in two states. In the first state, the
collation agrees with the above. Mr. Maugham's signature is found on
p. [1] which is otherwise blank, as is the verso. This leaf is conjugate

with p. [23]–[24], also blank. The first leaf is followed by a blank
leaf p. [3]–[4], which is conjugate with the colophon leaf, p. [21]–
[22].

In the second state, the colophon leaf is a stub.

Mr. Frederick R. Goff, then Chief of the Rare Book Division, the
Library of Congress, to whom I am indebted for this information,
tells me that from his own personal recollection 'the signed copies,
representing the first state, were issued first. They were distributed to
the audience who attended the presentation ceremony. Presumably
at the time the remaining 300 copies were being prepared for binding,
alterations took place which resulted in the colophon leaf being
mounted on a stub. Subsequently the second edition in wrappers was
issued to satisfy popular demand.'

A65   OF HUMAN BONDAGE   1946

An Address by W. Somerset Maugham

b. First and Trade edition: (separate impression from the same formes).
Of Human | Bondage | With a Digression | on the | Art of Fiction |
An Address By | W. Somerset Maugham | [*ornament*] | MCMXLVI [*in
fancy lettering, the whole enclosed in an ornamental head-and-tail frame*].

> *Collation:* (20) [paged (16)] pp. 10 leaves in one gathering, un-
> signed, stapled.
> Blank leaf, not included in pagination; p. [1], title; p. [2], blank;
> p. [3], [between head and tail type ornamental border] *This
> Address | was given by Mr. Maugham | in the Coolidge Auditorium, |
> The Library of Congress, on | the occasion of his presenting | the
> original manuscript of his | novel "Of Human Bondage" | to the
> Library/* p. [4], blank; pp. 5–16, text; p. [17], colophon [between
> head and tail type ornamental borders] *Designed and printed for |
> The Library of Congress at | the U.S. Government Print- | ing Office at
> Washington, in | an edition of 2,500 copies, of | which 1,000 are for
> sale by | the Superintendent of Docu- | ments at 25 cents a copy. |
> April 1946 |* SECOND PRINTING; p. 18, blank.
>
> *Binding:* Silver grey wrappers, printed in black; Of Human |
> Bondage | With a Digression | on the | Art of Fiction [*the whole
> enclosed in an ornamental head and tail frame*].
> All edges cut; leaves measure 21.7 × 13.4 cm.

Notes: This address was given by Mr. Maugham in the Coolidge
Auditorium, the Library of Congress, on the occasion of his presenting
the original manuscript of his novel *Of Human Bondage* to the Library.
In it, he tells how the novel came to be written, and makes other

observations of varying biographical interest. On the 11 October 1950, Mr. Maugham made a further presentation to the Library of the manuscript *The Artistic Temperament of Stephen Carey*, the first version of *Of Human Bondage* written shortly after he had received his degree in medicine. One of the stipulations of the gift is that it is never to be published.

A66   CREATURES OF CIRCUMSTANCE   (1947)

a. First edition:

CREATURES OF | CIRCUMSTANCE | BY | W. SOMERSET MAUGHAM | [*publisher's windmill device resting on base*] | WILLIAM HEINEMANN LTD | LONDON [*square of 4 dots*] TORONTO

Collation: [vi], 310 pp. A–I^{16} K^8 L^6.

p. [i], half-title; p. [ii], By w. somerset maugham [listing 27 non-dramatic and 24 dramatic works]; p. [iii], title; p. [iv], first published 1947 | printed in great britain at the windmill press | kingswood, surrey; p. [v], contents; p. [vi], blank; pp. 1–4, *The Author Excuses Himself*; pp. 5–310, text.

Binding: Smooth scarlet red cloth, blocked in silver on front with author's symbol and on back with publisher's device in blind; silver-lettered on front between triple rules: Creatures of | Circumstance; and on spine: maugham | [*triple rules*] | Creatures of | Circumstance | heinemann.

Advance Proof state: pp. [vi]+310 pp. Buff wrappers, printed in black. On inside of wrappers, front and back is an advert. for "Death Comes for the Archbishop" by Willa Cather. Possibly left over stiff sheets advertising different books were used by the binders so that in some proof copies the adverts. varied.

Hay end-papers; all edges cut; leaves measure 18½ × 12.2 cm.

Price: 10s. 6d. 50,000 copies were published on the 17 July 1947.

Notes: Throughout his professional career, Mr. Maugham showed a great reluctance to waste material, and time and again he has resurrected stories written in his youth, and revised them for book form. *The Mother*, to which he originally gave the title *La Cachirra*, *The Luncheon*, originally published as *Cousin Amy*, and *The Happy Couple*, are instances in point. He apparently kept no record of these stories, for in 1922 he wrote to Pinker asking if he could trace them.

Contents: The Colonel's Lady—Flotsam and Jetsam—Appearance and Reality—The Mother—Sanatorium—A Woman of Fifty—The Romantic

*Young Lady—A Casual Affair—The Point of Honour—Winter Cruise—
The Happy Couple—A Man from Glasgow—The Unconquered—Episode—
The Kite.*

A66   CREATURES OF CIRCUMSTANCE   1947

b. First American edition:
[*Title page in grey with decorative design and author's symbol in white and
lettered in black within white rule border*] CREATURES OF | CIR-
CUMSTANCE | By | W. SOMERSET MAUGHAM | [*author's
symbol*] | DOUBLEDAY & COMPANY, INC. | Garden City,
N.Y. 1947

> *Collation:* [vi], 314 pp. [unsigned 1–10^{16}].
> p. [i], half-title; p. [ii], BOOKS BY | W. SOMERSET MAUGHAM [listing
> 49 titles]; p. [iii], title; p. [iv], COPYRIGHT, 1934, 1935, 1938, 1940,
> 1942, 1943, 1946, 1947 | BY W. SOMERSET MAUGHAM | ALL RIGHTS
> RESERVED | PRINTED IN THE UNITED STATES | AT | THE COUNTRY
> LIFE PRESS, GARDEN CITY, N.Y. | FIRST EDITION.

> *Binding:* Smooth black cloth, blocked in gold on front with
> author's symbol; blocked on spine in gold with design incorporat-
> ing flowers and leaves and lettered in gold: W. SOMERSET |
> MAUGHAM | Creatures of | Circumstance | DOUBLEDAY.
> Plain end-papers; top edges cut and stained grey, other edges
> cut; leaves measure 19.8 × 13 cm.

> *Price:* $2.75. Number of copies unknown. Published in July 1947.

Notes: Each story has a title page printed in grey with decorative
design and border in white and title in black.

A67   CATALINA   (1948)

a. First edition:
CATALINA | A Romance | *by* | W. SOMERSET MAUGHAM |
[*publisher's windmill device resting on base*] | WILLIAM HEINEMANN
LTD | MELBOURNE [*square of 4 dots*] LONDON [square of 4
dots] | TORONTO

> *Collation:* [iv], 256 pp. A^{16+2} B–H^{16}. Sig. A gathering of 18
> leaves.
> p. [i], half-title; p. [ii], By W. SOMERSET MAUGHAM [listing 29
> non-dramatic and 24 dramatic works]; p. [iii], title; p. [iv],
> FIRST PUBLISHED 1948 | PRINTED IN GREAT BRITAIN | AT THE WIND-
> MILL PRESS | KINGSWOOD, SURREY; pp. [1] 2–256, text.

Binding: Scarlet red linen-grain cloth, blocked in silver on front with author's symbol and on back with publisher's device in blind; silver-lettered on front between triple-rules; Catalina; and on spine: MAUGHAM | [*triple rules*] | Catalina | HEINEMANN.

Binding Variant: The blocking on the casing of this book is silver on some copies and imitation gold on others. The publisher states that it was the original intention to use silver blocking, but that it proved unsatisfactory and a change over was made to imitation gold. A considerable number of silver copies, however, must have been blocked before the alteration was made, as gold copies are scarce. Both variations were delivered to the bookshops simultaneously. A few copies of the second impression with silver blocking on a matt cloth have been noticed, but the prevailing *motif* would appear to be gold. The gold is a brassy gilt which easily tarnishes and rubs off. The silver, on the other hand, has worn well.

Advance Proof state: pp. [i–iv], 256 pp. Buff wrappers, printed in black. 18.5×12.7 cm.

Hay end-papers; all edges cut; leaves measure $18\frac{1}{2} \times 12.3$ cm.

Price: 10s. 6d. 50,000 copies were published on 19 August 1948.

Notes: Catalina was serialised in 4 issues of *The Windmill*, the first two instalments appearing before book publication. It was also serialised in *Harper's Magazine* beginning with the June 1948 issue.

Somerset Maugham was looked upon by the reading public as such a fabulously successful novelist, that it came as a surprise to many to know how recent was his success. In 1930, Harper's were writing to Pinker 'Maugham still needs a good deal of advertising to put him across.' And this was after the publication of his most popular book of short stories *Ashenden.* He did not really come into the top-selling class in his own country until *The Razor's Edge* was published in a first edition of 50,000 copies. In America, however, he achieved recognition earlier through the serialisation of his short stories in the Hearst magazines *Cosmopolitan* and *Nash's.* For these contributions he was paid a dollar a word up to 6,000 words. In a letter to Eddie Marsh in the Berg Collection in the New York Public Library, Maugham writes: 'Since you toiled over the proof it may slightly interest you to know that by the end of its first month *The Razor's Edge* had sold 507,000 copies. I will not pretend that I am not staggered.'

K

A67   CATALINA   1949

b. First American edition:
Catalina | A ROMANCE | W. SOMERSET MAUGHAM | [*author's symbol*] | GARDEN CITY, N.Y. | DOUBLEDAY & COMPANY, INC. | 1948
Fancy or ornamental lettering has been ignored.

> *Collation:* [x], 278 pp. [unsigned 1–9¹⁶].
> pp. [i–ii], blank; p. [iii], blank; p. [iv], BOOKS BY | W. SOMERSET MAUGHAM [listing 50 titles]; p. [v], half-title; p. [vi], blank; p. [vii], title; p. [viii], COPYRIGHT, 1948, BY W. SOMERSET MAUGHAM | ALL RIGHTS RESERVED | PRINTED IN THE UNITED STATES | AT | THE COUNTRY LIFE PRESS, GARDEN CITY, N.Y. | FIRST EDITION; p. [ix], fly-title; p. [x], blank; pp. [1] 2–275, text; pp. [276–278], blank.

> *Binding:* Black ripple-grain cloth, blocked on front in blind with author's symbol; gold blocked on spine in ornamental lettering: Catalina | W. SOMERSET | MAUGHAM | DOUBLEDAY [*row of printer's ornaments at head*].
> Plain end-papers; top edges cut and stained yellow, fore and lower edges cut; leaves measure 19.8 × 13.2 cm.

> *Price:* $3. 50,000 copies were published on 26 October 1948.

A68   QUARTET   (1948)

a. First edition:
QUARTET | [*ornament*] | *Stories by* W. Somerset Maugham | *Screen-Plays by* R. C. Sherriff | [*publisher's windmill device*] | WILLIAM HEINEMANN LTD | MELBOURNE [*square of 4 dots*] LONDON | [*square of 4 dots*] TORONTO

> *Collation:* [viii], 244 pp. A–G¹⁶ H¹⁴.
> p. [i], half-title; p. [ii], BY W. SOMERSET MAUGHAM [listing 31 dramatic works, including *Quartet* and 24 dramatic works]; p. [iii], title; p. [iv], FIRST PUBLISHED 1948 | PRINTED IN GREAT BRITAIN | AT THE WINDMILL PRESS | KINGSWOOD, SURREY; pp. v–vii, Foreword by R. C. Sherriff; p. [viii], contents; p. [1], section-title; pp. 2–243, text p. [244], blank.

> *Binding:* Scarlet red matt cloth, blocked in gold on front with author's symbol and on back with publisher's device in blind; gold-lettered on front between triple rules: Quartet; and on spine: MAUGHAM | [*triple rules*] | Quartet | HEINEMANN.

Illustrations: Front. port., and 4 plates (stills from the film). Plain end-papers; all edges cut; leaves measure 19.7 × 13 cm.

Price: 8s. 6d. 5,000 copies were published on the 28 October 1948.

Notes: Script of the film, by R. C. Sherriff. Reprints also the four stories upon which the film is based. *The Facts of Life* from *The Mixture as Before*—*The Alien Corn* from *First Person Singular*—*The Kite* and *The Colonel's Lady* from *Creatures of Circumstance*. Mr. Maugham made a personal appearance in the film, introducing each story. These introductions are printed in the book.

A68 QUARTET (1948)

b. First American edition:
QUARTET | Stories by | W. SOMERSET MAUGHAM | Screen-Plays by | R. C. SHERRIFF | Garden City, N.Y. | DOUBLEDAY & COMPANY, INC. | 1949

> *Collation:* [xiv], 194 pp. [unsigned 1–5¹⁶ 6⁸ 7¹⁶].
> 1 blank leaf; p. [—], Books by | w. somerset maugham [listing 51 titles]; p. [—], blank; p. [i], half-title; p. [ii], blank; p. [iii], title; p. [iv], First published, 1949, in the United States | Copyright, 1931, 1939, 1942, 1946, 1948, by W. Somerset Maugham | Copyright, 1948, by R. C. Sherriff | All Rights Reserved | Printed in the United States | First Edition; pp. v–vii, Foreword; p. [viii], blank; p. [ix], Contents; p. [x], blank; p. [1], fly-title; p. [2], blank; pp. 3–189, text; pp. [190–194], blank.

> *Binding:* Black ribbed cloth, blocked in blind on front with author's symbol; [*running down spine*] [*purple jagged circle*] QUARTET [*ornament*] MAUGHAM and SHERRIFF [*in 3 lines*] DOUBLEDAY [*across*]. Plain end-papers: all edges cut; leaves measure 18.7 × 11.8 cm.

> *Price:* $2.50. Number of copies unknown. First published May 1949. Copyright copy deposited Library of Congress 12 May 1949.

A69 GREAT NOVELISTS AND THEIR NOVELS (1948)

a. First edition:
GREAT NOVELISTS | AND THEIR NOVELS | *Essays on the Ten Greatest Novels of the World,* | *and the Men and Women Who Wrote Them* | By W. Somerset Maugham | [*wavy rule*] | *Illustrated with pen and ink portraits of the authors* | By ROBERT W. ARNOLD | THE JOHN C. WINSTON COMPANY | Philadelphia [*dot*] Toronto

Collation: [viii], 248 pp. [unsigned 1–8¹⁶].

p. [i], half-title; p. [ii], blank; p. [iii], title; p. [iv], *Copyright, 1948 by* W. SOMERSET MAUGHAM [*wavy rule*] | *Copyright in Great Britain and in the British Dominions and Posses-* | *sions. Copyright in the Republic of the Philippines.* | FIRST EDITION [*wavy rule*] | *Made in the United States of America* [*wavy rule*]; p. v, contents; p. [vi], blank; p. [vii], fly-title; p. [viii], blank; pp. 1–245, text; pp. [246–248], blank.

Binding: Smooth crimson red cloth, blocked in gold on front and spine with ornamental single and double-rules and gold-lettered on front: Great Novelists | AND THEIR NOVELS | W. Somerset Maugham; and on spine: Great | Novelists | AND THEIR | NOVELS | Maugham | WINSTON.
Plain end-papers; all edges cut; leaves measure 20.8 × 14.3 cm.

Price: $3. Number of copies unknown. Published in September 1948.

Illustrations: Illustrated with 10 pen and ink portraits of the authors by Robert W. Arnold in the text.

Notes: This American edition was on sale in England and distributed by John Crowther (Publishers) Ltd., of Bognor Regis. The material of this book, which the author has described as his first book of essays, appeared in the American *Atlantic Monthly* under the title *Ten Best Novels*, issues commencing November 1947 onwards. These were again reprinted as introductions to new editions of the ten novels (issued by Winston) and edited by Mr. Maugham to omit 'everything but the story the author has to tell . . . some people have cultivated the art of skipping to their profit; but most people haven't; it is surely better that they should have their skipping done for them by someone of taste and discernment. If he has made a good job of it he should be able to give the reader a novel of which he can read every word with enjoyment.'

    There was an enlarged and revised edition published by Doubleday in 1955 under the title *Art of Fiction: and Introduction to 10 Novels and their Authors.* See B.24.

A69   TEN NOVELS AND THEIR AUTHORS   (1954)

a. First English edition:
TEN NOVELS AND | THEIR AUTHORS | *by* | W. SOMERSET | MAUGHAM | [*publisher's windmill device resting on base*] | WILLIAM HEINEMANN LTD | MELBOURNE [*square of 4 dots*] LONDON [*square of 4 dots*] TORONTO

Collation: [vi], 306 pp. A–I¹⁶ K¹².
p. [i], half-title; p. [ii], By SOMERSET MAUGHAM [listing 39 works
and the *Collected Plays*]; p. [iii], title; p. [iv], FIRST PUBLISHED 1954 |
PRINTED IN GREAT BRITAIN | AT THE WINDMILL PRESS | KINGSWOOD,
SURREY; p. [v], contents; p. [vi], 2 quotations; pp. 1–306, text.

Binding: Malachite green rough-grained cloth, blocked in blind
on front with author's symbol, on back with publisher's windmill
device, and on spine with a rectangular panel in pimento bordered
with a double frame and gold lettered: TEN | NOVELS | AND | THEIR |
AUTHORS [*these lines in frame*] | W. | SOMERSET | MAUGHAM | HEINE-
MANN.

Advance Proof state: pp. [vi]+1–306. Cream wrappers, printed in
black. 21.5×14.1 cm.

Plain end-papers; all edges cut; leaves measure 21.4×14 cm.

Price: 21s. 10,000 copies were published on 25 October 1954.

Notes: As pointed out in the note to the American edition, these
essays were written as introductions to a reissue of the ten novels.
They were written in a hurry and the author has, on reflection, seen
fit to revise extensively each biography. Considerable new material
has been added, the introduction has been extended, and there is an
interesting new chapter in which the author sums up the whole field of
creative literary activity—a subject that has always held for him a
singular fascination.
    A number of these essays, including the introduction and the
conclusion, were serialised in *The Sunday Times* (*see* D181) and in the
final instalment the Editor describes them as 'one of the most distinguished and successful serials ever to appear in these columns.
The negotiations for the publication of the series in *The Sunday Times*
were carried through by Ian Fleming who was then on its staff, and this
correspondence is in the Berg Collection in the New York Public
Library.
    There was also a Colonial edition issued on the 11 October 1954
at 21s. Reprinted in Heinemann's *Mercury Book* No. 38 (1963).

A70   A WRITER'S NOTEBOOK   1949

a. Preprint edition:
A Writer's | Notebook | BY W. SOMERSET MAUGHAM | Pre-
printed from | COSMOPOLITAN MAGAZINE | Hearst Magazine
Building, New York, N.Y. | 1949

Collation: [viii], 136 pp. [unsigned 1–9⁸].
pp. [i–ii], blank; p. [iii], half-title; p. [iv], LIMITED EDITION;
p. [v], title; p. [vi], "Copyright 1949 by Hearst Magazine Inc." |
"This book is a preprint of the con- | densed version of "A
Writer's | Notebook" being serialised in | Cosmopolitan Magazine.
It is not | for sale. The complete book will | be published in the
fall of 1949 | by Doubleday and Company, Inc. | Printed in the
United States of America | by Knickerbocker Printing Corpora-
tion, New York."; p. [vii], fly-title; p. [viii], blank; pp. 1–133,
text; pp. [134–136], blank.

Binding: Royal blue linen, blocked in gold on front on a dark
blue panel: A Writer's | Notebook | [*star*] | w. SOMERSET MAUGHAM
| Preprinted from | COSMOPOLITAN MAGAZINE; gold-lettered on
spine, reading downwards: MAUGHAM [double-rule] A Writer's
Notebook [*double-rule*] COSMOPOLITAN.
19½ × 14 cm. All edges cut.

Notes: Pp. 1–3 Editor's Preface to Part 1 (Herbert R. Mayes); p. 55
Editor's preface to Part II (Herbert R. Mayes); p. 93 Editor's Preface to
Part III.

This advance condensed version of *The Writer's Notebook* marked
a departure from normal procedure of publication, at least in the case
of this author. The text is not the full text, but is earlier than the
Doubleday edition, being contemporary with the serial publication
in *Cosmopolitan*. Although the book was stated to have been issued in a
limited edition 'not for sale', the edition was very substantial—about
6,000 copies. Later, most were said to have been withdrawn and sent
to military hospitals.

A70   A WRITER'S NOTEBOOK   (1949)

b. First and Trade edition:
W. Somerset Maugham | [*french rule*] | A WRITER'S | NOTEBOOK
| [*publisher's windmill device resting on base*] | WILLIAM HEINEMANN
LTD | MELBOURNE [*square of 4 dots*] LONDON [*square of 4 dots*]
TORONTO

Collation: xvi, 352 pp. [A]⁸ B–M¹⁶.
p. [i], half-title; p. [ii], By w. SOMERSET MAUGHAM [listing 33
non-dramatic and 24 dramatic works]; p. [iii], title; p. [iv],
FIRST PUBLISHED 1949 | PRINTED IN GREAT BRITAIN | AT THE WIND-
MILL PRESS | KINGSWOOD, SURREY; p. [v], dedication: In | Loving
Memory of My Friend | FREDERICK GERALD HAXTON | 1892–

1944; p. [vi], blank; pp. vii–xvi, preface; pp. 1–349, text; pp. [350–352], blank.

Binding: Smooth black cloth, blocked in silver on front with dagger-shaped filigree design incorporating author's symbol and divided at hilt by title: A WRITER'S NOTEBOOK; on spine with triangular filigree design and lettered: A WRITER'S | NOTEBOOK | W. | SOMERSET | MAUGHAM | HEINEMANN; on back author's symbol in blind.

Advance Proof state: pp. xvi+349+[1]+blank leaf. Cream wrappers, printed in black. 21.6+14.1 cm.

Plain end-papers; all edges cut; leaves measure 21.5 × 14 cm.

Price: 12s. 6d. 59,500 copies were published on 3 October 1949.

Notes: There is a later variant state of the first edition dust wrapper without the announcement of 'Maughamiana' on the back inner folder.

A70   A WRITER'S NOTEBOOK   (1949)

c. Limited edition: (separate impression from the same formes).
W. Somerset Maugham | [*spread rule*] | [*in red*] A WRITER'S | NOTEBOOK | [*publisher's windmill device resting on base*] | WILLIAM HEINEMANN LTD | MELBOURNE [*square of 4 dots*] LONDON [*square of 4 dots*] TORONTO

Collation: Same as in the copy described above.
Contents same as in the copy described above, except that the title-page is in black and red and verso of the half-title reads: This Edition of "A Writer's Notebook" | is limited to 1,000 copies and is signed | by the Author. | *Number. . . .*

Binding: Half vellum, navy blue buckram boards, divided by gold rule front and back; on front author's symbol blocked in blind; on spine black cloth label gold-lettered within a single frame: A WRITER'S | NOTEBOOK | W. SOMERSET | MAUGHAM.
Plain end-papers; top edges cut and gilt, other edges uncut and unopened; leaves measure 22.9 × 15½ cm. In slip case.

Price: £2.2. Published simultaneously with the ordinary trade edition, but in printing followed the trade edition. *See* Note to A46b.

A70   A WRITER'S NOTEBOOK   1949

d. American First and Limited edition:
W. SOMERSET MAUGHAM | [*in red*] A Writer's Notebook |
[*author's symbol*] | Garden City, New York | [*in red*] DOUBLEDAY &
COMPANY INC. | 1949

> *Collation:* xvi, 368 pp. [unsigned 1–12¹⁶].
> THIS EDITION IS LIMITED TO ONE THOUSAND | NUMBERED AND
> SIGNED COPIES, OF WHICH | NINE HUNDRED AND EIGHTY-FIVE ARE
> FOR SALE | This is number . . . ; verso, blank, inserted leaf: p. [i],
> half-title; p. [ii], Books by | W. SOMERSET MAUGHAM [listing 52
> titles]; p. [iii], title; p. [iv], COPYRIGHT, 1949, BY W. SOMERSET
> MAUGHAM | ALL RIGHTS RESERVED | PRINTED IN THE UNITED STATES |
> AT | THE COUNTRY LIFE PRESS, GARDEN CITY, N.Y. | FIRST EDITION;
> p. [v], dedication; p. [vi], blank; pp. vii–xvi, preface; pp. 1–367,
> text; p. [368], blank.
> Portrait by Sir Gerald Kelly, inserted.
>
> *Binding:* Red buckram, blocked on front with author's symbol in
> blind: on spine blocked in gold with ornamental borders and thin
> and thick rules and lettered in gold on black within a single
> rectangular frame: A Writer's | Notebook | [*author's symbol*] |
> W. SOMERSET | MAUGHAM | [*and at base in gold on black*] DOUBLEDAY.
> Cream end-papers; top edges gilt, fore and lower edges uncut;
> leaves measure 37 × 16 cm. In slip case.
>
> *Price:* $15. The first and limited edition was published on 20
> October 1949, simultaneously with the trade edition.

A70   A WRITER'S NOTEBOOK   1949

*e. First American and trade edition: (separate impression from the same
formes.)*
W. SOMERSET MAUGHAM | A Writer's Notebook | [*author's
symbol*] | Garden City, New York | DOUBLEDAY & COM-
PANY, INC. | 1949

> *Collation:* xvi, 368 pp. [unsigned 1–12¹⁶].
> p. [i], half-title; p. [ii], Books by | W. SOMERSET MAUGHAM (listing
> 52 titles); p. [iii], title; p. [iv], Copyright, 1949, by W. Somerset
> Maugham | All Rights Reserved | Printed in the United States
> at | The Country Life Press, Garden City, N.Y. | First Edition
> after the printing of a | limited edition of one thousand | num-
> bered and signed copies; p. [v], dedication; p. [vi], blank; pp. vii–
> xvi, preface; pp. 1–367, text; p. [368], blank.

Portrait by Sir Gerald Kelly inserted.

Binding: Black smooth cloth, blocked on front with author's symbol in blind; on spine, blocked in gold at head and tail with ornamental border and thick and thin rules and lettered in gold: A Writer's | Notebook | [*author's symbol*] | w. somerset | maugham. Red end-papers; top edges cut and stained brick red, lower edges cut, fore-edges uncut; leaves measure 21.4×14.6 cm.

Price: $4. Number of copies unknown. First trade edition was published on 20 October 1949 simultaneously with the signed limited edition.

A71   TRIO   (1950)

a. First edition:
Trio | [*ornament*] | *Stories by* W. Somerset Maugham | *Screen adaptation by* | W. Somerset Maugham, R. C. Sherriff | and Noel Langley | [*publisher's windmill device*] | WILLIAM HEINEMANN LTD | MELBOURNE [*square of 4 dots*] LONDON [*square of 4 dots*] TORONTO

Collation: [vi], 146 pp. [A]⁸ B–H⁸ I⁴ K⁸.
p. [i], half-title; p. [ii], By somerset maugham [listing 35 non-dramatic works (including *Trio*) and 6 vols. of the Collected Plays]; p. [iii], title; p. [iv], first published 1950 | printed in great britain | at the windmill press | kingswood, surrey; p. [v], contents and illus.; p. [vi], blank; p. [1], section title; p. [2] 3–145, text; p. [146], blank.

Binding: Signal red linen-grain cloth, blocked in gold on front with author's symbol and on back with publisher's device in blind; gold-lettered on front between triple-rules: Trio; and on spine: maugham | [*triple-rules*] | Trio | heinemann.

Illustrations: Front. port. and 3 plates (stills from the film).
Plain end-papers; all edges cut; leaves measure 19.7×13 cm.

Price: 7s. 6d. 12,500 copies were published on November 13 1950.

Notes: Screen adaptation by W. Somerset Maugham, R. C. Sherriff and Noel Langley. Reprints also the three stories upon which the film is based. *The Verger* from *Cosmopolitans*; *Mr. Know-All* from *Cosmopolitans*; *Sanatorium* from *Creatures of Circumstance*. Mr. Maugham made a personal appearance in the film, introducing each story. These introductions are printed in the book.

There was an odd sequel to the filming of *The Verger*. It appears that a Mr. Konrad Bercovici wrote a story closely similar in the early twenties, and made a claim on the grounds of breach of copyright. Mr. Maugham was rightly indignant, stating that it was strange that he should have waited 30 years (for *The Verger* was published in *Hearst's International Magazine* in 1929) before taking any action. Maugham had actually been told the story by Ivor Back, who was then Head Surgeon at St George's Hospital, but admitted that after the publication in *Hearst's International Magazine* he had received letters from various parts of the world informing him that it was an old Jewish story. The correspondence relating this incident appears in the A. P. Watt correspondence in the Berg Collection in the New York Public Library.

A71 TRIO 1950

b. First American edition:
[*In bold type*] Trio | *Original Stories by* | W. SOMERSET MAUGHAM | *Screenplays by* | W. SOMERSET MAUGHAM | R. C. SHERRIFF | NOEL LANGLEY | *Doubleday & Company, Inc.* | GARDEN CITY, NEW YORK, 1950

Collation: [iv], 156 pp. [unsigned 1–10⁸].
p. [i], half-title; p. [ii], Books by | W. SOMERSET MAUGHAM [listing 52 titles]; p. [iii], title; p. [iv], COPYRIGHT, 1924, 1929, 1938, 1950, BY W. SOMERSET MAUGHAM | ALL RIGHTS RESERVED | PRINTED IN THE UNITED STATES | FIRST EDITION; p. [1], Contents; [2], blank; p. [3], fly-title; p. [4], blank; pp. 5–156, text.

Binding: Black smooth cloth, blocked on front in blind with author's symbol and 3 circles; on spine lettered in gold: W. Somerset Maugham's Trio [*title in black with 3 circles on gold background*] Doubleday.
Plain end-papers; top and lower edges cut, fore-edges rough trimmed; leaves measure 18.7×11.7 cm.

Price: $2.50. First published in December 1950.

A72 THE WRITER'S POINT OF VIEW 1951

First edition:
THE WRITER'S POINT OF VIEW | W. SOMERSET MAUGHAM | LONDON | PUBLISHED FOR THE | NATIONAL BOOK LEAGUE | BY THE CAMBRIDGE UNIVERSITY PRESS | 1951

Collation: 24 pp. 12 leaves in one gathering, signed*.
p. [1], half-title; p. [2], N.B.L. Annual Lectures [listing 7 lectures];
p. [3], title; p. [4], The Ninth Annual Lecture of the National
Book | League, delivered by w. SOMERSET MAUGHAM, | at the
Kingsway Hall, W.C.2. on Wednesday | October 24 1951,
the Right Honourable | SIR NORMAN BIRKETT in the Chair. |
CAMBRIDGE UNIVERSITY PRESS | LONDON: BENTLEY HOUSE, 200
EUSTON ROAD, N.W.I. | NEW YORK: 32 EAST 57TH STREET, NEW
YORK 22 | CANADA: THE MACMILLAN COMPANY OF CANADA | *All
rights reserved*; pp. 5–23, text; p. [24], printer's imprint.

Binding: Stiff cream wrappers, printed on front in red THE |
WRITER'S | POINT OF VIEW | N.B.L. | W. SOMERSET MAUGHAM;
inside and back wrappers blank. Stapled.
All edges cut. 18½ × 12½ cm.

Price: 3s. Number of copies unknown. The first edition was
published in December 1951.

A73   ENCORE   (1952)

a. First edition:
ENCORE | [*ornament*] | *Stories by* W. Somerset Maugham | *Screen
adaptation by* | T. E. B. Clarke, Arthur Macrae | and Eric Ambler |
[*publisher's windmill device*] | WILLIAM HEINEMANN LTD |
MELBOURNE [*square of 4 dots*] LONDON [*square of 4 dots*]
TORONTO

Collation: [viii], 168 pp. [A]⁸ B–L⁸.
pp. [i–ii], blank; p. [iii], half-title; p. [iv], By w. SOMERSET
MAUGHAM [listing 34 non-dramatic works (including *Encore*) and
6 vols. of the Collected Plays]; p. [v], title; p. [vi], FIRST PUB-
LISHED 1951 | PRINTED IN GREAT BRITAIN | AT THE WINDMILL
PRESS | KINGSWOOD, SURREY; p. [vii], contents and illus.; p.
[viii], blank; p. [1], section title; pp. [2] 3–165, text; pp. [166–
168], blank.

Binding: Signal red linen-grain cloth, blocked in gold on front
with author's symbol and on back with publisher's device in
blind; gold-lettered on front between triple-rules: Encore; and
on spine: MAUGHAM | [*triple-rules*] | Encore | HEINEMANN.

Illustrations: Front. port., and 3 plates (stills from the film).
Plain end-papers; all edges cut; leaves measure 19.6 × 13 cm.

Price: 9s. 6d. 15,000 copies were published on 7 January 1952.

Notes: Screen adaptations by T. E. B. Clarke, Arthur Macrae and Eric Ambler. Reprints also the three stories upon which the films are based. *The Ant and the Grasshopper—Winter Cruise—*and *Gigolo and Gigolette*. The author makes a personal appearance in the film, introducing each story. These introductions are printed in the book.

A73   ENCORE   1952

b. First American edition:
[*in bold type*] ENCORE | *Original Stories by* | W. SOMERSET MAUGHAM | *Screen plays by* | T. E. B. CLARKE | ARTHUR MACRAE | ERIC AMBLER | Doubleday & Company, Inc. | GARDEN CITY, NEW YORK, 1952

> *Collation:* [i–ii], 158 pp. [unsigned 1–10⁸].
> pp. [i–ii], blank; p. [1], half-title; p. [2], Books by | w. somerset maugham [listing 54 titles]; p. [3], title; p. [4], Library of Congress Catalog Card Number 52–8052 | COPYRIGHT, 1924, 1935, 1943, 1952, BY W. SOMERSET MAUGHAM | ALL RIGHTS RESERVED | PRINTED IN THE UNITED STATES | AT | THE COUNTRY LIFE PRESS, GARDEN CITY, N.Y. | FIRST EDITION; p. [5], Contents; p. [6], blank; p. [7], fly-title; p. [8], blank; pp. 9–156, text; pp. [157–158], blank.

> *Binding:* Smooth black cloth, blocked in blind on front with author's symbol; on spine, running down, lettered in gold ENCORE [author's symbol] W. Somerset Maugham [*across*] Doubleday.
> Plain end-papers; all edges cut; leaves measure 18.7 × 11.3 cm.

> *Price:* $2.75. The first edition was published in June 1952.
> Copyright copy deposited with Library of Congress June 17 1952.

A74   THE VAGRANT MOOD   (1952)

a. First and Limited edition:
W. Somerset Maugham | [*french rule*] | THE VAGRANT | MOOD | *Six Essays* | [*publisher's windmill device resting on base*] | WILLIAM HEINEMANN LTD | MELBOURNE [*square of 4 dots*] LONDON [*square of 4 dots*] TORONTO
Title in red and black.

> *Collation:* [vi], 242 pp. A⁸⁺² B–O⁸ P⁸⁺². Sigs A and P gatherings of 10 leaves.
> p. [i], half-title; p. [ii], This Edition of "The Vagrant Mood" | is limited to 500 copies and is signed | by the Author. Number . . . ;

p. [iii], title; p. [iv], FIRST PUBLISHED 1952 | PRINTED IN GREAT
BRITAIN | AT THE WINDMILL PRESS | KINGSWOOD, SURREY; p. [v],
contents; p. [vi], author's note; pp. 1–241, text; p. [242], blank.

Binding: Half mushroom calf, navy blue calf boards, divided by
gold rule front and back; on front author's symbol blocked
in blind; on spine black cloth label gold-lettered within a single
frame, broken at top and tail: THE | VAGRANT | MOOD | W. SOMER-
SET | MAUGHAM.
Plain end-papers; top edges cut and gilt, other edges uncut,
unopened; leaves measure 22.8 × 15 cm. In slip case.

Price: £3 3s. The limited edition and the first trade edition were
published simultaneously on 27 October 1952.

A74   THE VAGRANT MOOD   (1952)

b. First Trade edition: (separate impression from the same formes).
THE VAGRANT MOOD | *Six Essays* | by | W. SOMERSET
MAUGHAM | [*publisher's windmill device*] | WILLIAM HEINEMANN
LTD | MELBOURNE [*square of 4 dots*] LONDON [*square of 4 dots*]
TORONTO
    Collation: [vi], 242 pp. [A]⁸ B–O⁸ P⁴ Q⁸.
    Contents same as in the copy described above, except that the
verso of the half-title reads: By w. SOMERSET MAUGHAM listing
33 non-dramatic and 18 dramatic works.

Binding: Pimento red cloth, blocked in blind on front with
author's symbol and on back with publisher's windmill device;
gold-lettered on front: THE VAGRANT MOOD; and on spine: THE |
VAGRANT | MOOD | W. | SOMERSET | MAUGHAM | HEINEMANN.

Advance Proof state: pp. [vi]+241+[1]. Cream wrappers printed in
black; at base: PROOF COPY | FOR YOUR PERSONAL READING.
21.6 × 14 cm.
There are small differences in the list of works by the author
facing the title page and in the note facing first page of text.

Plain end-papers; all edges cut; leaves measure 21½ × 14 cm.

Price: 12s. 6d. 40,000 copies were published on 27 October 1952.

Notes: Three of these essays appeared previously in *The Cornhill*.
The essay *Reflections on a Certain Book* formed a lecture given by
Mr. Maugham at the Philosophical Colloquium of Colombia Univer-
sity under the title *Beauty and the Professor*. It has, however, been re-

written for book form. Part of the final essay appeared in *Life and Letters* (June 1931).

A74   THE VAGRANT MOOD   1953

c. First American edition:
The Vagrant Mood | [*fine and heavy rule*] | SIX ESSAYS BY | W. Somerset Maugham | [*author's symbol*] | GARDEN CITY, N.Y. | Doubleday & Company, Inc. | 1953

> *Collation:* 256 pp. [unsigned 1–8¹⁶].
> Blank leaf not included in pagination; p. [1], blank; p. [2], Books by | W. SOMERSET MAUGHAM [listing 55 titles]; p. [3], half-title; p. [4], blank; p. [5], title; p. [6], *Library of Congress Catalog Card Number* 53–5283 | *First published, 1953, in the United States* | COPYRIGHT, 1949, 1950, 1952, BY W. SOMERSET MAUGHAM | COPYRIGHT, 1933, BY DOUBLEDAY & COMPANY, INC. | COPYRIGHT | 1940, BY THE CURTIS PUBLISHING COMPANY | ALL RIGHTS RESERVED , PRINTED IN THE UNITED STATES | AT | THE COUNTRY LIFE PRESS, GARDEN CITY, N.Y. | FIRST EDITION; p. [7], Contents; p. [8], blank; p. [9], fly-title; p. [10], blank; pp. 11–250, text; pp. [251–254], blank.

> *Binding:* Smooth black linen cloth, blocked in blind on front with author's symbol; on spine blocked and lettered in gold: THE | VAGRANT | MOOD | [*row of ornaments*] | W. | Somerset | Maugham | DOUBLEDAY.
> White end-papers; top and lower edges cut, fore-edges uncut; leaves measure 20.1 × 13.8 cm.

> *Price:* $3. Number of copies unknown. Published December 1953.

A75   THE NOBLE SPANIARD   (1953)

First edition:
ACTING EDITION | The Noble | Spaniard | *A Comedy in Three Acts* | by | W. SOMERSET MAUGHAM | adapted from the French of Grenet-Dancourt | [*publisher's device*] | LONDON | EVANS BROTHERS LIMITED | GENERAL EDITOR: LIONEL HALE [*within a broken-rule border, without a double-rule border*]

> *Collation:* 80 pp. [A]⁸ B–E⁸. Front. port., inserted.
> p. [1], title; p. [2], *First published* 1953 | COPYRIGHT | *Made and printed in Great Britain* | *by W. & J. Mackay & Co. Ltd., Chatham;* p. [3], cast and scenes; p. [4], copyright notice; pp. [5–7], intro-

duction (A. B. Walkley's criticism from *The Times*); p. [8], stage plan; pp. 9–76, text; p. [77], property plot; pp. [78–80], advts.

Binding: Cream pictorial wrappers, printed in cream and blue; on front in black within an oval panel; THE NOBLE | SPANIARD | *A Comedy in Three Acts* | by | w. SOMERSET | MAUGHAM | *from the French* | *by Grenet-Dancourt* | [*outside panel*] *Price 5s. net.*
Inner and outer back wrappers advts.; all edges cut; leaves measure 21.6 × 14 cm.

Notes: The wrappers issue was published in April; in the autumn the book was reissued in hard back in blue cloth, gilt, with dust wrapper at 8s. 6d. They were the same sheets, but slightly cut down.
The Noble Spaniard was written in 1908. The play was first produced at the New Royalty Theatre, London, on 20 March 1909 with Charles Hawtrey and Kate Cutler in the cast.

A76   THE MOON AND SIXPENCE   (1957)

a. First edition:
MUSIC BY JOHN GARDNER | The Moon and | Sixpence | OPERA IN THREE ACTS | *Libretto by* | PATRICK TERRY | *after the novel by* | W. SOMERSET MAUGHAM | *This opera was commissioned by the Sadler's Wells Trust Ltd.*

Collation: 44 pp. Unsigned.
p. [1], copyright note; p. [2], *First Performance Sadler's Wells Theatre* | 24th May, 1957; p. [3], title; p. [4], blank; p. [5], Characters in Order of Appearance; p. [6], description of Scenes; pp. 7–43, text of libretto; p. [44], blank.

Binding: Black stiff wrappers, lettered in yellow on front and back.

Notes: The booklet was sold in the Theatre (5s.) during the run of the Opera.
When the project of making *The Moon and Sixpence* into an opera was first mooted, Maugham wrote to A. P. Watt: 'I know of course there is no money to be made out of making an opera of *The Moon and Sixpence*, but if John Gardner has any talent it would be worth while giving him the rights if he wants them. I don't know how you can find out if the rights are free. I don't even know if Edith Ellis is still alive. I know that Warner Bros. sold the film rights, and the picture was eventually produced with success. I forget the name of the

present owners, but I don't think they would raise any objection to the story being made into an opera.'

When I next met Mr. Maugham soon after the opera had been produced (and so far as I know it was a success) he asked me what I thought of it, and I told him quite truthfully that though the music was written in such a way it sounded off-key, the cumulative effect was extremely impressive and when the curtain came down on the final scene, it left one strangely moved. Maugham listened with interest, but he made no comment.

A77   POINTS OF VIEW   (1958)

a. First edition:

W. SOMERSET MAUGHAM | [*double-rule*] | Points of View | [*publisher's windmill device*] | HEINEMANN | LONDON MEL-BOURNE TORONTO

Collation: [vi], 258 pp. A–G¹⁶ H⁴ I¹⁶.

p. [i], half-title; p. [ii], Books by Somerset Maugham [listing 41 titles; p. [iii], title; p. [iv], William Heinemann Ltd | LONDON MELBOURNE TORONTO | CAPE TOWN AUCKLAND | THE HAGUE | First published 1958 | c by WILLIAM SOMERSET MAUGHAM 1958 | *All rights reserved* | Printed in Great Britain | at The Windmill Press | Kingswood, Surrey; p. [v], contents and acknowledge-ments; p. [vi], publisher's note; pp. 1–255, text; pp. [256–258], blank.

Binding: Green linen grain cloth, blocked in blind on front with author's symbol and on back with publisher's windmill device; gold lettered on front on brick-red panel: Points of View; and on spine: Points | of | View | [*double-rule*] | W. Somerset | Maugham [*these words in a single rectangular frame with a brick-red background*] | HEINEMANN [*in a lozenge-shaped frame at tail with a brick-red back-ground*].

Advance Proof state: pp. [vi]+255 [256]+1 blank. Pale purple wrappers, printed in black and lettered: Uncorrected Proof Copy (not for sale). I have also noticed copies in cream wrappers.

Plain end-papers; all edges cut; leaves measure 21.3 × 14.1 cm.

Price: 21s. 15,000 copies were published on 3 November 1958.

Notes: Prior to publication Heinemann issued one of the essays *The Saint* in pamphlet form, presumably for the use of their travellers. The cover title was as follows: W. SOMERSET MAUGHAM | [double-

rule] | [in red] The Saint | [windmill device] | HEINEMANN | LONDON
MELBOURNE | TORONTO. Grey wrappers. 40p.
*Contents: The Three Novels of a Poet—The Saint—Prose and Dr. Tillotson
—The Short Story—Three Journalists.*

A77 POINTS OF VIEW 1959

b. First American edition:
POINTS OF VIEW | Five Essays by | W. SOMERSET MAUGHAM
| [*spread rule*] | *Garden City, New York* | DOUBLEDAY & COM-
PANY, INC. | 1959

> *Collation:* 288 pp. [unsigned 1–12¹²].
>
> p. [1], half-title; p. [2], blank; p. [3], BOOKS BY W. SOMERSET
> MAUGHAM [listing 61 titles]; p. [4], blank; p. [5], title; p. [6],
> Library of Congress Catalog Card Number 59–6997 | Copyright
> © 1958 by William Somerset Maugham | All Rights Reserved |
> Printed in the United States of America | First Edition; p. [7],
> acknowledgements; p. [8], Author's Note; p. [9], Contents;
> p. [10], blank; p. [11], fly-title; p. [12], blank; p. [13] 14–284,
> text; pp. [285–288], blank.
>
> *Binding:* Black calico grain cloth, blocked on front with broken
> red line and author's symbol in gold; spine blocked with broken
> red line and DOUBLEDAY in red; gold-lettered Points | of | View
> [*with author's name in gold running down spine*] W. SOMERSET
> MAUGHAM.
> Plain end-papers; top and lower edges cut; fore-edges rough
> trimmed; leaves measure 20.7 × 13.9 cm.
>
> *Price:* $4.50. 15,000 copies were published in 1959.

Notes: Mr. Maugham announced that this was the last book he would
ever publish and the publisher's note went on to say 'and since he seems
to have a way of doing what he says he is going to do, we may safely
assume that with this volume of essays he will take his leave of the
reading public and so put an end to a relationship that with "Liza of
Lambeth" began just over sixty years ago.'

A78 PURELY FOR MY PLEASURE (1962)

a. First edition:
PURELY | FOR | MY PLEASURE | [*author's symbol*] | W. SOMER-
SET MAUGHAM | [*publisher's windmill device*] | HEINEMANN |
LONDON MELBOURNE TORONTO

L

Collation: viii, 1–28 pp. Unsigned.
p. [i], half-title; p. [ii], blank; p. [iii], title; p. [iv], William Heinemann Ltd | LONDON MELBOURNE TORONTO | CAPE TOWN AUCKLAND | THE HAGUE | © W. S. Maugham 1962 | © S.P.A.D.E.M., Paris, 1962; plates of works of | Bonnard, Laurencin, Léger, Matisse, Monet | Picasso, Renoir, Rouault, Utrillo, Vuillard. | Made and printed in Great Britain | by William Clowes and Sons, Ltd | London and Beckles | Illustrations printed by | The Curwen Press; pp. v–viii, list of illustrations; pp. 1–28, text. Plates: Col. front., and 37 plates, numbered I–XXXVII.

Binding: Black buckram, blocked in gold, with author's symbol on front and gold-lettered on spine: W. S. MAUGHAM · PURELY FOR MY PLEASURE Heinemann.
Plain end-papers; all edges cut; leaves measure 28.6 × 22.4 cm.

Price: £3 3s. 5,000 copies were published on 9 April 1962.

A78   PURELY FOR MY PLEASURE   (1963 [1962])

b. First American edition:
PURELY FOR MY PLEASURE | [rule] | W. SOMERSET MAUGHAM | [*Coloured portrait of Maugham*]

Collation: [1–14] 15–92 [93–96] pp. Unsigned.
p. [1], author's symbol in black; p. [2], blank; p. [3], half-title; p. [4], author's symbol | DOUBLEDAY & COMPANY, INC., GARDEN CITY, NEW YORK, 1963; p. [5], title-page; p. [6], S.P.A.D.E.M., PARIS, 1962: PLATES OF WORKS OF | BONNARD, LAURENCIN, LÉGER, MATISSE, MONET, | PICASSO, RENOIR, ROUAULT, UTRILLO, VUILLARD. | [*rule*] | LIBRARY OF CONGRESS CATALOG CARD NUMBER 62–15961 | COPYRIGHT © 1962 BY W. SOMERSET MAUGHAM | ALL RIGHTS RESERVED | ILLUSTRATIONS PRINTED IN GREAT BRITAIN | TEXT PRINTED IN THE UNITED STATES OF AMERICA | FIRST EDITION IN THE UNITED STATES OF AMERICA: pp. [7–8], blank; p. [9–11], Illustrations; p. [12], blank; p. 13, fly-title; p. [14], blank; pp. 15–92, text; p. [93], author's symbol; pp. [94–96], blank.

Binding: Purple paper boards, with black cloth spine, blocked on front in gold with author's symbol; on spine in gold running down PURELY FOR MY PLEASURE [*vertical rule*] W. SOMERSET MAUGHAM [*vertical rule*] DOUBLEDAY.

Price: $20. The first edition was published in December 1962.

B

COLLECTED EDITIONS

THE COLLECTED WORKS OF W. SOMERSET MAUGHAM

The publication of the definitive edition of W. Somerset Maugham's works commenced with the issue of the author's selected 18 plays in six volumes in 1931, and was followed at intervals by the novels, short stories and travel books. There is still one or two books to come.

This was not intended to be a complete edition. As Mr. Maugham pointed out, he had chosen to put into it only those books and plays with which he was least dissatisfied. For the remarkable thing about this author is that he was not a born writer, perhaps not even a creative one in the D. H. Lawrence and Joseph Conrad sense. But like the famous short story writer that he so much admired, Guy de Maupassant, he was a very great craftsman and he acquired his skill by sheer dogged perseverance and hard work, and a determination to succeed. I cannot think of another writer who attained stardom after writing so many bad books. Mr. Maugham was fully aware of his deficiencies in this respect, and probably this accounted for his determination only to include those books which he wished to be remembered by; the others, as he stated in *The Summing Up*, he would have given much to suppress.

However, since his death a number of his early books have been added to the series, and presumably it is the intention of his publishers to include those that have so far not been reprinted since their first appearance.

Mr. Maugham always took an active interest in the formation of the series. Each work is printed as it was written, subject to certain revisions and corrections which are referred to in the preface to each volume of the plays and to the early volumes of the non-dramatic works. These prefaces contain much new information of considerable biographical and bibliographical importance.

The publishers list the volumes in the *Collected Edition* with a number, but since the numbering appears to vary and there are some duplications, it would seem preferable to list them chronologically. A number of the volumes, particularly the later ones, have no preface or introduction.

B1   DRAMATIC WORKS   1931–1934

The format is crown 8vo; issued in smooth chestnut cloth, with author's symbol in gold on front: on spine blocked and lettered in gold between double-rules; publisher's windmill device on back lower right-hand corner. Size 18.4 × 12.3 cm. In earlier volumes top edges trimmed and stained dark brown, other edges cut. White end-papers. Price 5s.

Vol. I

Lady Frederick; Mrs. Dot; Jack Straw. 1931. Preface 7 pp. 1 blank leaf+pp. xi+[i]+271+1 blank leaf.
2,000 copies were published on 24 August 1931.

Vol. II

Penelope; Smith; The Land of Promise. 1931. Preface 9 pp. 1 blank leaf+pp. xiii+[i]+310+1 blank leaf.
2,000 copies were published on 24 August 1931.

Vol. III

Our Betters; The Unattainable; Home and Beauty. 1932. Preface 7 pp. pp. xi+[i]+324.
2,000 copies were published on 15 August 1932.

Vol. IV

The Circle; The Constant Wife; The Breadwinner. 1932. Preface 7 pp. pp. xi+[i]+296.
2,000 copies were published on 15 August 1932.

Vol. V

Caesar's Wife; East of Suez; The Sacred Flame. 1934. Preface 8½ pp. 1 blank leaf+pp. xiii+[i]+319+[1].
2,000 copies were published on 19 March 1934.

Vol. VI

The Unknown; For Services Rendered; Sheppey. 1934. Preface 9 pp. 1 blank leaf+pp. xiii+[i]+304.
2,000 copies were published on 19 March 1934.

B2   NON-DRAMATIC WORKS   1934–69

The format is crown 8vo: issued in maroon or rose cloth, author's symbol blind-blocked on front: blocked in gold on spine with double-rules at head and base, or head only, and gold-lettered; publisher's windmill device blind-blocked on back lower right-hand corner. Size 18.4 × 12.4 cm. All edges cut. White end-papers.

Liza of Lambeth. 1934. Preface 21 pp.
pp. xxv+[iii]+171+[1].
Preface expanded from *The Traveller's Library* edition.

Ashenden. 1934. Preface 6 pp.
1 blank leaf+pp. x+[ii]+304+1 blank leaf.

The Painted Veil. 1934. Preface 5 pp.
pp. xi+[iii]+286.
This edition was reissued in 1949 when the author also re-wrote the last paragraph.

Cakes and Ale. 1934. Preface 6 pp.
1 blank leaf (not incl. in pagination)+pp. x+[ii]+270.

The Narrow Corner. 1934. Preface 4 pp.
pp. x+293+[1]

The Moon and Sixpence. 1935. Preface 6 pp.
1 blank leaf (not incl. in pagination)+pp. x+308.

On a Chinese Screen. 1935. Preface 4 pp.
pp. xii+228.

The Gentleman in the Parlour. 1935. Preface 4 pp.
1 blank leaf (not incl. in pagination)+pp. viii+[ii]+300.

The Trembling of a Leaf. 1935. Preface 4 pp.
1 blank leaf+pp. xiv+295+[1].

The Casuarina Tree. 1935.
pp. 311.
New edition, 1953. pp. viii, 232.

Ah King. 1936. Preface 6 pp.
1 blank leaf+pp. xii+335+[1]+1 blank leaf.

First Person Singular. 1936. Preface 5 pp.
pp. xi+[i]+307+[1].

Mrs. Craddock. 1937. Preface 3 pp.
pp. x+302. *See* **A5d**.

Of Human Bondage. 1937. Preface 4 pp.
1 blank leaf+viii+941+[1].

Don Fernando. 1937. Preface 3 pp.
pp. vii+[i]+251+[1]. *See* **A49d**.

Cosmopolitans. 1938. Preface 7 pp.
pp. xiii+[iii]+302+1 blank leaf.

Theatre. 1939. Preface 7 pp.
pp. xii+293+[1].

Christmas Holiday. 1941.
pp. [vi]+289+[1].

The Summing Up. 1948.
1 blank leaf+pp. [iv]+305+[1].

The Razor's Edge. 1949.
pp. [vi]+284+1 blank leaf.

Creatures of Circumstance. 1950.
1 blank leaf+pp. [vi]+310+1 blank leaf.

Catalina. 1948.
pp. [iv]+256.

A Writer's Notebook. 1951.
pp. xiii+[i]+297+[1].

The Magician. 1956. Preface 7 pp.
pp. xi+[i]+233+[1]. *See* **11e**.

Then and Now. 1959.
pp. [iv]+252.

Up at the Villa.
pp. [iv]+247.

The Explorer. 1967.
pp. [iv]+250.

The Merry-Go-Round. 1969.
p. [viii]+398.

B3   EAST AND WEST   1934

East and West. The Collected Short Stories of W. Somerset Maugham.
Garden City, New York, Doubleday, Doran & Company Inc. 1934.
1 blank leaf, not included in pagination+pp. xxiv+956+blank leaf.
The first edition was published on 8 August 1934. $3.

B4   ALTOGETHER   (1934)

Altogether. Being the Collected Stories of W. Somerset Maugham.
London, William Heinemann Ltd. (1934).
1 blank leaf, not included in pagination+pp. xxxiv+1,522+10

unnumbered pages, but forming part of last signature, containing Desmond MacCarthy's *Appreciation*.

15,000 copies of the first English edition was published on 20 August 1934. Price 8s. 6d.

Note: Altogether is the English title of *East and West*. A number of copies of the English edition lack the Maugham symbol on the upper cover. The publisher states that it was omitted 'probably from the first dozen early copies,' but all the Statutory libraries' copies are without the symbol and of the 30 odd copies I have examined in at least half of them the upper covers were blank. It is certain, therefore, that a considerably larger number than a dozen copies got into circulation, and they are not at all scarce. The colour of the cloth varies considerably from maroon to brownish red, but there is no evidence to suggest that copies in any one shade were issued earlier than the other. The edition was a very large one and more than one binder was employed. The book contains an important new 26 pp. preface on the art of the short story. The American edition lacks the MacCarthy *Appreciation*.

Copies exist with a misprint in the list of works facing the title-page. The publisher states that although this misprint was noticed it was not corrected. It must therefore be assumed that it occurred late in the run, as copies with the misprint are scarce.

Contents

Stories reprinted from *The Trembling of a Leaf—The Casuarina Tree—Ashenden—First Person Singular—Ah King.*

B5   TAUCHNITZ EDITION   1922–1935

(4585) The Trembling of a Leaf, 1922: (4690) The Painted Veil, 1925: (4841) Ashenden, or The British Agent, 1928: (4842) The Casuarina Tree, 1928: (4978) Cakes and Ale, 1931: (5026) The Moon and Sixpence, 1932: (5032) Six Stories Written in the First Person Singular, 1932: (5098) The Narrow Corner, 1933: (5138) Ah King, 1934: (5228) Don Fernando, 1936: (5295) Theatre, 1937: (5339) The Summing Up, 1938: (5253) Cosmopolitan, 1940: PLAYS: (5124) Lady Frederick: Mrs. Dot; Jack Straw, 1933: (5132) Penelope; Smith; The Land of Promise, 1934: (5145) Our Betters; The Unattainable; Home and Beauty, 1934: (5152) The Circle; The Constant Wife; The Bread Winner, 1934: (5180) Ceasar's Wife; East of Suez; The Sacred Flame, 1935: (5187) The Unknown; For Services Rendered; Sheppey, 1935.

B6   THE COLLECTED WORKS   1936–1938

Pocket Edition (William Heinemann Ltd.):
Ashenden, 1936; Cakes and Ale, 1936; Liza of Lambeth, 1936; On a
Chinese Screen, 1936; The Painted Veil, 1936; The Trembling of a
Leaf, 1936; The Narrow Corner, 1936; The Gentleman in the Parlour,
1936; The Moon and Sixpence, 1936; First Person Singular, 1936;
Ah King, 1936; Don Fernando, 1936; Cosmopolitans, 1938; Mrs.
Craddock, 1938.

Note: A beautiful little edition in green smooth cloth, that has become
very scarce. Only 16 titles appeared, further volumes being held up
owing to war conditions.
   The prefaces in this edition are identical to those in the *Collected
Edition.*

B7   PENGUIN BOOKS   1944–1970

Penguin Books in association with William Heinemann Ltd, Harmondsworth.

   468   The Moon and Sixpence. 1944. pp. 192. 9d.
         Also published by Harmondsworth, New York, with a portrait.

   651   Cakes and Ale. 1948. pp. 202.

   872   The Painted Veil. 1952. pp. 238. 2s. 6d.

   1852   The Summing Up. 1963. pp. 202. 3s. 6d.

   1859   The Narrow Corner. 1963. pp. 217. 3s. 6d.

   1860   The Razor's Edge. 1963. pp. 313. 3s. 6d.

   1861   Of Human Bondage. 1963. pp. 607. 6s.

   2643   Liza of Lambeth. 1967. pp. 125. 3s. 6d.

   2644   A Writer's Notebook. 1967. pp. 332. 5s.

   2645   Mrs. Craddock. 1967. pp. 255. 5s.

   2646   Christmas Holiday. 1967. pp. 251. 5s.

   2647   Then and Now. 1967. pp. 215. 5s.

   2668   The Magician. 1967. pp. 199. 3s. 6d.

   2669   Theatre. 1967. pp. 231. 5s.

   2670   Up at the Villa. 1967. pp. 94. 5s.

   2671   Catalina. 1967. pp. 239. 5s.

2905   Ten Novels and their Authors. 1969. pp. 301. 7s. 6d.

2906   The Explorer. 1969. pp. 204. 5s.

3373   The Merry-go-Round. 1972. pp. 340. 40p.

1871–74   Collected Short Stories. 4 vols. 1963. 5s.

PL43   Selected Plays. Sheppey—The Sacred Flame—The Circle—
       The Constant Wife—Our Betters. 1963. pp. 447. 5s.

B8   SAMUEL FRENCH'S ACTING EDITION   1948–51
                         OF PLAYS

239   Sheppey. A play in three acts. 1948. pp. 88. 4s.

268   The Circle. A comedy in three acts. 1948. pp. 70. 4s.

273   The Breadwinner. 1948. pp. 74. 4s.

274   Lady Frederick. 1948. pp. 78. 4s.

307   The Letter. A play in three acts. (1949). pp. 58. 4s.

316   The Constant Wife. 1949. pp. 70. 4s.

394   For Services Rendered. 1948. pp. 70. 4s.

396   The Sacred Flame. 1948. pp. 69. 4s.

1812   Home and Beauty. A farce in three acts. (1951). pp. 72. 4s.

B9   HERON BOOKS   1967–1969

The format is crown 8vo: a well produced edition of the complete
works of this author bound in deep blue skivertex, tooled in gold,
with bevelled edges, rounded corners, golden pattened endpapers,
silken headbands and silken bookmark, the author's symbol in gold
in a panel on front cover. All the volumes are specially illustrated,
with a frontispiece portrait of the author. The edition is a production
of Edito-Service S.A. of Geneva, and distributed in this country by
Heron Books. (In progress.) 24s. for subscribers to the series.

Liza of Lambeth: On a Chinese Screen. Original illustrations by
   Jeffery Frith. 1967. pp. [1–10] 11–382. 8 plates.

Of Human Bondage. Original illustrations by Charles Keeping.
   2 vols. (1967). pp. 478: 477. 8 plates: 8 plates.

Moon and Sixpence. With a General Introduction by John Raymond.
   Original illustrations by Ralph Brown. 1967. pp. xxiii, 251. 6 plates.

Cakes and Ale, or The Skeleton in the Cupboard. Original illustrations by Peter Snow. (1967). pp. xii, 267. 6 plates.

The Explorer: The Land of the Blessed Virgin. Original illustrations by Sandra Archibald. (1968). pp. 485. 10 plates.

Cosmopolitans. Original illustrations by Geoffrey Plant. (1968). pp. xi, 287. 8 plates.

The Mixture as Before. Original illustrations by Charles Keeping. (1968). pp. xi, 293. 7 plates.

Theatre. Original illustrations by Janina Ede. (1968). pp. xv, 293. 7 plates.

Creatures of Circumstance. Original illustrations by Pauline Ellison. (1968). pp. [viii], 309. 7 plates.

The Razor's Edge. Illustrations by David Knight. (1968). pp. [viii], 303. 7 plates.

Ashenden. Original illustrations by Robert Micklewright. (1968). pp. xxi, 247. 6 plates.

The Painted Veil. Illustrations by A. C. S. Laszlo. 1968. pp. 307. 7 plates.

The Merry-go-round. Original illustrations by Geoffrey Plant. 1969. pp. [5] 6–398. 9 plates.

The Vagrant Mood: Ten Novels, and their Authors. Illustrations. (1969). pp. [5] 6–556. 5 plates.

Orientations. Original illustrations by Frances Howes. 1969. pp. 266. 8 plates.

Ah King. Original illustrations by Andre Nicholas Suter. 1969. pp. xiv, 335. 10 plates.

A Writer's Notebook. Illustrations. (1969). pp. xv, 297. 7 plates.

The Narrow Corner: The Casuariana Tree. Original illustrations by Graham Byfield. 1968. pp. 491. 11 plates.

First Person Singular. Six Stories. Original illustrations by David Knight. (1968). pp. xii, 307. 6 plates.

Up at the Villa: Don Fernando. Original illustrations by Jutta Ash. (1968). pp. 413. 8 plates.

Mrs. Craddock. Original illustrations by C. A. M. Thole. 1968. pp. 338. 8 plates.

Christmas Holiday. Original illustrations by Sydney Harpley. (1969). pp. 289. 7 plates.

The Magician: The Gentleman in the Parlour. Original illustrations by Jane Darrington. pp. 413. 8 plates.

Catalina: Then and Now. Original illustrations by Michael Charlton. pp. 503. 12 plates.

The Trembling of a Leaf. Original illustrations by William Papas. pp. 295. 9 plates.

Plays, by W. Somerset Maugham: in three volumes.
> Vol. 1. Original illustrations by John Ward. 1969. pp. xxiii, 582. 7 plates.
> Vol. 2. Original illustrations by Peter Whiteman. 1969. pp. xxi, 620. 10 plates.

B10   SIX COMEDIES   (1937)

Six Comedies.
New York, Garden City Publishing Company, Inc.
1 blank leaf+pp. xiii+[i]+535+[1]. Black matt cloth, blocked in red.

Note: Contains a new 6½ pp. preface by the author. *The Unattainable* and *Home and Beauty* are published here for the first time in America.

Contents

The Unattainable—Home and Beauty—The Circle—Our Betters—The Constant Wife—The Bread Winner.

B11   THE FAVOURITE SHORT STORIES OF
                    W. SOMERSET MAUGHAM

The Favourite Short Stories of W. Somerset Maugham.
Garden City, New York, Doubleday, Doran. 1937.
pp. [ii]+xx+ii+464.

Note: Reprinted in 1940 by the *Book League of America.*

Contents

Rain—The Letter—Before the Party—The Outstation—Round Dozen—The Hairless Mexican—Guilia Lazzari—Mr. Harrington's Washing—The Human Element—The Alien Corn—The Vessel of Wrath—The Door of Opportunity—Neil McAdam.

B12   THE ROUND DOZEN   (1939)

The Round Dozen. A Collection of his Stories Selected by W.
Somerset Maugham.
London, The Reprint Society, (1939).
pp. [vi]+634.

Contents

*Rain—The Outstation—The Round Dozen—The Letter—The Alien
Corn—The Creative Impulse—Mr. Harrington's Washing—The Door
of Opportunity—Neil Macadam—The Vessel of Wrath—The Force of
Circumstances.*

B13   THE SOMERSET MAUGHAM SAMPLER   1943

The Somerset Maugham Sampler. Edited with an introduction by
Jerome Weidman.
Garden City, New York, Garden City Publishing Co. (1943).
pp. xxi+[i]+489.

Contents

Cakes and Ale—The Circle—Short Stories—Travel Sketches—Essays;
all previously published. Reprinted under title *The Somerset Maugham
Pocket Book*.

B14   HERE AND THERE   (1948)

Here and there: Short Stories by W. Somerset Maugham.
London, William Heinemann. (1948).
30,000 copies were published on 20 Sepetember 1948. Simultaneously,
The Reprint Society (London) issued the book as their monthly
choice.

Contents

All these stories appeared in *Cosmopolitans*, *The Mixture as Before* and
Creatures of Circumstance.

B15   EAST OF SUEZ   1948

East of Suez. Great Stories of the Tropics.
New York, Avon Publishing Co. 1948.
pp. 124.
Excerpts from *On a Chinese Screen*, and short stories from *The Casuarina
Tree*.

B16   THE MAUGHAM READER   1950

The Maugham Reader. With an Introduction by Glenway Wescott.
Garden City, N.Y., Doubleday & Company, Inc. 1950.
pp. xxvi+[ii]+1217+[3]. Front. portrait.

Apart from the ordinary trade edition of this book, there was also
what is called The Villa Mauresque Edition, a 'Presentation Edition,
Not for Sale' which the publishers handed out to book-sellers. The
principle feature of it is the reproduction on the free front endpaper
(repeated on the back lining paper pasted down) of Mr. Maugham's
letter of appreciation to booksellers generally. It begins 'Both as an
author and as a reader I am glad to have this opportunity to pay my
respects and send a cordial greeting to the booksellers to whom Doubleday & Co. are presenting this special edition. An author wishes to
reach as many readers as he can and on that account I for my part
welcome inexpensive reprints of my books so that no one who cares to
read them at all should be prevented from doing so because he cannot
afford to buy them. I know how much the bookseller can do for a
book he thinks well of, and I am grateful to those—and they are
many—whose efforts have been largely instrumental in obtaining the
not inconsiderable circulation (to put it modestly) that mine have
enjoyed. . . . The perfect bookseller is the reader's best friend.'

  This Presentation Edition was also issued with a different dust-
wrapper.

Contents

*The Painted Veil—Jane—The Opium Addict—The Facts of Life—Rain—
The Treasure—The Outstation—The French Governor—Our Betters—
The Summing Up—The Constant Wife—Red—A String of Beads—
The Door of Opportunity—September's Bird—The Alien Corn—The
Round Dozen—The Vessel of Wrath—Christmas Holiday—El Greco.*

B17   THE COMPLETE SHORT STORIES OF   (1951)
                          W. SOMERSET MAUGHAM

The Complete Short Stories of W. Somerset Maugham. 3 vols.
London, William Heinemann. (1951).
Vol. I. pp. viii+528. 20,000 copies were published on 8 October
1951. Vol. 2. pp. viii+529–1048. 15,000 copies were published on
3 December 1951. Vol. III. pp. viii+1049–1576. 15,000 copies were
published on 10 December 1951. All at 12s. 6d.

Note: These three volumes are the definitive edition of Mr. Maugham's
short stories and include those published after the appearance of *East*

and West. Each volume contains a new preface by the author. and he has himself arranged the order in which the stories appear.

B18   THE COLLECTED PLAYS OF   (1952)
          W. SOMERSET MAUGHAM

The Collected Plays of W. Somerset Maugham. 3 vols.
London, William Heinemann. (1952).
Vol. I. pp. xxi+[i]+310. 10,000 copies were published on 23 June 1952. Vol. II. pp. xix+[i]+296. 10,000 copies were published on 23 June 1952. Vol. III. pp. xxii+[i]+304. 10,000 copies were published on 25 June 1952. All at 15s.

Note: The Collected Plays were originally published in 1931–34 in six volumes. In this new edition the same eighteen plays are contained in three volumes, with six plays in each. The prefaces written by Mr. Maugham for the first edition are contained in the new edition just as he originally wrote them, except that the new arrangement has necessitated slight adjustments and revisions. These volumes are of the same size and format as the collected edition of his short stories.

B19   THE WORLD OVER   1952

The World Over; Stories of Manifold Places and People.
Garden City, N.Y., Doubleday. 1952.
pp. xv+[i]+681+[1].
A collection of stories, all previously published, and which were not contained in *East and West.* The volume contains a new eight page preface in which the author says 'I have written my last story.'

Contents

The Mixture as Before—Creatures of Circumstance—Cosmopolitans— three stories from *On a Chinese Screen* and four from *The Gentleman in the Parlour.*

B20   THE COMPLETE SHORT STORIES OF   1952
          W. SOMERSET MAUGHAM

The Complete Short Stories of W. Somerset Maugham. 2 vols.
Garden City, N.Y., Doubleday. 1952.
Vol. I. pp. xx+955+[1]. Vol. II. pp. xv+[i]+681+[1].
Volume I reprints *East and West*, and Vol. II reprints *The World Over.*

B21   THE SELECTED NOVELS OF   (1953)
                   W. SOMERSET MAUGHAM

The Selected Novels of W. Somerset Maugham. 3 vols.
London, William Heinemann. (1953).
Vol. 1. pp. (xvi) [paged xii+(ii)]+(94)+(2)+160+(2)+(206). Vol. II.
pp. (xvi) [paged xii+(ii)]+180+(2)+178+(2)+(182). Vol. III.
pp. (xiv) [paged xii+(ii)]+202+(2)+74+(2)+(286). 25,000 copies of
each volume were published on 30 November 1953.
Each novel separately paginated.

Note: The new preface to each volume contains important material of
biographical and bibliographical interest. Identical format with the
Plays and *Short Stories.*

B22   THE PARTIAL VIEW   (1954)

The Partial View.
London, William Heinemann. (1954).
pp. xii+[ii]+292. 12,000 copies were published on 27 Sepetember.

Note: Contains the two autobiographical works, *The Summing Up*
and *A Writer's Notebook*, with an extremely interesting new preface
(5½ pp.) presenting the author's philosophical view-point at the end
of his professional life.

B23   MR. MAUGHAM HIMSELF   ·(1954)

Mr. Maugham Himself. Selected by John Beecroft.
Garden City, N.Y., Doubleday. (1954).
pp. x+688.

Note: This volume contains *Of Human Bondage*—four short pieces:
Some Novelists I Have Known (from *The Vagrant Mood*), *Mr. Harrington's
Washing* (from *Ashenden*), *The Book Bag* (from *Ah King*), *El Greco* (from
Don Fernando), *The Summing Up* (from *A Writer's Notebook*).

B24   THE ART OF FICTION   (1954)–1955

The Art of Fiction: an Introduction to Ten Novels and their Authors.
Garden City, New York, Doubleday. 1955.
pp. 318.

Note: This is the first American edition of *Ten Novels and Their
Authors* which in turn was a revision and enlargement *of Great Novelists
and their Novels* first published in Philadelphia by John C. Winston in
1948. *Stanford University Library Cat.* (1958).

B25   THE TRAVEL BOOKS   (1955)

The Travel Books of W. Somerset Maugham.
London, William Heinemann. (1955).
pp. xv [xvi]+148+170+146. 10,000 copies were published 28
November 1955. 15s.

Advance Proof state: pp. [vi] vii–xv (v. blank)+[1–3] 4–146. White
wrappers, printed in green. 19.6×13 cm.

Note: Contains *On a Chinese Screen, Gentleman in the Parlour* and
Don Fernando with a new, long introduction (8½ pp.). Identical format
with the *Short Stories, Plays* and *Novels.*
An offset of the 'Preface' was issued prior to the publication of the
book (8 pp.), probably for the use of the publishers' travellers.

B26   THE BEST SHORT STORIES OF   (1957)
                    SOMERSET MAUGHAM

The Best Short Stories of Somerset Maugham. Selected, and with an
Introduction, by John Beecroft.
New York, The Modern Library. (1957). (*The Modern Library of the
World's Best Books, No.* 14).
pp. xi, 489.

Contents

*Alien Corn—The Book-Bag—Door of Opportunity—The Colonel's
Lady—Facts of Life—The Hairless Mexican—The Letter—Lord Mount-
drago—Mr. Harrington's Washing—Mr. Know-All—'P. & O.'— Rain—
Red—Round Dozen—The Treasure—The Verger—Vessel of Wrath—
Voice of the Turtle.*

B27   THE KITE AND OTHER STORIES   (1963)

The Kite and Other Stories. Introduced by Ian Serraillier.
London, William Heinemann. (1963). (*The New Windmill Series*).
pp. x, 133.

Contents

*Home—A Man from Glasgow—The Man with a Scar—The Traitor—
The Verger—A Friend in Need—The Kite—Salvatore—Mabel—A
Marriage of Convenience.*

B28   HUSBANDS AND WIVES   (1963)

Husbands and Wives. Nine Stories. Selected, and with an Introduction by Richard A. Cordell.

M

New York, Pyramid Publications. (1963). (*Pyramid Books*).
pp. 174.

Contents

Introduction—Mr. Know-All—The Kite—The Book-Bag—Jane—The Creative Impulse—The Colonel's Lady—The Social Sense—The Happy Couple—A Woman of Fifty.

B29   THE SINNERS   (1964)

The Sinners. Six Stories. Selected, and with an Introduction by Richard A. Cordell.
New York, Pyramid Publication. (1964). (*Pyramid Books.*)
pp. 174.

Contents

Introduction: Murder Without Regret—Before the Party—A Man with a Conscience—A Point of Law—The Letter—The Hairless Mexican—Giulia Lazzari.

B30   SELECTED PREFACES AND INTRODUCTIONS (1963)

Selected Prefaces and Introductions of W. Somerset Maugham.
Garden City, New York, Doubleday & Company Inc. 1963.
pp. [viii]+160.

B31   SELECTED PREFACES AND INTRODUCTIONS (1964)

Selected Prefaces and Introductions of W. Somerset Maugham.
London, William Heinemann. (1964).
pp. [viii]+152.

Note: An indifferent selection from the many absorbing introductions and prefaces written by W. Somerset Maugham to his own and other writer's work over the last forty years.

B32   A MAUGHAM TWELVE   (1966)

A Maugham Twelve. Stories selected and with an Introduction by Angus Wilson.
London, William Heinemann. (1966).
pp. x+340.

Contents

The Three Fat Women of Antibes—Mackintosh—The Lotus Eater—The

*Yellow Streak—Before the Party—Rain—Mr. Harrington's Washing—
The Force of Circumstance—Footprints in the Jungle—A Man with a
Conscience—'P. & O.'—Virtue.*

B33   CAKES AND ALE: 1967
                 AND TWELVE SHORT STORIES

Cakes and Ale, and Twelve Short Stories. Selected and with an
Introduction by Angus Wilson.
Garden City, New York, Doubleday. 1967.
pp. 512. Col. illus.

Note: Contents the same as above, except for the addition of the novel
Cakes and Ale.

B34   ESSAYS ON LITERATURE   (1967)

Essays on Literature.
New York and London, The New English Library Limited in association with William Heinemann Ltd. (1967). (*N.E.L. Signet Modern
Classics, 5027*).
pp. 192.

Contents

*The Three Novels of a Poet—After Reading Burke—The Short Story—
Some Novelists I have Known—The Detective and Fall of the Detective
Story—*from: *Ten Novels and their Authors.*

B35   MAUGHAM'S MALAYSIAN STORIES   1969

Maugham's Malaysian Stories. Selected and with an Introduction by
Anthony Burgess.
Singapore, Heinemann's Educational Books (Asia). 1969.
pp. xix+186.

B36   SEVENTEEN LOST STORIES   1969

Seventeen Lost Stories by W. Somerset Maugham. Compiled, and
with an Introduction by Craig V. Showalter.
Garden City, New York, Doubleday. 1969.
pp. x+273.

Note: According to a news item in *The Times* 29 April 1969 'Dr.
Showalter spent about two years tracking down the early stories.' If
he had consulted this bibliography, originally published in 1956, he
would have found all the so-called 'lost' seventeen stories without

stirring from his chair. As for Mr. Ken McCormick's remark, also quoted in *The Times*, that the discovery of the stories was 'like hearing early Beethoven—you could see the writer emerging,' Mr. Maugham told me he thought them all trivial and not worth republishing—hence why—with the exception of *The Mother* (*see* **C61**)—they were never republished in his lifetime.

Contents

Punctiliousness of Don Sebastian—A Bad Example—De Amicitia— Faith—The Choice of Amyntas—Daisy—Cupid and the Vicar of Swale— Lady Habart—Pro Patria—A Point of Law—An Irish Gentleman— Flirtation—The Fortunate Painter—A Marriage of Convenience—Good Manners—Cousin Amy—The Happy Couple.

B37   A BAKER'S DOZEN   (1969)

A Baker's Dozen. Thirteen Short Stories.
London, Heinemann. (1970).
pp. [iv]+291.

Contents

'P. & O.'—The Back of Beyond—A Casual Affair—The Letter—Before the Party—Louise—The Creative Impulse—A Woman of Fifty—The Three Fat Women of Antibes—Episode—The Fall of Edward Barnard— Lord Mountdrago—A Man with a Conscience.

B38   A SECOND BAKER'S DOZEN   (1970)

A Second Baker's Dozen. Thirteen Short Stories.
London, Heinemann. (1970).
pp. [iv]+367.

Note: The above two books were published during the run of the television dramatisations of his short stories by the B.B.C.

Contents

Footprints in the Jungle—The Book Bag—The Force of Circumstance— The Door of Opportunity—Jane—The Closed Shop—Rain—The Alien Corn—Flotsam—Jetsam—The Unconquered—Virtue—The Vessel of Wrath —The Human Element.

B39   W. SOMERSET MAUGHAM: (1970)
                          FOUR SHORT STORIES

W. Somerset Maugham: Four Short Stories. Illustrated with Drawings by Henri Matisse.

Kansas City, Mass., Hallmark Cards Inc. (1970).
p. 62. Front., and 4 illus.

Contents

The Ant and the Grasshopper—The Verger—Mr. Know-All—The Colonel's Lady.

C

BOOKS AND PAMPHLETS
EDITED, OR WITH CONTRIBUTIONS
BY
W. SOMERSET MAUGHAM

C1 QUEEN ALEXANDRA SANATORIUM, DAVOS (1909)

Queen Alexandra Sanatorium, Davos. Souvenir and Programme of Matinee. Edited by Arthur Croxton. Theatre Royal, Drury Lane. (Generously lent by Mr. Arthur Collins and the Directors.) Tuesday, 11 May 1909.

The first appearance in print of a scene from the Third Act of *Lady Frederick* by W. S. Maugham.

C2 THE BEST SHORT STORIES OF 1924 (1925)

The Best Short Stories of 1924. 1. English. Edited by Edward J. O'Brien and John Cournos.
London, Jonathan Cape Ltd. (1925).

Reprints *In a Strange Land* from *Cosmopolitan*. First appearance in book form.

C3 THE QUEEN'S DOLL'S HOUSE LIBRARY (1924)

The Book of the Queen's Doll's House Library. Edited by E. V. Lucas.
London, Methuen & Co. (1924).

An invitation was sent to many men of letters to contribute to the shelves of the Library and the request was accompanied by 'a little blank book in which the author was to write, as small as he could, with his own hand. ...' Most of these that contained new matter were printed in full in the above volume and among them was Somerset Maugham's *The Princess and the Nightingale*, pp. 242–249. A facsimile of one page of the MS. appears on p. 272. *The Book of the Queen's Doll's House* was published in a limited edition in two volumes. This is the second volume under the above title.

There was also an ordinary trade edition, much abridged, in one volume.

C4 THE TRUTH AT LAST (1924)

The Truth at Last. By Sir Charles Hawtrey. Edited by W. Somerset Maugham.
London, Thornton Butterworth. (1924).

With an introduction (4 pp.) by Somerset Maugham.

C5   WORLD BEST SHORT STORIES OF 1925   (1925)

World Best Short Stories of 1925.
New York, George H. Doran Company. (1925).

Reprints *The Letter*. First appearance in book form.

C6   GEORGIAN STORIES OF 1926   (1926)

Georgian Stories of 1926.
New York, G. P. Putnam's Sons: London, Chapman & Hall. (1926).

Reprints *Honest Woman*. First appearance in book form.

C7   TWO MADE THEIR BED   (1929)

Two Made Their Bed. By Louis Marlow. With a Preface by W. Somerset Maugham.
London, Willlam Heinemann. (1929).

C8   SHUDDERS   (1929)

Shudders. A Collection of Nightmare Tales. By Lady Cynthia Asquith (Ed.).
New York, Scribner's: London, Hutchinson. 1929.

Reprints *End of the Flight*. First appearance in book form.

C9   OUR PUPPET SHOW   (1929)

Our Puppet Show. By Francis de Croisset. With a Preface by W. Somerset Maugham.
London, William Heinemann. (1929)

C10   BITTER SWEET   1929

Bitter Sweet and Other Plays. By Noel Coward. With a Comment on the Young Dramatists by W. Somerset Maugham.
New York, Doubleday, Doran & Co. Inc. 1929.

The Maugham preface appeared only in the American edition.

C11   GALLERY UNRESERVED   1931

Gallery Unreserved. A Collection of Experiences, Opinions and Stories connected with the Gallery and Galleryites. By A Galleryite. With a Foreword by W. Somerset Maugham, and special Contributions by many famous Authors and Actors.
London, Heritage. 1931.

The author of this book was Fred Bason. It contains a description of a visit by Somerset Maugham to the old South London Theatre in company with Bason, in search of material for a new novel about Cockney London, later abandoned.

C12   A BIBLIOGRAPHY OF THE WRITINGS OF   1931
WILLIAM SOMERSET MAUGHAM

A Bibliography of the Writings of William Somerset Maugham.
Compiled by Frederick T. Bason.
London, The Unicorn Press. 1931.
Limited to 950 copies, numbered, and 50 copies, numbered and signed by W. Somerset Maugham, with a preface by him.

C13   WHAT A LIFE!   1932

What a Life! By Doris Arthur-Jones. With a Preface by W. Somerset Maugham.
London, Jarrolds. 1932.

C14   FAVORITE STORIES BY FAMOUS WRITERS   1932

Favorite Stories by Famous Writers. With an Introduction by Harry Payne Burton, Editor of *Cosmopolitan*.
New York, International Magazine Company. 1932.

Reprints *The Right Thing is the Kind Thing* from *Cosmopolitan*.
Appeared later in *Ah King* as *The Back of Beyond*. First publication in book form. The author made a number of small revisions in the text before it appeared in *Ah King*.

C15   THE TRAVELLERS' LIBRARY   (1933)

The Travellers' Library, compiled and with Notes by W. Somerset Maugham.
Garden City, New York, Doubleday, Doran. (1933).

An anthology edited by W. Somerset Maugham, with an 11-page general introduction, and short commentaries to each section. These appear on pp. 143–45, 409–12, 547–49, 575–81, 1135–36, 1317–20, 1513–14.
Reprinted under title *Fifty Modern English Writers*. No English edition.

C16   FIFTY MODERN ENGLISH WRITERS   (1933)

Fifty Modern English Writers, presented by W. Somerset Maugham.
Garden City, New York, Doubleday, Doran. (1933).

Contents identical with above. In Mr. Grenville Cook's copy of *The Traveller's Library* there is an inscription by Mr. Maugham to Desmond MacCarthy. 'Here at last is the omnibus book but with a stupid title not of my invention and contents pages all anyhow.'

C17 FLOWER PAINTINGS 1934

Flower Paintings. By Marie Laurencin.
London, The Mayor Gallery. 1934.

Catalogue of an exhibition of Marie Laurencin's work, with a preface by W. Somerset Maugham.

C18 THEATRE ROYAL DRURY LANE 1935

Theatre Royal Drury Lane. In the Presence of Her Majesty the Queen. Souvenir Programme of the Matinee organised by the Daily Telegraph as a tribute to Miss Marie Tempest on the occasion of her Jubilee. Tuesday, 28 May 1935.

Contains 'First Rehearsal' by Somerset Maugham. Other contributions by Sir James Barrie, Sir Edward German and Noel Coward. Coloured plates. A charming tribute.

C19 PORTRAITS AND SELF-PORTRAITS 1936

Portraits and Self-Portraits. By G. Schreiber (Ed.)
New York, Houghton, Mifflin. 1936.

Self-Portrait by W. Somerset Maugham. pp. 95–97.

C20 HOW WRITERS WRITE (1937)

How Writers Write. Essays by Contemporary Authors. Edited by N. S. Tillett.
Oxford, Toronto, Crowell. 1937.

How I write Short Stories by W. Somerset Maugham, pp. 69–82.

C21 THE HARVEST 1937

The Harvest. Being the Record of One Hundred Years of Publishing, 1837–1937. Offered in Gratitude to the Friends of the Firm by Bernard Tauchnitz.
Leipzig, Bernard Tauchnitz. MCMXXXVII.

A Souvenir octavo volume in gold wrappers, each copy being

printed with the name of the recipient. Contains a letter from W. Somerset Maugham.

C22   WISDOM OF LIFE   1938

Wisdom of Life: An Anthology of Noble Thoughts. By J. F. Green (Ed.). New edition, with additions by W. Somerset Maugham and Others.
London Watts, 1938.

C23   THE HOUSE WITH THE GREEN SHUTTERS   (1938)

The House with the Green Shutters. By George Douglas [Brown]. With a Preface by W. Somerset Maugham.
Oxford, Oxford University Press. 1938. (*World Classics*, 466).

C24   A NUMBER OF PEOPLE   (1939)

A Number of People. By Sir Edward Marsh. With a Preface by W. Somerset Maugham.
New York, Harper Bros. (1939).

The Preface does not appear in the English edition.

C25 W. SOMERSET MAUGHAM: AN APPRECIATION (1939)

W. Somerset Maugham: An Appreciation by Richard Aldington. Sixty-Five by W. Somerset Maugham. A Bibliography, an Index of Short Stories and Appreciations.
New York, Doubleday, Doran. (1939).

C26   TELLERS OF TALES   (1939)

Tellers of Tales. 100 Short Stories from the United States, England, France, Russia and Germany. Selected and with an Introduction by W. Somerset Maugham.
New York, Doubleday, Doran. (1939).

Contains an original 27-page introduction on the short story by the author. There is no English edition of this anthology, although one was advertised to appear shortly before the war broke out. Reprinted under the title *The Greatest Stories of all Times: Tellers of Tales.*

C27   IN THE BUS   (1940)

In the Bus. New York. The Allied Relief Ball Souvenir Program Hotel Astor. (1940).

With a foreword by W. Somerset Maugham.

C28   PETER ARNO'S CARTOON REVUE   1942

Peter Arno's Cartoon Revue. By Peter Arno.
London, Robert Hale. 1942.

With a foreword by W. Somerset Maugham.

C29   MODERN ENGLISH READINGS   1942

Modern English Readings. By R. S. Loomis and D. L. Clark (Eds.).
New York, Farrar. 1942.

Writing Prose by W. Somerset Maugham.

C30   GREAT MODERN READING   (1943)

Great Modern Reading. W. Somerset Maugham's Introduction to
Modern English and American Literature.
Garden City, New York, Doubleday. (1943).

There are two issues of this work, a De-Luxe edition limited to 2,000
copies and an ordinary trade edition. The trade edition differs from the
de-luxe edition only in lacking the numbered frontispiece of the Editor
and in having trimmed edges. The book has a 9-page introduction by
W. Somerset Maugham and a short commentary by him to each
section. The book was reprinted the same year from the publisher's
house in New York, and also in Philadelphia, in *The New Home
Library* under the title *Introductions to Modern English and American
Literature*.

C31   INTRODUCTION TO MODERN ENGLISH   (1943)
            AND MODERN LITERATURE

W. Somerset Maugham's Introduction to Modern English and
American Literature. A New Home Library Book.
Garden City, New York, Garden City Publishing Co. (1943).

Contents identical with **C30**.

C32   THE GREATEST STORIES OF ALL TIMES   (1943)

The Greatest Stories of All Times: Tellers of Tales, selected and with
and introduction by W. Somerset Maugham.
Garden City, New York, Garden City Publishing Co. (1943).

Contents identical with **C26**.

C33   THE ENGLISH SPIRIT   1944

The English Spirit. Edited with an Introduction by Anthony Weymouth. J. B. Priestley—Sir Philip Gibbs—Philip Guedalla—Somerset Maugham—Sir Hugh Walpole and Others.
London, George Allen & Unwin Ltd. 1942: New York, Norton. 1944.

Twenty Days in a Ship by W. Somerset Maugham, pp. 40–45. The twenty talks in this book were broadcast in the Empire Service of the B.B.C.

C34   DOROTHY PARKER   1944

Dorothy Parker: and with an Introduction by W. Somerset Maugham. New York, Viking. 1944. (*Viking Post Library*).

C35   THE STANDARD BOOK OF BIDDING   1944

The Standard Book of Bidding by C. H. Goren, with an Introduction by W. Somerset Maugham.
New York, Doubleday, Doran 1944: London, Walter Edwards. 1946.

C36   THE HISTORY OF TOM JONES   (1948)

Henry Fielding's The History of Tom Jones. A Foundling. Edited by W. Somerset Maugham, illustrated by Harry Diamond.
Philadelphia and Toronto, John C. Winston & Co. (1948).

C37   DAVID COPPERFIELD   (1948)

Charles Dickens' David Copperfield. Edited by W. Somerset Maugham. Illustrated by Everett Shinn.
Philadelphia and Toronto, John C. Winston & Co. (1948).

C38   MADAME BOVARY   (1949)

Gustave Flaubert's Madame Bovary. Edited by W. Somerset Maugham, in a new translation by Joan Charles. Illustrated by Ben Stahl.
Philadelphia and Toronto, John C. Winston & Co. (1949).

C39   OLD MAN GORIOT   (1949)

Honoré de Balzac's Old Man Goriot. Edited by W. Somerset Maugham, in a new translation by Joan Charles. Illustrated by Rafaello Busoni.
Philadelphia and Toronto, John C. Winston & Co. (1949).

C40   WUTHERING HEIGHTS   (1949)

Emily Bronte's Wuthering Heights. Edited by W. Somerset Maugham.
Illustrated by Michael Silver.
Philadelphia and Toronto, John C. Winston & Co. (1949).

C41   THE BROTHERS KARAMAZOV   (1949)

Fyodor Dostoevsky's The Brothers Karamazov. Edited by W.
Somerset Maugham in a new translation revised by Princess Alexandra
Kropotkin. Illustrated by Franklin Whitman.
Philadelphia and Toronto, John C. Winston & Co. (1949).

C42   THE RED AND THE BLACK   (1949)

Stendhal's The Red and the Black. Edited by W. Somerset Maugham
in a new translation by Joan Charles and illustrated by Frede Vidar.
Philadelphia and Toronto, John C. Winston & Co. (1949).

C43   PRIDE AND PREJUDICE   (1949)

Jane Austen's Pride and Prejudice. Edited by W. Somerset Maugham.
Illustrated by Douglas Gorsline.
Philadelphia and Toronto, John C. Winston & Co. (1949).

C44   MOBY DICK   (1949)

Moby Dick or The Whale. Written by Herman Melville. Edited by
W. Somerset Maugham. Illustrated by Anton Otto Fischer.
Philadelphia and Toronto, John C. Winston & Co. (1949).

C45   WAR AND PEACE   (1949)

War and Peace by Leo Tolstoy. Edited by W. Somerset Maugham in
a translation revised by Princess Alexandra Kropotkin. Illustrated by
Franklin Whitman.
Philadelphia and Toronto, John C. Winston & Co. (1949).

C46   WRITING FOR LOVE OR MONEY   1949

Writing for Love or Money. By Norman Cousins (Ed.).
New York, Longmans, Green. 1949.

15. *How I Write Short Stories*, pp. 99–108. Reprinted from *Saturday
Review of Literature*.

C47   NELSON DOUBLEDAY, 1889–1949   1950

Nelson Doubleday, 1889–1949.
New York, Privately Printed. 1950.

With a contribution by W. Somerset Maugham.

C48   AN EXHIBITION OF PAINTINGS   (1950)

An Exhibition of Paintings by Sir Gerald Kelly, P.R.A., with a
preface by W. Somerset Maugham.
London, The Leicester Galleries. (1950).

C49   ESSAYS BY DIVERS HANDS   1950

Essays by Divers Hands. Being the Transactions of the Royal Society of
Literature of the United Kingdom. New Series. Vol. 25.
With a foreword by Sir Edward Marsh.
London, Oxford University Press. MCML.

The Short Story by W. S. Maugham, pp. 120–134. Read before the
Society, 12 November 1947.

C50   THE LITTLE FELLOW   1951

The Little Fellow. The Life and Work of Charlie Chaplin. By Peter
Cotes and Thelma Niklaus. Foreword by Somerset Maugham.
London, Paul Elek. 1951.

The foreword is taken from some passages on Charlie Chaplin in
A Writer's Notebook.

C51   A CHOICE OF KIPLING'S PROSE   1952

A Choice of Kipling's Prose. Selected and with an Introductory
Essay by W. Somerset Maugham.
London, Macmillan. 1952.

C52   MAUGHAM'S CHOICE OF KIPLING'S BEST   1953

Maugham's Choice of Kipling's Best. Sixteen Stories Selected and
with an Introductory Essay.
Garden City, New York, Doubleday & Company Inc. 1953.

Note: In the conclusion to his introduction to Kipling's prose Somerset
Maugham wrote: "Rudyard Kipling is the only writer of short
stories our country has produced who can stand comparison with
Guy de Maupassant and Chekhov. He is our greatest story writer. I

can't believe he will ever be equalled. I am sure he can never be excelled."

This was indeed high praise coming from a man of Somerset Maugham's sensibilities for somehow one did not imagine that the two men had anything in common. Nevertheless despite temperamental differences Maugham did have a genuine admiration for Kipling as a short story writer and he had toyed for some time with the idea of making an anthology of his prose. He kept putting it off because of the pressure of other work, but it was always at the back of his mind. In March 1950, he wrote to his literary agent A. P. Watt: "With regard to the Kipling book. My intention of making an anthology and writing a preface has always been serious . . . I should hope to be able to gather the materials during the early part of next year. As you will realise, it would necessitate my reading again all the Kipling stories and making notes in them as I read. I should not want my work scrapped as Freddie Birkenhead had to scrap his owing to Elsie Bambridge's objection, and I couldn't undertake the work unless I had the assurance that I should not be interfered with. Obviously, I would never have made the suggestion if I hadn't a great admiration for Kipling's short stories, but my idea would be not to write a fatuous eulogy but a serious criticism." And then he adds a typical Maughamesque footnote: "NB. Some of the stories are awful."

C53 ROBERT ROSS: FRIEND OF FRIENDS 1952

Robert Ross: Friend of Friends. By Margery Ross.
London, J. Cape. 1952.

Letters to Robert Ross, pp. 157, 203.

C54 EDDIE MARSH 1953

Eddie Marsh. Sketches for a composite literary portrait of Sir Edward Marsh.
London, Lund Humphries. 1953.

A contribution by Somerset Maugham.

C55 WITHOUT VEILS (1953)

Without Veils. The Intimate Biography of Gladys Cooper by Sewell Stokes. With an Introduction by W. Somerset Maugham.
London, Peter Davies. (1953).

N

C56   MEMOIRS OF THE AGA KHAN   1954

Memoirs of the Aga Khan. With an Introduction by W. Somerset Maugham.
London, Cassell. 1954.

C57   THE ARTIST AND THE THEATRE   (1955)

The Artist and the Theatre. The Story of the paintings collected and presented to the National Theatre by W. Somerset Maugham. With an Introduction by W. Somerset Maugham.
London, William Heinemann. (1955).

C58   LETTERS FROM MADAME SEVIGNE   1955

Letters from Madame La Marquise de Sevigné: selected, translated, and introduced by Violet Hammersley with a preface by Somerset Maugham.
London, Secker & Warburg. 1955.

C59   SPEECH BY W. SOMERSET MAUGHAM C.H.   (1956)

Speech by W. Somerset Maugham C.H. on opening the exhibition of Authors as Artists at the Army & Navy Stores 15 October. 1956.
[London, Army & Navy Stores Ltd.]

A talk on "authors who have to a greater or lesser extent occupied themselves with the graphic arts" with reflections on Max Beerhbom Gordon Craig, Lawrence Whistler, D. H. Lawrence and Noel Coward (2 pp.).

C60   A COMPREHENSIVE EXHIBITION OF   1951
W. SOMERSET MAUGHAM

A Comprehensive Exhibition of W. Somerset Maugham drawn from Various Private Collections and Libraries with a preface by the Author. 25 May through 1 August, 1958. Albert M. Bender Room. Stanford University Press, California, in an edition of 1,000 copies. 1958.

One of the most comprehensive exhibitions of Maugham's works with a most informative catalogue.

C61   THE CASSELL MISCELLANY   (1958)

The Cassell Miscellany.
(London), Cassell & Co. Ltd. (1958).

Contains W. Somerset Maugham's *The Mother*. Reprinted from *The Story Teller*. First appearance in book form. *See* **D18**.

C62   VANITY FAIR   1960

Vanity Fair. Selections from America's Most Memorable Magazine. A Cavalcade of the 1920's and 1930's. Edited by Cleveland Amory and Frederick Bradlee.
New York, The Viking Press. 1960.

W. Somerset Maugham *On the Approach of Middle Age*.

C63   SOTHEBY'S SALE OF PICTURES   (1962)

Catalogue of the Collection of Impressionist and Modern Pictures formed by W. Somerset Maugham ... London, Sotheby & Co. (1962).

With a preface by W. Somerset Maugham.

D

CONTRIBUTIONS
BY W. SOMERSET MAUGHAM
TO
PERIODICALS

Nearly all W. Somerset Maugham's short stories and several of his novels were serialised in magazines before they appeared in book form. Nash's Magazine (London) and the American *Cosmopolitan* and *Hearst's International Magazine* and *Good Housekeeping* published most of the early and most famous short stories. These magazines have acquired considerable importance not only on account of their extreme scarcity but because a long period often elapsed (in some cases a decade) before the appearance of the stories in book form. Also, there are considerable textual differences in the early versions; occasionally the story was completely rewritten and the title changed, while nearly all the stories reveal the author's careful pruning before book publication. In a letter to Charles H. Towne, his American literary agent, in March 1925, Maugham wrote: 'I have posted to you today the typescript of six stories which I propose to publish as my next book ... These stories as you will have noticed have all appeared in *Cosmopolitan* or the *International* but I have written a great deal of them anew and I think have improved them.' The magazine stories were also illustrated, but none of these illustrations ever appeared in book form.

Usually the stories appeared first in America, but occasionally a story had prior publication in England or appeared simultaneously in *Nash's* and the *Cosmopolitan* or *Hearst's International*. The dates of English and American publication are given. If only one of these is indicated the story or article concerned was not published in the other country. The numerals in parentheses after some entries denote the book (listed in the A section) in which the story later appeared; items lacking this key were mostly not reprinted. The *Cosmopolitan* amalgamated with *Hearst's International* with the March 1925 issue.

D1 DON SEBASTIAN. *Cosmopolis*. October 1898. (**A3**)

> Mr. Maugham wrote his first published short story in a magazine called *Cosmopolis*, which was printed 'a third in English, a third in French, and a third in German ... The idea was that it would thus find readers in three countries; unfortunately, it found readers in none. It came to a sudden end and I was never paid for my work.' But the magazine was not quite the 'flash in the pan' that Maugham infers. It ran for nearly three years and 35 issues. Maugham's short story *San Sebastian* (reprinted in *Orientations*) appeared in the October 1898 issue and the magazine ceased publication the following November.

D2 CUPID AND THE VICAR OF SWALE. *Punch*. 7 February 1900. (**B36**)

D3 LADY HABART. *Punch.* 25 April, 2, 9 May 1900. (**B36**)

D4 SCHIFFBRÜCHIG. *The Venture.* 1903.

Contains Somerset Maugham's first published play *Schiffbrüchig*, a one-act play, translated into German with the help of an Anglo-German friend. It was produced in Berlin on 3 January 1902. In this volume it is in English under the title *Marriages are Made in Heaven*.

The Venture, an annual, was edited by Laurence Housman and W. Somerset Maugham. Only two volumes appeared, in 1903 and 1905.

D5 PRO PATRIA. *Pall Mall.* February 1903. (**B36**)

D6 A MAN OF HONOUR. *Fortnightly Review* (Supplement). March 1903. *See* **A6**

D7 A POINT OF LAW. *Strand Magazine.* September 1904. (**B36**)

D8 AN IRISH GENTLEMAN. *Strand Magazine.* September 1904. (**B36**)

D9 A REHEARSAL. A Novel in a Nutshell. *The Sketch.* 6 December 1905.

A Rehearsal is based on *Mademoiselle Zampa* the sketch that was used as a curtain raiser to the public production of *A Man of Honour* at the Avenue Theatre, but was taken off after twenty performances.

D10 FLIRTATION. *Daily Mail.* 3 February 1906. (**B36**)

This story was copyrighted in the British Museum in 1904. It was printed in the form of rough galley proofs and, when cut, made up 9 leaves (including a specially printed title page.) The imprint states 'Daily Mail. Price One Penny.' It is extremely unlikely that other copies now exist. Mr. Maugham (who had no recollection of it) thought it trivial when he re-read it and its manner suggestive of the now forgotten *Dolly Dialogues*. Nevertheless, the story is not without interest, if only on account of its typical Maugham twist at the end. The story did not appear in the *Daily Mail* until two years later.

D11 THE FORTUNATE PAINTER AND THE HONEST JEW. *Bystander.* 7 March 1906. (**B36**)

D12 A MARRIAGE OF CONVENIENCE. *Illustrated London News.* 23 June 1908.

This story was rewritten and reprinted in *The Gentleman in the Parlour.* pp. 194–204. *See* **D84**.

D13 THE MAKING OF A MILLIONAIRE. *The Lady's Realm* (Lond.). July 1906.

This short story, never republished, gives a glimpse of the later Maugham with its typical, cynical ending.

D14 GOOD MANNERS. *Windsor Magazine.* May 1907.

D15 COUSIN AMY. *Pall Mall Magazine.* March 1908. (**A50**)

Rewritten and reprinted as *The Luncheon.*

D16 THE HAPPY COUPLE. *Cassell's Magazine.* May 1908. (**A66**)

Karl G. Pfeiffer gives an interesting account of this story. 'Maugham told me that he wrote perhaps half a dozen short stories which he now has no record of. He thought they appeared during the ten years after *Liza.* I began a systematic search for them (which the war interrupted and I have never continued) . . . I found the one I refer to (*The Happy Couple*), sent Maugham a telegram (he was living in Hollywood then), told him what it was about and asked whether he wanted me to copy it and send it to him. He wrote back "I can't remember the story at all, am sure it's lousy, why waste your time?" But some time after I had it photostatted and sent it to him, whereupon he wrote back that he was surprised it didn't date more than it did and thought he would fashion a new story out of it. This he did, selling it to *Redbook* and giving me the MSS.' This second version of the story was reprinted in *Creatures of Circumstance.* The manuscript is in The University of Texas.

D17 A TRAVELLER IN ROMANCE. *Printer's Pie Annual.* 1909.

D18 THE MOTHER. *Story Teller.* April 1909. (**A66**).

The early purple patches of this somewhat lurid tale were toned down when the author revised it for inclusion in *Creatures of*

Circumstance, but he was sufficiently satisfied with it as a whole to let the greater part of it stand as it was first written. It was reprinted from the original version in *The Cassell Miscellany* (**C61**).

D19 PYGMALION AT HOME AND ABROAD. *English Review.* May 1914.

D20 GERALD FESTUS KELLY: Student of Character. *International Studio.* January 1915.

Sir Gerald Kelly painted between twenty and thirty portraits of his friend W. Somerset Maugham during his lifetime, and their friendship withstood the ravages of time and fame until the end. Sir Gerald once told me that he had kept the cutting of this article in his pocket for the best part of half a century. Maugham wrote another appreciation of Sir Gerald Kelly for an exhibition of his work at the Leicester Galleries in 1950 (**C48**)

D21 MACKINTOSH. *Cosmopolitan.* November 1920. (**A25**)

D22 MISS THOMPSON. *The Smart Set.* April 1921. (**A25**)

Appeared in book form as *Rain*. The late Charles Hanson Towne, I am informed by Mr. Lynwood Giacomini, placed *Miss Thompson* with *Smart Set* after it had been rejected in America by all other major magazines.

D23 RED. *Asia.* April. 1921 (**A25**)

A number of changes were made in the book version.

D24 ON WRITING FOR THE FILMS. *The North American Review.* May 1921.

D25 THE POOL. *Cosmopolitan.* September 1921. (**A25**)

D26 HONOLULU. *Everybody's.* October 1921. (**A25**)

D27 MY SOUTH SEA ISLAND. *Daily Mail.* 31 January 1922. (**A51**)

D28 FOREIGN DEVILS. *Asia.* February 1922. (**A28**)

Title changed to *Dinner Parties* in book form.

D29 FEAR. *Century*. March 1922. (**A28**)

Reprinted *Living Age*. 18 April 1925: *T. P. Cassell's Weekly* 25 October 1924.

D30 A CITY BUILT ON A ROCK. *Youth* (Lond.). March 1922. (**A28**)

D31 PHILOSOPHER. *McClure's Magazine*. 18 April 1922 (**A28**)

D32 TWO STUDIES: Mr. Pete; The Vice-Consul. *Saturday Review*. 8 July 1922. (**A28**)

Mr. Pete became *The Consul* in book form.

D33 TAIPAN. *Pearson's Magazine*. October 1922. (**A28**)

D34 THE PRINCESS AND THE NIGHTINGALE. *Pearson's Magazine* and *Good Housekeeping* (N.Y.). December 1922. (**A39**)

This story was later included in *The Gentleman in the Parlour*. In a caption to the story the Editor of *Pearson's* stated that 'this delightful story was written by Mr. Maugham for a very special purpose, the nature of which we are not, at the moment, permitted to disclose.' The special purpose was for inclusion in the miniature manuscript library of the Queen's Doll's House. Permission to publish in *Pearson's Magazine* was given on condition that the purpose was not disclosed.

D35 BEFORE THE PARTY. *Nash's Magazine*. December 1922. Reprinted *International Magazine*. January 1923.

D36 'P. & O.' *International Magazine*. February 1923, under title *Bewitched*. Reprinted *Nash's Magazine*, April 1923. (**A34**)

D37 JANE. *International Magazine*. April 1923. Reprinted *Nash's Magazine*. August 1923. (**A50**)

D38 THE IMPOSTERS. *Cosmopolitan*. November 1923. Reprinted *Nash's Magazine*. December 1923. (**A50**)

Appeared in book form under title *Raw Material*.

D39 MAYHEW. *Cosmopolitan*. December 1923. Reprinted *Nash's Magazine*. January 1924. (**A50**)

D40 GERMAN HARRY. *Cosmopolitan.* January 1924. Reprinted
Nash's Magazine. March 1924. (**A50**)

D41 THE FORCE OF CIRCUMSTANCE. *International Magazine.*
January 1924. Reprinted *Nash's Magazine.* February 1924. (**A34**)

D42 IN A STRANGE LAND. *Cosmopolitan.* February 1924.
Reprinted *Nash's Magazine.* April 1924. (**A50**)

D43 THE LUNCHEON. *Cosmopolitan.* March 1924. Reprinted
Nash's Magazine. June 1924. (**A50**)

A re-written version of *Cousin Amy* (**D15**)

D44 THE ROUND DOZEN. *Good Housekeeping* (Lond.). March
1924. Reprinted *International Magazine.* July 1924 under title
The Ardent Bigamist. (**A42**)

D45 THE WOMAN WHO WOULDN'T TAKE A HINT.
Cosmopolitan. April 1924.

D46 THE LETTER. *International Magazine.* April 1924. Reprinted
Nash's Magazine. May 1924. (**A34**)

D47 D47 A DREAM. *Cosmopolitan.* May 1924. Reprinted *Nash's
Magazine.* July 1924. (**A50**)

Appeared in book form as *The Dream.*

D48 THE OUTSTATION. *International Magazine.* June 1924.
Reprinted *Nash's Magazine.* August 1924. (**A34**)

D49 THE HAPPY MAN. *Cosmopolitan.* June 1924. Reprinted
Nash's Magazine. November 1924. (**A50**)

D50 SALVATORE THE FISHERMAN. *Cosmopolitan.* July 1924.
Reprinted *Nash's Magazine.* November 1925 (**A50**)

Appeared in book form as *Salvatore.*

D51 HOME FROM THE SEA. *Cosmopolitan.* September 1924.
Reprinted *Nash's Magazine.* November 1925. (**A50**)

Appeared in book form as *Home.*

D52 THE ANT AND THE GRASSHOPPER. *Cosmopolitan*. October 1924. (**A50**)

D53 MR. KNOW-ALL. *Cosmopolitan*. January 1925. Reprinted *Good Housekeeping* (London). September 1924. (**A50**)

D54 NOVELIST OR BOND SALESMAN: Letter to an Anxious Mother. *The American Bookman* February 1925. (**A72**)

Most of the material in this article was incorporated in the lecture given by Mr. Maugham at the Kingsway Hall in 1951, under the title *The Writer's Point of View*.

D55 A WIDOW'S MIGHT. *Cosmopolitan* February 1925. Reprinted *Nash's Magazine* September 1925. (**A50**)
This story was reprinted as *The Escape*.

D56 THE MAN WHO WOULDN'T HURT A FLY. *International Magazine* April 1925. Reprinted *Nash's Magazine*. August 1925. (**A50**)
Appeared in book form as *A Friend in Need*.

D57 THE CODE OF A GENTLEMAN. *International Magazine* June 1925. (**A50**)
Appeared in book form as *Portrait of a Gentleman*.

D58 THE YELLOW STREAK. *International Magazine* August 1925. Reprinted *Nash's Magazine* October 1925. (**A34**)

D59 THE MOST SELFISH WOMAN I KNEW. *International Magazine* September 1925. Reprinted *Good Housekeeping* December 1925 under title *Louise* (**A50**)
Appeared in book form as *Louise*.

D60 THE MAN WITH A SCAR. *International Magazine* October 1925. Reprinted *Nash's Magazine* December 1925 (**A50**)
Reprinted in the *Grand Magazine* May 1933.

D61 THE GREAT MAN. *International Magazine* November 1925. Reprinted *Nash's Magazine* January 1926. (**A50**)
Appeared in book form as *The Poet*.

D62   AN HONEST WOMAN. *International Magazine* December 1925. Reprinted *Nash's Magazine* February 1926. (**A50**)
Appeared in book form as *The Promise.*

D62a   THE END OF THE FLIGHT. *Harper's Bazaar* January 1926. Reprinted *Nash's Magazine* May 1926. (**A50**)

D63   ANOTHER MAN WITHOUT A COUNTRY. *International Magazine* January 1926. Reprinted *Nash's Magazine* March 1926. (**A50**)
Appeared in book form as *French Joe.*

D64   CONSUL. Golden Book April 1926. (**A28**)
First appeared in book form in 1922.

D65   THE CREATIVE IMPULSE. *Harper's Bazaar* August 1926. Reprinted *Nash's Magazine* November 1926. (**A42**)

D66   THE CLOSED SHOP. *Harper's Bazaar.* September 1926. Reprinted *Nash's Magazine* January 1927. (**A50**)

D67   FOOTPRINTS IN THE JUNGLE. *International Magazine* January 1927 Reprinted *Nash's Magazine.* March 1927 (**A46**)

D68   PEARLS. *International Magazine* February 1927. Reprinted *Nash's Magazine* April 1927. (**A50**)
Appeared in book form as *A String of Beads.*

D69   ADVICE TO A YOUNG AUTHOR. *New York Times* 2 March 1927.

D70   THE TRAITOR. *International Magazine* September 1927. Reprinted *Nash's Magazine* November 1927. (**A37**)

D71   ONE OF THOSE WOMEN. *International Magazine* October 1927. Reprinted *Nash's Magazine* December 1927. (**A37**)
Appeared in book form as *The Dark Woman.*

D72   HIS EXCELLENCY. *International Magazine* November 1927. Reprinted *Nash's Magazine* January 1928. (**A37**)

D73   THE HAIRLESS MEXICAN. *International Magazine* December 1927. Reprinted *Nash's Magazine* February 1928. (**A37**)

D74 MR. HARRINGTON'S WASHING. *International Magazine* January 1928. Reprinted *Nash's Magazine*. March 1928. (**A37**)

D75 THE BRITISH AGENT. *International Magazine* February 1928 Reprinted *Nash's Magazine* April 1928. (**A37**)
Appeared in book form as *Miss King*.

D76 THE FOUR DUTCHMEN. *International Magazine* December 1928. Reprinted *Nash's Magazine* February 1929. (**A50**)

D77 IN HIDING. *International Magazine* January 1929. Reprinted *Nash's Magazine* May 1929. (**A50**)
Appeared in book form as *The Wash Tub*.

D78 A DERELICT. *International Magazine* February 1929. Reprinted *Nash's Magazine* April 1929. (**A50**)
Appeared in book form as *The Bum*.

D79 THE EXTRAORDINARY SEX. *International Magazine* March 1929. Reprinted *Nash's Magazine* June 1929. (**A50**)
Appeared in book form as *The Social Sense*.

D80 STRAIGHT FLUSH. *International Magazine* June 1929. Reprinted *Nash's Magazine* July 1929. (**A50**)

D81 THE MAN WHO MADE HIS MARK. *International Magazine* June 1929. Reprinted *Nash's Magazine* August 1929. (**A50**)
Appeared in book form as *The Verger*.

D82 THROUGH THE JUNGLE. *Britannia and Eve* July August 1929.

The photographs which illustrate the articles were taken by Mr. Maugham's late secretary, Frederick Gerald Haxton, to whom *A Writer's Notebook* was dedicated.

D83 MIRAGE. *International Magazine* October 1929. Reprinted *Strand Magazine* November 1929. (**A39**)

D84 A MARRIAGE OF CONVENIENCE. *Strand Magazine* December 1929. Reprinted *International Magazine* January 1930. A rewritten version of the story which first appeared in the *Illustrated London News* in 1906. Appeared in book form in *The Gentleman in the Parlour*. *See* **D12**

D85 ON THE ROAD TO MANDALAY. *International Magazine* December 1929.

This story was offered to the Editor of *The Strand* under the title of *Masterson*, prior to its appearance in *The Gentleman in the Parlour*. It was turned down. It was not reprinted separately till 1951 when Maugham included it in *The Complete Stories* (**B17**), reverting to his original title for it of *Masterson*.

D86 CAKES AND ALE. *Harper's Bazaar* March – July 1930. The book was published in September 1930.

D87 MALTREAT THE DEAD IN FICTION. *Literary Digest* November 1930.

D88 THE HUMAN ELEMENT. *International Magazine* December 1930. Reprinted *Nash's Magazine* January 1931. (**A42**)

D89 VIRTUE. *International Magazine* February 1931. Reprinted *Nash's Magazine* March 1931. (**A42**)

D90 THE VESSEL OF WRATH. *International Magazine* April 1931. Reprinted *Nash's Magazine* May 1931. (**A46**)

D91 MAUGHAM DISCUSSES DRAMA. *The Living Age* May 1931.

D92 ARNOLD BENNETT. *Life and Letters* June 1931. (**A74**) Reprinted in *The Traveller's Library* (**C15**)

D93 THE RIGHT THING IS THE KIND THING. *International Magazine* July 1931. Reprinted *Nash's Magazine* September 1931. (**A46**)
Appeared in book form as *The Back of Beyond*. From this story comes the famous Maugham axiom "If to look truth in the face and not resent it when it's unpalatable, and take human nature as you find it. . .' Reprinted in *The Grand Magazine*, 1934.

D94 THE ALIEN CORN. *International Magazine* August 1931. Reprinted *Nash's Magazine* October 1941. (**A42**)

D95 THE DOOR OF OPPORTUNITY. *International Magazine*
October 1931. Reprinted *Nash's Magazine* December 1931.
(**A46**)

D96 THE TEMPTATION OF NEIL MACADAM. *International
Magazine* February 1932. Reprinted *Nash's Magazine* April
1932. (**A46**)
Appeared in book form as *Neil MacAdam*.

D97 THE NARROW CORNER. *International Magazine* October
1932–December 1932.
The novel was published in November 1932.

D97a FOR SERVICES RENDERED. *Sunday Express* (Lond.).
13 November–18 December 1932.
Today the Sunday Express begins publication of "For Services
Rendered" by W. Somerset Maugham, a play that is drawing
the whole of London. The Play is being acclaimed as a masterpiece, the "Journey's End" of the peace days.

D98 THE THREE FAT WOMEN OF ANTIBES. *International
Magazine* October 1933. Reprinted *Nash's Magazine* November
1933. (**A58**)

D99 THE BURIED TALENT. *International Magazine* February
1934. Reprinted *Nash's Magazine* March 1934.

D100 THE BEST EVER. *International Magazine* and *Nash's Magazine*
May 1934. (**A58**)
Appeared in book form as *The Treasure*.

D101 HOW I WRITE SHORT STORIES. *Saturday Review of
Literature.* 28 July 1934.

D102 THE SHORT STORY. *Nash's Magazine* October 1934.
This article was the Introduction to *East and West*.

D103 A CASUAL AFFAIR. *Nash's Magazine* November 1934.
Reprinted *International Magazine* April 1935. (**A66**)

D104 APPEARANCE AND REALITY. *International Magazine*
November 1934. Reprinted *Nash's Magazine* December 1934.
(**A66**)

OF
HUMAN
BONDAGE

By
W. Somerset Maugham

New York
George H. Doran Company

Title-page of the first (American) edition of *Of Human Bondage.*

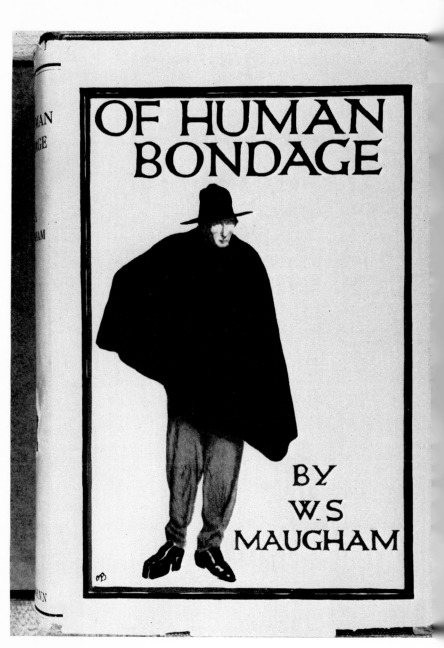

The suppressed dust wrapper of *Of Human Bondage*—the club foot on
the wrong foot.

The Humanities Research Center, The University of Texas at Austin.

D105 THE VOICE OF THE TURTLE. *Nash's Magazine* January 1935. Reprinted *International Magazine* November 1936. (**A58**)

D106 GIGOLO AND GIGOLETTE. *Nash's Magazine* March 1935. Reprinted *International Magazine* July 1935. (**A58**)

D107 THE LOTUS EATER. *Nash's Magazine* October 1935. Reprinted *International Magazine* April 1936. (**A58**)

D108 AN OFFICIAL POSITION. *International Magazine* July 1937. Reprinted *Nash's Magazine* August 1937. (**A58**)

D109 THE PROFESSIONAL WRITER. *Sat. Rev. of Lit.* 29 January 1939.

D110 THE LION'S SKIN. *International Magazine* November 1937. Reprinted *Good Housekeeping* (Lond.). February 1938
This story was not reprinted in book form.

D111 THE SANATORIUM. *International Magazine* December 1938.

D112 BOOKS AND YOU. *Sat. Eve. Post* 4 February 1939. (**A57**)

D113 DOCTOR AND PATIENT. *International Magazine* February 1939. (**A58**)
Appeared in book form as *Lord Mountdrago*.

D114 YOU AND SOME MORE BOOKS. *Sat. Eve. Post* 11 March 1939. (**A57**)

D115 THE FACTS OF LIFE. *International Magazine* April 1939. (**A58**)

D116 A MAN WITH A CONSCIENCE. *International Magazine* June 1939. (**A58**)

D116a CHRISTMAS HOLIDAY. *Redbook* August 1939–November 1939.
The novel was published in February 1939 in England, in October 1939 in America.

D117 PROOF READING AS AN AVOCATION (Sir Edward Marsh). *Publisher's Weekly* 14 October 1939.

o

D118 CLASSIC BOOKS OF AMERICA. *Sat. Eve. Post* 6 January 1940. (**A57**)

D119 THE VILLA ON THE HILL. *Redbook* February 1940–April 1940.
The novel was published in April 1941 as *Up at the Villa*.

D120 BRITAIN VIEWS THE FRENCH NAVY. *Living Age* July 1940.

D121 THE REFUGEE SHIP. *Redbook* September 1940.

D122 THE INSIDE STORY OF THE COLLAPSE OF FRANCE. *Redbook* October 1940.

D123 THE LION AT BAY. *Redbook* November 1940.

The above three articles were written after the author's escape from France in a cargo boat, and contain material which he incorporated in *Strictly Personal*.

D124 READING UNDER BOMBING. *Living Age* November 1940.

D125 GIVE ME A MURDER. *Sat. Eve. Post* 28 December 1940.

D126 WHAT TOMORROW HOLDS. *Redbook* January 1941

D127 THEY ARE STRANGE PEOPLE. *Redbook* February 1941.

D128 NOVELIST'S FLIGHT FROM FRANCE. *Sat. Eve. Post* 22 March 1941 (**A60**)

D129 LITTLE THINGS OF NO CONSEQUENCE. *Sat. Eve. Post* 29 March 1941. (**A60**)

D130 WE HAVE BEEN BETRAYED. *Sat. Eve. Post* 5 April 1941 (**A60**)

D131 ESCAPE TO AMERICA. *Sat. Eve. Post* 12 April 1941. (**A60**)
The above four articles represent the serialization of *Strictly Personal*.

D132 THEATRE. *Redbook* May 1941.

D133 MR. TOMKIN'S SITTER. *New Yorker* 7 June 1941.

D134 THE CULTURE THAT IS TO COME. *Redbook* August 1941.

D135 AN EXCITING PROSPECT. *Readers' Digest* October 1941.
Condensed from *Redbook* August 1941.

D136 PAINTINGS I HAVE LIKED. *Life* 1 December 1941.

D137 THE HOUR BEFORE THE DAWN. *Redbook* December 1941, January–April 1942.
This novel was published in book form in June 1942.

D138 WHY DO YOU DISLIKE US? *Sat. Eve. Post* 11 April 1942.

D139 TO KNOW ABOUT ENGLAND AND THE ENGLISH. *American Publishers' Weekly* 13 June 1942.

D140 MORALE MADE IN AMERICA. *Redbook* July 1942.

D141 THE HAPPY COUPLE. *Redbook* February 1943. *See* **D16**

D142 VIRTUE. *Redbook* April 1943.
Article on the war.

D143 UNCONQUERED. *Colliers' Magazine* 10 April 1943. **(A62)** and **(A66)**

D144 THE CAPTAIN AND MISS REID. *International Magazine* June 1943. **(A66)**
Appeared in book form as *Winter Cruise.*

D145 READING AND WRITING AND YOU. *Redbook* August 1943.

D146 WE HAVE A COMMON HERITAGE. *Redbook* August 1943.

D147 THE TERRORIST. *Redbook* October 1943.
This short story was based on Savenkoff, Grand Duke Sergius.

D148 WRITE ABOUT WHAT YOU KNOW. *Good Housekeeping* (N.Y.) November 1943.

D148a THE RAZOR'S EDGE. *Redbook* December 1943–May 1944. The novel was published in book form in April 1944.

D149 HOW I LIKE TO PLAY BRIDGE. *Good Housekeeping* (N.Y.) December 1944.

D150 IN DEFENCE OF WHO-DONE-ITS. *Scholastic* 25 May 1945.

D151 WHAT READING CAN DO FOR YOU. *Life Story* August 1945.

D152 THE COLONEL'S LADY. *Good Housekeeping* (N.Y.) March 1946. Reprinted *Good Housekeeping* (Lond.) August 1946. (**A66**)

D153 A WOMAN OF FIFTY. *Good Housekeeping* (N.Y.) May 1946. (**A68**)

D154 FUNCTION OF THE WRITER. *Writer* 25 May 1946.

D155 THEN AND NOW. *International Magazine* May–June 1946. (**A64**)

D156 BEHIND THE STORY. *Wings* June 1946.
Then and Now was *The Literary Guild*'s book choice for June. Mr. Maugham wrote about the novel in their house organ.

D157 EPISODE. *Good Housekeeping* (Lond.) March 1947. (**A66**)

D158 THE POINT OF HONOUR. *Good Housekeeping* (N.Y.) March 1947. (**A66**)

D159 WHAT SHOULD A NOVEL DO? *Scholastic* 3 March 1947.

D160 THE ROMANTIC YOUNG LADY. *New Yorker* 21 June 1947. (**A66**)

D161 GUSTAVE FLAUBERT AND MADAME BOVARY. *Atlantic Monthly* November 1947 (**A69**)

D162 HENRY FIELDING AND TOM JONES. *Atlantic Monthly* December 1947. (**A69**)

D163 HONORÉ DE BALZAC AND OLD MAN GORIOT. *Atlantic Monthly* January 1948.

D164 EMILY BRONTE AND WUTHERING HEIGHTS. *Atlantic Monthly* February 1948. **(A69)**

D165 FYODOR DOSTOEVSKY AND THE BROTHERS KARAMAZOV. *Atlantic Monthly* March 1948. **(A69)**

D166 STENDHAL AND THE RED AND THE BLACK. *Atlantic Monthly* April 1948. **(A69)**

D167 JANE AUSTEN AND PRIDE AND PREJUDICE. *Atlantic Monthly* May 1948. **(A69)**

D168 HERMAN MELVILLE AND MOBY DICK. *Atlantic Monthly* June 1948. **(A69)**

D169 CHARLES DICKENS AND DAVID COPPERFIELD. *Atlantic Monthly* July 1948. **(A69)**
The above nine articles were published under the general title *The Ten Best Novels of the World* and were collected in book form under the title *Great Novelists and their Novels*. The tenth best novel was *War and Peace* but as there had already been an article on Tolstoy in a recent issue of the *Atlantic Monthly*, Mr. Maugham's essay on the Russian author did not appear in the magazine series.

D169a CATALINA. The Windmill. Nos 9–12. March–December 1948 **(A67)**
The first two numbers preceded book publication.

D170 CATALINA. *Harper's Magazine* June, July and August 1948. The novel was published in book form in America in October 1948.

D171 SPANISH JOURNEY. *Continental Daily Mail* 11 August 1948.

D172 TEN BEST SELLERS. *Good Housekeeping* September 1948.

D173 A WRITER'S NOTEBOOK. *International Magazine* June–August 1949. **(A70)**
This work was published in book form in America in October 1949.

D174 AUGUSTUS. *Cornhill Magazine* Winter 1949/50. **(A74)**

D175 ZURBARAN. *Cornhill Magazine* Summer 1950. (**A**74)

D176 AFTER READING BURKE. *Cornhill Magazine* Winter 1950/51.

D177 SOMERSET MAUGHAM TELLS A STORY OF THE LADY FROM POONA. *News Chronicle* (Lond.) 3 May 1951.
Mr. Maugham's speech at the Royal Academy Banquet reported verbatim.

D178 THE BIDDING STARTED SLOWLY. *The Connoisseur* June 1952.

D179 A letter to the Editor of John O'London's Weekly from Somerset Maugham on the revival of the weekly under date 8 October 1952.

D180 LOOKING BACK ON EIGHTY YEARS. *The Listener* 28 January 1954.
Mr. Maugham's famous broadcast talk on his eightieth birthday.

D181 SOMERSET MAUGHAM AND THE GREATEST NOVELS. *Sunday Times* June–October 1954.
The English serialisation of *Great Novelists and their Novels*, considerably revised and augmented, with a new preface and epitaph, later reprinted by Heinemann under the title *Ten Novels and their Authors*. It was originally intended to run the series for from four to six articles for which Maugham was to receive £3,000 but it was so phenomenally successful that he allowed the serialization to be extended to fifteen weeks—an unprecedented span. The full story is told and Ian Fleming's role in the negotiations in John Pearsons' *The Life of Ian Fleming* (1966).

D182 THE PERFECT GENTLEMAN. Adapted from Molière's *Le Bourgeois Gentilhomme* by W. Somerset Maugham. Photographs by Roderick MacArthur. *Theatre Arts* November 1955.
This play was produced in London in 1915, with Beerbohm Tree in the part of Jourdain. It was published in *Theatre Arts* to celebrate the debut in New York of the Comédie Française Company in their opening performance of Molière's *Le Bourgeois Gentilhomme*. It had not been published before and

Mr. Maugham makes no reference to it in any of his biographical writings.

D183 ON HAVING MY PORTRAIT PAINTED. *Horizon* January 1959.

D184 CREDO OF A STORY TELLER: excerpts from *Points of View*. *Sat. Eve. Post* 21 March 1959.

D185 ON THE APPROACH OF MIDDLE AGE. *Vogue* 15 November 1960.

D186 LOOKING BACK. *Show* (N.Y.) June, July, August 1962. The first appearance of the now notorious autobiography, later serialised in part in the *Sunday Express* from 9 September till 28 October 1962.

E

PLAYS NOVELISED
OR BOOKS DRAMATISED
BY OTHERS

E1   SMITH   1911

SMITH. A novel based on the play by W. Somerset Maugham.
By David Gray.
New York, Duffield & Company. 1911.
pp. [x]+307+[3]. Front., 3 plates.

Note: This novel was issued in two bindings—light greyish green
ribbed cloth, lettered in white, with a cut-out photograph of a scene
from the play pasted on to the front cover, and blue cloth, lettered in
blue, without the photograph on the cover. There are 4 illustrations
taken from the scenes in the play. $1.20. See Muir *Points: Second
Series*, pp. 127–8.

E2   THE LAND OF PROMISE   (1914)

THE LAND OF PROMISE. A Novelization of W. Somerset
Maugham's Play by D. Torbett. Illustrated from Photographs of the
Play. New York, Edward J. Clode. (1914).
pp. [vi]+312. Front., 3 plates. Red ribbed cloth, with title on front in
a circle. $1.25.

E3   THE LAND OF PROMISE   (1915)

THE LAND OF PROMISE. A Novelization of W. Somerset
Maugham's Play by D. Torbett. Illustrated from Photographs of
Scenes from the Play.
New York, Grosset & Dunlap, n.d.
pp. [vi]+312. Front. ,3 plates. 75 c.

E4   THE CANADIAN   (1927)

THE CANADIAN. Photoplay Title of The Land of Promise. A
Novelization of W. Somerset Maugham's Play by D. Torbett.
Illustrated with Scenes from the Photoplay. A Paramount Picture
Starring Thomas Meigham.
New York, Grosset & Dunlap. n.d.
pp. [vi]+312. Front. (different from the above), 3 plates. On cover:
The Land of Promise. This book was issued in two bindings, one in
brown buckram and the other in green cloth, probably a remainder
issue.

E5   RAIN   (1923)

RAIN. A Play in Three Acts, founded on W. Somerset Maugham's
story "Miss Thompson" by John Colton and Clemence Randolph.

New York, Boni and Liveright. (1923).
pp. xiv+243+[1]+1 blank leaf. Blue cloth, paper label on spine, printed in black.

Note: The book has an introduction by Ludwig Lewisohn. The play was originally produced at the Garrick Theatre on 12 May, 1925, with Olga Lindo in the *Sadie* role.

E6 RAIN (1948)

RAIN. A Play in Three Acts by John Colton and Clemence Randolph.
London, New York, Samuel French. (1948).
pp. 86+1 blank leaf. Buff wrappers, printed in red and black, with cover design by Joyce Dennys. *Samuel French's Acting Edition of Plays*, 391.

E7 THE TENTH MAN (c.1937)

THE TENTH MAN from the play by W. Somerset Maugham. Story re-told and edited by C. M. Martin, with illustrations from the film.
[London, Wardour Films (?) c.1937].
pp. 64. Green stiff wrappers, printed in red and black. Illus. in the text, taken from the stills of the film.

Note: A novelisation of the play, probably issued by the film distributors for publicity purposes.

E8 THEATRE (1942)

THEATRE. A Comedy in 3 Acts by Guy Bolton and W. Somerset Maugham.
New York, London, Samuel French. (1942).
pp. 124+[2]+1 blank leaf. Reddish brown wrappers, printed in black. French's *Standard Library Edition*.

Note: A later issue has a slip, drawing attention to certain reservations about the performing rights, pasted on to the verso of p. [8]. The dramatisation was by Guy Bolton, not "Guy Bolton and Somerset Maugham" as stated on the wrappers.

E9 LARGER THAN LIFE (1951)

LARGER THAN LIFE. A Comedy in Three Acts by Guy Bolton. Based on the novel *Theatre* by W. Somerset Maugham.
London, New York, Samuel French. (1951).

pp. 82+1 blank leaf. Blue wrappers, printed in dark blue. Front. *Samuel French's Acting Edition of Plays*, 1955.

Note: This is the same play as *Theatre*, under another title, and with the authorship corrected.

E10   BEFORE THE PARTY   (1950)

BEFORE THE PARTY. A Play in Four Acts by Rodney Ackland, based on a short story by W. Somerset Maugham.
London, New York, Samuel French. (1950).
pp. iv, 83+[1]. White wrappers, printed in black and red with cover design by Joyce Dennys. *Samuel French's Acting Edition of Plays*, 1097.

E11   JANE   1952

JANE. A Comedy, based upon an original story by W. Somerset Maugham, by Samuel Nathaniel Behrman.
New York, Random House. 1952.
pp. 195. Illus. Boards. Also published in *Samuel French's Acting Edition of Plays*. (1953).

F

CHECK-LIST OF WORKS
CONCERNING
W. SOMERSET MAUGHAM

F1 FINDLATER, Jane Helen. Stories from a Glass House. London, James Nisbet & Co. 1904.
Slum Movement in Fiction (Liza of Lambeth), pp. 65–88.

F2 DREISER, Theodore. W. Somerset Maugham's | Great Realistic Novel | OF HUMAN BONDAGE | [*thick rule*] | A Review from The New Re- | public, by Theodore Dreiser | *double-thick rule*] | [*thin rule* | New York: George H. Doran Company. n.d. (1916)
p. 8. 16×9 cm.
The famous review in The New Republic which first drew attention to *Of Human Bondage* in America. Few are aware that it was reprinted in pamphlet form and it is now very scarce.

F3 MARCOSSON, Isaac F. and FROHMAN, Daniel. Charles Frohman. Manager and Man. London, John Lane, The Bodley Head. 1916.
Charles Frohman, whom everybody liked and never had a contract with anyone—his word was always good enough—sponsored several of Maugham's plays, and gave him the idea for *The Land of Promise*. He was drowened when the *Lusitania* was torpedoed in 1915.

F4 WILLIAMS, Harold. Modern English Writers. London, Sidgwick & Jackson. 1918.
W. Somerset Maugham, pp. 267–69, 387.

F5 COLLINS, Joseph. Idling in Italy. Studies of Literature and of Life. New York, Scribner's. 1920.
W. Somerset Maugham, pp. 148–58.

F6 OVERTON, Grant M. When Winter Comes to Main Street. New York, George H. Doran. 1922.
W. Somerset Maugham, pp. 270–92.
Grant Overton was with Doran for some years and handled the promotion side of many of Maugham's books, and was well liked by him.

F7 LEWISOHN, Ludwig. The Drama and the State. New York, Harcourt, Brace. 1922.
Somerset Maugham Himself, pp. 184–87.

F8   ADCOCK, A. St. J. Gods of Modern Grub Street. London, Sampson, Low, Marston. 1923.
W. Somerset Maugham, pp. 213–19.

F9   MAIS, S. P. B. Some Modern Authors. London, Grant Richards. 1923.
Somerset Maugham, pp. 115–28.

F10   TYLER, George C. Whatever Goes Up. The Hazards and Fortunes of a Born Gambler. New York, The Bobbs-Merrill Co. 1924.
A long, fascinating account of how *Lady Frederick* nearly came to be produced first in America.

F11   WARD, Richard Heron. Aspects of the Short Story. London, London University Press. 1924.
Many references to Somerset Maugham.

F12   OVERTON, Grant M. Authors of the Day: Studies in Contemporary Literature. New York, George H. Doran. 1924.
Heterogeneous Magic of Maugham, pp. 344–65.

F13   DUTTON, Graham. Some Contemporary Dramatists. New York, George H. Doran. 1925.
V. W. Somerset Maugham, pp. 95–117.

F14   CLARK, Barrett Harper. A Study of the Modern Drama: a Handbook for the Study and Appreciation of the Best Plays . . . of the last Half Century. New York, D. Appleton & Co. 1925.
W. Somerset Maugham, pp. 123, 143, 242, 248, 265, 320–27.
Contains an admirable analysis of the technique of *The Circle*.

F15   SWINNERTON, Frank. Georgian Scene. London, William Heinemann. 1925.
Black and White, pp. 168–207.

F16   TOWNE, Charles Hanson [and Others]. W. Somerset Maugham: Novelist, Essayist, Dramatist. [New York, George H. Doran, 1925].
John Farrar, 'W. Somerset Maugham: Novelist and So Forth': Charles Hanson Towne, 'Mr. Somerset Maugham at Home': Carl Van Doren and Mark Van Doren, 'W. Somerset Maugham': Dorothea Lawrence Mann, 'Somerset Maugham in

his Mantle of Mystery': M. Aurelius Goodrich, 'After Ten Years of *Of Human Bondage*'.

F17 NICHOLS, Beverley. Twenty-Five. London, Jonathan Cape. 1926.
In which William Somerset Maugham makes a Delicate Grimace, pp. 232–239.

F18 DREW, Elizabeth A. The Modern Novel: Some Aspects of Contemporary Fiction. London, Jonathan Cape. 1926.
W. Somerset Maugham, pp. 93, 96, 98–100, 252.

F19 NICHOLS, Beverley. Are They the Same at Home? London, Jonathan Cape. 1927.
W. Somerset Maugham, or Dark and Difficult, pp. 240–44.

F20 MORGAN, Louise. Writers at Work. London, Jonathan Cape. 1927.
An unusually interesting and revealing article on Somerset Maugham's working methods, gleaned in an interview by a very observant journalist.

F21 DOTTIN, Paul. W. Somerset Maugham et ses Romans. Paris, Perrin et Cie. 1928.

F22 BALMFORTH, Ramsden. The Problem Play and Its Influence on Modern Thought and Life. London, Allen & Unwin. 1928.
Somerset Maugham's *The Unknown*. The Problem of Agnosticism, pp. 108–121.

F23 MARBLE, Annie Russell. A Study of the Modern Novel. British and American since 1900. New York, D. Appleton & Co. 1926.
Dramatic Novelists: W. Somerset Maugham, pp. 148–52.

F24 RASCOE, Burton. A Bookman's Daybook. New York, Horace Liveright. 1929.
A Chat with Somerset Maugham, pp. 148–151.

F25 MANSFIELD, Katherine. Novels and Novelists. London, Constable. 1930.
W. Somerset Maugham (*The Moon and Sixpence*), pp. 17–20.

THE
PAINTED VEIL

BY

W. SOMERSET MAUGHAM

LONDON
WILLIAM HEINEMANN LTD.

The first state of the title-page of *The Painted Veil* before cancellation.

ROYALTY AGREEMENT

Memorandum of Agreement made this 6th April 1897 between W. S.
Maugham of St. Thomas's Hospital hereinafter called the author,
for himself his executors administrators and assigns of the one
part and Thomas Fisher Unwin of 11 Paternoster Buildings hereinafter called the publisher for himself his executors administrators and assigns of the other part. Whereas the author is
the proprietor of copyright in a work at present entitled "A
Lambeth Idyl" which he has requested the publisher to publish
on the terms and conditions hereinafter appearing. It is
hereby agreed between the author and the publishers as follows:-
1.   That in consideration of the hereinafter mentioned payments
the author hereby agrees to sell and assign and the publisher
agrees to purchase the exclusive right of printing and publishing
the above work in serial and book form in Great Britain its Colonies abd Dependencies in the U.S.A. and in English on the con-
tinent of Europe and in all other countries. The author shall
deliver the complete manuscript not later than June 30th 1897
and the publisher shall publish the same not later than
December 30th 1897.
2.   That all details as to the time and manner of production
publication and advertisement and the number and destination of
Free Copies shall be left to the sole discretion of the Publisher
who shall bear all expenses of production publication and Advertisement except the printers' errors at per printers' in-
voice exceeds an average of 5/- per sheet of sixteen pages of
printed matter which amount shall be borne by the author.
3.   That the published price of the first edition shall on
publication be 3/6 per copy but the publisher shall have power
in his discretion to alter the published price of any edition
as he may think fit and to sell the residue of any edition at
a reduced price,or as a remainder.
4.   That the publisher shall deliver to the author on the 30th
September of each year a statement of the number of copies sold
whether singly or in editions or remainders and whether in the
British Dominions or elsewhere during the year before the pre-
ceding 31st March with the price or prices at which such copies
were sold.
4a.   That the first 750 copies sold shall be free of Royalty.
5.   That the publisher shall at the time of the delivery of the
said statement pay to the author on all such copies after the
first 750 at above half their published price a royalty of 10%
on their published price and on all such copies sold after the
first 750 at or below their published price a royalty of 10%
on the net receipts of such sales, and on all copies sold as
remainder that is at below $\frac{1}{4}$ of the published price the royalties shall be 5% on the net receipts of such sales.   In
calculating such royalties 13 copies shall be reckoned as 12
and no royalties shall be paid upon any copies presented to the
author or others or to the press or upon copies destroyed by
fire. But after the sale of 2000 copies the royalty shall
be 12½% and after the sale of 4000 copies the royalty shall be
15% and after the sale of 6000 copies the royalty shall be 20% on
all copies sold at ordinary rates, but on all copies sold at or

Royalty Agreement between W. Somerset Maugham and T. Fisher
Unwin for *Liza of Lambeth*.

The Beinecke Rare Book and Manuscript Library, Yale University

F26 MANNIN, Ethel. Confessions and Impressions. London, Jarrolds, 1930.
Somerset Maugham. Portrait of a Dramatist, pp. 333–37.

F27 BREWSTER, Dorothy and BIRRELL, Angus. Adventure or Experience. Four Essays on Certain Writers and Readers of Novels. New York, Columbia University. 1930.
A sensitive and enlightened essay on Maugham's *Of Human Bondage*, pp. 42–53.

F27a ANON. I HOPE THEY WON'T MIND. London, Eveleigh Nash & Grayson Ltd. (1930).
W. Somerset Maugham, (91, 151, 166.

F28 JONES, Doris Arthur. The Life and Letters of Henry Arthur Jones. London, Victor Gollancz Ltd. 1930.
W. Somerset Maugham, pp. 93, 347.

F29 EPPINGER, Dora W. Somerset Maugham: Regeny es Short Story. Budapest, Kiralyi Magyar Egyetemi Nyomda. 1930.

F30 RIPOSTE, A. Gin and Bitters. New York, Farrar & Rinehart. 1931.

MORDAUNT, Elinor. Full Circle, London. Martin Secker. 1931.

The American edition appeared anonymously and contains a foreword that is lacking in the English edition. *Full Circle* is a vicious and scarcely veiled attack on Somerset Maugham and according to Hart-Davis gossips were quick to whisper that Hugh Walpole had written it in revenge for *Cakes and Ale* and Walpole had sent off an immediate disclaimer to Maugham, who had answered reassuringly. Heinemann persuaded Maugham—reluctantly because he felt it would be better to treat it with the contempt it deserved—to issue a writ for libel and the book was withdrawn, but only after a number of copies had been distributed. I was under the impression that Elinor Mordaunt was a friend of Hugh Walpole's and had written the book as a reprisal for Maugham's portrayal of Walpole in *Cakes and Ale*. Elinor Mordaunt's title *Gin and Bitters* suggested this, but Mr. Hart-Davis told me that she had never known Walpole. Equally cryptically, Martin Secker told me that Elinor Mordaunt had once told him that she had never met Maugham, but had once passed him on the doorstep of her London hotel as he was leaving it. So one is thrown back upon the other principal character in *Cakes and Ale* upon whom the public's attention was first focussed, at least in America, namely Edward Driffield, whose career bore a remarkable resemblance to that of Thomas Hardy's. The novelist had died only two years previously and because he was venerated as the Grand Old Man of literature it was felt unseemly to portray him as not being averse to dropping in at the local and singing ribald comic songs and making a moonlight flight to avoid accumulated debts. But there were few grounds really for censuring Maugham for "libelling the dead" for he never detracted from the accepted belief that Driffield was a distinguished writer.

It is still necessary, however, to find a motive for the loathing that manifests itself on almost every page of *Full Circle*. Looking around for a clue one's attention is drawn to another character in *Cakes and Ale* whose portrait was delineated in none too flattering terms, and that was the second Mrs. Driffield. Nothing was ever said to suggest that she was anyone but of unblemished reputation but a hint that she might have lacked some of the warmer feminine qualities was subtly inferred. The second Mrs Hardy of course was still alive and though there is no record to indicate what were her feelings when she read the book, for she never revealed them at least in public, she would not have been human not to have felt aggrieved. Among her friends she numbered Elinor Mordaunt, and the theory that here lies the explanation would seem to be borne out by a copy of *Gin and Bitters* used by the novelist for preparing the English version, now in the Grenville Cook Collection. She had tried to tone down the portrait of Maugham, cutting out such passages as "He had got a good play out of China, apart from several short stories," but there was enough truth remaining in the book to make it a libellous portrait. The opening paragraphs of Chapter XII have been entirely re-written on a separate blank sheet hinged in. In addition to the extensive revisions the title has been changed to *Full Circle* (she first thought of calling it 'Travellers Tales') and the author has replaced the nom-de-plume 'A Riposte' with her own name.

Possibly the key to the mystery is to be found in a marked passage towards the end of the book. It reads "The widow of the man who he had most grievously lampooned spoke of his great work [*Cakes and Ale*] as 'That silly book', and in the margin Elinor Mordaunt has written 'Thomas Hardy really said this.' "

I doubt if Hardy who was then an old man could have been greatly concerned—"that silly book" probably summed up a momentarily irritation that soon passed and if he had been younger he would perhaps have been more amused than angry. But it was a different matter for the second Mrs. Hardy who had no public reputation to sustain her. She had been a nurse when she married Hardy and now kept his house and worked as his amanuensis and business manager. The slight upon her was real and formidable.

It is perhaps difficult for the normal male to understand the intensity of feeling that must have prevailed when Elinor Mordaunt wrote her book, but if the friendship between the two women had been very close and the second Mrs. Hardy had been more upset than was generally supposed then 'a riposte' could take many guises, and 'no fury like a woman scorned' could be one of them.

F31 SAWYER, Newell W. The Comedy of Manners from Sheridan to Maugham. Philadelphia, University of Pennsylvania Press: London, Oxford University Press. 1931.
W. Somerset Maugham, pp. 152, 197, 198, 204, 217, 224–28, 238.

F32 BENNETT, Arnold. Journal 1929. London, Cassell & Co. 1930.
On pp. 20–24 Bennett describes a picnic Maugham took him on when he was staying with him in the South of France, and it is illuminating to compare this description with Maugham's in *The Vagrant Mood* on pp. 228–29.

F32a BENNETT, Arnold. The Journals of. Newman Flower (Ed.). 3 vols. London, Cassell & Co. 1932–33.
W. Somerset Maugham: Vol. 1. pp. 208, 220, 221, 288. Vol. 3. pp. 86, 134–35, 158, 200, 215–16, 240.
Maugham once said that he and Bennett were not intimate friends but intimate acquaintances, but in later years he grew to like him and they got on well together. In 1905 before Bennett had written *The Old Wives' Tale* one gets the impression that Maugham was inclined to look down on Bennett and had very much the pose of a suave man about the world.

F33 EDGAR, Pelham. The Art of the Novel. From 1700 to the Present Time. New York, Macmillan. 1933.
The Way of Irony and Satire: Maugham, Douglas, Huxley, Lewis, pp. 268–76.

F34 CARICATURES BY LOW. Twelve Biographies. Limited edition of One Hundred Copies. London, New Statesmen and Nation. [December] 1933.
W. Somerset Maugham, with a biography.

F35 GUERY, Suzanne. La Philosophie de Somerset Maugham. Paris, Editions de France. 1933.

F36 ERVINE, St John. The Theatre in My Time. London, Rich & Cowan, 1933.
W. Somerset Maugham, pp. 118–19, 169.

F37 MacCARTHY, Desmond. William Somerset Maugham. "The English Maupassant." With a bibliography. London, William Heinemann. 1934.
One of the best critical studies of Mr. Maugham and his work. First published in Nash's *Pall Mall Magazine*, then in the above pamphlet form. It was again reprinted in *Altogether* and finally in MacCarthy's autobiographical *Memories*.

F38 LEGGETT, H. W. The idea in Fiction, London. George Allen & Unwin. 1934.
W. Somerset Maugham, pp. 45, 65, 111, 112, 120, 142.

F39 MacCARTHY, Desmond. Experience. London, Putnam. 1935.
With the Red Cross in France 1914–1915. Though Maugham is not mentioned by name he served in MacCarthy's unit in France and had his share in some of the incidents described.

F40 MILLETT, F. B. Contemporary American Authors. London, Harrap & Sons. 1935.
Check-list of Maugham's works and some biographical contributions.

F41 CHRONICLES OF BARABBAS 1884–1934. By George H. Doran. New York, George H. Doran, 1935: London, Methuen. 1935.
Somerset Maugham, pp. 143–48, 165, 264, 349.
The book was republished by Rinehart & Co. in 1952 with additional matter.

F42 BENNETT, Arnold, Letters to his Nephew. With a Preface by Frank Swinnerton. New York. Harper Bros. 1935.

W. Somerset Maugham, pp. 125, 138, 145, 148, 198, 219, 267, 275, 279, 290, 316.

F43 DREISER, Theodore. The New Republic Anthology 1915–1935. New York, Dodge Publishing Co. 1936.
As a Realist Sees *Of Human Bondage*, pp. 24–30. *See* **F2**.

F43a BUCHANAN, Donald. James Wilson Morrice. A Biography. Toronto, The Ryerson Press, (1936).
W. Somerset Maugham, pp. 50–52, 57, 59–60, 62–63, 67–73; *The Magician*, pp. 51, 57, 59, 67, 72; *Of Human Bondage*, pp. 67–71. An important source of Maugham's early life in Paris, and the group of artists and writers who used to congregate at the *Chat Blanc*. Maugham used Morrice for the portrait of Warren in *The Magician* and later on the painter Cronshaw in *Of Human Bondage*. See also **F143**.

F44 SCHREIBER, Georges. Portraits and Self-Portraits. Boston, Houghton, Mifflin & Co. 1936.
William Somerset Maugham, pp. 95–105.

F45 McIVER, Claude Searcy. William Somerset Maugham. A Study of Technique and Literary Sources. Upper Darby, Pa., The Author, 6 S. Brighton Ave. 1936.

F46 CORDELL, R. A. William Somerset Maugham. Toronto, New York, Edinburgh, Nelson. 1937. Revised edition: Bloomington, Ind., Indiana University Press: London, William Heinemann. 1961.

F47 DOTTIN, Paul. Le Théâtre de W. Somerset Maugham. Paris, Perrin et Cie. 1937.
Dottin was the first critic to attempt a serious appraisal of Somerset Maugham's work.

F48 WARD, Richard Heron. W. Somerset Maugham: an appreciation. London, Bles. 1937.

F49 MULLER, H. J. Modern Fiction. Studies of Values. New York, Funk & Wagnalls. 1937.
Realism of the Center: Bennett, Galsworthy, Maugham.

F50 CONNOLLY, Cyril. Enemies of Promise. London, George Routledge & Sons. 1938.

W. Somerset Maugham, pp. 37–38, 76–77, 85–88, 92–93, 117–19, 151, 155, 158.

F51 BROWN, John Mason. Two on the Aisle. Ten Years of American Theater in Performance. New York, W. Norton. 1938.
W. Somerset Maugham and Noel Coward Compared, pp. 108–113.

F52 KNOBLOCK, Edward. Round the Room. An Autobiography. London, Chapman and Hall. 1939.
W. Somerset Maugham, pp. 208, 265, 196–98, 341–2, 443.
Although they were great friends and collaborated together on several projects, Knoblock is not very forthcoming about Maugham.

F53 SAVINI, Gertrud. Das Weltbild in William Somerset Maughams Dramen. Erlangen, Junge & Sohn. 1939.
University Thesis.

F54 DOREN, Carl Van & DOREN, Mark Van. American and British Literature since 1890. Revised and enlarged edition. New York, D. Appleton-Century. 1939.
W. Somerset Maugham, pp. 226–31, 271–73, 377.

F55 BATES, H. E. The Modern Short Story. London, Jonathan Cape. 1941.
Somerset Maugham, pp. 7, 15, 74, 105, 141–45, 146, 222.

F56 MOSES, Montrose J. Dramas of Modernism and their Fore-runners. Edited, with Introduction and Bibliographies. Revised, and supplemented, by Oscar J. Campbell. Boston, Little, Brown. 1941.
W. Somerset Maugham, pp. 413–17, 922–23. Also reprints *The Circle*.

F56a VOSKA, Emanuel Victor and Will Irwin. Spy and Counter Spy. London, George G. Harrap & Co. Ltd. (1941).
Voska, who was mixed up with Maugham in the espionage business in Russia, tells the tale of the American business man whom Maugham used as his model for the Ashenden story *Mr Harrington's Washing*.

F57   CARBUCCIA, Horace. Adieu à mon ami anglais. Paris, Editions de France. 1942.

F58   KUNITZ, Stanley J. 20th Century Authors. New York, 1942. William Somerset Maugham, pp. 934–37.

F59   CHURCH, Richard. British Authors. London, Longmans, Green. 1945.
W. Somerset Maugham (with portrait), pp. 69–72.

F90   GOLDRING, Douglas. South Lodge. Reminiscences of Violet Hunt, Ford Madox Ford and the English Review Circle. London, Constable & Co. 1943.
Violet Hunt, popularly supposed to be the original of Rose Waterford in "The Moon and Sixpence" was a great friend of Somerset Maugham and she used to correct his proofs. A collection of his letters to her are preserved in the Berg Collection in the New York Public Library.

F61   SCULLY, F. Rogues Gallery: Profiles of My Eminent Contemporaries. [Hollywood, Murray & Gee. 1943].
W. Somerset Maugham, pp. 15–36.

F62   CONNOLLY, Cyril. Condemned Playground. Essays 1927–44. London, Routledge & Sons, 1945; New York, Macmillan. 1946.
The Art of Being Good, pp. 250–59.

F63   SATURDAY BOOK, THE. Fifth Year. London, Hutchinson. 1945.
Mr. Somerset Maugham, by Fred Bason.
An article of some significance for future biographers. In the early thirties Maugham made a return visit to Bermondsey and got Fred Bason, a genuine Cockney bookseller, to accompany him round his old haunts. Although nothing came of the visit, he did not drop the idea of writing a sequel to *Liza of Lambeth* and after World War II he again revisited the district but when he saw what the war had done to it he was disenchanted. He describes his feelings in *A Writer's Notebook*: "I entered upon a world that was strange to me. I have no doubt that it still offers ample material for a novel, but that which I had in mind was a picture of conditions that have ceased to exist, and I see no point in writing it."
He remained friends with Bason for some years and as the

correspondence[1] between the two men reveals Bason undertook various tasks for him, one of the last—the attempted disposal of his manuscripts in 1936—culminating in a break. But although a Cockney with little education, Fred Bason is a shrewd looker-on and occasionally comes out with some striking observations when writing about Maugham.

F64 WILSON, A. E. Playwrights in Aspic. London, Hume & Van Thal. 1946.
The Inconstant Wife by Somerset Maugham, pp. 56–61. A parody.

F65 VAN GELDER, Robert. Writers and Writing. New York, Charles Scribner's. 1946.
Mr. Maugham on the Essentials of Writing, pp. 139–41.

F66 HITCHENS, Robert. Yesterday, The Autobiography of Robert Hitchens. London, Cassell. 1947.
Some very important references to Maugham, pp. 169, 225, 253–55, 272, 387, 422.

F67 PENGUIN NEW WRITING, THE. Harmondsworth, Middlesex, Penguin Books. 1947.
Men of the World by V. S. Pritchett, pp. 135–41.

F67a WESTCOTT, Glenway. Somerset Maugham and Posterity. *The Windmill* (Lond.) December 1948.

F68 SWAN, Michael. Ilex and Olive: an account of a journey through France and Italy. London, Hume & Van Thal. (1949). Conversations with Maugham, pp. 73–76.

F69 ALLEN, Walter. The English Novel: a short critical history. London, Phoenix House, 1949.
W. Somerset Maugham, pp. 271, 287, 312–14.

F70 BURKE, Billie. With a Feather on My Nose. New York, Appleton-Century-Crofts. 1948: London, Peter Davies, 1950.
W. Somerset Maugham, pp. 31, 74, 86, 91–2, 104, 125, 171.

F71 BASON, Fred. Fred Bason's Diary. Edited, and with an introduction by Nicholas Bentley. London, Wingate. 1950.
Many references to Somerset Maugham.

[1] Letters in the Grenville Cook collection.

F72 TOOLE STOTT, R. Maughamiana. The Writings of W. Somerset Maugham. Being a Handlist of Works by William Somerset Maugham and of his contributions to certain selected periodicals. London, William Heinemann. 1950: New York, Doubleday. 1950.
A handlist, useful for checking publication dates and the novelist's periodical work.

F73 JONAS, K. W. A Bibliography of the Writings of W. Somerset Maughan. [South Hadley, Mass.] 1950.
This check list is almost wholly based on Toole Stott's *Maughamiana*.

F74 MAUGHAM, The Rt. Hon. Viscount. At the End of the Day. London, William Heinemann. 1950.
Robin Maugham writes a very amusing account of an interview with his father when he was writing his autobiography. "I have already written nearly a quarter of a million words," his father said, "and so I'm afraid I can't spare the family very much space. I must therefore ask you to write out for me a brief description of your three sisters and of yourself and of my brother Willie—*in that order.*
"How brief?" his son asked.
"Four lines," his father replied.
In fact Lord Maugham relented and gave his brother Willie three brief mentions by name in all the five hundred and eighty-seven pages of the book.

F75 WILSON, Edmund. Classics and Commercials. A Literary Chronicle of the Forties. New York, Farrar, Strauss. 1950: London, W. H. Allen, 1951.
The Apotheosis of Somerset Maugham, pp. 319–26. The notorious attack on Somerset Maugham, which probably harmed the author more than it did its victim.

F76 EDMAN, Irwin. Proceedings of the American Academy of Arts and Letters and the National Institute of Arts and Letters. Second Series. No. 1. [New York]. 1951.
The Philosopher as Man of Letters, pp. 59–62. An address given at the dinner of the National Institute of Arts and Letters on the 17th October 1950 when Maugham addressed the meeting on the occasion of his being made an Honorary Associate of the Institute.

F77 TREWIN, J. C. The Theatre since 1900. Illustrated. London, Andrew Dakers. 1951.
Many references to Maugham, including the tribute that *Our Betters* and *The Circle* are "two classic plays, fit to stand by Congreve's patterned flourish like frost flowers in glass."

F78 HUDSON, Lynton. The English Stage: 1850–1950. London, George Harrap. 1951.
Maugham's early career in the theatre discussed, pp. 125–27.

F79 BROPHY, John. Somerset Maugham. London, Longmans, Green (for The British Council and the National Book League). 1952.
An excellent study of the novelist.

F80 PAPAJEWSKI, Helmut. Die Welt-, Lebens- und Kunstanschau-ung William Somerset Maughams. Köln, Kölner Universitäts-Verlag. 1952.
This is the complete work of a study of the novelist, part of which first appeared in the Anglia Zeitschrift für englische Philologie. (1944).
I sent Mr. Maugham a copy of the revised edition of Papa-jewski's book and he replied "I am trying to make up my mind to read it again. I thought there was nothing to complain about in the earlier book, except perhaps that he was inclined (in his German way) to reproach me because I had not contrived to raise myself by my boot-straps."

F81 BANKHEAD, Tallulah. Tallulah. My Autobiography. New York, Harper & Bros. 1952.
Maugham wrote to his agent in New York in September 1925 [1] "When I think of the possibility of Tallulah Bankhead playing the part [of Sadie] my blood runs cold and I am resigned to almost any alternative", but according to Rowland Leigh, the playwright, Somerset Maugham later admitted that the biggest professional mistake he had made in his life was "not letting Tallulah Bankhead play *Rain*". 10 years later she played Sadie Thompson in a revival of *Rain* at the Music Box in New York.

F82 KRONENBERGER, Louis. The Thread of Laughter: chapters on English Stage Comedy from Jonson to Maugham. New York, Alfred A. Knopf. 1952.
"Maugham", pp. 289–98.

[1] In the Charles H. Towne Collection in Yale University Library.

F83 HART-DAVIS, Rupert. Hugh Walpole, a Biography. London, Macmillan & Co. 1952.
Cakes and Ale, 316; his letter of denial, 316–17; his later admission, 317 n.; his reflections on, 318, 319, 320; and *Gin and Bitters*, 323–4, 326.
Part of the Mordaunt story is told in Hart-Davis's biography but he deals only with Walpole's kindly intervention on Maugham's behalf and does not attempt an explanation. He said that in the end all was well and the book was not published in England, so he was evidently unaware that Secker had published *Full Circle*.

F84 POUND, Reginald. Arnold Bennett. A Biography. London, William Heinemann. (1952).
W. Somerset Maugham, pp. 6, 23, 31, 129–40, 292, 294, 315, 345, 353, 362.
A useful reference work for the picture it gives of the early days in Paris at the Chat Blanc.

F85 MacCARTHY, Desmond. Memories. London, MacGibbon & Kee. 1953.
William Somerset Maugham, pp. 61–68.

F85a KUNER, Mildred C. The Development of William Somerset Maugham. Ann Arbor, Michigan, Columbia University. 1953.
Doctoral dissertation.

F86 MARLOW, Louis. Seven Friends. London, Richards Press. 1953.
William Somerset Maugham, pp. 142–70. A rewrite of the article he wrote for Writers of Today. Ed. by Denys Val Baker. 1948.

F87 JONAS, K. W. (Ed.). The Maugham Enigma. An Anthology. London, Peter Owen Ltd. 1954.
A scrap book of articles, reviews etc., all previously published.

F88 MacCARTHY, Desmond. Theatre. London, MacGibbons & Kee. 1954.
Somerset Maugham, pp. 119–39.

F89 WILLIAM SOMERSET MAUGHAM. Aetat 80. London, William Heinemann. (1954).
A pamphlet on Maugham to celebrate his 80th birthday.

F90 WILLIAM SOMERSET MAUGHAM. An exhibition of manuscripts, first editions, and associated items in honour of his eightieth birthday. London, The Times Bookshop. (1945). Most of the exhibits came from the Toole Stott Collection, now preserved in The University of California Library, Santa Barbara.

F91 BASON, Fred. Fred Bason's 3rd Diary. Edited, and with an introduction by Michael Sadleir. [London], Andre Deutsch. 1955.
W. Somerset Maugham, pp. 48, 49, 81, 117–19, 167.

F92 GREEN, Julian. Journal 1950–1954. Paris, Librairie Plon. 1955. A visit made by Julian Green to Somerset Maugham in 1952, p. 154.

F93 MANDER, Raymond & MITCHENSON, Joe. Theatrical Companion to Maugham. A Pictorial Record of the First Performances of the Plays of W. Somerset Maugham. With an Appreciation of Maugham's Dramatic Works by J. C. Trewin. London, Rockcliff. (1955).

F94 SWINNERTON, Frank. Background with Chorus. London, Hutchinson. 1956.
W. Somerset Maugham, pp. 27, 102, 124, 139, 162, 176.

F95 BELL, Clive. Old Friends. Personal Recollections of Clive Bell. London, Chatto & Windus. 1956.
W. Somerset Maugham, pp. 151–53. Reminiscences of Maugham in Paris in the early part of the century.

F96 JONAS, K. W. The Gentleman from Cap Ferrat. With a preface by W. Somerset Maugham. New Haven, Conn. 1956. A re-hash of biographical material garnered from Maugham's writings. The booklet has a letter of Maugham's inserted as a preface. The photographs, taken by a photographer in Nice, are excellent.

F97 PEARSON, Hesketh. Beerbohm Tree. His Life and Laughter. London, Methuen & Co. Ltd. 1956.
p. 163: In 1913 Strauss's *Ariadne in Naxos* was sandwiched between *The Perfect Gentleman*, an English version of Molière's *Les Bourgeois Gentilhomme* by W. S. Maugham who writes: "Tree

asked me to put it into modern English which I did, and both he and I were rather violently attacked in consequence. If Tree hadn't wanted this, he could have used the very good 18th century translation. Mine was never published, and has long been lost sight of."

In August 1949 Glynbourne were making enquiries about Maugham's translation, and wrote to A. P. Watt [1] asking who owned the copyright. When the enquiry was put to Maugham, he replied "I cannot tell you whether Tree's executors have any rights in the play . . . In point of fact, only part of my translation was used or otherwise, with Strauss's opera, the performance would have lasted all night. I myself think that for the short part of *Le Bourgeois Gentilhomme* that was used, the Glynbourne people would do much better to use an 18th century translation. It would fit in much better with the costumes and music than my deliberately colloquial version."

F98 JENSEN, Sven Arnold. William Somerset Maugham. Some Aspects of the Man and his Work. Oslo, University Press. 1957. A University thesis.

F99 BISHOP, George W. My Betters. London, W. Heinemann. 1957.
W. Somerset Maugham, pp. 96–99, 180–81.
The author was literary Editor of the Daily Telegraph for 20 years.

F100 HASSALL, Christopher. Edward Marsh. Patron of the Arts. A Biography. [London], Longmans. (1959).
This definitive biography contains a great deal of interesting information on Maugham including a number of unpublished letters, and reproduces some of the proofs of 'The Summing Up' with Marsh's critical notes. These proofs were auctioned at Sotheby's in the Sir Gerald Kelly sale and are now in the Library of the University of Texas.

F101 DAVIS, H. Pilgrims not Strangers. London, Oxford University Press, 1959.
A Mirror of the Ministry in Modern Novels, pp. 113–36.

F102 PFEIFFER, Karl G. W. Somerset Maugham. A Candid Portrait. Introduction by Jerome Weidman. New York, W. W. Norton & Co. Inc. (1959): London, Gollancz. 1959.

[1] In the A. P. Watt letters in the New York Public Library.

In a full-page splash interview in The Sunday Express (London)
under date 19 April 1959, Mr. Maugham disassociated himself
from his biographer and stated that he had not 'set eyes on him
for 10 years' and in all his life 'I suppose I have been in his
company for 10 days.'

F103 JONAS, K. W. (Ed.). The World of Somerset Maugham. An
Anthology. New York, British Book Center. (1959).
Described on the title page as an anthology this is a collection of
5 essays all previously published. The book has a letter of
Maugham's inserted as a foreword which was also used as a
preface to '*The Gentleman from Cap Ferrat*'.

F104 SATURDAY REVIEW GALLERY. Selected from the com-
plete files. Introduction by John Winterich. New York, Simon
& Schuster. 1959.
Somerset Maugham by Frank Swinnerton, pp. 362–69.

F105 BASON, Fred. The Last Bassoon, from the diaries of Fred
Bason. Edited, and introduced by Noel Coward. London, Max
Parrish. (1960).
W. Somerset Maugham, pp. 8, 34–5, 36, 88, 102, 132.

F106 COOPER, Douglas. The Work of Graham Sutherland. London,
Lund Humphries. 1961.
W. Somerset Maugham, pp. 39, 50, 52 n., 56–7.
Interesting account of the genesis of the portrait now in the
National Gallery and the *Cakes and Ale* drawings.

F107 SIMOES, Joao Gaspar. Quatro Estudos. Brasil, Ministerio da
Educacao e Cultura. (1961).
III. Somerset Maugham, Dramaturgo.

F107a YOUNG, Jessica Brett. Francis Brett Young. A Biography.
With a preface by C. P. Snow. London, Heinemann. 1962.
W. Somerset Maugham, pp. 13, 128, 172, 179, 247, 249, 289;
Walpole and, pp. 172, 176.

F108 LAWRENCE, D. H. The Collected Letters of. Edited, with an
Introduction by Harry T. Moore, 2 vols. London, Heinemann.
1962.
Vol. 2. W. Somerset Maugham, pp. 815–16, 817 n., 908, 1230 n.
Maugham understandably was not Lawrence's 'cup of tea'. He

and Wells were "rolling their incomes round Nice", while poor Lawrence "coughed in his little 'square box' of a villa." Lawrence unkindly referred to Maugham as "a narrow-gutted 'artist' with a stutter".

F109 BOOTHBY, Lord. My Yesterday. Your Tomorrow, London, Hutchinson, 1962.
The Maugham Legend, pp. 224–28.

F109a RUSSELL, Leonard (Ed.). The Sunday Times Book Encore. (London), Michael Joseph. (1963).
Somerset Maugham reviles University Scum, pp. 294–95.

F110 LAND, Myrick. The Fine Art of Literary Mayhem. A Lively Account of Famous Writers and their Feuds. New York, Holt, Rinehart and Winston. 1962: London, Hamish Hamilton. (1963).
The 'Ridiculous' Mr. Walpole Endures Agonies at the Hands of Mr. Maugham, pp. 161–79.

F111 BRANDER, Laurence. Somerset Maugham. A Guide. Edinburgh. London, Oliver & Boyd. 1963: New York, Barnes & Noble. 1963.
A not uninteresting study of Somerset Maugham's work, with some occasional shrewd comments.

F111a STEWART, J. I. M. Eight Modern Writers. Oxford, The Clarendon Press. 1963.
W. Somerset Maugham, pp. 13, 245, 263.

F112 FLEMING, Ian. Thrilling Cities. London, Jonathan Cape. 1963.
An afternoon spent with Maugham in Tokyo, pp. 52–4.

F113 WYNDHAM, Violet. The Sphinx and Her Circle. A Memoir of Ada Leverson by her Daughter. London, Andre Deutsch. 1963.
W. Somerset Maugham, pp. 38, 76–7.
Ada Leverson, the friend of Oscar Wilde, and many literary people of her day, kept up an acquaintance with Maugham for some years, and he wrote her many letters in his early days which are in Yale University Library.
Ada Leverson also wrote a novel in 1911 *The Limit* in which one of the characters was Hereford Vaughan, a recognisable portrait of Somerset Maugham.

F114 SWINNERTON, Frank. Figures in the Foreground. Literary
Reminiscences 1917–40. London, Hutchinson. 1963.
Sophisticated Cavemen, pp. 31–26: Maugham and Walpole,
pp. 89–94.

F115 McKINNEY, John F. Review Notes and Study Guide to
Maugham's *Of Human Bondage*. Edited by Ralph Ronald. New
York, Distributed by Monarch Press. (1964). (*Monarch Review
Notes and Study Guides*, 622).

F116 WEINTRAUB, Stanley. Reggie. A Portrait of Reginald
Turner. New York, George Braziller. 1965.
W. Somerset Maugham, pp. 3, 153, 158–60, 163, 167, 185,
192–3, 212, 223, 224–5, 231, 232–33, 244.
Reginald Turner knew everyone in the literary world of his
day, and was a friend of Maugham. See App. **11**

F117 MACLAREN-ROSS, J. Memories of the Forties. London,
Alan Ross. 1965.
How W. S. Maugham's *The Decline and Fall of the Detective
Story* came to be rejected by Cyril Connolly, editor of *Horizon*,
pp. 77–78. In the March 1940 issue of *Horizon* the Editor
announces that he will publish Somerset Maugham on the
Thriller next month, but did not. Not next month or ever!

F118 MACKENZIE, Compton. My Life and Times. Octave Four.
1907–1914. London, Chatto & Windus. 1965.
W. Somerset Maugham, pp. 111, 233.
The Island of Capri was a favourite resort of the English literary
celebrities before the first world war and Maugham shared a
villa with E. F. Benson and John Ellingham Brooks, who was the
prototype for Cross in *The Artistic Temperament of Stephen Carey*
and later far more prominently as Hayward in *Of Human
Bondage*. Compton Mackenzie provides much valuable information about the Island and the colourful literary folk who
made it so notorious at that time.

F119 PURCELL, Victor. The Memoirs of a Malayan Official. London,
Cassell. 1965.
W. Somerset Maugham, pp. 109, 248, 249, 253, 256, 257, 271.
This book throws quite a lot of light not only on the scandals
which undoubtedly gave Maugham the idea for many of his
plots (i.e. pp. 249–50) but also on the charge that he abused

hospitality by ferreting out the family skeletons and putting them into his books, *The Letter* which was based on a local *cause célèbre*, being the most notorious.

F120 MENARD, Wilmon. The Two Worlds of Somerset Maugham. Los Angeles, California, Sherbourne Press Inc. (1965).

F121 STANLEY, Louis T. People, Places and Pleasures. London, MacDonald. 1965.
Somerset Maugham, pp. 126–29.

F122 W. SOMERSET MAUGHAM: an appreciation with biographical sketches and a bibliography. Garden City, New York, Doubleday. (1965).
Mr. Maugham in America by Ellen Doubleday.

F123 ALLSOP, Kenneth. Scan. London, Hodder & Stoughton. 1965.
Grand Old Maugham, pp. 93–97.

F124 NAKANO, Yoshio. Sansetto Momu Kenkyu [trans: W. Somerset Maugham. Tokio. 1966].

F125 MACKENZIE, Compton, My Life and Times. Octave Five 1915–1923. London. Chatto & Windus. 1966.
W. Somerset Maugham, pp. 71, 150, 166, 231, 247.

F126 NAIK, M. K. W. Somerset Maugham. Norman, University of Oklahoma Press. (1966).

F127 BENNETT, Arnold. Letters of. Edited by James Hepburn. 2 vols. London, Oxford University Press. 1966.
Vol. 1. Letters to J. B. Pinker, pp. 4, 63, 78, 80, 108.

F128 HEWETSON, Cecil (Ed.). Wit and Wisdom of Somerset Maugham. Collected by Cecil Hewetson. [London], Duckworth. (1966).
A very superficial selection, which omits many of the most noteworthy passages which are to be found only in the author's fiction.

F129 NICOLSON, Harold. Diaries and Letters 1930–1939. Edited by Nigel Nicolson. London, Collins. 1966.
W. S. Maugham, p. 58; his stories about Lily Langtry, p. 167;

Q

his demon chauffeur, pp. 273–74, 276; Virginia Woolf's praise for *The Summing Up*; Nicolson at the Villa Mauresque, p. 351; the Windsors come to dinner, pp. 351–52.

F130 SATURDAY BOOK, THE. 26th Year. London, Hutchinson. 1966.
Postscript to Maugham, by Fred Bason. A sad postscript indeed!

F131 PEARSON, John. The Life of Ian Fleming. London, Jonathan Cape. 1966.
W. Somerset Maugham, pp. 223–24, 234–35, 242, 243–45, 329.

F132 NICHOLS, Beverley. A Case of Human Bondage. London, Secker & Warburg. (1966).

F133 [Nichols, Beverley]. Preview of A Case of Human Bondage. By Beverley Nichols. Coming from Secker & Warburg on Thursday May 19th at 21s.—"The Most Controversial Book of 1966 . . . could sell 100,000 copies."
An advertising blurb for Beverley Nichols' book, containing extracts picked at random. Whether it sold 100,000 is doubtful, but the publishers came in for some caustic criticism for publishing this attack on one of their own authors.
A biography of Syrie Maugham is being written by an American Richard Fisher with the help and approval of Syrie's daughter Lady Glendevon.

F134 MAUGHAM, Robin. Somerset Maugham and All the Maughams. London, Longmans-Heinemann. 1966: [New York], New American Library. (1966).
There has been some criticism of Robin Maugham's book, but apart from the passages dealing with his Uncle, it is a fascinating and absorbing study in family history, particularly the Appendices which add a sad and final note to Robin Maugham's researches into the past. Although there is some truth in what the 'blurb' to the book claims that as a contribution to the understanding of Somerset Maugham it is of incomparable value and interest, it should not be overlooked that his nephew arrived late on the scene and that many of his deductions are second-hand or are based on the recollections and sensibilities of a very old man. Mr. Robin Maugham sold the film rights of his book to Mr. Joseph F. Levine's Embassy Picture Corporation, and he wrote the screen play of the film. Much of the shooting of "Willie"—

if it has not been shelved—will take place in the grounds of the Villa Mauresque. But because it has changed so much with the building of luxury chalets in the ground and alterations to the Villa itself, a replica will have to be built in the studio. Mr. Alan Searle told me that when he visited the Villa shortly after the developers had moved in, he just "stood there and cried!"

F135 COWARD, Noël. A Song at Twilight. A Comedy in Two Acts. London, Samuel French. (1967).
It was generally assumed by the critics at the first night of the play that the character of Sir Hugo Latymer was based on Somerset Maugham, but this was denied by the author. The play was originally published by Heinemann (1966) as one of three plays by Noël Coward.

F136 WINN, Godfrey. The Infirm Glory. London, Michael Joseph. 1967.
W. Somerset Maugham, pp. 92, 128, ,77, 180, 202, 245–6, 247, 248–60, 261–76, 279–88, 317, 2337, 339.

F137 TAYLOR, John Russell. The Rise and Fall of the Well-Made Play. London, Methuen: New York, Hill & Wang. 1967.
Many references to Maugham's dramatic work.

F138 HENRY, William H., Jr. A French Bibliography of W. Somerset Maugham. Charlottesville, The Bibliographical Society of the University of Virginia. 1967.

F139 WAUGH, Alec. My Brother Evelyn and Other Profiles. London, Cassell. 1967.
10. The Nail in the Coffin. Hugh Walpole, pp. 128–40. 18. W. S. M.: R.I.P., pp. 271–94.
A kind, sympathetic portrait that warms the cockles of the heart.

F140 CHANNON, Sir Henry. Chips. The Diaries of. Edited Robert Rhodes James. London, Weidenfeld & Nicholson. 1967.
W. Somerset Maugham, pp. 32, 392, 417–19, 435–36, 448, 450.

F141 SOTHEBY'S CATALOGUE of the Contents of the Villa Mauresque, the property of the late W. Somerset Maugham. Day of Sale Monday 20th November 1967 at 10.30 precisely. Sotheby & Co.

The Villa Mauresque was left to Mr. Maugham's daughter Lady Glendevon, the contents of the Villa and the income from the copyright of his works for life to Mr. Alan Searle, his secretary and companion for more than 30 years. The income will then go to the Royal Literary Fund which helped aged authors in difficulties and of which Mr. Maugham was Vice-President.

F142 BEACHCROFT, T. O. The Modest Art. A Survey of the Short Story in English. London, Oxford University Press. 1968. W. Somerset Maugham, pp. 4–5, 8, 12, 25–6, 66, 84, 125, 127, 195, 196–204, 216–17, 228; comparison with Kipling, 137; with Maupassant, 201; his influence on post-war writers, 214; writing on Chekhov, 5, 128, 196–97, 214, 233; on development of short story form, pp. 1, 64, 197–200, 233–34.

F143 MORRICE, James Wilson. Catalogue of an exhibition of his paintings. London, Wildenstein's Gallery. July 4–August 2 1968. Morrice was one of the group of painters Maugham met at the *Chat Blanc* in 1905, and the author used him as a model for Cronshaw in *Of Human Bondage*.

F144 BARNES, Ronald F. The Dramatic Comedy of William Somerset Maugham. The Hague, Paris, Mouton. 1968. (*Studies in English Literature*, Vol. XXXII.).

F145 GREENE, Graham. Collected Essays. London, Bodley Head. 1969.
Notes on Somerset Maugham, pp. 197–205.

F145a FOWLER, W. B. British-American Relations 1917–1918. Princeton, N.J., Princeton University Press. 1969. W. Somerset Maugham, pp. 114–18. Important official account of Maugham's role in allied espionage in Russia in 1917. Fowler also reveals the location of Maugham's reports to Sir William Wiseman, head of the British intelligence operations in the United States. A number of these important documents are published for the first time in Robert L. Calder's *W. Somerset Maugham* (1972).

F146 HOUSE AND GARDEN. Weekend Book. London, Condé Nast Publications Ltd. 1969.

Ann Fleming writes about her visit to Somerset Maugham in his home in the South of France a decade ago.

F146a CROWLEY, Aleister. The Confessions of Aleister Crowley. An Autobiography. Edited by John Symonds and Kenneth Grant. London, Jonathan Cape Ltd. 1969.
W. Somerset Maugham, pp. 348, 349, 570–72, 931 n.
Crowley's first wife was Sir Gerald Kelly's eldest sister.

F147 SANDERS, Charles (Ed.). W. Somerset Maugham. An Annotated Bibliography of Writings About Him. De Kalb, Illinois, Northern Illinois University Press. (1970).
This work lists criticisms, reviews and what has been said in books and articles about Maugham (much of it ephemera) over three quarters of a century. What the Editor means by the statement "except for solving certain bibliographical problems and correcting some inaccuracies, the Editor has refrained from rendering personal judgements" is not clear, since none are propounded. But the work will no doubt be of interest to students and scholars seeking to ascertain the reaction of critics to Maugham at different periods of his literary career.

F148 DEAN, Basil. Seven Ages. An Autobiography 1886–1927. London, Hutchinson, (1970).
W. Somerset Maugham, pp. 175–78, 233–34, 250–51, 255, 304–06, 312, 322.

F149 ALDINGTON, Richard. Richard Aldington: selected critical writings, 1928–1960. Edited by Alister Kershaw: with a preface by Harry T. Moore. Carbondale, Ill., Southern Illinois University. Press. 1970.
Somerset Maugham, pp. 32–39.

F150 STERLING, Nora B. Who Wrote the Modern Classics? New York, The John Day Co. (1970).
W. Somerset Maugham (with portrait), pp. 9–41.

F151 BROWN, Ivor. W. Somerset Maugham. London, International Profiles. 1970.
The text is indifferent, but the photographs illustrating the book are a delight!

F152 ACTON, Harold. More Memoirs of an Aesthete. London, Methuen. 1970.

W. Somerset Maugham, pp. 16, 62, 214, 253, 323, 325–28, 334–37, 365.

F153 BROWN, Ivor. Old and Young. London, The Bodley Head. 1971.
W. Somerset Maugham, pp. 15, 60, 61, 65, 145, 165.

F154 DAUBENY, Peter. My World of Theatre, London. Jonathan Cape. (1971).
A severely critical account of a visit to Somerset Maugham at the Villa Mauresque and in London, pp. 67–69, 97–101.

F154a GORDON, Ruth. Myself Among Others. New York, Atheneum Publications. (1971).
Ruth Gordon, the American actress, was a friend of Maugham's for many years.

F155 CANTERBURY, England. King's School. Books given by W. Somerset Maugham. Canterbury, Kent, King's School. n.d. Folio.
Catalogue of the Maugham Library of 5,000 books bequeathed to King's School, classified according to subjects. The best part of the books were his working library and many are annotated by him. The remainder are mostly books sent to him by their authors and inscribed by them. There is for instance a charming double inscription in a book of poems by Edith Sitwell in which she has written "For W. Somerset Maugham with homage from Edith Sitwell and for Willie with love from Edith." There is also a set of the works of H. G. Wells Vol. 1 of which is inscribed "To Willie. God bless him. H. G. Xmas. 1934," with a comic sketch of himself in the nude. There are one or two which belonged to his wife Syrie and a number of Gerald Haxton's.
The Library is kept locked and can only be entered by the pupils for purposes of study. It is a delightful building and admirable for lectures and such like activities and the school is obviously very sensible of the kindness of their benefactor in providing it.
The ashes of W. S. M. are buried in a mahogany casket in the wall of the Library and a plaque marks the spot.[1] Mr. Alan Searle told me that Mr. Maugham wanted to be buried in Canterbury Cathedral but the Dean and Chapter would not

[1] *See illustrations.*

consent because he was an agnostic "which he was not," said Mr. Searle, "at least towards the end."

F156 BEHRMAN, S. N. People in a Diary. A Memoir. Boston, Toronto, Little, Brown & Co. 1972.
xxi. W. Somerset Maugham.

F157 —— Tribulations and Laughter: a memoir. London, Hamilton. 1972.
xxi. W. Somerset Maugham.
A somewhat barbed portrait.

F158 MAUGHAM, Robin. Escape from the Shadows. Robin Maugham His autobiography. London, Hodder & Stoughton. (1972).
One of the shadows being his Uncle William Somerset Maugham.

F159 CALDER, Robert L. William Somerset Maugham and the Quest for Freedom. London, Heinemann. (1972).

F160 ROBERTS, Cecil. Sunshine and Shadow. Being the fourth book of an Autobiography 1930–1946. London, Hodder & Stoughton. (1972).
W. Somerset Maugham, pp. 40, 91, 98, 201, 274, 275, 293, 294–5, 296, 328, 330, 332, 351, 353, 364, 367, 376, 410. A fascinating autobiography, which contains much of interest on Maugham.

G

CHECK LIST OF PERIODICALS CONCERNING W. SOMERSET MAUGHAM

G1 TRAGEDY OF MAUGHAM'S DRAMATIC SUCCESS. *Current Literature*. August 1908.

G2 MR. WILLIAM SOMERSET MAUGHAM. *Bookman* (Lond.). June 1908.

G3 PLAYWRIGHT WHO STUMBLED INTO FAME. By W. P. Eaton. *Harper's Weekly*. 10 October 1908.

G4 W. SOMERSET MAUGHAM. By Max Beerbohm. *Saturday Review*. 9 January 1909.

G5 COLLES v. MAUGHAM. *Times*. 21 December 1909. Also in E. J. MacGillray's *Copyright Cases* (1911).

G6 W. SOMERSET MAUGHAM. *Ally Sloper*. Vol. 27. p. 1342. 1910. (Interview).

G7 PYGMALION AT HOME AND ABROAD. *English Review*. May 1914.

G8 OF HUMAN BONDAGE (review). *Times*. 12 August 1915.

G9 AS A REALIST SEES IT. By Theodore Dreiser. *New Republic*. 25 December 1915.

G10 A BRITISH CLYDE FITCH. By Louis De Foe. *Green Book Magazine*. November 1916.

G11 W. SOMERSET MAUGHAM: Playwright and Novelist. By J. P. Collins. *Bookman* (Lond.). October 1919.

G12 TAHITI FROM MELVILLE TO MAUGHAM. By H. T. Craven. *The Bookman* (N.Y.). November–December 1919.

G13 SOMERSET MAUGHAM. By Desmond MacCarthy. *New Statesman*. 14 August 1920.

G14 W. SOMERSET MAUGHAM. By Rebecca West. *New Statetman*. 5 November 1921.

G15 GOSSIP ON MISS WEST AND MR. MAUGHAM. By Burton Rascoe. *Arts and Decoration*. December 1923.

G16 TOM JONES AND PHILIP CAREY: heroes of two centuries. By C. Van Doren. *Century*. May 1925.

G17 LE REALISME DE SOMERSET MAUGHAM. By Paul Dottin. *Revue de France*. 1 June 1925.

G18 PHYSICIAN, NOVELIST AND PLAYWRIGHT. By G. W. Gabriel. *The Mentor*. December 1926.

G19 SOMERSET MAUGHAM AT HOME. By Frank Scully. *World To-Day*. August 1928.

G20 THE SKIRMISHERS 1. By Desmond MacCarthy. *Life and Letters*. February 1931.

Of all the outstanding critics who have written about Somerset Maugham, Desmond MacCarthy is probably the only one who ever really understood him and knew what he was striving to achieve in his literary work.

G21 MAUGHAM DISCUSSES THE DRAMA: interview. *Living Age*. May 1931.

G22 MR. MAUGHAM ISSUES WRIT FOR LIBEL AGAINST MRS. E. MORDAUNT. *Times*. 6 October. 1931.

G23 THE EXOTICISM OF SOMERSET MAUGHAM. By Leslie A. Marchand. *La Revue Anglo-Américaine*. April 1932.

G24 SOMERSET MAUGHAM. An Appreciation. By Desmond MacCarthy. *Nash's Magazine*. May 1933.

G25 W. SOMERSET MAUGHAM—SOME BIBLIOGRAPHIC-AL OBSERVATIONS. By Percy H. Muir. *Book Collectors' Quarterly*. January–March; April–June 1933.

G26 SOMERSET MAUGHAM—THE MAN AND HIS METHOD. By Godfrey Winn. *Strand*. June 1933.

Recalling that Mr. Maugham had once written a short story— *The Voice of the Turtle*—said to have been based on Godfrey Winn who had spent some weeks at the Villa Mauresque soon after the publication of his first novel, I once asked him what he thought of Godfrey Winn, who was then a very successful columnist. He looked at me blandly for a moment and then said, after a slight pause, "he is a very good bridge player."

G27 LUCK IN AUTHORSHIP. By F. A. Beaumont. *John O'London's Weekly.* 7 October 1933.

G28 MY GREATEST HOUR: the Play that Changed My Life. *John Bull.* 28 October 1933.

The play of course that changed his life, was *Lady Frederick.*

G29 THE STORY TELLING ART OF MR. MAUGHAM. By Louis Kronenburger. *New York Times Book Review.* 12 August 1934.

G30 ANGRY AUTHOR'S COMPLAINT. By Malcolm Cowley. *New Republic.* 22 August 1934.

G31 BOOKS OF THE DAY. By Sylvia Lynd. *Observer* (Lond.). 26 August 1934.

Sylvia Lynd, a noted critic in her day, goes sadly awry in attempting to sum up the literary achievements of Somerset Maugham.

G32 SOMERSET MAUGHAM STANDS CORRECTED: Tallulah Bankhead gives an exciting, arresting performance in *Rain. Literary Digest.* 23 February 1935.

G33 BIOGRAPHICAL SKETCH. By E. K. Taggard. *Scholastic.* 9 March 1935.

G34 THE PLAYS OF SOMERSET MAUGHAM. By St John Ervine. *Life and Letters.* March 1935.
A paper read to the Royal Society of Literature, 9 January 1935.

G35 BRITISH COMEDY. By Ivor Brown. *Theatre Arts Monthly.* August 1935.

G36 THE SPAIN OF SOMERSET MAUGHAM. By Osbert Sitwell. *London Mercury.* September 1935.

G37 "MR MAUGHAM". By Raymond Mortimer. *New Statesman.* 29 June 1935.

G38 SOMERSET MAUGHAM. By L. A. Mackay. *Canadian Forum*. May 1936.

G39 SOMERSET MAUGHAM. By Claude S. McIver. *Reading and Collecting*. July 1937.

Check list of the novelist's works.

G40 AU CAP FERRAT: CHEZ SOMERSET MAUGHAM, ROMANCIER ET ARBORICULTEUR. By Edmond Epardaud. *Les Nouvelles Litteraires*. 24 July 1937.

G41 CAP FERRAT—W. SOMERSET MAUGHAM. By Albert Flament. *La Revue de Paris*. 5 October 1937.

G42 THE MAUGHAM ENIGMA. By Malcolm Cowley. *New Republic*. 30 March 1938.

G43 A SELF-TAUGHT TRADE: Advice to Young Writers from Two Recent Autobiographies. By Stephen Vincent Benét. Sat. Rev. Lit. 16 April 1938.

G44 HISTORY OF THE WRITER'S MIND. M. M. Colum. *Forum*. May 1938.

G45 SOMERSET MAUGHAM: AN APPRAISAL. By Richard Aldington. *Sat. Rev. Lit.* 19 August 1939.

G46 FIVE-DAY ADVENTURE. By Richard A. Cordell. *Sat. Rev. Lit.* 21 October 1939.

G47 W. SOMERSET MAUGHAM. By V. S. Pritchett. *New Statesman*. 15 June 1940.

G48 ASHENDEN'S ESCAPE. *Time*. 22 July 1940.

Story of Mr. Maugham's escape from France.

G49 ENGLISH MAUPASSANT. By W. R. Benet. *Sat. Rev. Lit.* July 27 1940

G50 MR. MAUGHAM ON THE ESSENTIALS OF WRITING. By Robert Van Gelder. 20 November 1940.

G51 SOMERSET MAUGHAM VISITS U.S. AFTER FLEEING CONQUERED FRANCE: *Life.* 2 December 1940.

G52 DEVIL A MONK WAS HE. By Malcolm Cowley. *New Republic.* 1 May 1941.

G53 COOL HAND. By M. D. Zabel. *Nation.* 3 May 1941.

G54 CLOSE-UPS OF THOMAS MANN AND SOMERSET MAUGHAM. *House and Garden.* August 1942.

G55 IMPERTURBABLE MR. MAUGHAM. By H. Smith. *Sat. Rev. Lit.* 22 April 1944.

G56 TRADE WINDS. By B. Cerf. *Sat. Rev. Lit.* 27 May 1944.

G57 LIFE CALLS ON SOMERSET MAUGHAM. *Life.* 18 September 1944.

G58 SOMERSET MAUGHAM'S GIFT TO KING'S SCHOOL, CANTERBURY. *Times* 24 October 1944.

G59 SOMERSET MAUGHAM: A PROFILE. By Hamilton Basso. *New Yorker.* 6 January 1945.

G60 W. SOMERSET MAUGHAM: his attitude toward the drama and his dictum on the theatre. By Sewell Stokes. *Theatre Arts.* February 1945.

G61 MAUGHAM—AS I KNOW HIM. By Karl G. Pfeiffer. *Redbook.* May 1945.

G62 SOMERSET MAUGHAM: SOVIET STAGE PRODUCTIONS OF HIS WORKS. By N. Volkov. *Theatre World.* April 1946.

The Soviets get very confused when they attempt to interpret Maugham's dramatic work. They know they should dub him 'decadent' and 'bourgeois' but they grudgingly admit that they enjoy seeing his plays performed.

G63 AN INTERVIEW WITH SOMERSET MAUGHAM. By Robert Van Gelder. *New York Times Book Review.* 21 April 1946.

G64 MR. SOMERSET MAUGHAM. *Times Lit. Suppl.* 27 April 1946.

Article written on the occasion of Maugham's presentation of his manuscript *Of Human Bondage* to the Library of Congress.

G65 MAUGHAM EPIGRAMS. Selected by Karl G. Pfeiffer. *Vogue.* July 1946.

G66 MAUGHAM AND THE TWO MYTHS. By David Paul. *Cornhill Mag.* Autumn 1946.

G67 ENGLISH LAUGHTER PAST AND PRESENT. By J. M. Brown. *Sat. Rev. Lit.* 23 November 1946.

G68 THE MYSTERIOUS MR. MAUGHAM. *Sat. Rev. Lit.* 26 July 1947.

G69 SOMERSET MAUGHAM AND POSTERITY. By Glenway Wescott. *Harper's Magazine.* October 1947.

Reprinted in *The Windmill* (Heinemann). A fine, critical study.

G70 OF INNOCENCE AND EXPERIENCE. *Time.* 22 March 1948.
The Somerset Maugham Award.

G71 MAUGHAM'S FOLLY. *Desiderata.* 3 September 1948.
A shrewd, penetrating article, written anonymously.

G72 HOW TO WRITE—BY MAUGHAM. By Harry Gilroy. *New York Times Book Review.* 16 January 1949.

G73 MAUGHAM CINEMATIZED. By R. Rhodes. *Sat. Rev. Lit.* 18 June 1949.

G74 HAPPY HOUSE. *New Yorker.* 27 August 1949.

G75 De senectute. By W. O'Hearn. *Commonweal.* 16 September 1949.

G76 W. SOMERSET MAUGHAM. A STORY OF SUCCESS. By Kay Dick. *Leader.* 1 October 1949.

G77   MAUGHAMIANA 1892–1949. By W. R. Benet. *Sat. Rev. Lit.* 22 October 1949.

G78   W. SOMERSET MAUGHAM. *Ladies Home Journal.* November 1949.

G79   W. SOMERSET MAUGHAM. By Trevor Allen. *The Queen.* 7 December 1949.

G80   SOMERSET MAUGHAM. *Sunday Times* (Lond.). 11 December 1949.

   The famous photographic portrait by Douglas Glass, with a short biographical note.

G81   W. SOMERSET MAUGHAM. By C. Angoff. *American Mercury.* January 1950.

G82   SOMERSET MAUGHAM. By L. Kochan *Contemporary Review.* February 1950.

G83   SOMERSET MAUGHAM. An Evaluation. By Luke Parsons. *Fortnightly Review.* November 1950.

G84   A PLAY TO ENCOURAGE YOUNG WRITERS. W. Somerset Maugham proposes an Academy and how it should be conducted. *New York Herald Tribune.* 1 November 1950.

G85   LIFE SPENDS A DAY WITH SOMERSET MAUGHAM IN NEW YORK. *Life.* 20 November 1950.

G85a   SOMERSET MAUGHAM AT REHEARSAL. By Julian Hall. *Radio Times.* 19 January 1950.

G86   MAUGHAM'S "OF HUMAN BONDAGE": The Making of a Masterpiece. By Robert Spence. *Library Chronicle* (University of Pennsylvania). Spring–Summer 1951.

G87   ENCORE. By Georgian. *Woman's Journal.* September 1951.

G88   MERE STORYTELLERS. *The Times* (Lond.). 25 October 1951.
   Leading Article.

G89 SOMERSET MAUGHAM. By Allen Walter. *Journal of the National Book League.* November 1951.

G90 PROFILE—W. SOMERSET MAUGHAM. *Books of the Month* (Lond.). September 1952.

G91 MR. MAUGHAM TO THE RESCUE. By Raymond Mortimer. *Observer* (Lond.). 14 September 1952.

G92 THE OLD PARTY GOES TO LONDON. *Esquire.* December 1952.
Reprinted from the Preface to his *Collected Plays* Vol. 1.

G93 W. SOMERSET MAUGHAM. Författarens Syn pä Saken. *Bonniers Litterära Magazine.* February 1953.

A fine critical article.

G94 REMBRANCE OF H. G. WELLS. *Sat. Rev. Lit.* 11 April 1953.

G95 DEAN OF THE SMOOTHIES. By H. Alpert. *Sat. Rev.* (N.Y.). 25 April 1953.

G96 MAUGHAM AND THE YOUNG IDIOT. By D. Taylor. *Vogue.* 1 September 1953.

G97 SOMERSET MAUGHAM AT EIGHTY. By Cyril Ray. *Sunday Times.* 1 November 1953.

G98 HE PLANNED HIS LIFE LIKE ONE OF HIS NOVELS. By Allan Chappelow. *D. Mail* (Lond.). 21 January 1954.

G99 JOHN O'LONDON'S WEEKLY. 22 January 1954.

Nearly the whole of this issue is devoted to W. Somerset Maugham, with articles by G. B. Stern *Somerset Maugham Comes of Age*, O. Blakeston *Somerset Maugham and the Critics*, Frank Swinnerton *Somerset Maugham as a Writer*, etc.

G100 SOMERSET MAUGHAM. *Times Lit. Suppl.* 22 January 1954.
Appreciation of W. Somerset Maugham's literary career on the eve of his 80th birthday.

G101 OLD FRIENDS. By Sir Gerald Kelly. *Sunday Times.* 24 January 1954.

R

G102 SOMERSET MAUGHAM. Aet. Suae: LXXX. By Harold Nicolson. *Observer* (Lond.). 24 January 1954.

G103 THE EIGHTY YEARS OF MR. MAUGHAM. By Thomas F. Brady. *New York Times Magazine.* 24 January 1954.

G104 LES 80 ANS DE W. SOMERSET MAUGHAM. By Jacques Duesberg. *Syntheses* (Brussels). February–March 1954.

G105 HIS PEN EARNED HIM £750,000. By Frederick Laws. *News Chronicle.* 10 June 1954.

G106 SOMERSET MAUGHAM FESTIVAL. An Evening with Somerset Maugham. By Howard Agg. *Radio Times.* 29 October 1954.
Portrait on front cover.

G107 MR. MAUGHAM'S MAGIC CUP. By J. Chambrun. *Readers Digest.* December 1954.

G108 HOME OF THE GRAND MASTER ON THE RIVIERA'S EDGE—Somerset Maugham's Villa Mauresque. *Woman's Journal.* January 1955.
Finely illustrated.

G109 A PERPETUAL STUDENT. *St Thomas's Hospital Gazette.* April 1955. (Front. port.)
St Thomas's Hospital was of course the hospital where Mr. Maugham obtained his medical degree.

G110 ASPECTS BIOGRAPHIQUES de l'Oeuvre de Somerset Maughams Enfance. By J. Dobrinsky. *Etudes Anglaises.* October–December 1955.

G111 MANN AND MAUGHAM. By J. H. Durston. *House and Garden.* November 1955.

G112 PHYSICIAN FOR THE THEATRE'S ILLS. By J. C. Trewin. *Theatre Arts.* June 1956.

G113 EVEN AT 83 YOU'RE NEVER TOO OLD. *D. Mail.* 16 May 1957.

Somerset Maugham re-visits Heidelberg. Illustrated.

G114 TEA WITH SOMERSET MAUGHAM. By H. Lash. *Library Journal*. 1 October 1957.

G115 THE 'SCUM' AND I. Somerset Maugham takes a long look at the new crop of Angry Young Men, in a talk with Gordon Young. *Sunday Dispatch*. 6 October 1957.

> The now famous remark that raised a storm of protest. Mr. Maugham diplomatically recants in this interview but one imagines that this conception of the new generation of writers is not confined to Mr. Maugham, though he was the first to express it.

G116 ANGRY YOUNG MEN—I ADMIRE THEM. Somerset Maugham discusses 'that rumpus' with Godfrey Smith. *Sunday Times*. 6 October 1957.

G117 SOMERSET MAUGHAM MAKES A VERY ODD RE-QUEST. *D. Mail*. 12 November 1957.

> The interview following the published request to his friends to destroy all his letters.

G118 OF HUMAN BONDAGE. By E. J. Kahn. *New Yorker*. 11 January 1958.

G119 SOMERSET MAUGHAM. A full-page interview with Philip Toynbee. *Observer*. 20 January 1958.

> An odd interview indeed!

G120 SOMERSET MAUGHAM SUMS UP. In an interview with William Hickey. *D. Express*. 20 January 1958. (Illustrated).

G121 SOMERSET MAUGHAM. By Ann Fleming. *House and Garden*. March 1958.

> A long, finely illustrated article describing Somerset Maugham's famous villa at Cap Ferrat.

G122 SOME NEW SHORT STORIES BY SOMERSET MAUGHAM. Told in London Yesterday—and all about Himself. *D. Express*. 4 October 1958. (Interview).

G123 MAUGHAM: A FREE MAN AT EIGHTY-FIVE. By J. Beavan. *New York Times*. 25 January 1959. (Illustrated).

G124 THE THEATRE OF SOMERSET MAUGHAM. By Richard A. Cordell. *Modern Drama*. February 1959.

G125 YACHTS? CAVIAR? NOT FOR ME, SAYS MR. MAUGHAM. An interview with Robert Pitman on the eve of the publication of the Pfeiffer biography *Somerset Maugham as a Candid Portrait*. *Sunday Express*. 19 April 1959.

G126 IT'S AGAINST DOCTOR'S ORDERS: but Maugham (at 85) still Dives. *D. Mail*. 18 May 1959.

G127 OLD PARTY AT TWILIGHT. By Robert Muller. *D.Mail*. 12 October 1959.

G128 GEISHA GAMBOL FOR SOMERSET MAUGHAM. *Life*. 14 December 1959.

G129 SUBSTANCE AND SHADOW. The Originals of the Characters in *Cakes and Ale*. Papers of the Michigan Academy of Science Arts and Letters. XLV. 1960.

G130 A VISIT WITH SOMERSET MAUGHAM. By Edward M. Korry. *Look* 5 January 1960.

Interview with Mr. Maugham on the eve of his 86th birthday.

G131 MASTER OF FICTION—AND MIRROR OF FACT. By Hannen Swaffer. *T.V. Times* (London). 29 January 1960.

G132 EDWARD KORRY VISITS SOMERSET MAUGHAM, THE WORLD'S RICHEST WRITER. *Woman's Day* (Australia). 7 March 1960.

Reprinted from *Look*. Lavishly illustrated in colour.

G133 SOMERSET MAUGHAM TALKS ABOUT LIFE. By Joel Lieber. *This Week*. 22 January 1961 (Interview).

G134 LIVING LEGENDS. By A. Robin. *Today's Health*. April 1961.

G135 MR. MAUGHAM'S NOTIONS. By Kingsley Amis. *Spectator* (Lond.).

G136 THE IBSENITE MAYHEM. By John S. Fielden. *Modern Drama*. September 1961.

G137 MAUGHAM BY THE SEA. By Leonard Lyons. *Saturday Review* (N.Y.). 14 October 1961.

G138 MAUGHAM UNDER THE HAMMER. By John Russell. *The Sunday Times Colour Section* (Supplement). April 1962.

The dispersal of the famous Maugham collection of pictures at Sotheby's.

G139 MAUGHAM. WILLIAM SOMERSET. (1874–1965). British Author. By Anon. Madame Tussaud's Biographies. On sale at the Exhibition. (c. 1962).

An effigy of the most widely read writer since Dickens was added to the waxworks in November 1962. When Maugham saw it, he said "Quite a good likeness."

G140 THE KING'S SCHOOL, CANTERBURY. The Hugh Walpole Collection. The Somerset Maugham Library. By H. M. P. Davies. *Etudes Anglaises*. January–March 1963.

G141 MAUGHAM AT NINETY. Stephen Coulter reports on a visit to the Villa Mauresque. *Sunday Times*. 19 January 1964.

G142 SUMMING UP SOMERSET MAUGHAM AT 90. By Walter Allen. *New York Times Book Review*. 19 January 1964.

G143 SOMERSET MAUGHAM AT 90. By Robin Maugham. *Sunday Telegraph*. 26 January 1964.

Talking to his nephew, a great story-teller recounts some tales he has never written.

G144 I HAVE ONE DESIRE LEFT—TO RETURN TO MY LAST VILLAGE IN THE JUNGLE. Somerset Maugham talking to Ewan MacNaughton. *Sunday Express*. 26 January 1964.

G145 A WILLIAM SOMERSET MAUGHAM.N APPRECIA- TION AND A PROBE. By Joseph B. Lurie M.B. *Medical Proceedings*. 16 January 1965.

A doctor who trained at St. Thomas's Hospital, and became interested in Maugham.

G146 CONFIDENTIAL QUESTION. *NEA Journal.* April 1965.

G147 WILLIAM SOMERSET MAUGHAM. By F. J. S. (Canon F. J. Shirley). The Canturian. December, 1965. (Magazine of King's School, Canterbury.)

One of the great Headmasters of his day, Canon Shirley was responsible for bringing the School back to prosperity when it was in very low waters, and he had the great gift of being able to talk influential people into providing funds for projects to help the School expand. Under his guidance Maugham was brought back to the fold, for after he had left the school he took no further interest in it until Canon Shirley became Headmaster. Then his gifts became frequent and substantial, and these are described in this article. Quotations from Maugham's letters add to its biographical interest.

G148 POSTHUMOUS PUBLICATION BANNED BY MAUGHAM, EXECUTOR REPORTS. By Harry Gilroy. *New York Times.* 16 December 1965.

G149 SOMERSET MAUGHAM. "... THE MOST ASSURED ENGLISH WRITER OF HIS TIME." *Times.* 17 December 1965. (Obituary).

G150 SOMERSET MAUGHAM. *New York Times.* 17 December 1965. (Obituary).

G151 SOMERSET MAUGHAM. By Norman Sherry. *The Guardian.* 18 December 1965. (Obituary).

G152 SOMERSET MAUGHAM. By Malcolm Muggeridge. *Observer.* 19 December 1965. (Obituary).

G153 MAUGHAM. COMPASSIONATE CYNIC. A Summing Up by Cyril Connolly. *Sunday Times.* 19 December 1965. (Obituary)

G154 W. SOMERSET MAUGHAM: 1874–1965. By Anthony Burgess. *Listener.* 23 December 1965.

G155 SOMERSET MAUGHAM. During a simple funeral ceremony at the King's School, Canterbury, yesterday the ashes of W. S. M. an old boy of the School, were buried by the wall of the Library that he gave to the school some years ago. *Times.* 23 December 1965.

G156 VERY OLD PARTY. By J. Lehmann. *New Republic.* 8 January 1966.

G157 SOMERSET MAUGHAM. By Raymond Las Vergnas. *La Revue.* 15 January 1966.

G158 SOMERSET AND ALL THE MAUGHAMS. By Robin Maugham. *Sunday Telegraph.* 16, 23 and 30 January 1966.

Pre-publication serialisation of parts of Robin Maugham's book which was published in April.

G159 MAUGHAM NEVER FORGOT THE DAY I TRUMPED HIS ACE. By C. Goren. *Sports Illus.* 17 January 1966.

G160 THE OTHER SOMERSET MAUGHAM. By Hector Bolitho. *Medical News.* 21 January 1966.

G161 "MY UNCLE WILLIE." By Robin Maugham. *Sat. Eve. Post.* 29 January 1966.

Pre-publication excerpts from Robin Maugham's book on his ancestors.

G162 WHY MAUGHAM WAS MISERABLE. By W. G. S. *Books and Bookmen.* February 1966.

G163 MAUGHAM'S BONDAGE. By F. Clinton. *Nat. Review.* 22 February 1966.

G164 A CASE OF HUMAN BONDAGE. By Beverley Nichols. *Sunday Express.* 10 February–3 June 1966.

The book was serialised in full.

G165 PRINCIPLES AND PROFITS. Publication "Freedom". By Graham Greene. *Daily Telegraph.* 10 June 1966.

The devastating letter written by Mr. Greene, protesting against the publication by Maugham's publishers of B. Nichols' "A Case of Human Bondage".

G166 REMEMBERING MR. MAUGHAM. By Garson Kanin. *Vogue.* 15 August 1966.

G167 SOMERSET MAUGHAM AND HIS WORK. By Sir John Pollock. *Quarterly Review.* October 1966.
An important article about Maugham's literary work.

G168 THE TWISTED MARRIAGE OF SOMERSET MAUGHAM: excerpts from *A Case of Human Bondage*, by Beverley Nichols. *Look* 18 October 1966.

G169 W. SOMERSET MAUGHAM (1874–1965): A Medical Truant. By Fred B. Rogers. *Transactions and Studies of the College of Physicians of Philadelphia.* January 1967.

A well illustrated article.

G170 MAUGHAM FOR SALE. By Colin Simpson. *The Sunday Times Magazine Supplement.* 19 November 1967.

The contents of the Villa Mauresque, some of which are here illustrated in colour, were left to Alan Searle, and were sold at Sotheby's.

G171 SOMERSET MAUGHAM: Encounters with Peril. By Wilson Menard. Blackwood's Magazine. March 1969.

G172 SOUNDINGS. Collections of the University Library. Santa Barbara, University of California. 1971.

Recollections of Somerset Maugham by R. Toole Stott. His article is a slightly revised transcript of a recorded talk.

G173 A VISIT TO MAUGHAM, AND A VISIT FROM COWARD. By Peter Daubeny. *Sunday Times.* 10 April 1971.

Pre-publication excerpts from Daubeny's book *My World of Theatre*.

G174 SOMERSET MAUGHAM'S QUEST FOR FREEDOM by Cecil Roberts. *Books and Bookmen* January 1973.
A fine very long article on Somerset Maugham by Cecil Roberts in his 81st year.

APPENDICES

I   MANUSCRIPTS

II   MISCELLANEOUS MANUSCRIPTS

III   UNPUBLISHED PLAYS

IV   UNPUBLISHED PLAYS ADAPTED BY OTHER WRITERS

V   NOTES

APPENDIX I

MANUSCRIPTS

AS few authors today compose their manuscripts in long-hand but rattle them off on typewriters, we are fortunate that W. Somerset Maugham never became a devotee of the machine but set down in longhand everything he ever wrote. A number of manuscripts have disappeared and several have been destroyed, some by Maugham himself. It is known he tore up one or two of the early manuscripts which he thought immature and not worth preserving, and it is also known that in his old age he spent one infamous day, now known as the 'holocaust', when he put in the fire every manuscript and letter he could lay his hands on, despite the endeavours of his friend and Secretary Alan Searle, to dissuade him. Fortunately, however, by that time he had already distributed among Institutions and Universities both here and in America most of the manuscripts which, in the 30's, he was trying to sell for £10,000 to provide a fund to help young authors—a project happily that came to nought. A number remained in private hands but since his death several of these have been disposed of by their owners, so that now less than two or three remain in private hands. I have been fortunate in tracing one or two 'lost' manuscripts and I do not doubt that one or two others may turn up in course of time. Meanwhile, the following list is as complete a census of the manuscripts still surviving it is possible to compile. They have been listed in chronological order based on date of publication and it can be assumed that any not so listed have been lost or destroyed. I have seen most of the manuscripts, but not all, and I have to thank the curators of Special Collections in the American Universities, particularly those outside New York and Washington, for their cooperation in providing me with all the information I needed to complete the cataloguing.

The plays, since most of them are now the property of the National Theatre, perhaps deserve a special mention. At the present time they are preserved at the Victoria and Albert Museum, but when the National Theatre, the foundation stone of which was laid in 1951, is completed, space will be provided for a Museum or Gallery in which Maugham's plays and his fine collection of theatrical pictures will be on permanent exhibition. The plays are uniformly bound in dark blue or black morocco and written on quarto ruled paper or, as is the case with most of the early plays, on paper torn from exercise books of not always uniform size. Probably because he had not the money to buy fresh paper, he had to make do with what he had. Usually he wrote on ordinary school exercise books bought for a penny, but he would also use all kinds of odd sheets, and even the back of discarded typescripts. The writing has changed somewhat over the years. In the early days the manuscripts were untidy and the writing at times almost illegible but in later years they were both legible and carefully wrought. He hardly ever dated his manuscripts and if it were not for the admirable prefaces, it would be difficult to state with any certainty when his books were written. This reluctance to date his manuscripts applies also to his letters. He would write the day of the month, but invariably not the year.

It is gratifying to know that all the plays Maugham wished to preserve and which were included in the *Selected Plays* with the exception of *Our Betters*, stolen by a friend, and one act of *Lady Frederick*, are now safe for posterity in institutional libraries.

I would like to acknowledge here my indebtedness to Mr. J. T. Bender, the compiler of the excellent catalogue of the Maugham exhibition held at The Stanford University Library in 1958 upon which I have drawn.

LIZA OF LAMBETH

The manuscript of *Liza of Lambeth* is written in 3 differently sized school exercise books in marbled boards and cloth sides, with a stationer's label inside 'Papeterie F. Brocchi, 30 Faubourg Saint-Honoré, Paris.' In the first volume is still preserved the piece of blotting paper he used during the writing of it. The writing is recognisable, but it has none of the evenness of his later years and is sometimes difficult to decipher. The title originally stood as *A Lambeth Idyll* and the author's name is given as William Somerset, whether because he was training as a doctor and did not want his identity revealed, or he wished to remain anonymous in case his book was not a success, are matters for conjecture.

The first volume, which has a map of France on the inside cover, runs to 84 pp. and is written on one side of the sheet only. Vol. 2 is paginated 85–148 and Vol. 3 149–212. The last few pages of the original manuscript have been torn out and six pages added in Maugham's handwriting with the explanation 'The last four pages of this MS. written on loose sheets have vanished in the course of years, so to complete it I have re-written them. 15 July 1931.' And he added a postscript. 'P.S. This novel, my first, was written in 1895 at 11 Vincent Square, Westminster. W. Somerset Maugham.'

It was a strange, eerie sensation to hold these three precious volumes in one's hands in the school grounds where 80 odd years ago Maugham must have passed with his school books under his arm and now, in the wall of the Library, after a lifetime of wonderful story telling, all that remained was a simple plaque bearing his name behind which his ashes rested and where perhaps he had found at last the peace for which he craved.

King's School, Canterbury, through the gift of the author.

THE ARTISTIC TEMPERAMENT OF STEPHEN CAREY

Mr. Maugham presented this manuscript to The Library of Congress on condition that it was never to be printed. He gave as his reason its immaturity and that he was then too young to make proper use of his subject, but the real reason may have been that in it he gave too much of himself away and could not disguise it as he was able to do later when he became a professional writer. For the biographer, this is probably the most important and revealing document in the entire Maugham canon.

The story begins with Stephen in his nursery. He is playing with a toy theatre and his nurse comes in to tell him his mother has died, and the moving scene (repeated in *Of Human Bondage*) describing the young child going into his mother's bedroom, opening a cupboard filled with dresses and burying his face in them so he could smell her scent, is told with a poignancy suggesting it may really have happened.

In this first draft Stephen has no club-foot or infirmity of any kind, his Uncle is not a parson or his Aunt a foreigner, and they have a daughter May (the original of Sally) whom Stephen marries in the end.

He goes to Tercanbury School and is bullied by the other boys, not because of any infirmity but because of his dislike of games and his aptitude for work. The revulsion he has for school, more dramatically expressed in *Of Human Bondage* when the club-foot is the cause of so much humiliation, is not apparent here, and his years at Tercanbury are no more than a passing phase in the life of a sensitive schoolboy.

He leaves school at the age of sixteen and goes to France (instead of Germany in the later version) ostensibly to learn the language but little emphasis is given to his studies. Here he meets Hayward (named Cross in this draft) but he bears little resemblance to the important figure he became in *Of Human Bondage*. After two years in France, spent mostly idling, he returns to England where his Uncle obtains for him a position in a solicitor's office, where he remains until he qualifies.

His Uncle and Aunt live at Woodbridge (the equivalent of the Rectory in the later version) and here Stephen meets his neice's governess Miss Wilkinson, the only character to retain her name when the book is re-written. His affair with her brings the book alive for the first time, and the author uses quite a substantial part of this text when he re-rewrites the story.

While living in London one of the clerks in the office takes him to the tea-shop where Rosie Cameron (the original of Mildred) works as a waitress. And here one gets the impression that this story of unrequited love still fresh in his memory is the motive for writing the book, for apart from the few disgressions in the early chapters, the rest of the novel revolves round Rosie and ends with her.

Miller, the commercial traveller, makes his appearance in much the same way as he does in *Of Human Bondage*, and events succeed each other after much the same pattern, with Miller offering to marry Rosie but does not do so, and she becomes pregnant and he deserts her. She returns to Stephen and the affair miserably drags on for two more years and then she drifts out of his life.

His Uncle dies and Stephen goes down to Woodbridge and meets May again, who is now grown up. He tells her about Rosie and afterwards proposes to her, and though she is unhappy about the influence Rosie still seems to wield over him, she agrees to marry him. Then out of the blue Rosie comes into his life again. He receives an importunate letter from her, insisting she must see him. He is reluctant to do so but May, knowing he will not be able to get her out of his mind until he makes a final break, urges him to go. And against all reason and all his good intentions, Stephen succumbs once again to the hopeless and inexplicable passion he still has for this worthless slattern. He wakes up next morning in a cheap Shaftesbury Avenue hotel with her beside him, realising he has shattered his happiness and can never return to May.

This is undoubtedly how the young Maugham intended to end his novel, but the story is continued on several loose foolscap sheets (filed in a pocket at the end of the second volume) describing his return to Woodbridge and his marriage to May, leading one to believe that a publisher had hinted that if he would give the story a happy ending, he might re-consider it. But the author's heart is not in it and it is laboured writing.

Nevertheless, here was the core of the later draft—the harrowing story of a young and inexperienced boy's passion for a worthless slut that became in the hands of an experienced and accomplished writer one of the great novels in the English language.

The full text of this novel is written on one side of the paper of ruled exercise books measuring 21×15 cm and bound into two volumes. Vol. I ends on p. 299 with Chapter XXXIII and Vol. II on p. 302 with Chapter LIX. The conclusion of the last chapter is continued on sheets of loose ruled foolscap. The title page of Vol. II reads 'An Artistic Temperament' but this is crossed out and changed to 'The

Artistic Temperament of Stephen Carey'. In the top left-hand corner, also crossed out, is written 'Mr. Payne, Albany Chambers, York St, S.W.' Added later under the author's name is the inscription 'This manuscript is presented to The Library of Congress on the condition it is never printed. WM.' In Vol. II the author has made a design of a series of ruled coloured lines as a border to the title-page and at the bottom of the page has written '44,220 words'.

The handwriting is irregular and uncertain, there are numerous corrections, substantial parts having been re-written, and the manuscript has all the signs of having been written in a hurry. Vol. I is bound in brown morocco and Vol. II in blue morocco.

The Library of Congress, through the gift of the author.

THE MIDDLE OF NEXT WEEK

On p. 63 of his delightful *Remembering Mr. Maugham* Garson Kanin tells the story of a play that Maugham wrote for Charles Hawtrey, the actor manager. He did not give it a name but he said that when Hawtrey read it he came round full of excitement and all enthusiasm for the play and for his role. But he wanted to make changes, first one and then another, and though Maugham demurred Hawtrey was such an important figure in the theatre at that time he did not wish to offend him and he promised to give his ideas consideration. When he had gone he picked up the manuscript and became very angry for the pages were full of scribblings and parentheses indicating cuts. Maugham said "I was soon at a boil. I destroyed the manuscript and all the other copies save one—for my files. That one we put into that flame a few nights ago ... I saw Hawtrey many times after that," continued Maugham "and we remained good friends until his death—but he never mentioned my play again. Nor did I."

In the late fifties I went down into the vaults of a bank in St James St and went through a lot of Maugham manuscripts stored there in an old deeds box. Among them was one entitled *The Middle of Next Week*— the first title had been *One of These Days*, but this had been crossed out. I had never heard of the play nor could I recognise it from the names of the characters. When I mentioned it to Mr. Maugham he told me it had been written for Charles Hawtrey and he thought it had been destroyed. That was all.

The play, judging from the handwriting, which is erratic and at times almost illegible, must have been written very early in Maugham's career, round about the turn of the century. It may have been the second draft of the play for leaves written with a very thick nib on paper of smaller size have been inserted possibly from an earlier manuscript. The handwriting resembles that in the manuscript of *A Man of*

Honour and judging from the inks employed was written over a period and not continuously.

It is quite an amusing play and the main character the Duke of St Erth was a typical 'Hawtrey part'. Maugham gives the Time as 'One Hundred Years (changed to 'A Number of years.) after the abolition of the House of Lords', but what the future has got to do with the play is anybody's guess since all the changes the author sees in the future is the impecuniosity of the well-to-do. It is a straight forward story of a member of the aristocracy endeavouring to sustain his financial position in the world by 'inviting ladies and gentlemen of means to join in the refined and elegant house parties which he proposes to give in his historic castle during the summer holidays.' He makes his terms very high so that only the 'very nicest people could accept the invitation'.

> Act I. The Scene. The Hall at Bulkeley Castle. It is a magnificent specimen of late Gothic architecture. Bulkeley Castle is one of the stately homes of England and this is its most gorgeous feature. People come from far and near to see it. There is an open roof, with great black—— (indecipherable), and an imposing elaborate fireplace. The doors have pointed arches and are surmounted with delicate tracery.
> The furniture is of the Jacobean period of dark oak, stately, beautiful and very uncomfortable.
> It is a summer afternoon at the beginning of August. Through the window may be seen the fine old trees of the Park and the blue sky.

As this is a farce, the author adds a Note which is evidently intended to go in the programme: The Management in consultation with eminent politicians, divines, social reformers, and other persons concerned with the future, had spared no expence [*sic*] in providing the exact costumes worn at the period of the play. But there was some doubt whether men would then wear braces or belts, and though it would not have been visible to the audience the management felt that an inaccuracy would be inartistic.

The last sentence was crossed out and changed to 'But there was some doubt whether ladies would then adjust their stockings by means of constriction or of suspension. The management felt that an inaccuracy, though invisible to the audience, would be inartistic.'

The manuscript is written on 127 leaves of ruled thick and thin paper of different dimensions and quality measuring from 21.8 to 25.4 cm. The author has numbered the pages Act I 1–38, Act II 1–56, Act III 1–37. The ending to the play has been accidentally misbound at the beginning of Act III. There are some revisions to the dialogue and all in the author's hand. A label of Ethel Christian's Typewriting Office,

Strand, W.C. is attached to the back of one of the leaves, so it was probably a typed copy that Hawtrey saw and not the manuscript. Bound into a single volume of black morocco with the title in gilt on the front cover.
The National Theatre, through the gift of the author.

THE HERO

This extensively revised and corrected working manuscript is written in seven 6d school exercise books with linen spines and marbled boards. This is probably one of the most interesting of the Maugham manuscripts, not only because the author's handwriting has still not matured but also because it is so extensively revised and altered that one could say it has been completely rewritten; indeed, at first sight it looks as though the author had used both sides of the leaf when writing his story. The foliation in the author's hand is as follows: (1) 1–65, (2) 1–67, (3) 9 leaves unnumbered, 10–67, (4) 1–64, (5) 1–66, (6) 1–37, (7) 1–39. The end is written on the backs of 3 sheets of discarded typescript of the play *The Explorer* and folded into the back of the last notebook. Unlike most of the author's manuscripts, this one is dated 1900 October 8–1901 January 14, and at the top of the title page the author has written '76,000 words'. The seven notebooks are preserved in two black half morocco boxes, red labels on spine.
The University of Texas, Austin.

THE MERRY-GO-ROUND

The first draft of this novel written entirely in the author's hand in four school exercise books with linen spines and marbled paper sides. The first book contains chapters I–VIII (part) of Part I and is foliated in the author's hand 1–138; the second book contains chapters VIII–XV and is foliated 1–142; the third book commences with Part II and contains chapters I–VIII (part) and is foliated 1–140; the fourth book contains chapters VIII–XIV and is foliated 1–139. The novel is written of course on one side of the leaf only, but it has been so heavily corrected and added to that the back of the previous leaf is often completely filled with corrections and additions, here and there in red ink. The writing and inks differ so much that one gets the impression that the alterations and revisions were made at different periods and at long intervals. The title of the first two notebooks is *The Old and the New*, changed in the final version to *The Merry-go-Round*. The original inscription, which is crossed out, was to 'Gerald' (Gerald Haxton) but this was changed at a much later date to 'Jerry' (Jerry Zipkin). In the third book not crossed out is the inscription 'for dear

Gerald. W. S. M.' The four books are preserved in two half black morocco box cases, with red labels on spine.
The University of Texas, Austin.

MRS. CRADDOCK

The manuscript of *Mrs. Craddock* is written in black ink in five small quarto volumes (Vols. I and II of about 200 leaves each, bound in blue cloth, Vols. II–V in school exercise notebooks of about 40 leaves each, bound in marbled wrappers). It is undated and entirely in the author's hand, the main text written on recto leaves with additions, corrections and revisions on versos, with numerous stapled and pasted insets throughout. It is not paginated, and the extensive corrections in red ink all in the author's handwriting are very legible and complete. The manuscript was originally given by Maugham to Mr. A. S. Frere, head of Heinemann's for many years, but it has now changed hands and in the possession of Mr. Lew David Feldman of New York.

A MAN OF HONOUR: a play in four acts.

The first draft of Maugham's first full length play written on the back of 98 leaves of the typed corrected version of *Mrs. Craddock*, measuring 25.5 × 22 cm., now bound into a single volume of limp blue morocco. The manuscript has the appearance of having been written over a period, as different inks are used, the first 8 pages being in purple ink. The writing is very uneven and sometimes difficult to decipher. The author has numbered the leaves boldly Act I 1–27, Act 2 1–28, Act 3 1–25 and Act 4 1–20. The names of some of the characters have been changed but there are very few alterations or amendments.
The National Theatre, through the gift of the author.

A MAN OF HONOUR: printed version.

Mr. Maugham undoubtedly learnt a lot from watching the rehearsals and the first performance of *A Man of Honour*. For one thing he discovered that some scenes of 'flirtations bandinage' in the first act were amusing, and he decided that he could write a comedy. The other thing he noticed was that the scenes in Act III did not develop as he had hoped, and some of them fell quite flat. When, therefore, he heard the play was going to be put on for public performance at the *Avenue Theatre* he decided drastically to revise Act III, and this he did in collaboration with the leading lady Miss Wyford. He used for this purpose a copy of the printed version of the play that had been on sale the first night of the Stage Society's production, and this is the actual copy with the many revisions set down in his own hand. In the Grenville Cook collection there is a letter from Maugham to J. T.

S

Grein dated 25 May 1922 in which he expresses the opinion that he did not think it worth while reviving *A Man of Honour* for a stage production. 'I have not read it for 15 years but my recollection is that the construction of the 3rd Act even in those days was clumsy.'
The University of Texas.

LADY FREDERICK: a comedy in three acts.
The first act of the play that changed the fortunes of Somerset Maugham overnight. It is written on the backs of discarded typescript because, as the author says in his preface to the Stanford University catalogue "being then very short of money, very short indeed, I could not afford to waste pages of good clean paper." It was written in 1905. There are 52 sheets written entirely in the author's hand with numerous corrections and alterations. Maugham states in the above preface that two acts had survived, but so far as is known this single act is the only extant fragment. Included with the manuscript is a presentation letter to Jerome R. Zipkin dated Xmas 1957 in which the author says "the other two acts must have been destroyed years ago." Boxed.
The University of Texas, Austin.

JACK STRAW: a farce in three acts.
The first draft of this play written entirely in the author's hand with a great many changes and interpolations on 141 sheets measuring 20.4 × 18½ cm., the first 41 sheets on lined exercise book paper, the next 46 on similar paper but larger, with the remainder on the earlier size, now bound into a single volume of blue limp morocco. The sheets have been numbered by Maugham Act 1 1–48, Act 2 1–41 and Act 3 1–48. The author described the play originally as a Farce in Three Acts, but crossed this out and changed it to A Very Light Comedy in Three Acts. In the printed version he reverted to the first description and called the play 'a Farce'. This was one of the four plays that he had running in London simultaneously in 1908.
The National Theatre, through the gift of the author.

The first draft of the play originally entitled *Worthley's Entire* is written entirely in the author's hand on 127 leaves of ruled exercise book paper, measuring 23.8 × 19.7 cm. Act II is on larger sized ruled paper. There are very few alterations but the ending of the first act was changed, the old ending still being present. The author gave up numbering the leaves after fol. 24, and another hand has written in the foliation in pencil as follows: Act 1 1–39, Act 2 1–40, Act 3 1–38. Bound in limp blue morocco.
When Maugham first started writing plays he had one play after

another turned down because—as with *Loaves and Fishes*—it was felt he had held up a clergyman to ridicule; and as with *Lady Frederick*, no actress would be seen on the stage with no make-up on and her hair dishevelled. So he made up his mind to devise a play in which no one would find anything to object to. He wrote *Mrs. Dot.* It suffered the same fate as the others.

The managers complained there was not enough action, and a popular actress suggested he added a burglary to make it more exciting. When *Mrs. Dot* eventually found a backer, it ran for over a year.

The National Theatre, through the gift of the author.

PENELOPE: a comedy in three acts.

The first draft of the play written entirely in the author's hand with a number of corrections in red ink on 161 leaves of lined exercise book paper, bound into a single volume of dark blue morocco.

The University of Texas, Austin.

THE TENTH MAN: a tragic comedy.

The manuscript of *The Tenth Man* is written on 199 leaves of ruled and plain paper measuring 25.5×22 cm. with many alterations and additions, especially to Act 2 and Act 3, and several rewritten leaves have been inserted. The pagination is erratic, particularly of Act I, where letters of the alphabet are used as well as numbers. Act I runs a–c, 1–11a, 1–22a, Act II 1–65, Act III 1–71. Bound in limp blue morocco.

The National Theatre, through the gift of the author.

LANDED GENTRY: a comedy in four acts.

Described as a Play in Four Acts this manuscript is written entirely in the author's hand on 131 leaves of blue and white ruled paper, measuring 25.6×22 cm. Apart from one scene excised in Act IV, there are very few revisions or amendments. The leaves are numbered in the author's hand Act I 1–36, Act II 1–32, Act III 1–30 and Act IV 1–29. Bound in limp blue morocco.

The National Theatre, through the gift of the author.

SMITH: a comedy in four acts.

The first draft of this play written in 1909 entirely in the author's hand on 133 leaves of blue ruled exercise books measuring 25.5×21.5 cm. The writing is uneven and sometimes illegible. There are numerous changes and interpolations, particularly in the last two acts. The leaves have been foliated by the author Act I 1–32, Act II 1–37, Act III 1–36 and Act IV 1–35. Bound into a single volume of limp blue morocco. *The National Theatre, through the gift of the author.*

THE LAND OF PROMISE: a comedy in four acts.
The first draft of this play written entirely in the author's hand on 148 leaves of school exercise books with ruled red lines measuring 25.6×21.5 cm. The leaves have been numbered by the author Act I 1–33, Act II 1–37, Act III 1–36 and Act IV 1–38. Bound in a single volume of limp blue morocco.
The author went to Canada and spent some time on a farm in the Middle West to get the background for this play which has as its theme *The Taming of the Shrew* in modern guise. It was one of his most popular plays.
The National Theatre, through the gift of the Author.

OF HUMAN BONDAGE
Described by The Library of Congress as one of the great literary manuscripts of contemporary English literature, *Of Human Bondage* fills some sixteen medium sized notebooks measuring 26×17.4 cm. In addition to the text, it contains copious annotations and amendments in the author's hand. The manuscript consists of 125 chapters, reduced in the printed book to 122, and the pagination of each volume runs as follows: 1–90, 1–85, 1–85, 1–95, 1–85, 1–85, 1–87, 1–86, 1–86, 1–87, 1–86, 1–87, 1–85, 1–85, 1–87, 1–58. Bound in blue niger morocco, all edges gilt or marbled, and lettered in gold on spine MAUGHAM| OF HUMAN BONDAGE.
In Vol. 1 the title page written in the author's hand, reads: "Beauty for Ashes" by W. S. Maugham" and this was not changed until much later when the author discovered this title had recently been used. Looking around for something else he hit upon the title of one of the books in Spinoza's *Ethics* and called it *Of Human Bondage*. It was an inspired thought, and though his publishers did not much care for it, it has undoubtedly contributed in no small measure to its continuing success.
It will interest collectors to know that the author when writing this novel must have had beside him the manuscript of the first draft for there are many passages copied from it almost word for word.
The Library of Congress, through the gift of the author.

THE MOON AND SIXPENCE
The first draft of this novel written entirely in the author's hand on 281 blank leaves bound into two volumes (one with loose pages) and heavily revised. It was purchased by Mr. Jerome Zipkin at the sale of

Sir Gerald Kelly's library in 1950 and obtained a record price for a contemporary literary manuscript. Unlike most of Maugham's manuscripts, this one has a date May–August 1918. Included with the manuscript is a single sheet of lined paper in which the author briefly but imaginatively demonstrates the underlying purpose behind the writing of the book. "Since some readers of this novel have found its title obscure the author ventures upon the following explanation. In his childhood he was urged to make merry over the man who, looking for the moon, missed the sixpence at his feet, but having reached years of maturity he is not so sure that this was so great an absurdity as he was bidden to believe. Let him who will pick up the sixpence, to pursue the moon seems the most amusing diversion." The manuscript was given to his old friend Sir Gerald Kelly, but the inscription has been erased and there is now a new one to "Jerry". Boxed.
The University of Texas, Austin.

THE UNKNOWN: a play in three acts.
First draft of the play written entirely in the author's hand with only minor alterations, apart from one page which has been excised, on 108 sheets of thin while lined paper measuring 25.4 × 22 cm. Maugham has numbered the sheets Act I 1–34, Act II 1–41 and Act III 1–29. Bound in a single volume in limp black morocco.
The National Theatre, through the gift of the author.

THE CIRCLE: a comedy in three acts.
First draft of this play written entirely in the author's hand with only a few alterations and deletions on 84 sheets of lined paper measuring 33 × 23½ cm., now considerably browned and brittle. The leaves have been numbered by the author Act I 1–27, Act II 1–33 and Act III 1–32, but another hand has added a continuous foliation 1–94. The manuscript has been bound into a single volume in dark blue limp morocco with stiff blue end-papers, the title on the spine in gold. Maugham says in the preface to his *Collected Plays* that *The Circle* was generally thought the best play he had written.
The National Theatre, through the gift of the author.

THE TREMBLING OF A LEAF
The first drafts of all seven of the stories which make up this book written entirely in the author's hand with many corrections and alterations on sheets of lined paper now bound into a single volume of dark blue morocco and preserved in a slip case. In the manuscript the stories are differently arranged to the sequence in which they appeared in book form, and read *Rain*, 1–75, *Red*, 76–113, *Honolulu*, 114–155,

The Pool, 156–220, *The Fall of Edward Barnard*, 221–270 and *Mackintosh*, 271–323. *Mackintosh* is spelt without a 'k' and *The Fall of Edward Barnard* has a separate title page. The leaves have been numbered consecutively by Maugham 1–323 but another hand has paginated each story in pencil. *Pacific* and *Envoi* were probably written when the author was rearranging the stories for book publication.

On the holograph title page of the volume is the inscription—"For Bertram Alanson in memory of a long friendship this book dedicated to him is presented by the author January 11, 1947." Bertram Alanson flew from San Francisco to the Mauresque (quite an ordeal in those days) to be with Maugham on his 80th birthday, a pact Maugham told me that they had made when they had first met in the Mauresque nearly 50 years previously.

In the Berg Collection is a letter from A. S. Frere, Chairman of Heinemann, which reads: "Once in San Francisco, on his way to Tahiti, where he got the material for *Rain* and other stories, he met a San Francisco Stock Broker, Bert Alanson, and gave him a thousand pounds to invest, and the Broker turned that into a million dollars—stocks and bonds, nothing to do with writing!"

CEASAR'S WIFE: a comedy in three acts.
The manuscript of this play is written on 129 leaves of blue ruled paper measuring 25.5 × 21.5 cm. and numbered by the author Act I 1–43, Act II 1–46, and Act III 1–36. Apart from two pages which have been heavily revised, there are only minor alterations to the text. The play has two endings. The first

> V. I wish we could have a baby, Arthur. I should be so proud.
> A. Well, my dear, I don't see why we shouldn't.
> V. Put your arms round me closer.

The second ending on white paper, added later, and used for the the printed version

> V. I want to be a good wife to you. I want your love. I want your love so badly.
> A. My dear one.
> V. Put your arms round me. I'm so tired.
> (Her eyes are closed. He kisses her gently. In the distance there is heard again the melancholy wail of a Beduin (*sic*) love song.)

The National Theatre, through the gift of the author.

EAST OF SUEZ: a play in seven scenes.
First draft of the play written entirely in the author's hand on 166

sheets of thin and thick ruled paper, foliated in rubber stamp and pencil but not by the author. It is made up of seven scenes written after a trip to China and was the author's first attempt to write a play of spectacle. It was written from a scenario which may account for the few revisions, but part of Scene VI has been rewritten in red ink on three ruled leaves and inserted into the manuscript. Folios 122–166 are written on larger sized paper with ruled margins. The title page has been added later and is on different paper. Bound in a single volume of dark blue morocco with stiff blue end-papers.
The National Theatre, through the gift of the author.

ON A CHINESE SCREEN
The first draft of this book written entirely in the author's hand on 236 sheets of lined paper with many corrections and alterations in red ink. *On a Chinese Screen* is not a travel book written after he had returned home, but records notes jotted down during the journey of people he had met and sights he had seen and published more or less as they were. This accounts for the numbering of the sheets which were changed frequently as the author altered the sequence of the short chapters to make them conform to the pattern he had in mind for the published book. In presenting the manuscript to the Library, Mr. Maugham wrote in his letter to Mr. Donald G. Wing 22 October 1954 "I am sending you for your Library the manuscript of a book called *On a Chinese Screen* which I have always had a prediliction for. It was written as a result of a long stay in China in 1920. I notice the manuscript hasn't got the preface I wrote when these notes of mine were eventually published, and I suppose I wrote that separately." Bound into a single volume of dark blue morocco, with title and author's name stamped in gold.
The Yale University Library, through the gift of the author.

HOME AND BEAUTY: a farce in three acts.
Written entirely in the author's hand on 131 leaves of ruled paper measuring 25.5×22 cm. with very few alterations. The play was originally called *The Return*. The pagination has been done by the author in ink Act I 1–40, Act II 1–47, Act III 1–53, but another hand has added a continuous pagination in pencil. Bound in limp dark blue morocco.
Home and Beauty was written by Maugham in a Scottish sanatorium during the last winter of the first world war. He contracted tuberculosis of the lungs through exposure to the rigours of a sojourn in Russia, where he had been on a diplomatic mission.
The National Theatre, through the gift of the author.

THE UNATTAINABLE: a farce in three acts.
This is the play that Maugham wrote in 1915 in Switzerland when he was engaged in intelligence work. He had written the whole play up to a great comic scene in the last act. He obtained leave and went to London for the final rehearsals. To his dismay the climax to the great scene did not amuse him at all. He asked the producer to give him twenty-four hours, took the script home and re-wrote the last act. He left out the scene that had so much disappointed him and with it the actor who had been engaged to play it.
This is the original manuscript and the last act is as it was first written with very few revisions. There is nothing to indicate that it had been rewritten, so it would seem the revised text was left with the producer or destroyed.
The Unattainable, the title of which the producer persuaded the author to change during rehearsals to *Caroline*, is written entirely in the author's hand on 144 leaves of blue ruled marginal paper measuring 25.3×21.7 cm. The leaves have been numbered by Maugham in ink Act I 1–41, Act II 1–59, Act III 1–48, but another hand has added a continuous foliation in pencil. There are very few revisions. Bound in a single volume of limp blue morocco.
The National Theatre, through the gift of the author.

LOAVES AND FISHES: a comedy in four acts.
The first draft of the author's second full-length play written entirely in his own hand on 143 leaves of blue tinted bond paper measuring 25.6×22 cm. with some revisions especially in the earlier pages. The end of the play may also have been rewritten as the last four leaves are on white paper and appear to have replaced the original leaves. The pagination is continuous and in another hand. The acts run as follows: Act I 1–31, Act II 1–29, Act III 1–35 and Act IV 1–34. The play was originally described on the title page as A Very Light Comedy, changed to A Satire.
In the preface to *Liza of Lambeth* the author reveals that his novel *The Bishop's Apron* was made out of a play that he had been unable to place. He neglected to mention that the play had been made out of a novel called *Loaves and Fishes* which he had put aside with the intention of rewriting. Then The Stage Society accepted his first full-length play *A Man of Honour* and one or two scenes in it made the audience laugh. This gave him the idea of writing a comedy, so instead of rewriting the novel, he turned it into a play and gave it the novel's original title *Loaves and Fishes*.
The National Theatre, through the gift of the author.

THE CASUARINA TREE
The manuscript of *The Casuarina Tree* is written entirely in the author's hand on 319 leaves of lined loose leaf paper with a number of corrections and alterations in red ink, now bound into a single volume of blue morocco, the title stamped in gold.
Lady Glendevon, through the gift of the author.

THE CONSTANT WIFE: a comedy in three acts.
The first draft of the play written entirely in the author's hand on 156 leaves of thin ruled paper measuring 25.4 × 22 cm. with very few alterations or additions, now bound into a single volume of limp blue morocco. The author has numbered the leaves Act I 1–43, Act II 1–57 and Act III 1–53. It would appear the author was going to call the play *The Painted—* but changed his mind and crossed it out.
The National Theatre, through the gift of the author.

THE LETTER: a play in three acts.
First draft of the play written entirely in the author's hand with some minor corrections in red ink to the first act, on 121 sheets of thin white paper measuring 25.4 × 21.5 cm. The author has not numbered the leaves of the first act, but the other two acts are numbered 1–43 and 1–40. Another hand has added a pagination in pencil 1–121. Bound in a single volume of limp black morocco.
The National Theatre, through the gift of the author.

ASHENDEN
The Bodleian Library possesses a manuscript of *Ashenden* which was presented to the Library by Mr. Maugham in 1952. It is written in school exercise book type paper and bound into a single volume, but although the catalogue says 'holograph' there appears to be some doubt whether it is in the author's hand. There are numerous alterations and additions but again doubt has been expressed whether they were made by the author. It is believed the original manuscript was des-destroyed in the 'holocaust' in 1960 when Maugham made a clean sweep of every manuscript and letter that still survived, but Mr. Alan Searle says that it was not the manuscript he destroyed but fourteen short *Ashenden* short stories that were never published. These were the stories that he showed to his friend Sir Winston Churchill, who expressed the opinion that they should not be published, presumably because of the risk of prosecution under the Official Secrets Act. I have not seen the manuscript so I am unable to express an opinion, but consider from the information that has been vouchsafed me, it is the authentic original manuscript.
The Bodleian Library, through the gift of the author.

SACRED FLAME: a play in three acts.
The first draft of the play originally entitled *Stella* written on 131 leaves of thin lined paper wlth many alterations and additions throughout the manuscript. The leaves have been numbered by the author Act I 1–30 (the first two leaves not included in the pagination), Act II 1–41, Act III 1–44, but another hand has added a continuous pagination in pencil. Bound into a single volume of limp black leather with the title on the spine in gold.
In this play Maugham attempted a greater elaboration of dialogue than he had been in the habit of using and this no doubt accounted for the re-writing of much of the dialogue.
The National Theatre, through the gift of the author.

THE GENTLEMAN IN THE PARLOUR
The first draft written entirely in the hand of the author with numerous corrections and alterations on sheets of paper which at one time formed part of school exercise books. The author has numbered the leaves 1–322 and they are now bound in a single volume of dark blue morocco.
Lady Glendevon, through the gift of the author.

CAKES AND ALE
The first draft of this book written entirely in the author's hand with a number of alterations and additions on 286 sheets of lined paper now bound into a single volume.
The University of Texas, Austin.

THE BREADWINNER: a comedy in One Act.
The first draft of this play originally described as a Comedy in Three Acts, but altered on the title page to "in One Act," with a note "the action of the play is continuous . . . in order to rest the audience the curtain is lowered twice during the performance." The manuscript is written entirely in the author's hand on 126 leaves of white paper with two holes punched at the top so they could go on a file. A number of the scenes have been rewritten, and they were again revised in typescript before being finally sent to the printer. Bound into a single volume of black morocco and lettered in gold on front cover.
The National Theatre, through the gift of the author.

SIX STORIES WRITTEN IN THE FIRST PERSON SINGULAR
The first drafts of all six of the stories that make up this book written entirely in the author's hand on 382 leaves of lined paper now bound

into a single volume and preserved in a box. Like all Maugham's manuscripts these stories show evidence of considerable revision. They again underwent further changes in magazine form so that the type-script which went finally to the printer varies considerably from the manuscript. There is an inscription on the title page to "Jerry".
The University of Texas, Austin.

TO ACCOUNT RENDERED
First draft of the play the title of which was changed to *For Services Rendered* when it was put into rehearsal, written entirely in the author's hand with only a few minor alterations in the text, on 128 sheets of thin white ruled paper measuring 25.4 × 20.5 cm. The leaves have been numbered by the author Act I 1–41, Act II 1–43, Act III 1–42. Bound into a single volume of black morocco with lettering in gold on spine.
For Services Rendered was one of the four plays Maugham said he had to write before finishing his career as a practising dramatist. He did not expect it to be successful and it was not, but he had got it off his mind and he was content.
The National Theatre, through the gift of the author.

AH KING
The first draft of all six of the stories plus the introduction which make up this book written entirely in the author's hand in ruled exercise books measuring 25.9 × 22 cm. now bound into a single volume. It comprises 408 sheets numbered in pencil by the author. Two of the stories have been substantially revised in red ink. The ending of *The Back of Beyond* (re-titled in the International *The Right Thing is the Kind Thing*) was completely re-written, and *Neil MacAdam* was considerably revised throughout. After appearing in magazine form the author again wrote a great deal of them anew, the text of the manuscript therefore differs greatly from that of the first edition. The manuscript is bound in full black morocco, with blue end-papers.
The Pierpont Morgan Library, through the gift of the author.

SHEPPEY: a play in three acts.
Written entirely in the author's hand on 175 leaves of thin white ruled paper measuring 25.4 × 20 cm. with many alterations and revisions in red ink, some considerable. Three leaves of a rewritten scene are loosely inserted. The leaves have been foliated by the author Act I 1–54, Act II 1–49, Act III 1–65, but there is no title page or list of characters. Bound in limp blue morocco.

After the production of *Sheppey* Maugham announced that he would write no more plays.
The National Theatre, through the gift of the author.

DON FERNANDO: or Variations in Some Spanish Themes.
W. Somerset Maugham was 23 when he went to Spain and spent nine months in Seville where "it was heavenly to live in the flower of one's youth." Some 35 years later he incorporated in *Don Fernando* much of the fascination that he found there and which remained with him always. The manuscript which, except for sheets 188 to 205 typed on plain paper, is entirely in the author's hand with many deletions, corrections and alterations in red ink on 301 sheets of lined paper. These are probably single sheets rather than lined exercise books and are bound into a single volume. The inscription on the fly-leaf reads "A belated present for Lord Beaverbrook. W. Somerset Maugham. 30.12.1960."
The University of New Brunswick, through the gift of Lord Beaverbrook (to be kept in his Special Collections).

COSMOPOLITANS
The stories that make up the volume *Cosmopolitans* were originally written on commission for the *Cosmopolitan Magazine*. They had to be short enough to print on opposite pages of the magazine, with an accompanying illustration. They were written over a period of about five years. This probably accounts for the fact that the 286 sheets of lined white paper on which they were written is not quite of uniform size, measuring 26.2 or 28×21.5 cm. All the stories and the preface are written entirely in the author's hand with many deletions, corrections and alterations in red ink. They are bound together in a single volume of full blue morocco in the same order in which they appeared in the printed volume, suggesting that they were bound as a manuscript at some later period. The story *Mr. Know-All*, however, is not present and the story *Raw Material* appears in the manuscript as *The Imposters*. *Cosmopolitans* was one of a number of manuscripts given by their authors for a sale at Christie's in aid of the British Red Cross Fund. The sale was on the 24th and 25th July 1940. The manuscript was bought by an English bookseller for £70. He sold it to Barnet B. Ruder, an American bookseller, who in turn sold it to Mr. Cranford. Accompanying the manuscript is a letter from Mr. Maugham to Ruder, in which he expressed his pleasure that it had been bought by someone interested in him and went on to say that if, after the war when things were more normal, his client would care to make an offer for any of the manuscripts remaining, he would be glad to consider it, as it was

still his intention to put such monies towards the educational purpose he had always had in mind.

It was the bookseller Barnet Ruder, incidentally, who had offered— through Fred Bason—to buy all the Maugham manuscripts for £10,000, but had made conditions that were unacceptable to Maugham and the deal fell through and Bason lost his £1,000 commission.

Mr Duncan Cranford.

THEATRE

The first draft of this book on 425 sheets of lined paper measuring 25×23 cm. written entirely in blue ink in the author's hand. The extensive revisions have been written in red ink on the blank reverse sides of the sheets, now bound into a single volume with the title and author's name blocked in gold.

The University of Princeton, through the gift of the author.

THE SUMMING UP

The first draft of this book written entirely in the author's hand is bound into a single volume, but it is evident from the pagination and the fact that the sheets are conjugated they probably at one time comprised six separate copy-books. The sheets measuring 25.5× 20.5 cm. have been numbered by Maugham 1–20, 1–49, 1–88, 1–84, 1–98, 1–94, later re-numbered by the British Museum 1–463. The two totals do not tally because the author substituted re-written pages with the numbering a, b, c etc., and a few of these sheets are of different quality paper. The manuscript is bound in the author's usual black morocco binding with the title and author's name in gilt on the front cover.

The author spent more time re-writing and revising *The Summing Up* than any of his other works. Substantial passages have been re-written or added in red ink but even much of the unaltered text has been re-written or excised at a later stage and does not appear in the printed book. Indeed, it is doubtful whether more than half of the original writing ever reached the final printing.

The British Museum, through the gift of the author.

TYPESCRIPT. The second stage in the book evolution is the type-script of 467 loose pages with numerous deletions and alterations secured in four red paper folders and bound. Inscribed on the title page "For Gerald Haxton this typescript W. S. Maugham". Above this there is another and later inscription "This typescript once given to G. H. I now give in recollection of him to his friend and mine. W.M." *The University of Texas, Austin.*

FIRST PROOF STAGE. The full set of first proofs heavily corrected in the author's hand and running to 323 pages. There is a pencilled note on the covering sheet "Author's corrections made 23.9.37." The printed date 1937 appears on the title page. Bound and boxed. *The University of Texas, Austin.*

SECOND PROOF STAGE. Second Galley Proofs. These galley proofs which have also been heavily amended and altered in the author's hand were run off from the type after the corrections in the first proofs had been made. These proofs were cut down to page size and comprise 323 pages, which have been bound and boxed. The printed date has been altered by the author from 1937 to 1938. Tipped in at the end are 13 sheets of further revisions and notes covering both sides. *The University of Texas, Austin.*

CHRISTMAS HOLIDAY
The manuscript of *Christmas Holiday* was given by Maugham for a charity sale sponsored by The League of American Writers and the Bookseller's Guild of America. The money was to be devoted to the relief of Italian, Spanish, German and Czech writers both in America and abroad whom political regimes had made homeless. Some of those to be assisted included Leon Feuchtwanger, Heinrich Mann, brother of Thomas Mann, Oscar Maria Graf and Egon Kish.
The sale was to take place on 14 January 1940 at the Hotel Pierre, and some of the writers and musicans who had made gifts of manuscripts proposed to auction off their own works. Maugham had been approached by Vincent Sheen and Louis Bromfield and in a letter dated November 16 said he was sending them the manuscript of *Christmas Holiday*. On the 9th January he cabled that the manuscript would arrive by clipper. On the day of the sale, however, the manuscript was still in transit and as no one apparently had thought to inquire what type of MS it was, the bid was made two ways—one, if it was a typescript and the other if it turned out to be in the author's hand. Of course, it proved to be in the author's hand and Mr Cranford acquired it through the bookseller Barnet Ruder.
The manuscript is the first draft of the novel written entirely in the author's hand with a number of corrections and alterations in red ink on 506 sheets of lined paper measuring 26.5×21.5 cm, now bound into a single volume of full blue morocco, lettered in gold and preserved in a blue morocco slip case.
Mr. Duncan Cranford.

THE PRINCESS AND THE NIGHTINGALE

The first draft of the short story written entirely in the author's hand with a number of corrections and alterations in red ink on 17 sheets of lined paper now bound into a single volume of full blue morocco. It was first published in *Pearson's Magazine* in 1922 with a note stating that it had been written for a 'special purpose'. This special purpose is revealed on the sheet bearing the title on which the author has inscribed "This story was written for the Queen's Doll's House and copied into a long volume which was afterwards bound and placed in the Library. W.M."

Maugham gave this manuscript to The Personal Service League to be sold for charity, and there is a newspaper cutting accompanying the manuscript describing the event. Also included is a cutting from the catalogue of a bookseller who acquired the manuscript at the sale and sold it to the University. When Maugham decided to include the story in *The Gentleman in the Parlour* he must have gone to the trouble of copying it from this manuscript, for the revisions he made in it are included in the later version. The miniature volume which is in the Queen's Doll's House at Windsor is described below.

The University of Texas, Austin.

MINIATURE EDITION

In Queen Mary's Doll's House in Windsor Castle there is a Library containing 200 books written in their author's own hands and bound in exquisite bindings by such noted craftsmen as Sangorski & Sutcliffe, Robert Riviere & Son, Zaehnsdorf and Birdsall & Son of Northampton.

The authors approached were asked to contribute either original work or something already published and (according to the Preface in *The Book of the Queen's Doll's House*) the request was accompanied by "a little blank book in which the author was to write, as small as he could, with his own hand; or, if he could not reduce his calligraphy minutely enough he was to provide the material and it would then be inscribed professionally and he would be asked to sign it."

This indeed may have been the intention, but as the Editor points out it is by no means easy to write neatly in a fat little volume about the size of two postage stamps, and in actual fact what happened was the author was sent the sheets for the miniature book already cut and folded but not bound. This is borne out by the manuscript of *The Princess and the Nightingale*, an examination of which reveals that the writing on some leaves has been cut into by the guillotine, establishing that the book was bound after, and not before, the author had completed writing the story.

The manuscript, measuring $3\frac{1}{2} \times 3 \times 1.2$ cm., is written on 53 leaves entirely in the author's hand. The writing of course is very small and it must have been physically a very exhausting task to write such a long story in such a minute hand. There is no pagination and as there are no alterations or additions, it would seem the author copied the story from the original manuscript. There are two blank leaves before the title page which reads: The Princess and | The Nightingale | by | William | Somerset Maugham, followed by a single leaf on the recto of which is written The End, followed by two further blank leaves. The book is bound in yellow calf, blocked on front with the Royal insignia and similarly on back: the spine is elaborately gilt with a red label lettered in gold THE PRINCESS | AND THE | NIGHTINGALE and a green label W. S. | MAUGHAM. The top edges are gilt. The endpapers are dark green and Queen Mary's book plate is attached to the inside cover.

In the Royal archives is a letter to Mr. Maugham granting him permission to publish the story in *The Book of the Queen's Doll's House* Volume II.

Queen Mary's Doll's House, Windsor Castle, through the gift of the author.

THE MIXTURE AS BEFORE

The manuscript of *The Mixture as Before*, measuring 25 cm., is written entirely in the author's hand in blue ink on 381 leaves of lined paper with corrections and revisions in red ink. The foreword which was probably written at a later date, is not present, and the first page of *The Lotus Eater* is missing. An early draft of pages 25 and 26, in that order, of *A Man with a Conscience* follow *An Official Position*. In the manuscript copy the stories are differently arranged to the printed version, *An Official Position* being the second story and *A Man with a Conscience* the ninth story. In the printed version the position of these two stories is reversed. Bound in oasis niger, with the title in gold.

The Lilly Library, Indiana University.

UP AT THE VILLA

The first draft of the novel written entirely in the author's hand with numerous alterations and amendments in red ink on 213 sheets of lined paper now bound into one volume. This novel was first written in the form of a short story with the same characters and identical plot, but it did not find a publisher and the author put it aside for the best part of 25 years before deciding to re-write it as a novel.

The University of Texas, Austin.

STRICTLY PERSONAL
First draft of this book which was mostly written in the home of his friend Bertram Alanson after his hazardous journey from France in a small collier. It is written entirely in the author's hand on 157 sheets of lined paper with many deletions, alterations and corrections in red ink. Bound into a single volume of dark blue morocco, with title and author's name stamped in gold.
The Yale University Library, through the gift of the Author.

THE UNCONQUERED
The full text of this short story written entirely in the author's hand with a number of alterations and interpolations in red ink on 44 leaves of lined paper. There is an inscription on the title page to "Jerry" Christmas 1943. This is the rewritten version of the story that appeared in *Colliers' Magazine* in an expurgated form.
The University of Texas, Austin.

THE RAZOR'S EDGE
This long novel suggested by a theme in an unproduced and un-published play *The Road Uphill* (1924) is written entirely in the author's hand in a series of exercise books which from his earliest days had been his favourite form of writing material. They comprise 540 sheets with extensive revisions written on the reverse side of the sheets and now bound into a single volume. There is an inscription on the flyleaf "For Nelson Doubleday from his deeply obliged and very affectionate friend the author. Christmas 1944." When Maugham went to America after his flight from France it was Nelson Doubleday, his American publisher, who built him a large comfortable house called Parker's Ferry on his plantation in South Carolina where he wrote *The Razor's Edge*.
Princeton University Library

THEN AND NOW
The first draft of this book written entirely in the author's hand with a number of alterations and additions on 286 sheets of lined paper now bound into a single volume.
The University of Texas, Austin.

CREATURES OF CIRCUMSTANCE
This book is a collection of short stories written at different times over a long period of years. A number of them are stories resurrected from his youth and re-written. It is not surprising, therefore, that when he died the manuscript was not complete. Some stories had been given

T

away, some lost and some destroyed. The following are all that are known to have survived and are together in one place: *The Author Excuses Himself—Flotsam and Jetsam—Appearance and Reality—Sanatorium—The Romantic Young Lady—A Casual Affair—The Point of Honour—[A Man from Glasgow] Robert Morrison—The Happy Couple—Episode—The Kite.*

All these stories are written entirely in the author's hand with a number of alterations and interpolations in red ink on lined and plain paper and number together 528 leaves. *The Happy Couple* was rewritten from the story published in *Cassell's Magazine* in 1908 and the manuscript and typed version given to Professor Karl Pfeiffer. The two versions are preserved together in the Library.

The University of Texas, Austin.

CATALINA

The first draft of the novel written entirely in the author's hand on 381 sheets of lined paper, beautifully bound in pale blue calf. This is probably the cleanest and neatest manuscript that Maugham ever wrote. The writing is wonderfully clear and even and the whole a model of what a publisher likes a manuscript to be. There is not much revision and what there is, is equally neat and tidy. It is dated 28 January 1947, and this (I think) is the third MS. of this author's that I have seen dated. His old school thus possesses his first novel and his last.

King's School, Canterbury, through the gift of the author.

TEN NOVELS AND THEIR AUTHORS

Described by the author as his first book of essays, this manuscript consists of 10 essays with an introduction and a postscript, all written entirely in the author's hand on white lined paper not always of uniform size, now bound into a single volume in black morocco. The numerous revisions are in red ink or on leaves added to the manuscript. Each chapter is paginated separately in the author's hand, and runs as follows: Introduction 1–21, (2) Fielding 1–35, (3) Jane Austen 1–37, (4) Stendhal 1–32, (5) Balzac 1–32, (6) Dickens 1–42, (7) Flaubert, 1–33 (8) Melville 1–32, (9) Bronte 1–41, (10) Dostoevsky 1–38, (11) Tolstoy 1–38, (12) In Conclusion 1–28. The Jane Austen essay is only in typescript as the original manuscript was given to Mrs. Robert Tritton (see below). As leaves have been added later either to add to or re-write the text and numbered with a letter, the pagination is only approximate. There is an inscription on the title page "For Alan, who typed all these essays their grateful Author W. Somerset Maugham. October 1955 in London." Included with this manuscript is a typescript of the same work with alterations and lengthy additions

in the author's hand adding up to approximately 350 pp, but chapter 7 and 8 are missing.
The University of Texas, Austin.

JANE AUSTEN & PRIDE AND PREJUDICE

The first draft of the Jane Austen essay written entirely in the author's hand on 25 leaves of lined quarto paper, lightly revised by him in red ink. A comparison of the manuscript with the printed version reveals however that the whole essay was gone over again by Maugham in typescript and considerably rewritten and added to. Maugham wrote the essay when he was staying with Mrs. Tritton at Godmersham Park, Canterbury, which was once owned by Jane Austen's brother. She often used to visit him when he was there.
Mrs. Robert Tritton, the gift of the author.

A WRITER'S NOTEBOOK

For the best part of his life Maugham kept a notebook in which he jotted down—as he said in the preface to *A Writer's Notebook*—thoughts and emotions of a personal nature with the intention of ascribing them sooner or later to creatures of his invention or when on his travels, impressions while still fresh "of such persons and places as seemed likely to be of service to me for the particular purpose I had in mind at that moment."
These notebooks amounted to fifteen stoutish volumes, but all that seems known to have survived are two lined tablets, one of about 90 sheets made during his journey to the South Seas and entitled *Honolulu* —the raw material that produced *The Trembling of a Leaf*—and the other a similar tablet of about 60 sheets comprising notes made on the journey from Sarawak to Macassar. With these tablets are preserved five loose sheets and the cover of a blank book from which they have been torn. It may be that other tablets still exist. All the above material was used in *A Writer's Notebook*.
The University of Texas, Austin.

ANOTHER FRAGMENT

Written entirely in the author's hand in blue ink on 14 sheets of unlined paper with corrections in red ink and foliated in upper right-hand corner 346–360, bound in blue boards, decorated in gold. It is prefaced by a sheet of lined paper on which the author has written "For Tamie—an unpublished MS. being the last pages of a note book. Xmas 1944. W. Somerset Maugham." This is part of the epitaph to *A Writer's Notebook* which in book form was extended.
From the collection of Grenville Cook.

ANOTHER FRAGMENT

The preface (only) to *A Writer's Notebook*, of which I have no particulars, is owned by Mr. David Randall, Lilly Librarian of the Indiana University.

TRIO

First draft written partly in the author's hand and partly in typescript of the dramatization of the short story *Mr. Know-All* with some corrections and alterations on 37 sheets of plain lined paper. This was one of the three stories filmed in *Trio*. Boxed.
The University of Texas, Austin.

TRIO

First draft of three love scenes from *Sanitorium* written by the author in his own hand on 8 sheets of lined blue paper. In forwarding them to Mrs. Tritton, Maugham commented "I thought you might like the 3 love scenes I wrote for *Sanitorium* because they were written at Godmersham. They of course mean nothing out of the context, but as one of these days you will doubtless see them on the screen it may amuse you to think that they were written over the weekend at your house."
Mrs. Robert Tritton, the gift of the author.

THE VAGRANT MOOD

The Vagrant Mood is another book that comprises essays written at different periods. *Reflections on a Certain Book* was delivered as a lecture at the Philosophical Colloquium of the University of Columbia under the title *Beauty and the Professor*. The author re-wrote it and included it in *The Vagrant Mood* "in the hope of making it more easily readable." *Some Novelists I Have Known* included the well known essay on Arnold Bennett published in *Life and Letters* in June 1931. *Augustus* was published in *The Cornhill* in the Winter of 1949/50. These are the only three out of six essays that make up this book of which the whereabouts are known. They are written entirely in the author's hand with extensive revisions in red ink on 54, 71 and 56 sheets respectively of lined paper.
The University of Texas, Austin.

POINTS OF VIEW

The first draft written entirely in the author's hand on lined exercise books now bound into one volume of black morocco lettered in gold Points of View. The five essays are divided into sections and separately paginated in the author's hand and add up to 314 leaves. Extensive revisions have been made by the author in red ink. The

second essay entitled *The Maharshi* was changed to *The Saint* in book form. The manuscript was given by the author to Lord Beaverbrook in 1961.
The University of New Brunswick, through the gift of Lord Beaverbrook (to be kept in his Special Collections).

PURELY FOR MY PLEASURE
The University of New Brunswick, Fredericton, N.B., where the Beaverbrook Special Collections in the Harriet Irving Library are preserved, can find no trace of this manuscript, but Mr. Alan Searle tells me that he delivered it to Lord Beaverbrook personally at his Villa in Cap Ferrat. It would appear, therefore, that it is still retained by the family.
Lord Beaverbrook, the gift of the author.

LOOKING BACK
The notorious autobiography written during the last years of the author's life and which only appeared abridged serially in *Show* and *The Sunday Express* (D186). It is written on his usual lined paper, and was very little revised. Mr. Searle tells me it contains "some very brilliant things".
Mr. Alan Searle, the gift of the author.

APPENDIX II

MISCELLANEOUS MANUSCRIPTS

THE MAYFAIR MURDER
The Mayfair Murder. By W. Somerset Maugham and Edward Knoblock. Typescript. (Carbon copy, autographed notes): [n.p., n.d.] Maugham m.s. corrections and additions. In 5 folders.
Numerous minor amendments and corrections in the author's hand. It would appear that this film scenario was written by Knoblock, perhaps from a synopsis or short story by Maugham, but nothing ever came of it, probably because it was a very indifferent piece of work.
The Berg Collection at The New York Public Library

THE RAZOR'S EDGE
Holograph of the film play, unsigned and undated. 51p.
—— Typescript, incomplete, with the author's manuscript revisions, dated July 12–19 1945, unsigned. 106p., with the above.

The script is in the author's own hand, on his usual lined exercise book paper, with his opening notes:
"The following is not to be looked upon as a script and will be incomprehensible unless it is read in conjunction with Lamar Trotti's. It should be looked upon only as a story in dialogue. To save time I have left all descriptions of the various scenes and all indication of the feelings or expressions of the various characters. I know nothing about photographic effectiveness and so have left that to be dealt with by Lamar Trotti and George Cukor.'
[The script was not used. Maugham's instructions on p.1 refer to Lamar Trotti's script, a mimeographed copy of which dated 22 March 1946 is in the Theatre Collection.]
Bound in blue buckram and lettered in gold on spine THE | RAZOR'S | EDGE | [ornament] | MAUGHAM 31.4×20 cm.
The Berg Collection at The New York Public Library.

THE CASTILLYONS
Complete outline of a scenario based on an incident taken from the third story in *The Merry-go-Round* and written entirely in the author's hand on four sheets of lined exercise book paper measuring 33×20.4 cm. This is the same provenance as the manuscript of *Penelope*, so it would seem that it is a very early draft, probably the period when, as the author says in *The Summing Up* "from 18 to 20 I wrote down scenes from the plays I had in mind." There is however no record that the author ever proceeded further with it.
There is an inscription on the first page "Given to me by W. Somerset Maugham in February 1905 partly written in my cottage at St Margaret's Bay. —— Wylford. (The christian name is indecipherable.)
Bound in blue morocco with a gold rule border and lettered on spine W. S. MAUGHAM | THE CASTILLYONS | (SCENARIO). | ORIGINAL MANUSCRIPT.
The University of Texas, Austin.

THE LOTUS EATER
The complete text of this short story from *The Mixture as Before* typed on 30 sheets of plain paper with many revisions in the author's hand and notes and markings to the printer. This is apparently all that is known to survive of this manuscript.
The University of Texas, Austin.

[UNTITLED ESSAY ON CHEKHOV]
The draft of an unfinished essay on Chekhov written entirely in the author's hand with numerous revisions on ten sheets of lined paper. It

is, I believe, unpublished, though it may have been the notes for the essay on Chekhov in *The Summing Up*.
The University of Texas, Austin.

ADDRESS DELIVERED IN AMERICA APPEALING FOR FINANCIAL AID FOR THE BENEVOLENT FUND OF THE R.A.F. n.d.
The complete text of this speech written entirely in the author's hand with some additions and corrections on two sheets of plain paper. Included with this is an ALs to André David dated Sepetember 11 (no year).
The University of Texas, Austin.

BROADCASTS OF SHORT STORIES
The complete text of the Introductory and concluding remarks made before and at the end of the broadcasts of the short stories on television. It is written entirely in the author's hand on 19 leaves of lined paper with some amendments. Boxed. The broadcasts were made on American television in 1950.
The University of Texas, Austin.

ADDRESS DELIVERED TO AN UNIDENTIFIED AUDIENCE n.d.
The complete text of this speech beginning "We are living in troublous times..." typed on seven sheets of lined blue paper with several amendments in the author's hand.
The University of Texas, Austin.

ADDRESS DELIVERED AT THE ACADEMY OF ARTS AND LETTERS IN NEW YORK, 1950
The complete text of this speech written entirely in the author's hand with numerous corrections and additions on five sheets of lined blue paper. The text was published in the *Proceedings of the American Academy of Arts and Letters*. No. 1. 1951 under the title *The Philosopher as Man of Letters*.
The University of Texas, Austin

ADDRESS DELIVERED BEFORE THE HERALD TRIBUNE FORUM IN NEW YORK, 1950.
The complete text of this speech written entirely in the author's hand with numerous corrections and amendments on ten sheets of blue lined paper. The text of this paper was published in the New York Herald Tribune on November 1 1950.
The University of Texas, Austin.

ADDRESS DELIVERED BEFORE THE FRIENDS OF THE PIERPONT MORGAN LIBRARY IN NEW YORK. 1950.
The complete text of this speech written entirely in the author's hand with amendments and corrections on seven sheets of lined blank-book paper on the occasion of the presentation to the Friends of the manuscript of "Ah King". Boxed.
The University of Texas, Austin.

ADDRESS DELIVERED AT THE LIBRARY OF CONGRESS IN WASHINGTON, D.C. October 11, 1950.
The complete text of this speech written entirely in the author's hand with deletions and corrections on three sheets of blue lined paper on the occasion of the presentation to the Library of the manuscript of *The Artistic Temperament of Stephen Carey.*
The University of Texas, Austin.

ADDRESS DELIVERED TO AN UNIDENTIFIED AUDIENCE n.d.
The full text of a short speech beginning "I thank you for the great honour . . ." typed on one sheet of plain paper with several corrections, deletions and additions in the author's hand.
The University of Texas, Austin.

ADDRESS DELIVERED AT THE OPENING OF THE HEINE-MANN WINDMILL PRESS EXTENSION 24 June 1952.
The complete text of this speech typed on four sheets of plain paper with some corrections in the author's hand, signed. There is another typewritten copy framed in the Chairman's office at William Heinemann Ltd.
The University of Texas, Austin.

A CHOICE OF KIPLING'S PROSE
The final draft of the introduction to Kipling's short stories written entirely in the author's hand with numerous deletions and alterations in red ink on 73 sheets of lined paper. The first draft formed the talk which he gave before the Kipling Society at a luncheon in 1951.
The University of Texas, Austin.

ADDRESS DELIVERED AT THE BANQUET OF THE ROYAL ACADEMY OF ART IN LONDON. 1951.
The complete text of this speech typed on five sheets of plain paper with several corrections in the author's hand in red ink on the occasion of Mr. Maugham being invited to speak "In Response to the Toast to Literature." His speech was reported verbatim in the *News Chronicle*

(Lond.) on May 3 1951 under the title *Somerset Maugham Tells a Story of a Lady from Poona.*
From the Felton Library at Stanford University, through the gift of Mr. Bertram E. Alanson.

ADDRESS DELIVERED ON THE OPENING OF THE EX-HIBITION OF AUTHORS AS ARTISTS AT THE ARMY AND NAVY STORES (London) 15 October 1956.
The complete text of this speech typed on three sheets of plain paper with several corrections and additions in the author's hand. This talk was later published as a pamphlet. *See Appendix V.*

THE MAGICIAN. A Fragment of Autobiography.
This is the manuscript of the seven page preface Mr. Maugham wrote for this new edition of *The Magician* in which he deals with his literary career after leaving St. Thomas's. It is written entirely in his own hand on eight leaves of plain lined paper with several corrections and alterations. With it is included a typescript revised by the author and the first page proofs with additions and corrections. There is an inscription to Jerry Zipkin giving him the manuscript as "a trifling Christmas present".
The University of Texas, Austin.

GALLERY UNRESERVED
Foreword to *Gallery Unreserved* by Fred Bason, written on four sheets and containing about 500 words.
Accompanying the Maugham foreword is the typed manuscript of *Gallery Unreserved*, together with a proof copy in the original wrappers, and a letter from Maugham to Bason about his book.
Mr. Duncan Cranford.

LETTERS, AGREEMENTS

YALE UNIVERSITY LIBRARY
4 ALS to Dorothy Stanley Allhusen—London, Venice. No year.
45 letters and cards to Lady Marion Bateman 1939–1956—various places.
ALS to Mrs. Ruth Buddington [1935]—Villa Mauresque
5 ALS to William Morris Colles 1899–1905—London, Capri
ALS to Mary Cadwalter Jones 1910—Boston
TLS to Mr. Knollenberg 1942—New York
38 ALS and 1 APCS to Mrs. Ada Leverson 1908–1911—various places
TLS to Sinclair Lewis 1922—Taunggyi, Shan States

ALS to Benjamin Moore n.d.—Villa Mauresque

2 TLS to Miss Morse of George H. Doran 1916–1926—Savoie, Capri.

19 ALS and 3 TLS to William Lyon Phelps 1938–[1943]—various places

4 ALS and 9 TLS to John W. Rumsey 1924–1927—various places

7 ALS and 11 TLS to Charles Hanson Towne 1924–1926—various places

2 TLS to Carl Van Vechten 1924—New Orleans, Havana

TLS to Mr. Wilensky. No year. Villa Mauresque

ALS and 2 TLS to Donald G. Wing [1945]—San Francisco, Cap Ferrat

Royalty Agreement—typed copy of an agreement between Maugham and T. Fisher Unwin of London about *Liza of Lambeth* (1897 April 6 London)

Royalty Agreement—typed copy of an agreement between Maugham and T. Fisher Unwin of London about *The Making of a Saint* (1898 April 4, London)

Royalty Agreement—typed copy of an agreement between Maugham and William Heinemann of London about *The Merry-go-Round* (1904 April 6 London)

Royalty Agreement—typed copy of an agreement between Maugham and Lewis Waller of the Lyric Theatre, London, about *The Explorer* (1907 May 24, London)

NEW YORK PUBLIC LIBRARY, BERG COLLECTION

Letters etc. in the Berg Collection at the New York Public Library, described in the card index:

6 ALS (one undated as to year but fitting in with the period of the typed letters), 72 TLS, all signed, and a Telegram. Various addresses but mostly from Villa Mauresque, Cap Ferrat 1947–1954. 83 pp.

Characteristically succinct instructions and suggestions to Watt concerning rights and fees involved in new editions or reprints of his earlier novels and stories, stage, television and film adaptations (such as the stories used in the films *Quartet* and *Trio*), and the operatic version of *The Moon and Sixpence*. New works discussed frequently include Notebooks (*A Writer's Notebook*), essays (particularly on Jane Austen and Dickens) which Ian Fleming was interested in securing for *The Sunday Times*, and his preface to the Aga Khan's *Memoirs*, over which a misunderstanding as to payment had taken place. The longest letter (2 pp. 4to. 3 June 1951) and several others concern *A Choice of Kipling's Prose*. In 1952 Maugham was shocked by Compton Mackenzie's loss on a tax appeal over the sale of rights: " . . . the stories sold to Rank for me were regarded as capital sales, and so not liable for income tax . . . your lawyers told us that I was perfectly safe . . . I am not very en-

thusiastic at paying over something like £30,000 if it can be avoided!"
The later letters concern negotiations over the *Ten Novels and Their
Authors* (of which Jane Austen and Dickens essays were part). The last
letter (4to October 1954) comments on a Central Office of Information
suggestion that he write a tribute to Sir Winston Churchill "as man
and writer" to mark Sir Winston's 80th birthday; ". . . you were
right in declining on my behalf . . . I have known Winston for over
40 years, and could only write about him from an intimate standpoint,
which I should not want to do. [G.M.] Trevelyn OM. is the person
indicated . . ." The Telegram ("Nothing Doing") is an answer to a
cable from *Collier's Magazine* requesting an informal piece on lunch
with Sir Winston at $2,000 for "not more than two thousand words."
with Brief ALS from H. H Aga Khan to Maugham, 1 page 8vo, about
the Preface to the *Memoirs:* 2 short TLS from Harold Macmillan
concerning the Kipling selection (1951); 2 TLS from Ian Fleming,
1954, 3 pp. 4to: a lawyer's letter concerning the dispute about payment
for the Aga Khan preface, 1954: the Collier's cablegram, 1953: the
Central Office of Information letter about the Churchill article, 1954:
carbon copies of 9 TLS from Watt to Maugham; 1947–1954: 9 pp. 4to,
8vo., also A. P. Watt's autograph draft of a letter of congratulations on
Maugham's 80th birthday, 25 January 1954, and Memoranda. Togethet
24 pp. 4to & 8vo.
The majority of Maugham's letters are written from Villa Mauresque
and are characteristically business like instructions or agreements with
Watt's suggestions on serial rights, reprints and allied matters. References are to the selection of Kipling's prose, *Catalina*, *The Quartet* and
Trio stories, film rights in various works (including a reference to
Isherwood having prepared a script of *Up at the Villa* for Warner
Bros.), *The Hero*, *The Vagrant Mood* and subsequent works. The
longest ALS (3 pp. 8vo.) expresses sympathy at the death of one of the
Watt Bros. and the death of Nelson Doubleday—"I was in some small
measure able to help in the settlement of the grave disagreement that
had arisen between Nelson and Ellen on one side and Doug Black and
Dorothy Doubleday (as was) on the other, so that his last days were
relieved of anxiety and the action has of course been dropped."
There is also in the Berg Collection a large number of letters from
Maugham to prominent personalities, including 9 ALS Beverley
Nichols; several to Maurice Colles; 11 ALS Violet Hunt; Edward
Knoblock, Richard Madden, Sir Edward Marsh, V. Payen-Payne,
J. B. Pinker, Jane Ruben, Clement King Shorter, Fisher Unwin,
Sybil Colefax, Carl Van Vechten, A. P. Watt & Sons (27 folders),
William Archer, Max Beerbohm and Sidney Box.

A. S. FRERE COLLECTION

Collection of 74 Autograph and Typewritten letters signed "Willie" "Willie S.M.", "W. S. Maugham", and "WSM" to Maugham's editor and publisher A. S. Frere (54 letters), and Mrs. Frere (17 letters) as described in the House of El Dieff Inc's Catalogue Seventy Two.

This important correspondence spans about thirty years in W. Somerset Maugham's relations with his principal publishing house, William Heinemann Ltd and with his editor, and later chairman of the firm, A. S. Frere. It includes both personal and business letters to Mr. Frere and his wife, Pat (Edgar Wallace's daughter) together with a few related pieces, and provides a first hand record in length and in depth, of the intriguing, and not always smooth, course of their relationship during a period when the firm published many of his finest and most enduring works.

The earliest letter dated (from Ormonde House, London, November 14, 1932) is an invitation to Frere to attend "a little cocktail party for the cast of my play" (probably *For Services Rendered*), and the last (from Villa Mauresque, January 27 1962) confirms *Looking Back* as the title for the notorious autobiography, which was about to be serialised in the American *Show* magazine, and later in the London *Daily Express*. Through the years Maugham called upon Frere for editorial advice of varying kinds. In a series of letters in 1935 he sought help with *Don Fernando*, and in 1944 worried about *The Razor's Edge* and its likely appeal to an English audience. There are many amusing and tart comments on his own early books which he read, apparently for the first time since publication, in preparation for the collected editions. He frequently sought Frere's opinion on financial matters and his plans for the disposal of his copyrights and the preparation of his will. In the early 1940's a bit of what Maugham called "sharp practice" over the American rights of *France at War* caused a falling out, but it was apparently soon smoothed out and the letters in subsequent years maintain the same friendly tone as the earliest. There are several very interesting letters about Maugham's reasons for giving the original manuscript of *Of Human Bondage* to the Library of Congress, and his trepidation about the "jollification" proposed by the librarian, Luther Evans, which would accompany the occasion.

Maugham spent many of the years of the second World War in America and provided in many of his letters insights into the American character as he saw it, and reflections on our institutions. He wrote Frere in 1946 that the proposal to send Harold Laski to Washington as British Ambassador "would be disastrous. He would have too many prejudices to overcome in too many quarters."

Frere was the author's literary executor and Maugham wrote in 1951 to remind him about his prohibition against any biography especially by his nephew, Robin. The year after Somerset Maugham's death on December 16, 1965, Robin Maugham's book *Somerset and All the Maughams*, was published jointly by Longmans and William Heinemann Ltd. Maugham's acid wit is well displayed in many of his letters. On a visit to Turkey in 1953 he summed up his reception by hordes of interviewers and photographers with the phrase: "If hell is gratifying this is." Maugham's gift of his copyrights to the Royal Literary Fund was supplemented by scholarships he set up for young authors and they were the subject of several letters to Frere and the correspondence between Frere and J. B. Priestley. Maugham also quietly helped pay the bills for at least one ageing author with Frere acting as agent for him. Several letters concern the publication of books, about the author, including Stott's bibliography, Richard Cordell's biographical and critical study, and the biography by Karl Pfeiffer, which Maugham considered trying to prevent before publication. He finally decided to ignore it. The letters to Mrs. Frere are mainly charming and pleasant thank-yous for gifts and favours. At the bottom of a typed letter from one of the publisher's staff in 1932, and on the blank verso of an attached sheet, Maugham wrote comments on a series of short stories he was judging for a contest. They contain some short but pithy observations on writing.

A collection of major biographical and critical importance of unpublished letters by one of the most versatile 20th century authors. *House of El Dieff, Inc., New York.*

BERTRAM ALANSON COLLECTION

In the Stanford University Library there is a collection of 600 letters written to his old friend and financial adviser Bertram Alanson. The letters date from 1921 when they met for the first time in the South Seas to 1958, when Alanson died. They contain interesting comments on prominent figures both in the political and literary world, and pertinent information concerning Maugham's works. A large number of letters relate to Maugham's financial interests.

Bertram Edward Alanson, born January 6, 1877, was an investment broker and President of San Francisco Stock Exchange. He was a personal friend and stock broker of W. Somerset Maugham, and possessed a fine collection of his works, mostly inscirbed, and some manuscripts. These were left to the Stanford University Library.

Mr. Maugham put a restriction on these letters of twenty years from the date of his death, and they may not therefore be read or examined by scholars until the expiry of this period.

The collection is preserved in containers, divided up as follows:

Container No.	Contents
1–15	Maugham's letters to Alanson 1921–1958
16	Maugham's letters to Alanson undated
19	Letters from Sir Gerald Kelly to Alanson 1928–1956
20–21	Letters from Alan Searle to Alanson 1939–1958
22	Letters from Robin Maugham to Alanson 1937–1958
31–32	Newspaper clippings and notices concerning Maugham.
34	Photographs
35	Letters to Terry Bender (1958) re Maugham Exhibit —"By Way of a Preface" which Maugham wrote for the Exhibit. Speech by Maugham to the Toast to Literature," 1951.

THE LILLY LIBRARY COLLECTION, INDIANA UNIVERSITY

The Lilly Library, Indiana University, possesses a collection of 32 letters written by Somerset Maugham to Richard Albert Cordell dating from December 1928 to May 1961. They contain comments on his travels to the East, political conditions in France, on critics and modern fiction and various literary matters. He also mentions his annoyance with Karl Pfeiffer's book. In the letter in 1957 he makes known that he has instructed the executors of his Will not to assist biographers—he alone knows the facts, and adds that the best book on his work is by Papajewski. When Cordell sent him his biography, Maugham thanks him, but says that he is sorry not to have read it, but can't read anything about himself unless forced to do so.

The Library also possesses 7 letters to Ian Fleming, mostly acknowledging receipt of his Bond books, turning down a suggestion that he write a piece about Sir Winston Churchill for The Sunday Times, and commenting on an article by Fleming entitled *A Visit to Mr. Maugham by Atticus*. "I have read your article with great amusement. I don't see that it is undignified. There is nothing less I want than to have anyone take me for a stuffed shirt."

THE UNIVERSITY OF TEXAS LIBRARY COLLECTION

In the University of Texas Library, Austin, there is a collection of some 968 letters, comprising possibly one of the most important sources of biographical material now extant. The letters date from 1909 until a year before Maugham's death. A description is given below of the more important letters to specific individuals.

Barbara Back, 1926–1962.

The 149 letters to Barabra Back, wife of the famous surgeon Ivor Back, include some of the finest and most poignant letters Maugham has probably ever written. They reveal his delight in corresponding with someone for whom he has a great personal regard and whose letters obviously enchant him, and he unburdens himself to a far greater degree than is noticeable with other correspondents. He tells her about a visit to a French penal settlement where he and Gerald Haxton are looked after by a couple of murderers serving life sentences, which gave him the idea for the short story *An Official Position*. A number of letters report his literary progress, and of meetings with fellow authors. He tells of a visit paid him by John Van Druten, who had bought himself a ranch in the desert and was so successful as an adapter of stories for films that he could get all the work he wanted. He discusses the difficulties he has with his play *Sheppey* in adapting it for the New York production, and bemoans the deterioration in the quality of his Parker pens—'they don't seem to hold the ink like they used to'—and ruefully thinks that he will have to go back to the old Waterford of his youth. In a number of moving letters he unburdens himself on the subject of Gerald Haxton, his friend and secretary, and bewails his inability to influence him to lead a more upright life. He thinks that his trouble is that he hasn't enough to do. When the breakdown comes and it is apparent that he is doomed, Maugham tells of his visit to the hospital to see him and poignantly recalls the days when they travelled the world together. He reveals how forlorn and lost he feels when it is all over, and how his grief is assuaged by the arrival of Robin, back from the war with a head wound, and later on Alan Searle, who is a great comfort to him and on whom he comes implicitly to rely. He tells an amusing story about Alan who has to undergo an operation and is nursed back to health by nuns. When Maugham comes to fetch him he is astounded to see him kiss the Mother Superior on both cheeks and if she was a bit taken aback he had the impression she liked it. Maugham makes the observation that he didn't suppose she had been kissed for fifty years!

(N.B. *Cecil Roberts has described Mrs. Ivor Back in his autobiography. "Slim, beautiful, intense, she was famed for her wit and common sense, which had an earthy quality."*)

Robin Maugham (Viscount Maugham of Hartfield). 1933–1964.

These letters do not in any way appear to bear out the suggestion in Robin Maugham's autobiography that all was not well in the relationship between Uncle and Nephew. All the 99 letters are written in affectionate terms and largely in the role of literary mentor, usually beginning 'Robin dear' and ending 'yours ever' or 'affectionately yours'. The first letter dated 23 December 1933 is an acknowledgement of a magazine produced when Robin was at Eton. It contains what was probably his first short story and his Uncle commends it, but remarks that it has a slight sentimentality 'surprising in anyone who bears your name'. He was insistent in the early years that Robin obtained his parents' permission before coming to stay with him. If they held the view that his house was likely to corrupt his morals, then it was not for him to say 'stuff and nonsense'. He was equally correct when his brother came to stay with him, and though he might make some wry comments to his nephew about his behaviour, it never went further than that. There are many letters giving his opinion of manuscripts submitted to him. Occasionally, he would express disapproval of the way his nephew had treated his subject and recommend how it could be improved, and sometimes he would suggest a better ending as with *The Servant*. He was always encouraging and never begrudging in his admiration when a novel or a play met with success. If Maugham had any mental reservations about his nephew they were never revealed in these letters. Much of the correspondence not unnaturally deals with family affairs, the effect the war was having in the South of France, and there is a fine description of the cottage his friend Nelson Doubleday built for him in South Carolina which would give him 'a wonderful opportunity to write a thrilling book'. (He began there *The Razor's Edge*). The last letter is dated 27 April 1964 and despite the then rapid deterioration in his health, there is no change in the friendly tone that markedly prevails throughout the correspondence.

COLLECTION OF REGINALD TURNER LETTERS
A collection of 35 letters written by Somerset Maugham to Reginald Turner dated from January 18 1915 to October 24 1938. The dates are often only approximate as Maugham invariably wrote only the month and the day and not the year and the dates on the envelopes have been blocked out by heavy French, Italian or German postmarks. The majority of the letters are mostly of literary interest, discussing his books or the plays that he has in production and mentioning the people with whom he has come into contact—Beerbohm Tree, who is producing *Pygmalion*, Charles Frohman in New York, Billie Burke, Compton Mackenzie and many others. He tells Turner in a letter dated June 14 (1932?) that he has finished with the theatre and is so thankful that he can hardly contain himself. "I know that my decision to have done with it cost me nothing." In a letter dated October 24 1938 he mentions that he has been suffering from what the doctors called delayed shock—he had been involved in a car accident near Nice

in which he barely escaped with his life. When Reginald Turner wrote to congratulate him on receiving the "Rosette"—the Legion of Honour—he pointed out that it made a very fine effect on the lapel of an evening coat but that he wore it with a certain diffidence because it seemed to him that the lips of various old gentlemen whom he knew would curl with scorn. But he expected to live the scandal down! Reginald Turner, who had the courage to stand by Oscar Wilde in his darkest hour, was a friend of most of the literary celebrities of his day and was trusted and liked by them.
Duncan Cranford

Golding Bright, theatrical agent. 1909–1928.
A series of 32 autograph and typewritten letters, dealing mostly with business matters but also touching on his private affairs. Writing from Brighton (no date) Maugham protests that Bright's conclusion that he does not want money is hasty, but that he does prefer to go on pigging it in the squalor of Mount Street than sell his soul for hire. He is much irritated by the paragraph Waller had sent round to the press to the effect that he had rewritten the last act of *The Explorer* to accord with the views of the critics—'I think it is very stupid and undignified to crawl before the critics in this manner,' and anyway it wasn't true; his delight at the news that *Lady Frederick* had been accepted. 'You letter filled me with exaltation; now the likelihood of an early pro- duction makes me realise that the world is not hollow and foolish . . '; a letter dated 2 October (no year) informing Bright that he is about to write a play which he is going to call *Smith;* suggestions about casting, views on theatrical machinations, and warning Bright that each play may be the beginning of the end of his career as a dramatist. The last letter touches on his position in the world of the theatre, and reminds Bright that he is no longer in need of an agent, he really only wants someone to collect the money and for that service he thinks 5% is adequate compensation.

Gladys Bertha Stern. 1938–1954.
These 49 letters to a well known prolific and versatile English novelist, reveal another side of Somerset Maugham—the letters are written in a half facetious, skittish vein, and begin variously 'Peter dear' 'Delilah' 'Sweetheart' 'My Precious Peter Petrovina' or 'Dear Mr. Dick'. But they never go very deep or give anything away. They touch lightly on the literary work of both of them, on mutual friends or acquaintances, expressions of his opinions and moods, of books he has read, and places he has been to. They are friendly, lively letters tossed off to someone of

v

whom one is very fond but who does not occupy a very important niche in one's life.

Hugh Walpole. 1927–1937.
The 25 Walpole letters are very much as one would expect from what is known about the two men. They are mostly short and written in friendly vein. They refer to invitations to dinner, and suggestions for meeting, and one letter discusses Walpole's visit to America, which had been a great success. There is a telegram from Maugham dated 14 May 1937 congratulating him on his knighthood. The correspondence, however, contains two letters of considerable biographical significance, the famous letter to Walpole dated 24 December 1930 denying that Alroy Kear in *Cakes and Ale* was a portrait of Walpole, and the other the letter replying reassuringly when Walpole sent off a disclaimer that he was not, as was rumoured, the author of the bitter diatribe *Gin and Bitters*.

Paul Dottin. 1926–1947.
Paul Dottin, President of the University of Toulouse, was the first critic to attempt a serious appraisal of Somerset Maugham's work. These 46 letters, which are mostly replies to questions put to him, deal almost exclusively with various aspects of his work as a playwright and novelist, and are interesting in that they reveal his early approach to literary techniques and style.

Karl Graham Pfeiffer. 1931–1958.
Karl Pfeiffer and Somerset Maugham were once close enough friends to exchange working manuscripts in the mid 1940's; the relationship cooled as Pfeiffer became interested in writing Maugham's biography. The 52 letters show the writer's reticence about being the subject of biographical investigation.

The remaining letters in the Collection include the important Pinker letters (99) of which a full description appeared in my 1956 bibliography; 32 letters to William Lyon Phelps which contain a fairly extensive reference to antecedents of the characters in *Cakes and Ale*, and letters to numerous other correspondents who wrote to him 'out of the blue'.

Royalty Agreement—typed copy of an agreement between Maugham and William Heinemann of London about *The Land of the Blessed Virgin* (1904 August 9).

APPENDIX III

UNPUBLISHED PLAYS

(Plays written or adapted by W. Somerset Maugham that have never been published. A number of these have been filed for the purpose of copyright with the Library of Congress).

MDLLE. ZAMPA. A Play in One Act.
[Rome, 1900?]
Produced at the Avenue Theatre as a curtain-raiser to *A Man of Honour* in 1904, but was taken off after 20 performances.

MRS. BEAMISH. A Comedy in Three Acts.
[n.p. 1917]
1 p.i., 37, 35, 32. A typewritten (carbon) copy is lodged with The Library of Congress, Washington. (PR6025.A86M46). Unproduced.

UNDER THE CIRCUMSTANCES. A Comedy in Three Acts.
[n.p., n.d.]
2 p.i., 39, 44, 33. A later and revised transcript version of *Mrs. Beamish*, fastened into linen cover of the American Play Company in the Berg Collection, New York Public Library.

THE KEYS TO HEAVEN, a Comedy in Three Acts.
[New York? 1917?]
2 p.i., 42, 42, 35. Typewritten (carbon) copy lodged with the Library of Congress, Washington. (PR6025.A86K4). Unproduced.

LOVE IN A COTTAGE, a Comedy in Four Acts.
[New York? 1917]
2 p.i., 28, 34, 29, 26. Typewritten (carbon) copy lodged with the Library of Congress, Washington. (PR6025.A86L65)
Produced 27 January 1918 at the Globe Theatre with Marie Lohr and Haidee Wright in the cast.

THE CAMEL'S BACK. A Play in Three Acts.
[n.p. 1924]
Produced 29 October 1923 at Worcester Theatre, Worcester Mass and in London at the Playhouse 31 January 1924.

THE ROAD UPHILL. A Play in Three Acts.
[n.p. 1924]
Unproduced. The theme of this play inspired the novel *The Razor's Edge*.

THE FORCE OF NATURE. A Play in Three Acts.
[Cap Ferrat, France? 1928]
4 p.i., 26, 34, (i.e. 35), 40. Typewritten copy is lodged with The Library of Congress. Washington. (PR6025.A86F65). Unproduced.

THE MASK AND THE FACE. A Play in Three Acts.
[New York? 1933].
This play by Luigi Chiarelli was translated by W. Somerset Maugham and produced in Boston at the Colonial Theatre in May 1933. A typewritten (carbon) copy is lodged with The Library of Congress, Washington. (PR4809.H34M32).

APPENDIX IV

UNPUBLISHED PLAYS ADAPTED
BY OTHER WRITERS

(N.B. The Berg Collection at The New York Public Library acquired the files of the American Play Company which handled Maugham's dramatic interests in the States. They therefore possess similar type-written carbons to those lodged with The Library of Congress for copyright purposes.)

AKINS, Zoe. The Human Element, a play in three acts by Zoe Akins; adapted from the short story of that title by W. Somerset Maugham.
[New York? c. 1933].
3 p. I.,2–31, 37, 31. Typewritten (carbon) copy is lodged with The Library of Congress, Washington. (PR6025.A86H82). Unproduced and unpublished.

ELLIS, Edith. "Strickland". A Drama in Two Acts and Six Episodes by Edith Ellis, based on W. Somerset Maugham's novel "The Moon and Sixpence".
120 leaves. Typewritten (carbon) copy, leaves variously numbered, lodged with The Library of Congress, Washington. (PR6025.

A86M66). First presented by Howard Wyndham and Bronson Albery at the New Theatre, London, September 24 1925 (75 performances).

BRENT, Romney. Man-Hunt, a play in three acts by Romney Brent, based on the story "The Vessel of Wrath" by W. Somerset Maugham.
[New York? c. 1935].
2 p.i., 63, 40, 48. Typewritten (carbon) copy lodged with The Library of Congress, Washington. (PR6025.A86V43). Unproduced and unpublished.

DIXON, Campbell. "Secret Agent" by Campbell Dixon. From the novel "Ashenden: or The British Agent" by W. Somerset Maugham.
[New York? c. 1932].
2 p.i., 33, 54, 34. Typewritten (carbon) copy lodged with The Library of Congress, Washington. (PR6025.A86A88). Unproduced and unpublished, but Hitchcock's film *Secret Agent* was partly founded on this play.

CORMACK, Bartlett. W. Somerset Maugham's *The Painted Veil* arranged for the stage by Bartlett Cormack.
[New York? 1930].
4 p.i., 30, 33, 25. Typewritten (carbon) copy lodged with The Library of Congress, Washington. (PR6025.A86P29).
Produced at The Playhouse 19 September 1931 with Gladys Cooper and Lewis Casson in the cast (129 performances). Unpublished.

JEROME, Helen. Theatre, a comedy by Helen Jerome, made from Somerset Maugham's novel of the same name.
[New York? 1937].
3 p.i., 2–66, 44, 37. Typewritten (carbon) copy; part of the title supplied in manuscript, lodged with The Library of Congress, Washington. (PR6025.A86T45). Unproduced and unpublished.

DIETZ, Howard & MAMOULIAN, Rouben. Sadie Thompson, a musical version of the play, with music by Vernon Duke, based on W. Somerset Maugham's *Rain*.
[New York? 1944?].
Typescript (carbon) unsigned and undated. 92p.
Stamped December 13 1944 on cover. Script stamped "Richard

J. Madden Play Company". Presented at the Alvin Theatre, New York, November 16 1944 and closed January 6 1945. Unpublished.
The Berg Collection, New York Public Library.

JACKSON, Felix. The Letter, adapted for television from the play by W. Somerset Maugham.
[New York?] 1950 January 30. "Robert Montgomery presents—Your Lucky Strike Theatre."
62 pp. Duplicated script, signed.
The University of Texas, Austin.

APPENDIX V

NOTES

1. (**A8**) The letters from W. S. Maugham to J. B. Pinker & Sons, his literary agents, quoted or referred to throughout Section A, are now in the possession of the University of Texas.

2. (**A10c**) Mr. Maugham had a brother, Henry Neville Maugham, who was also a novelist. He published a travel book and two novels, one of the latter *Richard Hawkwood*—an Italian romance in the Maurice Hewlett style—posthumously in 1908. The business arrangements for the latter were carried through by his brother. Mr. Maugham's grandmother was also a writer and made a substantial income from writing novels and children's books in French, to the number of about 70. There is a delightful account of her in Robin Maugham's *Somerset and All the Maughams* Appendix VI.

3. (**A21a**) The first edition of *Of Human Bondage*, was published on 12th August, 1915, and the details showing how the edition was printed and distributed were supplied to me by Mr. H. T. Downey, who was a Doran man and is now with Doubleday's. There appears some discrepancy in the total showing how the 5,000 was arrived at, but I give the figures as they were supplied to me.

OF HUMAN BONDAGE: Pub. date: August 12, 1915. Price $1.50. Apparently for the first edition 5,000 copies were ordered and of this order 4,336 copies were delivered.
On March 31, 1916, there were 548 copies delivered, which I

presume was part of the balance of the binding of the original edition of 5,000, and there were 461 copies in stock on hand.

On September 30, 1916, they bound 172 copies, which were probably part of the original edition of 5,000, and there were 135 copies on hand. A second edition [impression] was made in 1919 and 1,125 copies were manufactured. A third edition [impression] of 1,101 copies was manufactured.

A fourth edition [impression] was manufactured. Here the record stops.

As will be noted from the above details, the first impression was exhausted probably some time in 1916. The second impression, comprising 1,125 copies, was run off in 1919, *four years later*. A third impression, comprising 1,101 copies, was run off in 1919, and a fourth impression, comprising 1,204 copies, in 1920. Mr. Downey describes these impressions as 'editions', but as they were printed from the original typesetting in the form of plates, they are still part of the first edition and, bibliographically, are 'impressions'.

In view of these facts, the possibility cannot altogether be discounted that the second impression may have been bound in a similar style of casing with identical lettering, in which event it would be impossible to differentiate between the two impressions, but—and here is the crux of the matter—four years elapsed before a second impression was printed, and in the interim a war had intervened, bringing with it inevitable economies in the employment of gold leaf and cheaper paper.

I have examined a number of impressions of this novel published between 1921 and 1926, and although they were all printed from the original typesetting in the form of plates—the typeface, number of leaves and pagination being common to all—all of them differed from the first impression in that the title and half-title pages had been re-set, and they were bound not in the original green cloth with a gold panel on front, but in a red cloth with no colour stamping in front or a green cloth with a brown panel on front and spine. The paper, also, was of a cheaper quality.

I consider it unlikely, therefore, that the impressions published in 1919 and 1920 had the same binding as the first impression. Indeed, it is feasible that the balance of the first impression published in 1916 (the first re-binding) was also differently cased, in which event the number of copies in the original green cloth would not exceed 4,336 copies. Few of the leading American libraries seem to possess a copy of the first American edition.

4. (**A33c**) To remove every reference to Hong Kong, Canton, etc., the following thirty leaves required cancelling:

pp.	15–16	pp.	75–76	pp.	237–238
	17–18		111–112		245–246
	33–34		117–118		247–249
	35–36		123–124		249–250
	37–38		133–134		251–252
	43–44		137–138		253–254
	45–46		147–148		255–256
	49–50		189–190		267–268
	55–56		193–194		269–270
	61–62		235–236		273–274

This makes a total of 60 pages, but in fact only 27 of these leaves, making 54 pages, were corrected. Pages 56, 133 and 267 were not cancelled at all and only one or two necessary corrections were made on p. 34.

To effect the corrections Heinemann's prepared sixteen cancel leaves and also reprinted the whole of sections 3 and 16. These two sections, of eight leaves each, contained only 11 offending pages but it was more convenient to reprint the whole sections than to insert eleven cancel leaves in them. Consequently, five unoffending leaves, three in Section 3 and two in Section 16, were also reprinted. The second issue, first state, of the first English edition thus contains fifty-four revised text pages and ten pages which were reprinted without revision. The cancel title page and the inserted *Author's Note* were printed separately. For the record, it may be of interest to set down the details of the whole transaction as extracted from the publisher's files. I am indebted to Messrs. William Heinemann for this privilege.

THE PAINTED VEIL *by William Somerset Maugham*
Official Publication Date: 23 April 1925
Price: 7s. 6d.
Printings listed to Publication: 5 printings as follows: 4,000
                                                                                        4,000
                                                                                        5,000
                                                                                        5,000
                                                                                        5,000

Copies on File: No. 1 . 1st edition.
                              Reverse title page "First published 1925"
                              Cancel title page

The location *HONG KONG* used throughout
File copy stamped: "*This edition called in.*
Next edition April 23 1925"

No. 2. 1st edition
Reverse title page "First published 1925"
Cancel title page
Author's Note inserted after title page
The location changed to TCHING-YEN with
the following exceptions:
Page 34. 1st line "Hong-Kong"
Page 56. 4th line "Hong-Kong"
File copy stamped: "*Published April 23 1925*"

No. 3. Reprint
Reverse title page:
"*First published, April 1925*
New impressions, April, May 1925"
Title page not cancel
Author's Note inserted after title page
The location is TCHING-YEN throughout

The Binding on all three copies is identical.

Copy of information on file card:
Maugham, W. S.
The Painted Veil   April 23 1925
7/6 1st Printing. Press copies sent out and called in
    Hong-Kong instead of Tching-Yen.
7/6 1st Printing with numerous cancel pages
    288 pages. April 23 1925
7/6 Third Printing. Two errors in previous edition rectified.

Daily Sketch (no date given)
    "In front of me lies the latest and what (out of regard for author and
    publishers) I must hope is the final version (for the present edition)
    of Somerset Maugham's new novel 'The Painted Veil'. Somehow
    its misfortunes do not seem quite over, for Messrs. Heinemann's
    note requests me not to notice it before April 34rd, a date which I
    have failed to discover in the calendar."

    "*Thickening the Veil:*—Without waiting for this somewhat mystify-
    ing date of release, however, I suppose there is no harm in mention-
    ing that the temporary withdrawal of the book after printing has

enabled the author to change the scene of his narrative from Hong-Kong to the mythical colony of Tching-Yen, where the "Happy Valley" becomes the "Pleasant Vale", the "Peak" the "Mount" and so on.

But (so persistent is ill-luck) in one instance 'Hong-Kong' still survives in the text.

'Kitty' who was once 'Mollie' continues 'Kitty' and to make security doubly secure for the sensitive the author prefixes a completely disarming note."

[1] Both file copies list twenty-six works on the reverse of the half-title page.

5. (**A22d**) Under a license granted to them by William Heinemann William Collins published in cheap editions five Maugham titles, each title running for a period of seven years from the date of publication. The complete series is set out below:

COLLINS OWN CATALOGUES [Not always showing Year of publication]			ENGLISH CATALOGUE OF BOOKS [Showing Year of publication]
TITLE/LENGTH	1/- NOVELS Bound $6\frac{1}{4}'' \times 4\frac{1}{4}''$	7d NOVELS	
THE MOON AND SIXPENCE 250pp.	September 30 31 31 37 38	November 34 35 36	1/- 31 32 L. Bk. Co. 6d 33 7d. 34
THE PAINTED VEIL 248 pp.	30 31 32 37	July 34 35 36	1/- 30 36 L. Bk. Co. 6d 32 7d 34
ASHENDEN 254 pp.	30 31 32 37	36	1/- 30 L. Bk. Co. 6d 34 7d 36 37
THE CASUARINA TREE 254 pp.	31 32 37 38	October 34 35 36	1/- 31 L. Bk. Co. 6d 34 7d 36
THE TREMBLING OF A LEAF	32 37 38	July 35 36	1/- 32 7d 35 37
THE LETTER [The Casuarina Tree]			Detective Club 6d 30 33

6. **(A29)** In 1923, some students at St Thomas's Hospital, where Mr. Maugham studied medicine, wrote to him and asked if he would write a sketch for their Xmas show. By return he sent them a short skit, in which the characters—a doctor, a nurse, a theatre porter and a patient on a trolley—got jammed in a lift as a cry of 'fire' was heard. My informant (now an eminent figure in the medical profession) could not recall all the details but he said there was much discussion in committee whether or not they should put it on. Eventually, despite its wit, it was decided that it was altogether too macabre and might create panic in the audience. No one now appears to know the whereabouts of the original script.

7. It has been stated in print (*The Book Collector*, Spring 1957) that the address given by Mr. Somerset Maugham at the opening of the new Heinemann Windmill printing works has been published in pamphlet form. This is not correct. The only record apart from the MS. of the address is a framed typewritten copy hanging on the wall in the Chairman's office. *See Appendix II.*

8. A unique piece of Maughamiana is a cigarette card in the possession of Mr. Grenville Cook, being a coloured photograph of the author and on the back a brief description of his career and writings, and the following caption: FAMOUS BRITISH AUTHORS. 22. W. Somerset Maugham. W. D. & H. O. Wills (c. 1933).

9. A decorative Xmas card (14.2×11.2 cm.) issued by Doubleday, Doran Book Shops with the following quotation: "The danger of making friends is that you may not be able to drop them when you want to; the advantage of reading a book is that if it bores you, you can put it aside without compunction. But perhaps you will want to finish this one. W. Somerset Maugham."
From *The Berg Collection at The New York Public Library.*

INDEX OF TITLES

Advice to a Young Author, D69
Ah King, A46
Alien Corn, A42; D94
Allied Relief Ball Souvenir Program *see* In the Bus
Altogether, B4
An Official Position, A58; D108
Andalusia: Sketches and Impressions, A8
Another Man Without a Country *see* French Joe
Ant and the Grasshopper, A50; D52
Appearance and Reality, A66; D104
Ardent Bigamist, D44
Arnold Bennett, A74; C15; D92
Art of Fiction, B24
Artist and the Theatre, C57
Artistic Temperament of Stephen Carey, A65; App. I
Ashenden, or The British Agent, A37; App. I, II
Augustus, D174

Back of Beyond, A46; C14; D93
Bad Example, A3
Bakers' Dozen, B37
Beauty and the Professor, A74
Before the Party, A34; D35
Before the Party (play), E10
Behind the Scenes, A37
Best Ever *see* The Treasure
Best Short Stories of W. Somerset Maugham, B26
Bewitched *see* 'P. & O.'
Bibliography of the Writings of W. Somerset Maugham, C12
Bidding Started Slowly, D178
Bishop's Apron, A9, 32
Bitter Sweet, C10
Book Bag, A43, 46
Books and You, A57; D112
Bread-Winner, A41; App. I
British Agent *see* Miss King
Bum, The A50; D78
Buried Talent, D99

Cachirra, La *see* The Mother
Caesar's Wife, A26; App. I
Cakes and Ale, A40; D86; App. I
Canadian *see* Land of Promise
Camel's Back, App. III
Captain and Miss Reid, The *see* Winter Cruise
Caroline *see* The Unattainable
Cassell's Miscellany, C61
Castillyons, The, App. 11
Casual Affair, A66; D103

Casuarina Tree, A22, 34
Catalina, A67; D169a, 170; App. I
Chance Acquaintance, A37
Choice of Amyntas, A3
Choice of Kipling's Prose, C51-52, App. II
Christmas Holiday, A54; D116a
Circle, The, A24; App I
City Built on a Rock, D30
Classic Books of America, D118
Closed, Shop, A50; D66
Code of a Gentleman *see* Portrait of a Gentleman
Collected Plays, B18
Collected Works, B12
Collins Cheap Editions, App. V. Note 5
Colonel's Lady, A66; D152
Complete Short Stories of W. Somerset Maugham, B17, 20
Comprehensive Exhibition of W. Somerset Maugham, C60
Constant Wife, A35; App. I
Consul, D64
Cosmopolitans, A50
Cousin Amy *see* The Luncheon
Creative Impulse, A42; D56
Creatures of Circumstance, A66 App. I
Culture that is to Come, D134
Cupid and the Vicar of Swale, D2
Daisy, A3
Dark Woman, A37; D71
De Amicitia, A3
Derelict *see* The Bum
Doctor and Patient *see* Lord Mountdrago
Domiciliary Visit, A37
Don Fernando, A49; App. I
Don Sebastian *see* Punctiliousness of
Door of Opportunity, A46; D95
Dorothy Parker, C34
Dream (The, A), A50; D47

East and West, B3
East of Suez (play), A27; App. I
East of Suez (collection), B15
Eddie Marsh, C54
Encore, A73
End of the Flight, A50; C8; D62a
English Spirit, C33
Episode, A66; D157
Escape, The, A50; D45
Essays on Literature, B34
Essays by Divers Hands, C49
Exhibition of Paintings by Sir Gerald Kelly, C48
Explorer, The, A10, 25
Explorer, The (play), A16
Extraordinary Sex *see* The Social Sense

Facts of Life, A58; D115
Faith, A3
Fall of Edward Barnard, A25
Favorite Short Stories of W. Somerset
  Maugham, B11
Fear, D29
Fifty Modern English Writers, C16
First Person Singular *see* Six Stories in the
First Rehearsal, C18
Flip of a Coin, A37
Flirtation, D10
Flotsam and Jetsam, A66
Flower Paintings, C17
Footprints in the Jungle, A46; D67
For Services Rendered, A45; D97a; App. I
Force of Circumstance, A34; D41
Force of Nature, App. III
Foreign Devils, D28
Fortunate Painter and the Honest Jew, D11
Four Dutchmen, A50; D76
France at War, A56
French Acting Edition, Samuel, B8
French Joe, A50; D63
Friend in Need, A50; D56
Full Circle, F30
Function of the Writer, D154

Gallery Unreserved, C11 App. II
Gentleman in the Parlour, A39, App. I
Gerald Festus Kelly, D20
German Harry, A50; D40
Gigolo and Gigolette, A58; D106
Gin and Bitters, F30
Give Me a Murder, D125
Good Manners, D14
Great Man *see* The Poet
Great Modern Reading, C30
Great Novelists and their Novels, A69;
  C36–45; D161–69, 181; App. I
Greatest Stories of All Times, C26, 32
Greek, The, A37
Guilia Lazzari, A37
Gustave, A37

Hairless Mexican, A37; D73
Happy Couple, A66; D16, 141
Happy Man, A50; D49
Harvest, C21
Here and There, B14
Hero, The, A4; App. I
Heron Books, B9
His Excellency, A37; D72
Home, A50; D51
Home and Beauty, A30; App. I
Home from the Sea *see* Home
Honest Woman *see* The Promise
Honolulu, A25; D26
Hour Before the Dawn, A61; D137
House with the Green Shutters, C23

How I Like to Play Bridge, D149
How I Write Short Stories, C46, D101
How Writers Write, C20
Human Element, A42; D88; App. IV
Husbands and Wives, B28

Imposters, The *see* Raw Material
In a Strange Land, A50; C2; D42
In Defence of Who-Done-Its, D150
In Hiding *see* The Wash Tub
Inside Story of the Collapse of France,
  A60; D122
In the Bus, C27
Introduction to Modern English and
  American Literature, C31
Irish Gentleman, D8

Jack Straw, A13, App. I
Jane, A42; D37
Jane (play), E11
Judgement Seat, A48, 50

Keys of Heaven, App. III
King's School, Canterbury, F115
Kite, The, A66
Kite and Other Stories, B27

Lady Frederick, A10, 12; C1; App. I
Lady Habart, D3
Land of Promise, A20, App. I
Land of Promise (novel), E2–4
Land of the Blessed Virgin, A8
Landed Gentry, A18; App. I
Larger than Life, E9
Letter, The, A34; C5; D46
Letter, The (play), A36; App. I, IV
Letters from Madame Sevigne, C58
Lion at Bay, D123
Lion's Skin, A58; D110
Little Fellow, C50
Liza of Lambeth, A1; App. I
Loaves and Fishes, A32; App. I
Looking Back, D186
Looking Back on Eighty Years, D180
Lord Mountdrago, A58; D113
Lotus Eater, A58; D107; App. II
Louise, A50; D59
Love and Russian Literature, A37
Love in a Cottage, App. III
Luncheon, The, A50; D15, 43

Mackintosh, A25; D21
Mademoiselle Zampa, D9; App. III
Magician, The, A11; App. II
Making of a Millionaire, D13
Making of a Saint, A2
Malaysian Stories, B35
Maltreat the Dead in Fiction, D87
Man and Wife *see* Penelope

Man from Glasgow, A66
Man Hunt, App. IV
Man of Honour, A6; D6; App. I
Man Who Made his Mark *see* The Verger
Man Who Wouldn't Hurt a Fly *see* A Friend in Need
Man with a Conscience, A58; D116
Man with a Scar, A50; D60
Manuscripts, App. I
Marriage of Convenience, A39; D12, 84
Mask and the Face, App. III
Maugham Discusses Drama, D91
Maugham's Malaysian Stories, B35
Maugham Reader, B16
Maugham Twelve, B32
Maughamiana, F72
Mayfair Murder, App. II
Mayhew, A50; D39
Memoirs of Aga Khan, C56
Merry-go-Round, A5, 7; App. I
Middle of Next Week, App. I
Mirage, D83
Miss King, A37; D75
Miss Thompson *see* Rain
Mixture as Before, A58
Moon and Sixpence, A22, 25; App. I
Moon and Sixpence (opera), A76
Most Selfish Woman I know *see* Louise
Mother, The, A66; C61; D18
Mr. Harrington's Washing, A37; D74
Mr. Know-All, A50; D53
Mr. Maugham Himself, B23
Mr. Pete, D32
Mr. Tomkin's Sitter, D133
Mrs. Beamish, App. III
Mrs. Craddock, A5; App. I
Mrs. Dot, A14; App. I
My South Sea Island, A51; D27

Narrow Corner, A44; D97
Neil MacAdam, A46; D96
Nelson Doubleday, 1889–1949, C47
Night in June, A *see* Up at the Villa
Noble Spaniard, A75
Novelist or Bond Salesman, D54
Number of People, C24

Of Human Bondage, A21; App. I, V Note 3
Of Human Bondage (address), A65
On a Chinese Screen, A28; App. I
On Having My Portrait Painted, D183
On the Road to Mandalay, D85
One Of Those Women *see* The Dark Woman
On Writing for the Films, D24
Orientations, A3
Our Betters, A29
Our Puppet Show, C9

Outstation, The, A34; D48

P. & O., A34; D36
Pacific, The, A25
Painted Veil, The, A22d, 33; App. V Note 4
Painted Veil (play), App. IV
Paintings I Have Liked, D136
Partial View, B22
Pearls *see* A String of Beads
Penelope, A15; App. I
Penguin Books, B7
Perfect Gentleman, D182
Peter Arno's Cartoon Review, C28
Philosopher, D31
Plays of Somerset Maugham, B1; 18
Poet, The, A50; D61
Point of Honour, A66; D158
Point of Law, D7
Points of View, A77; App. I
Pool, The, A25; D25
Portrait of a Gentleman, A50; D57
Princess September, A55; C3; D34; App. I
Professional Writer, D109
Promise, The, A50; C6; D62
Proof Reading as an Avocation, D117
Pro Patria, D5
Punctiliousness of Don Sebastian, A3; D1
Purely for My Pleasure, A78
Pygmalion at Home and Abroad, D19

Quartet, A68
Queen Alexandra Sanatorium, Davos, C1
Queen's Doll's House, C3

R, A37
Rain, A25; D22
Rain (play), E5–6
Raw Material, A50; D38
Razor's Edge, A63; D148a; App. I, II
Reading and Writing and You, D145
Reading Under Bombing, D124
Red, A25; D23
Refugee Ship, D121
Right Thing is the Kind Thing *see* Back of Beyond
Road Uphill, The, App. III
Robert Ross: Friend of Friends, C53
Romantic Young Lady, A66; D160
Round Dozen, A42; D44
Round Dozen (collection), B12

Sacred Flame, A38; App. I
Sadie Thompson, A25
Sadie Thompson (musical), App. IV
Saint, The, A77
Salvatore, A50; D50
Salvatore the Fisherman *see* Salvatore
Sanatorium, A66; D111
Schiffbruchig *see* The Venture

Second Baker's Dozen, B38
Secret Agent, App. IV
Selected Novels, B21
Selected Prefaces and Introductions, B30, 31
Sergel *see* NOTE
Seventeen Lost Stories, B36
Sheppey, A47; App. I
Short Story, The, D102
Sinners, The, B29
Six Comedies, B10
Six Stories Written in the First Person Singular, A42, App. I
Sixty-Five, C25
Smith, A6, 19; App. I
Social Sense, A50; D79
Somerset Maugham Pocket Book, B13
Somerset Maugham Tells a Story of the Lady from Poona, D177
Somerset Maugham Sampler, B13
Spanish Journey, D171
Standard Book of Bidding, C35
Straight Flush, A50; D80
Strickland, App. IV
Strictly Personal, A60; D121–23, D128–31; App. I
String of Beads, A50; D68
Summing Up, A53; App. I

Taipan, A28; D33
Tauchnitz Edition, B5
Teller of Tales, C26
Tempest, Marie *see* First Rehearsal
Temptation of Neil MacAdam *see* Neil MacAdam
Ten Novels and their Authors *see* Great Novelists and their Novels
Tenth Man, A17; App. I
Tenth Man (novel), E7
Terrorist, The, D147
Theatre, A52; App. I
Theatre (play), E.8; App. IV
Theatrical Companion to Maugham, F93
Then and Now, A64; D155; App. I
They are Strange People, D127
Three Fat Women of Antibes, A58; D98
Through the Jungle, D82
Times Book Club, A5b
To Account Rendered *see* For Services Rendered
Too Many Husbands *see* Home and Beauty
Traitor, The, A37; D70
Travel Books, B25
Traveller in Romance, D17
Traveller's Library, C15
Treasure, The, A58; D100

Trembling of a Leaf, A21, 22, 25
Trio, A71, App. I
Trip to Paris, A37
Truth at Last, C4
Twenty Best Short Stories in Ray Long's 20 Years as an Editor, A43; 43a
Two Made Their Bed, C7
Two Studies, D32

Unattainable, The, A31; App. I
Unconquered, The, A62, 66; D143; App. I
Under the Circumstances *see* Mrs. Beamish
Unknown, The, A23; App. I
Up at the Villa, A59; D119; App. I

Vagrant Mood, A74; App. I
Vanity Fair, C62
Venture, The, D4
Verger, The, A50; D81
Vessel of Wrath, A46; D90
Vice-Consul, The, D32
Villa on the Hill *see* Up at the Villa
Virtue, A42; D89
Voice of the Turtle, A58; D105

W. Somerset Maugham: An Appreciation, C25
W. Somerset Maugham: 4 short stories, B39
W. Somerset Maugham: the English Maupassant, B4; F37, 85
Wash-Tub, The, A50; D77
We Have a Common Heritage, D146
What a Life! C13
What Reading Can Do for You, D151
What Should a Novel Do? D159
What Tomorrow Holds, D126
Why Do You Dislike Us, D138
Widow's Mite, D55
Winter Cruise, A66; D144
Wisdom of Life, C22
Without a Country *see* Another Man Without a Country
Without Veils, C55
Woman of Fifty, A66; D153
Woman Who Wouldn't Take a Hint *see* The Escape
World Over, B19
Worthley's Entire *see* Mrs. Dot
Write About What You Know, D148
Writer's Notebook, A70; D173; App. I
Writer's Point of View, A72

Yellow Streak, A34; D58
You and Some More Books, D114

Zurbaran, A74; D175